SYAMA PRASAD MOOKERJEE

LIFE AND TIMES

TATHAGATA ROY

INTRODUCTION BY BIBEK DEBROY

PENGUIN
VIKING
An imprint of Penguin Random House

VIKING

USA | Canada | UK | Ireland | Australia
New Zealand | India | South Africa | China

Viking is part of the Penguin Random House group of companies
whose addresses can be found at global.penguinrandomhouse.com

Published by Penguin Random House India Pvt. Ltd
7th Floor, Infinity Tower C, DLF Cyber City,
Gurgaon 122 002, Haryana, India

Penguin
Random House
India

First published as *The Life and Times of Dr Syama Prasad Mookerjee: A Complete
Biography* by Prabhat Prakashan, New Delhi 2012
Published in Viking by Penguin Random House India 2018

Copyright © Tathagata Roy 2012, 2018
Foreword copyright © L.K. Advani 2012
Introduction copyright © Bibek Debroy 2018

10 9 8 7 6 5 4 3 2 1

ISBN 9780670090419

Typeset in Adobe Garamond Pro by Manipal Digital Systems, Manipal
Printed at Replika Press Pvt. Ltd, India

www.penguin.co.in

MIX
Paper from
responsible sources
FSC® C016779

To
my dear daughters,
Malini Roy (Rao)
and
Madhura Roy (Khedekar)

In his public life he was never afraid of expressing his inmost convictions. In silence the cruellest lies are told. When great wrongs are committed it is criminal to be silent in the hope that truth will one day find its voice. In democratic society one should speak out, especially when we are developing an unequalled power of not seeing what we do not wish to see.

—Dr Sarvepalli Radhakrishnan, in his condolence message after Dr Mookerjee passed away

Contents

Acknowledgements

My thanks are first of all due to Lal Krishna Advani—former Deputy Prime Minister of India, elder statesman and senior-most leader of the Bharatiya Janata Party (BJP), successor to the party that Dr Mookerjee founded—because a casual remark by him during one of his speeches at a party meeting provided me with the idea and the inspiration to write this biography. He also kindly consented to write the foreword. Thanks are due next to Bibek Debroy, chief of the Economic Advisory Council to the Prime Minister, outstanding economist and Sanskrit scholar rolled into one, who wrote the introduction to this edition.

I also wish to specially thank the Dr Mookerjee Smruti Nyas (Dr Mookerjee Memorial Trust), New Delhi, and especially M. Venkaiah Naidu (now Vice President of India), chairman, and Nand Kishore Garg of the Nyas for their invaluable help in meeting the expenses of researching the material for and writing the book, as also otherwise.

I particularly wish to thank Prashanto Chatterji, formerly head, department of history, Bardhaman University, West Bengal, for drafting two chapters of this book. In fact this book was originally intended to be co-authored by him, but owing to the severe problems that he developed with his heart and eyesight he had to withdraw from the effort after the work that he had managed to do.

I also particularly wish to thank Dinesh Sinha, formerly
assistant registrar, Calcutta University, and a survivor of the
Noakhali Carnage. Sinha, while battling cancer, has been
forthcoming with a wealth of information on Dr Mookerjee,
especially his educational phase, and for that reason deserves the
most unstinted praise.

Thanks are due to the interviewees, all of whom readily agreed
to be interviewed upon being requested, some of them despite
their advanced age and associated problems. Among them the
names of Dr Mookerjee's daughters, the late Sabita Banerjee and
Arati Bhattacharji, and those of his close political associates Balraj
Madhok and Kidar Nath Sahni should be specially mentioned.
Together with Madhok's, I should also mention the name
of Prafull Goradia who kindly put me in touch with Madhok.
Sabita Banerjee died while the book was being written, but I was
lucky enough to be able to interview her a year before that when
she was in good health and spirits.

The president and other functionaries of the Asutosh Mookerjee
Memorial Institute, notably Justice Chittatosh Mookerjee (retd),
the late Amitabha Chatterjee (both nephews of Dr Mookerjee) and
Reena Bhaduri (a niece), have been the soul of cooperation, and
have been forthcoming with a large volume of literature as well as
a number of anecdotes about his personal life and also rendered
invaluable help in checking parts of the typescript.

Apart from Sabita Banerjee and Amitabha Chatterjee, another
person who died while this book was being written was Bansi Lal
Sonee, a senior Sangh Pracharak and sometime office secretary
at the BJP's central office in New Delhi. He was present during
the historic meeting between Dr Mookerjee and Param Pujaniya
Guruji (M.S. Golwalkar) at Calcutta, and as such supplied an
anecdote of inestimable value.

I am especially grateful to the late Mihir Saha, secretary of
the Syama Prasad Mookerjee Smarak Samiti, and to Ashok

Chakrabarti for carefully preserving the photographs of different phases of Dr Mookerjee's life and for making them available.

Special thanks are due to veteran journalist Sukharanjan Sengupta of Calcutta whose books in Bengali contain priceless information on Dr Mookerjee, and upon coming to know that I was writing this biography, he made a very kind gift of those books to me.

Among Dr Mookerjee's kin thanks are also due to his grandchildren Sandip C. Bhattacharji of New York for kindly assisting his ailing mother, Arati, to answer my questions; Subha Prasad Mookerjee and his wife, Sumita Mookerjee, bar-at-law; and Dr Mookerjee's great-grandniece Debdutta Chakraborty, niece Amita Roy Choudhury and nephew Janatosh Mookerjee (Jirat).

Among Dr Mookerjee's associates in West Bengal, Sukumar Banerjee, an ex-president of the state BJP, advocate Shyama Prasad Mukherjee and Sudhir Bera have helped with anecdotes and I wish to thank them.

I am thankful to Dr Shuvo Dutta, MD, FRCP (Lond.), FACC, consultant cardiologist, and Dr R.N. Das, MD, FRCP (Lond. and Edin.), consultant in internal medicine, for medical advice with respect to Dr Mookerjee's illness of 1945 and his fatal illness of 1953.

I am thankful to Prabhat Prakashan, Delhi, and its proprietor, Prabhat Kumar, for publishing the earlier edition of this book.

I am thankful to Subrata Chowdhury of UltraTech Cement Ltd who made a gift of a good digital camera to me. The camera was very useful for photographing Dr Mookerjee's laminated photographs.

I am particularly thankful to Premanka Goswami, Aditi Muraleedharan and others of Penguin Random House for picking up this book for publication and their subsequent guidance and help in editing, and to Penguin Random House, the worldwide publishers.

I also wish to thank Kabindra Purkayastha and Paritosh Pal Choudhury of Silchar for information on the Sylhet referendum; Mahamahopadhyay Dhyanesh Narayan Chakraborty for enlightenment on Hindu scriptures; advocate and ex-minister Kashi Kanta Maitra for information and literature on his father, Pandit Lakshmi Kanta Maitra; my sister-in-law, Sumita Ghosh, my brother, Saugata Roy, my erstwhile colleague Bela Banerjee, my good friend Priyadarsi Dutta (a staffer of Arun Jaitley) and Shailendra Singh, Tripura's resident commissioner at New Delhi, for help in library work; Rana Nandy for help with computers and peripherals; my personal assistant, Ashok Das, my chauffeur, Bibhuti Jana, and my aide-de-camp, Major S.S. Bajwa, for continuous help; and Sudhangsu and Chirasree Chakraborty, Satyajit and Debjani Changdar, Ramtanu Maitra (Washington DC, USA) and Shantanu Mukherjee (Frankfurt am Main, Germany), all relatives and friends, who helped me with informed and active encouragement. There may be others whose names I have missed for which I ask forgiveness, and to all of them I express my heartfelt thanks.

And lastly, this book would not have been possible without the encouragement, help, cooperation and love from my immediate family, and to them I express my thanks—my wife, Anuradha, my daughters, Malini and Madhura, my sons-in-law, Kiran Rao and Ajinkya Khedekar, and my grandchildren, Surya Kiran Rao, little Uma Rao and littler Leon Khedekar-Roy.

Foreword

Tathagata Roy, the author of this book, was the president of our party's West Bengal unit at one point of time. When he met me in Kolkata he presented to me his manuscript of Dr Syama Prasad Mookerjee's biography and requested me to write a foreword for the book.

His request was an honour for me. I regard Dr Mookerjee as the first martyr for independent India's unity and integrity.

I was born in 1927 in Karachi (now in Pakistan). In 1947, as a result of the sacrifices and struggles of thousands of patriots, India was able to wrest freedom from British rule. But the independence of our motherland was accompanied by the trauma of Partition—an event that witnessed the massacre of tens of thousands, and the uprooting of millions from their hearths and homes.

I left Karachi a month after Partition. My first ten years after Independence, from 1947 to 1957, were spent in Rajasthan. So when in 1951 Dr Mookerjee launched the Bharatiya Jana Sangh (BJS), a political party committed to nationalism, democracy and good governance, besides a polity based on *Bharatiya sanskriti* and values, many of us associated with the Rashtriya Swayamsevak Sangh (RSS) since childhood decided to join this new party and serve the country through politics.

I can list several young men, then in their twenties or early thirties—Pandit Deen Dayal Upadhyaya, Atal Bihari Vajpayee, Nanaji Deshmukh, Balraj Madhok, Yagya Dutt Sharma, Sunder Singh Bhandari, Jagannath Rao Joshi, Gopal Rao Thakur, Kailashpati Mishra, Vasant Rao Bhagwat, Nathabhai, Jagdish Prasad Mathur, P. Parameswaran, Ram Prasad Das, Kusha Bhau Thakre et al.—along with whom I was also drawn into this first political party born after Independence.

The activists I have listed above together constituted a galaxy of highly talented youth, whose dedicated labour in those early decades of a developing democracy have today made the BJP a formidable force to be reckoned with.

As I have mentioned, at the time the Jana Sangh was founded, I was in Rajasthan. And within a couple of years of the party's launching, Dr Mookerjee defied the Jammu and Kashmir government's order forbidding him to enter the state. Midway on the bridge linking Punjab with Jammu and Kashmir state, Dr Mookerjee was arrested and taken to a place near Srinagar where he kept in detention for a couple of months.

On 23 June 1953, the whole country was shocked to learn that after a short illness at his place of detention, Dr Mookerjee was shifted to the state hospital in Srinagar where after a brief while he breathed his last.

I was in Jaipur those days. I vividly remember how that morning around 4.30 a.m. I was woken up from sleep by the loud wailing sounds of someone outside our party office (he turned out to be a local newsman) who kept shouting, while weeping, 'Advaniji, they've killed Dr Mookerjee!'

Till today, it is a mystery how he died. Was proper medical assistance made available to him? Or was it a case of medical elimination? The then Chief Minister of West Bengal, Dr B.C. Roy, and Dr Syama Prasad's revered mother, Jogomaya Devi, carried on a prolonged correspondence with Pandit Nehru urging that the tragedy be thoroughly probed and the full facts brought to light. Such a monumental tragedy occurred, and yet not even an inquiry was ordered.

Jogomaya Devi's letter to Pandit Nehru in reply to his condolence message is really heart-rending. She wrote:

> I am not writing to you to seek any consolation. But what I do demand of you is justice. My son died in detention—a detention without trial. In your letter you have tried to impress that Kashmir Government had done all that should have been done. You base your impression on the assurances and information you have received. What is the value, I ask, of such information when it comes from persons who themselves should stand trial? You say, you had visited Kashmir during my son's detention. You speak of the affection you had for him. But what prevented you, I wonder, from meeting him there personally and satisfying yourself about his health and arrangements?
>
> His death is shrouded in mystery. Is it not most astounding and shocking that ever since his detention there, the first information that I, his mother, received from the Government of Kashmir was that my son was no more, and that also at least two hours after the end? And in what a cruel cryptic way the message was conveyed! Even the telegram from my son that he had been removed to the hospital reached us here after the tragic news of his death. There is definite information that my son had not been keeping well practically from the beginning of his detention. He had been positively ill a number of times and for successive periods. Why did not, I ask, the Government of Kashmir or your Government send any information whatsoever to me and my family?

We in the BJP owe our position in Indian politics to the sacrifices of thousands who have preceded us, and above all to the vision and martyrdom of Dr Mookerjee. We have known our great leader closely only during the closing years of his life. Tathagata Roy has done a signal service to history and to the nationalistic cause we are pursuing in politics by doing all the research work he could. He has compiled voluminous details about this great hero's life, right from his birth and preparing what he has called a complete biography. All compliments to him.

New Delhi   L.K. Advani
June 2012

Introduction

In October 2017, there was a question on the *Kaun Banega Crorepati* show, 'Which member of Jawaharlal Nehru's cabinet resigned and founded a new party in 1951?' It wasn't one of the early-rung questions. Even then, I was surprised when the participant got the answer right. Perhaps I am being unfair. But I suspect, twenty years ago, in a similar situation, not too many participants would have known. Independent India's discourse has been shaped in a certain way. Moulded through that jaundiced view, Dr Syama Prasad Mookerjee hasn't got his due. The naming of educational institutions, roads, bridges, buildings, swimming pools, towns and schemes after him is a relatively recent phenomenon. Perhaps the only exception is the University of Delhi's Shyama Prasad Mukherji (spelt thus) College. However, even for this college, the preference seems to be to refer to it as SPM College, as if one has Suspended Particulate Matter in mind. Had it not been for SPM, not only India's legacy, independent India's geography too would have been remarkably different. More likely than not, the state of Punjab would have been part of Pakistan and the state of West Bengal would have been part of Bangladesh. This may sound exaggerated, but it is part of documented history. If this sounds exaggerated, that's because of Dr Syama Prasad Mookerjee's marginalization in popular renderings of India's Independence movement and because good books on him are rare.

What books can one possibly think of? (1) Anil Chandra
Banerjee (2000), but that covers a brief (1937–46) period of his
life; (2) Prashanto Kumar Chatterji (2010), but that covers only
one aspect (political) of his life; (3) Manoj Das Gupta (2001),
but that is essentially the printed version of a talk and is more
a monograph than a book; (4) a brief profile published by the
Dr Syama Prasad Mookerjee Research Foundation (2016); (5)
the compilation of documents, speeches and correspondence
by Harish Chander Padmini (2001); (6) the Lok Sabha
Secretariat's monograph on eminent parliamentarians (1990);
(7) Balraj Madhok's brief portrait (1954); (8) Syama Prasad
Mookerjee's diaries (1993), that too, only for a certain period
in his life; and (9) various collections of his speeches, including
a recent (2017) compilation by the Dr Syama Prasad Mookerjee
Research Foundation of speeches on education.[1] For a person
who left such an indelible impression, this is all too brief a list,
almost perfunctory. If one extends coverage beyond English and
includes Bengali, in the realm of books and monographs, one
will at best add half a dozen more. One of these, mentioned in
the Bibliography, is in Bengali and is titled *Syama Prasad Ke Na
Jana Aparadh*. This translates as 'It is a crime not to know about
Syama Prasad'. If there has to be atonement for the crime and
amnesia, and the biased telling of history, both deliberate and
inadvertent, there has to be a good book about SPM—the man
and his times. Tathagata Roy has produced exactly that and the
subtitle 'Life and Times' is entirely justified.

Who was Dr Syama Prasad Mookerjee? 'After Syama
Prasad demitted the office of the vice chancellor, the university
conferred an honoris causa doctorate degree on him. The prefix
of "Dr" somehow fitted him well, and gradually, he came to be
universally known as "Dr Mookerjee".' This was in 1938, the
same year that Banaras Hindu University conferred another
honoris causa doctorate degree on him. To step back a bit,

SPM was the son of the legendary Sir Asutosh Mookerjee. If one were to follow in the illustrious father's footsteps, one could have become an educationist or a lawyer. Academically, he was prepared for either, having topped the BA Honours in English and also having topped the MA in Bengali. He then went on to do a BL and became a barrister.

> Syama Prasad took to working for the Calcutta University as a duck takes to water. Sir Asutosh, multifaceted genius that he was, apparently chose his first son [Rama Prasad] to succeed him principally at the High Court, and the second one at the University. It is interesting that he made both his sons wear both hats—Rama Prasad was also a member of the university syndicate, while Syama Prasad studied for the bar in India and England and became a barrister.

SPM became the vice chancellor (VC) of Calcutta University in 1934. He was all of thirty-three, and unless I am wrong, this record of the youngest VC ever (in India) still stands. Even before becoming the VC, he had succeeded Sir Asutosh on the university syndicate. With a combination of youth and his father's shadow, being a VC couldn't have been easy. Changing the university's logo couldn't have been easy. Getting a convocation address delivered in Bengali couldn't have been easy. Bringing in the vernacular as a medium and standardizing Bengali spellings couldn't have been easy. Who was SPM? He was an educational administrator and educationist, with clear thoughts about how education should be delivered. The aforementioned compilation by the Dr Syama Prasad Mookerjee Research Foundation of speeches on education is a refreshing collection of SPM's thoughts on the subject.

But politics beckoned, through the Bengal Legislative Council seat from the Calcutta University constituency. The plight of minority Hindus in what was then Bengal transformed this beckoning into a full-time career through the Hindu Mahasabha. Eventually, this path led to his becoming finance minister of Bengal between 1941 and 1942 in A.K. Fazlul Haq's coalition government and subsequent resignation. Compared to other episodes in his career, his role as finance minister and engagement in famine relief is relatively ignored in biographies other than this one. More than 2 million people died in the Bengal Famine of 1943–44, some because of starvation, others because of subsequent disease and adverse health effects. In recent times, a lot has been written by economists and historians on the Bengal Famine, arguing that it was the outcome of faulty distribution, deliberate or otherwise, rather than a shortfall in supply. A bibliography will be as long as an arm. In such explorations, rarely, if at all, will SPM's views feature, though all this subsequent academic research merely vindicated his views.

> The famine was an important landmark in the life of Dr Mookerjee for three reasons. First, he had shown remarkable foresight in trying to dissuade the Governor from impoverishing the countryside in the name of collection of foodstuff for military personnel, and had resigned when he found that the Governor would not listen to him. Secondly, when the famine became a reality, he had organized a massive relief effort, which saved innumerable lives—a task which should have been undertaken by the government, but was not done, or done properly. And thirdly, he had ruthlessly exposed the crimes of omission and commission by the British administration and the Muslim League ministry, the horrible acts which would have never come to light without Dr Mookerjee's initiative, mostly through speeches in the Legislative Assembly.

The opposition to the Quit India movement was natural. As was mentioned earlier, had it not been for SPM, who knows what

Bengal would have looked like today? This is after the possibility of partition of the country became a reality and after the Calcutta Killings and Noakhali, the latter deservedly given an entire chapter in this book. Once partition was certain, what of Bengal?

> Dr Mookerjee, who had so long campaigned so indefatigably to prevent the partition of the country, by this time realized that the dreaded partition was inevitable, a certainty. He had no doubt in his mind that if the whole of Bengal went to Pakistan then the condition of the 47 per cent Hindus of the undivided province would be worse than miserable . . . He therefore decided to make partition of the province a necessary corollary to partition of the country.

In hindsight, once the deed was done, it seems obvious that Bengal (and Punjab) would have to be partitioned. But it was by no means obvious then, and an undivided Muslim majority (even if the majority was thin) landing up with Pakistan might well have become a fait accompli. Once partition was accepted for Bengal, by logical extension, it followed for Punjab. Yet another detail for a proper retelling of history needs to be mentioned.

> Even here, Dr Mookerjee intervened and convinced Radcliffe that while deciding the population balance for deciding whether to award a particular unit of area to India or Pakistan, the unit to be considered should be the thana, the police station area, and not the district or subdivision. It is on this basis that a number of districts themselves came to be partitioned; and the Krishnanagar and Ranaghat subdivisions of the Nadia district, the bulk of Malda district, the Balurghat and Raiganj subdivisions of Dinajpur district, the Bongaon subdivision of Jessore district and many other parts came to India.

Because my family had been affected by the partition of Bengal, I did know that the unit used was the thana. However, had it not been for this volume, I would not have known that SPM had a hand in this. Indeed, this decision about the unit affected the lives of thousands, but I cannot recall this aspect being mentioned in any standard book on the history of India's Independence and Partition.

SPM's post-Independence career is probably better known, at least outside Bengal. He was inducted into the interim central government as the minister for industry and supply. Sure, he had been finance minister of undivided Bengal. But one wonders what would have happened had he been made education minister instead? As Tathagata Roy also argues, that would have been a more natural fit. However, the question need not perhaps be asked. He wasn't going to last long as a minister, something he himself seems to have anticipated, given his differences with Jawaharlal Nehru. For the limited period that he was a member of the cabinet, the Industrial Policy Resolution of 1948 (significantly different in emphasis from the Industrial Policy Resolution of 1956) reflected his views. Eventually, in 1950, he resigned from the cabinet because of the Delhi Pact with Liaquat Ali Khan. The background to SPM's opposition to the Delhi Pact lay in the incidents in East Pakistan.

If continuation in the cabinet was untenable, there also needed to be an alternative to the Congress party. Thus it was that the Bharatiya Jana Sangh was set up in 1951. This was just before the general elections of 1952. As a start-up, the Bharatiya Jana Sangh won three seats in the Lok Sabha, two from West Bengal and one from Rajasthan. Despite the limited number of seats, SPM was the de facto leader of the Opposition. This brings one close to the end, Jammu and Kashmir, the Dogra agitation and Article 370.

There were, as Dr Mookerjee astutely observed, two principal dimensions to the crisis in the state. One stemmed from Sheikh Abdullah's pretensions to independence of the state vis-à-vis India. The other was the preferential treatment he gave to the Vale of Kashmir and Kashmiri Sunni Muslims as compared to the other parts of the state, principally the Jammu region, whose people he considered almost pariah.

The protagonists may have changed, but the issues, unfortunately, have not changed even in 2017.

Finally, there are the events of May–June 1953, on which there is a lot of misreporting of facts.

It is important to note here that many are under the impression that Dr Mookerjee was imprisoned for entering Jammu and Kashmir state without a permit. This is a canard deliberately spread by Sheikh Abdullah himself, as he had done in a broadcast, for reasons best known to him. Dr Mookerjee mentioned this in a handwritten note to his council U.M. Trivedi for drafting of his habeas corpus petition. In fact on 11 May the state government of Jammu and Kashmir issued an ordinance through the Sadr-i-Riyasat that it is an offence to enter the state without a state permit, but as the order of Prithvinandan Singh, inspector-general of police reveals, Dr Mookerjee was not (and could not have been) arrested under that ordinance. On the day of the arrest, the only permit that could have been issued was one by the Government of India and not by the government of Jammu and Kashmir. But as we have already seen, the deputy commissioner of Gurdaspur told him that the Government of India had already decided to allow Dr Mookerjee to enter Jammu and Kashmir state without a permit. This reveals a very strange and suspicious chain of circumstances.

Events got murkier when he fell ill. The illness was mishandled, as this book explains. Overt indifference does invariably raise suspicions about covert intent. There is, and probably never will be, a satisfactory explanation of the events.

After SPM's death, Harindranath Chattopadhyay wrote a poem, quoted by Tathagata Roy. 'The sun of a colossal intellect has set / The giants are departing one by one / To whom our mourning nation owes a debt.' A colossal intellect, who was the son of another colossal intellect. However, before acknowledging the debt that the country owes to Dr Syama Prasad Mookerjee, the country must know about the man, his life and times. This is certainly the first complete biography that we have and Tathagata Roy must be complimented for painstakingly researching and writing it.

New Delhi   Bibek Debroy
November 2017

Preface

If one walks into any office of the BJP, be it the imposing central office in New Delhi or some humble local office in an obscure corner of India, one is sure to come across two pictures, side by side. One of them shows a portly gentleman with a shining bald pate, a thick moustache, a powerful chin and eyes shining with determination. The other is of a quiet, self-effacing, nondescript person with a shy smile who could have been a rural schoolteacher—except for the same streak of resolution in his visage. The first is Dr Syama Prasad Mookerjee, the founder of the Bharatiya Jana Sangh (BJS), the predecessor of the BJP. And the second, Pandit Deen Dayal Upadhyaya, who took over the BJS after the death of Dr Mookerjee under mysterious circumstances at the early age of fifty-two and nursed it to maturity—till his own, even more mysterious, death, also at the early age of fifty-two! But that is another story.

For the uninitiated, the BJS was the pre-1977 incarnation of the BJP. The BJS had merged into a party called the Janata Party at the call of Jayaprakash Narayan in 1977. The ex-BJS people, plus a few others, separated again in 1980 to form the BJP.

This book is about Dr Syama Prasad Mookerjee and his times. A truly multifaceted personality, Dr Mookerjee encapsulated within himself a politician, an educationist, a bit of a religious and social reformer and a humanitarian. He excelled as a parliamentarian and he has had few equals to this day. As an educationist he had risen to dizzy heights at a very early age, and if he had pursued this line he might have surpassed his very illustrious father, Sir Asutosh Mookerjee. And he not only founded a party, but also led a political movement that swam against the prevailing current of the times and a great deal of the subsequent times. And all this in a life span of only fifty-two years, of which only the last fourteen years were devoted to politics. In the history of achieving an enormous amount in a very short life, perhaps he stands in the same league as Acharya Sankara and Swami Vivekananda.

In spite of his superlative qualities, and due to his choosing to fight the current, it was his lot to have become a controversial person—a lot more so than other prominent personalities of his time who really deserved to be controversial, or worse. This book concerns itself to a great extent with this debate and the reasons for the same.

A lot of this dispute, the reader would find, hinges around the word 'secular' and its Indian-context antonym, 'communal', arguably the two most misused words in Indian politics today. In the context of Indian politics these words do not at all mean what any standard dictionary would say they mean. For example, to people who call themselves 'secular', according to a concept (more on this later) made popular by some political stalwarts, Dr Mookerjee was 'communal', not 'secular'.

Then there are people who do not subscribe to the Nehruvian-left idea of secularism, who often call it pseudo-secularism, and who consider that Muslims are no different from other Indians, that they should be adversely spoken of should they do any wrong, just as a Hindu, Christian or Sikh should be adversely spoken of should any of them do any wrong. Time and again, such people are dubbed 'anti-Muslim' or 'anti-minority' and therefore 'communal' by a group of people. Such people do not subscribe to this definition of 'secularism' or 'communalism' and consider Hindu communalism and Muslim communalism to be equally reprehensible; to them, a wrong is a wrong, and must be denounced no matter who did it.

Dr Syama Prasad Mookerjee was a person devoid of any religious or communal bias, and a patriot par excellence. However, he has been dubbed 'communal', because he never hesitated to take up the cause of Hindus if he found that Hindus were being wronged. In an article in Bengali in the 1952 Durga Puja (October) number of the fortnightly *Swastika*, Dr Mookerjee had written, '[M]ost political parties of India literally squirm at the mention of the word "Hindu". If reminded that their leaders are Hindus themselves, they appear to die from shame . . . but somehow if they can discover any wrong, even an imagined one, done by a Hindu to a Muslim they explode, almost bringing down the sky.'

The problem Dr Mookerjee posed to his detractors was that he could not care less about such considerations. He was singularly capable of clear thinking and equally incapable of being hypocritical (for which the current euphemism is 'politically correct') about it, or letting those thoughts get obfuscated by the fashionable dogma of the times. But more than anything else, he was an incredibly courageous person, both in the moral and physical sense, considering some of the adversaries and adversities that he had braved, some parts of the system that he had defied and some of the things that he had done including one that eventually led to his death.

It is indeed surprising that the biography of such a person took all these years to begin. There is, of course, the life-sketch by Balraj Madhok, his ardent follower and sometime president of the BJS, but it falls far short of being a complete biography, focusing heavily on only the last three years of his life, and being somewhat coloured by the author's idiosyncrasies. There is also a short sketch in English by S.C. Das, and a number of similar short sketches in languages other than English, most of them in Bengali, by Sushil Kumar Sahityaratna, Nikhilesh Guha, Shyamalesh Das and others, but the latter are accessible only to those who read Bengali. As a result of this paucity of material many of his admirers do not know of him in totality. In fact, even within the BJP many know only of the Kashmir phase of his life.

The material for the biography has been gleaned from printed material available in English and Bengali on the man, and on interviews of his political co-workers as well as of his kin. More than sixty years have gone by since Dr Mookerjee's death, and the memories of the persons interviewed have not remained exactly photographic, but whatever has remained is invaluable. Two of his family, namely Sabita Banerjee, his elder daughter, and Amitabha Chatterjee, his nephew (sister's son), breathed their last while the book was being written—it is the biographer's good fortune that he could interview them in time. It is, however, a matter of great regret with the biographer that he could not interview Atal Bihari Vajpayee, the former Prime Minister of India and his private secretary for a short while, because of the extremely delicate state of his health.

For the removal of doubts, I would like to make absolutely clear and put on record here that I have made no effort in the book to be politically correct and prove that Dr Mookerjee was a 'secular' person as defined by the so-called 'secularist' political parties and media of India. In other words, I am not at all defensive about the way Dr Mookerjee did things, and I am under no compulsion to justify his actions before the 'secularists'. It is necessary to say this in so many words because certain passages in the book may seem, at first sight, to give that impression. Take for example, the observations of A.K. Fazlul Haq, the Premier of Bengal, or his acolyte Abul Mansur Ahmad on the man, or the eulogies by his friend Dr Sarvepalli Radhakrishnan, the second President of India and a celebrated philosopher. Or the appointment of Hasan

Suhrawardy as the Vageshvari Professor of Comparative Art in Calcutta University. Or, even more poignantly, the heart-rending letter written by the celebrated Bengali poet Kazi Nazrul Islam. Nazrul would, in all probability, simply not have survived beyond 1942 but for the support offered by Dr Mookerjee. These actions came naturally to Dr Mookerjee, and he promptly did what his conscience dictated him to do. The mention of these may seem to indicate that I am trying to show how 'secular' Dr Mookerjee was. I am not. I do not, nor did Dr Mookerjee, subscribe to the idea or concept of 'secularism' preached (whether believed in or practised is a different matter) by the 'secular' parties and media in India. I shall, therefore, leave it entirely to the reader to draw his or her own conclusions as to what Dr Mookerjee was and was not.

Some may find some references to some political leaders of the times not as respectful as they would have liked them to be. I would like to assure them that I am second to none in paying respect where I consider respect to be due, but at the same time I am not prepared to deify anyone. No one in politics is a saint. Similarly, even though I have been critical of many leading men and women of the times, I have refrained from using strong language in respect of any of them. There are, however, two exceptions: Sir John Arthur Herbert, Governor of Bengal, 1939–43; and Huseyn Shaheed Suhrawardy, Premier of Bengal, 1946–47. The reader will understand why when he reads about them.

A word about names of places and people: In this book I have used the old spellings, such as 'Calcutta', 'Bombay' and 'Dacca' and not 'Kolkata', 'Mumbai' and 'Dhaka', because the first mentioned were the spellings in use at the relevant time. It does not make sense to keep saying 'Calcutta (now Kolkata)'. For the same reason I have usually attached the definite article 'the' to 'Punjab', although this practice is no longer in vogue. As for names, many Bengali Hindu given and family names have alternative spellings and variations, and some of these may be difficult for the uninitiated to follow. Among the most common ones are Mukherjee = Mukhopadhyay, Banerjee = Bandyopadhyay, etc. The first mentioned ones are the common ones and they have been spelt as they are commonly spelt, but in the case of the subject of this book and his family, I have used the spelling that they used and still use, namely 'Syama Prasad Mookerjee', and not the more common, phonetically closer, 'Shyama Prasad Mukherjee'.

To end, this is an effort to put on record the life of a person deliberately made to be misunderstood by his political adversaries and little known to many people in India, including many people in his home state of West Bengal.

This book is intended to be a biography for popular reading and reference and not a learned historical treatise. It is a combination of a chronicle and an estimate of the man. And finally, this is a book, in common with almost all biographies, by an admirer.

All possible care has been taken to check the completeness and authenticity of the facts stated in the book. Any suggestions for correction of factual errors and for improvement will be gratefully received. If this book helps in dispelling the lack of knowledge and misconceptions that exist about this great man, showing him in a true light and countering the malicious propaganda that was done and is still being done against him, the author will consider his efforts amply rewarded.

Genealogical Table

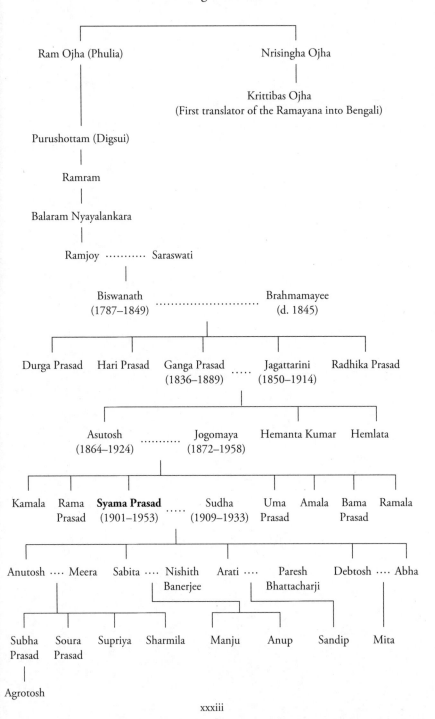

1

Ancestry and Early Life

It is believed that sometime in the twelfth century AD, the chieftain Adishura (some say Maharaj Ballal Sen, the Hindu king of Gaud in central Bengal) had decided that it was necessary to improve and preserve the racial purity of his subjects. To achieve his end, he decided to 'import' five Brahmins and five Kayasthas (a sub-caste specializing in accounting and clerical work) of good birth from faraway Kanyakubja or Kanauj (in present-day Uttar Pradesh) and give them the right to marry any number of times among themselves. This was presumably to create some sort of a Bengali *herrenvolk*. The name given to this herrenvolk was Kulin. Some of the descendants of these Kulin Brahmins settled in the part of present-day West Bengal west of the Ganga (also known as Bhagirathi or Hooghly) River, in the area still known as Rarh Bhumi. They came to be known as Rarhi Brahmins. With the passage of time, they lost all their north Indian traits and became thoroughly *Bengalized*. Their surnames (though they rarely used them and usually called themselves Sharma or Dev Sharma) also underwent several changes, and eventually they came to be called Bandyopadhyay, Mukhopadhyay, Chattopadhyay, Gangopadhyay and Ghoshal, depending on their *gotra* (presumed descent from an ancient sage). The colloquial forms of these names were Banrujjey, Mukhujjey, Chatujjey and Ganguly respectively—Ghoshal was presumably not difficult to pronounce. When the British arrived,

1

and needed clerks for their burgeoning Indian Empire, they drew them from among these Brahmin and Kayastha castes who had meanwhile not only taken to the Macaulay-inspired English education but had excelled in it. For their interaction, the British needed names that their Anglo-Saxon tongues could pronounce and with that in view, they distorted proper names right and left. Thus, an area of present-day central Kolkata, which had once housed Job Charnock's (founder of Calcutta) parlour, known as Baithak-khana became Boytaconnah, Chuchura became Chinsurah and Chattogram Chittagong. The River Ganga became the Ganges. And the first four of the five Brahmin surnames mentioned earlier became Banerjee, Mukherjee, Chatterjee and Ganguly.

The Brahmins, as a rule, though respected because of their supposed 'proximity to divinity', were anything but rich. Many of them used to eke out a miserable existence by acting as *purohit* (priests) to non-Brahmins, called their *yajman*s, and living off the rice, vegetables and articles offered in puja, together with the little *dakshina* (cash) they used to get. The rest ran *chatushpathi*s or *toal*s—schools of Sanskrit learning and Hindu scriptures—and lived off whatever their pupils could pay them in kind or cash. Among them, the few who had rich yajmans, were relatively well-to-do. There never was, and still is not, any organized clergy in Hinduism. As a result, the rich yajmans were generally on top, although the Brahmins had an edge because of the superiority of their caste—they were always called *varnashreshtha*, belonging to the topmost caste. Still, quite often, a yajman would sack a Brahmin from his family priesthood, and the Brahmin would have to look for a new yajman, which was not easy. The Brahmins therefore had to move from place to place quite often in search of territory where there was a shortage of their caste brothers.

Because of the Kulin system of multiple marriages contracted by men, it was quite often the case that a man well into his sixties or even older would marry a nine-year-old girl. In many such cases, the men died at their due age, leaving behind an orphaned child wife and often their young offspring as well. Even otherwise, the life expectancy in those days in Bengal was very low. When the husband died, either from old age or from disease, the child wife would generally have to go back to her parents' house and be condemned by society to live a life of strict celibacy and vegetarian food. One such girl, called Saraswati, had been married off to a Brahmin called Ramjoy in the village of Digsui in the district of Hooghly. The girl gave birth to a child soon after, and in due course, was widowed and came back to live with her parents in the nearby village of Jirat in the same district. She came with her two-year-old son, Biswanath, who was born on 18 October 1787. Jirat is located on the west bank of the Bhagirathi or Ganga River, not far from the subdivisional town of Kalna in the Bardhaman district.

The child Biswanath, however, inherited the surname of the father whom he had never seen. This surname was Mukhopadhyay or Mookerjee, a Samvedi Rarhi Brahmin name, and his gotra, Bharadwaj. He also inherited direct descent from a cousin of Krittibas Ojha, the celebrated translator of the epic Ramayana into Bengali. Because the Ojha family was from the village of Phulia in the Nadia district, the Mookerjees belonged to the Phulia Mel, *mel* being an element in the complicated caste system of the time.

In due time, Biswanath grew up and was married to Brahmamayee (it is not as if every Kulin Brahmin indulged in polygamy), the great-granddaughter of Sarbabhaum Chatterjee, the famous court purohit at the court of the maharaja of Bardhaman. Biswanath became a moneyed man in the course of time, and is credited with writing one of the earliest travelogues in Bengali, describing his travel by boat from Jirat to Rangpur in north Bengal (now Bangladesh). His wife, Brahmamayee, was very fond of going on pilgrimage. She, with a few other women of her village, decided to trudge all the way to Puri in Orissa—a distance of about 500 kilometres—on one such pilgrimage. This was at a time when the railway line to the place had not yet come into operation. She reached Puri all right, but contracted smallpox there (some say cholera) and breathed her last. Some seven years later, while Biswanath was taking a holy dip in the Ganga, the mast of a passing boat accidentally broke off and collapsed on him, hitting him on the head. Biswanath succumbed to the injury, leaving behind his four sons, Durga Prasad, Hari Prasad, Ganga Prasad and Radhika Prasad, aged seventeen, fifteen, thirteen and ten, respectively.

A Kayastha woman named Jahnavi, who used to work in the Mookerjee household and had brought up the four boys, took it upon herself to look after the orphaned boys. The boys were, however, all very bright and pursued their studies with great vigour. Biswanath, when he died, was heavily in debt. Although the debt was due to expire shortly thereafter, Durga Prasad, the eldest son, decided that to maintain the honour of his family he would have to repay it. With this in mind, he moved to a place called Andul in Howrah district after a while, to work as a schoolteacher. He took his brothers along as well. He was a parent to his brothers at this stage, not only earning for them, but even cooking for them. For in those days a Brahmin could eat food cooked only by another Brahmin. He moved to other places like Tamluk and tried to train himself in more lucrative trades than schoolteaching. He chose to study civil engineering and eventually rose to be the district engineer in the district of Ghazipur in the United Provinces (now Uttar Pradesh). With the money that he could make this way, he finally collected enough to move to the imperial capital, Calcutta (he moved to Ghazipur later). Here, he got his brothers admitted to schools for them to complete their education.

Among his brothers, the third one—Ganga Prasad—was especially meritorious. He got admitted to the Hare School, founded by the British educationist David Hare, then considered the best school in the city. Calcutta University was founded in 1857, and Ganga Prasad sat for the school-leaving examination, then known as the 'entrance examination', conducted by the university the same year. He not only cleared it but also won a scholarship and a free studentship to Presidency College, then considered the best college in all of Bengal. The boy had incredible determination and perseverance. In spite of very strained financial circumstances, he continued with his studies and kept excelling in them. Often, his brother could not afford the oil for a lantern and Ganga had to study under the street light or sitting in the nearest grocer's shop. He got a bachelor's degree in arts in 1861. This was a time when a simple BA degree was a passport to a plum job (fit for Indians of course)—usually the post of a deputy magistrate—with the government or with one of the merchant houses of Calcutta. And, with one such step, Ganga Prasad could put an end to the financial stringency that he had been living through practically since his birth. Instead, he decided to study modern medicine and enrolled at the newly established Medical College in Calcutta and graduated with credit in 1866. Here again, he could have got an appointment as an assistant surgeon in government service and could have lived comfortably with the salary offered. Instead, he chose private practice as a career.

While in Medical College, Ganga Prasad was married to Jagattarini, daughter of Harilal Chatterjee. At this time, the Mookerjees were living in Malanga Lane, amid a congested labyrinth of narrow lanes in the Bowbazar area of central Calcutta. On 28 June 1864, while Ganga Prasad was still a student, Jagattarini gave birth to their first child, a son named Asutosh. This was the time of the famous Bengal Renaissance, and it was no wonder that this son of Ganga Prasad would eventually grow up to be one of the greatest sons of Bengal of all time, and would sire the great man about whom this book is.

The medical practice of Dr Ganga Prasad flourished beyond all expectation, and he was very soon in a position to move out of the congested confines of Malanga Lane. The plot of land he chose to build his home on would be the spot that would see a lot of history being made in later years. This was 77 Russa Pagla Road (now 77 Asutosh Mookerjee Road) in Bhawanipur. The road was so named because it led to the ashram (abode) of a sadhu (sage) called Russa Pagla Baba in Tollygunge (some believe that the name owes its origin to the fact that it led to the lunatic asylum at Russa). Russa Pagla Road was later renamed Russa Road North, and the section where the building stands would be later renamed Asutosh Mookerjee Road, and still later, another section would be renamed Syama Prasad Mookerjee Road. The building is rather majestic to look at. It is still intact and in good shape, housing a number of organizations related to Asutosh Mookerjee and his descendants. At that time, Bhawanipur was one of the southern suburbs of Calcutta, but eventually the city grew well beyond it, so that today it is very much a part of south Calcutta. Ganga Prasad made his *griha pravesh*, the Hindu ceremony of entering one's own home for the first time, on the auspicious day of the first of 'baisakh', the Bengali New Year's Day, in April 1873. Although founded by a medical practitioner, eventually this house became the scene of a lot of action in the fields of law, education and, eventually, politics.

A feature worth mentioning about the Mookerjees is that the males in these successive generations of Mookerjees have all been given names following a set custom. Alternate generations have had the given middle name of 'Prasad', and the suffix of '-tosh' in their first names, as in Ganga Prasad–Asutosh, Syama Prasad–Anutosh, Subha Prasad–Agrotosh, and so on. In truth, 'Prasad' is not really a middle name at all, but a part of one's first name, but the way the names are written, it has come to be taken as a middle name. All Hindu names are supposed to have meanings, and

'Prasad', used in such a context as in given names, means 'pleasure of (usually a Hindu god or goddess)'. Thus, 'Ganga Prasad' means 'one with whom the Goddess Ganga is pleased'. The suffix '-tosh', on the other hand, means the act of being pleased, and can be used either actively or passively, depending on the context. Thus, 'Asutosh' means 'one who is easily pleased', 'Chittatosh' means 'one who pleases the mind', 'Shivatosh' means 'one who pleases Lord Shiva', and so on. Sir Asutosh and Mahamahopadhyay (great Sanskrit scholar) Hara Prasad Shastri were great friends, and it is believed that this friendship gave rise to this custom. The descendants of Sir Asutosh have followed this custom to the present generation.

Ganga Prasad had two sons, Asutosh and Hemanta Kumar (born in 1866), and a daughter, Hemlata (born in 1874). Both the siblings of Asutosh died early—Hemanta from typhoid at the age of twenty-one in 1887 and Hemlata at twenty-nine in 1903. It is believed that Ganga Prasad's death was precipitated by the death of his younger son, of whom he was very fond. A road commemorating Ganga Prasad's name runs parallel to the one named after his more famed and illustrious son Asutosh. His wife Jagattarini survived him and was a great influence on Asutosh's life. In those days, orthodox Hindus believed that 'crossing the seas' (going to England) was a mortal sin, and she forbade Asutosh to do so. Asutosh obeyed her and never travelled to England, something considered de rigueur in those times. His knighthood was conferred on him in absentia.

Asutosh Mookerjee, the eldest son of Ganga Prasad, later knighted by the British sovereign and usually referred to as 'Sir Asutosh', hardly needs any introduction, particularly in Bengal. A bronze statue of his stands at one of the most prominent road junctions of Calcutta, in front of CESC House (formerly Victoria House) at Chowringhee Square. He was a remarkable man in many ways, of which his physical appearance was not the least. Most photographs of him show him either in the robes of the university standing up, as in the statue, or bare-bodied, as was customary for Brahmins of that age to be—his more than ample torso adorned only by his *upaveeta* (*paita, janeu*), the sacred thread.[1] The most distinguishing feature of his face, his moustache, was nothing less than intimidating, and till this day, anyone in Bengal sporting a similar moustache is likened to him. It was a veritable bush. Never trimmed, it hung down from his nose almost to cover his entire mouth. His hair was cut short and parted in the middle, all of which together had the effect of giving him a very stern look. He laughed easily, but because of his formidable moustache, the laughter was not visible on his lips, only in his eyes. He had a booming voice that at once carried total authority, and together with it, a lot of compassion. He had the qualities that make a dictator, or at least a very authoritative person, but he used to put that quality to use only when strictly necessary. The rest of the time he was a person of consensus. Probably as much for his achievements as for his appearance, he had earned the sobriquet *Banglar Bagh* (Bengal Tiger).

Syama Prasad Mookerjee, about whom this book is, was the second son of Sir Asutosh. It is the unanimous view of his surviving kin that he inherited many of the qualities and characteristics of Sir Asutosh. Indeed in Syama Prasad, they saw fruition in public life, particularly politics, a field into which Sir Asutosh never ventured. A contemporary of Syama Prasad, Dr Dhirendra Nath Sen, has remarked,[2] 'Syama Prasad owed to his father his amazing capacity for work, his knowledge of men and affairs, his passionate devotion to the cause he had made his own, his tender care and consideration for scholars and students, his broad human sympathy and his courage and self-confidence. But it would be wrong to think that Syama Prasad was great because his father was great, that the son was no more than the sire's pale shadow. The son watched the father with admiration, followed him devotedly and utilized to the fullest extent both his rich inheritance and personal qualities, so that in the fullness of time he became a fighter, a builder and a leader.'

Asutosh joined the bar of the Calcutta High Court in 1893 and was elevated to the bench in 1904, where he served till his retirement in 1923. While at the bar, he took in and trained many juniors, then called articled clerks. His very last articled clerk was a young man, a very meritorious student, just like him in both mathematics and law, uncharacteristically from humble Atrap[3] Muslim peasant stock from the East Bengal district of Barisal. His name was Abul Kashem Fazlul Haq. He became a powerful and captivating speaker and an outstanding parliamentarian, and rose to become the premier of Bengal and Chief Minister of East Pakistan and is called *Sher-e-Bangla* (Tiger of Bengal) in Bangladesh. His association with Syama Prasad was intimate, and his name will recur many times in this biography.

Asutosh was married, as was the custom then, while in his early twenties and still a student, to the daughter of Ram Narayan Bhattacharyya of Krishnanagar, a district town about 100 kilometres north of Calcutta. Ganga Prasad, considering his standing in society then, could have got his son married to the daughter of a much richer man and got thousands of rupees in dowry, but opted for the daughter of Ram Narayan, a simple, learned, pious Brahmin. Additionally, he did not take a paisa in dowry. Asutosh's wife had been named Rakhali by her parents, but following marriage she was renamed Jogomaya. This marriage was in 1886, and the first child, a daughter, came quite late, in 1895. In those days, this was an inexcusable delay, and invariably led to the conclusion that the wife was barren, and the son had to be married again. Male sterility was habitually ruled out in those days and polygamy among Hindus was very much legal. In fact, tongues had started wagging in the direction of another marriage for Asutosh, and this made Ganga Prasad aghast. In the meantime, he had lost his second son and was very near his own end, but he made a will bequeathing his new house, not to Asutosh, but jointly to his wife, Jagattarini, and his daughter-in-law Jogomaya. In fact, Asutosh did not even become part owner of the house till 1914, when Jagattarini died.

After the birth of the first child, a daughter named Kamala (pronounced *Kaw-mo-lah*), a large family followed in quick succession. The eldest son, Rama (*Raw-mah*) Prasad, followed Kamala in 1896, Syama (*Sham-ah*) Prasad in 1901, the third son Uma (*Oo-mah*) Prasad in 1902, another daughter Amala (*Awe-mo-lah*) in 1905, the fourth son Bama Prasad in 1906, and the last, the third daughter Ramala (*Raw-mo-lah*) in 1908. Of the sons, other than Syama Prasad, Rama Prasad was later to become a judge of the Calcutta High Court, while Uma Prasad remained a bachelor, a famed trekker and travel writer in Bengali. But after all these children, the eldest—Kamala—remained Asutosh's favourite.

But all his love could not do anything about the terrible misfortune that seemed to have been ordained for her. Kamala was married in 1904 at the age of nine to Shubhendu Sundar Banerjee, a grandson of the great writer Bankim Chandra Chatterjee, creator of the immortal 'Vande Mataram', the national song of India. Shubhendu was a very handsome man, and as his only son-in-law, a great favourite of Asutosh. But he contracted typhoid fever within a few months of his marriage, for which there was no cure then, and succumbed to it. Asutosh was not the type to take misfortune lying down and lament and watch his dearest child spend the rest of her life as a Hindu widow. Remarriage of Hindu widows had, through the efforts of Pandit Ishwar Chandra Vidyasagar, been legalized only a short time ago, but was still very much frowned upon by orthodox Hindus, especially Brahmins. Asutosh obtained the consent of his mother and proceeded to get Kamala remarried, to Brajendra Nath Kanjilal, an advocate of the high court. He faced tremendous resistance in this action, not only from his colleagues and other orthodox Brahmins of Calcutta, but also from Shubhendu Sundar's mother (Bankim Chandra Chatterjee's daughter), who not only sued Sir Asutosh for custody of her minor widowed daughter-in-law, but tried to storm the Mookerjee house to forcibly take Kamala back. She failed in both attempts. Asutosh also had to face estrangement in his native village, Jirat. Braving all the resistance, he got his daughter remarried. But as poor Kamala's ill luck would have it, after all her father's herculean efforts, her second husband Brajendra also died shortly after marriage, probably from a heart attack.

Into such a family was born Syama Prasad Mookerjee on 6 July 1901.

* * *

His *daak naam* was Beni, but he was also called Bhutu or Bhuti. He grew up to be a stout child and darker than his brothers, about which he was somewhat sore. As a child, even before he had learnt to sit up he had gained some notoriety for having a voracious appetite like his father. He was fond of driving around the house on a tricycle, as his teacher Haridas Kar (later the headmaster of Bhawanipur Mitra Institution, Syama Prasad's school) recalled.

Food in the Mookerjee household consisted of rice as a staple, and was substantially vegetarian, with a lot of milk, both of which are distinctly un-Bengali traits. Among the menfolk, only Asutosh and Syama Prasad ate meat and fish. The other three brothers and the senior women, Jagattarini and Jogomaya, were strict vegetarians—no meat, no fish, no onions. Fish (always freshwater) was the usual non-vegetarian staple, and Sir Asutosh used to like *morola* and the head of the bigger fish. Milkmen used to look after and milk the cows in the compound. Asutosh was fond of the milk as well as the sandesh and other Bengali sweets made from that milk. Meat was a relative rarity, but occasionally meat from goats sacrificed at the Kali temple in Kalighat and offered to the goddess was brought in—this meat had to be cooked without onions, in the sattvic style. As for morning and afternoon snacks, home-cooked food was the rule, and eating snacks bought from the market was practically forbidden. One reason for this was that both Asutosh's wife and his mother were very orthodox about food, and would eat only food they themselves had cooked (*swapak*) and drink only water from the River Ganga (*Ganga-Jal*). In fact, they were orthodox not only about food but other things as well—Jogomaya never used to sit on a chair, and even on the ground, she would first spread her little mat which she used to carry wherever she went. Asutosh himself was not particularly orthodox by the standards of the times, but even he steered clear of tea or food served at the establishment of a Britisher, including the Government House.

Asutosh was a religious Hindu Brahmin, though unorthodox in his own way, but he did not try to inculcate his specific kind of religiosity in his children and preferred that they grew up according to the beliefs that they themselves developed along the way. The Hindu ambience in his family, combined with the liberated attitude of Sir Asutosh, must have worked to create in Syama Prasad his particular brand of religiosity, but there was more to it. Consider an entry (in Bengali) that he made in his diary[4] in the year 1946:

> I never learnt to look up to God with all my heart and soul— this is a great failing that I have. I believe in God. But I don't know, nor do I want to know who He is, and in which of our deities he resides. I am not a devotee of any particular deity. But I see nothing wrong in those who worship one deity or another . . . If one thinks that the deity is the God, then God must laugh at such action—but if the deity is only a medium

to invoke Him, and that gives one satisfaction, then that should
be all right. The important thing is to do it with heart and soul.
When does one look up to Him, pray to Him? When one's son
is ill, when one gets into trouble, loses one's job, incurs a loss,
is about to lose property . . . But how many of us pray to him
when there is no reason to do so? He must be invoked, prayed
to, when there is no earthly reason to do so, dispassionately,
without self-interest in mind.

And again, in another diary[5] entry in 1939, this time in English,
he writes:

Oh God! Give me faith, strength, courage and peace of mind.
Give me the will and the power to do good to others. Give me
your blessings that I may think of you in times of prosperity
and woe and merge myself in your boundless affection. Forgive
me for all the wrongs that I have done and lead me on to you
and you alone.

And again, written in Bengali, in his diary, on 27 January 1946:[6]

It is not possible to achieve anything if one does not have
physical and mental well-being. That is why I thank God
for whatever he has given me and I pray to Him to give me
the strength and devotion to dedicate myself to Him. I have
now come to realize that one's ailments and sorrows vanish
if one just concentrates on Him. I feel a sense of serenity that
I could never have imagined I was capable of attaining. But
I am still unable to invoke Him in right earnest. I suppose
that profound ability too lies in His hands. Previously, I had
never felt the urge to invoke Him thus. It is His grace that
has taught me to feel this way. So, I am confident that He,
in his infinite mercy, will show me the right way to do it. I

do not aspire for wealth, fame or glory. I will get only what I deserve and what I have laboured for. And I only seek the right to offer myself to Him. I do not wish to make any irrational demands on those whom I love dearly and whom I crave to have around me. I wish them happiness and peace. Living in this world is like living in a world of make-believe. It contains both truth and falsehood. If one achieves truth which I have had the good fortune to attain, why should He wish to forsake it? I want to cling to it with all my might.

Some of the words are very close to those found in Christian prayers, and the invocation is to the singular God. How is it that Syama Prasad, born in a family of devout Brahmins, the product of a Brahmanical education, is praying in this manner? The answer to this question probably lies in the realization of the universal God, to whom Syama Prasad was praying, something that came naturally to him and many enlightened people.

What sort of a person did Syama Prasad grow up to be—mentally or spiritually? For one thing, he has more than once mentioned in his writings that he was basically an introvert, a rather insular, reflective person; he was also an emotional person, and someone who needed someone else by his side to give him emotional support. He was seriously affected by the early death of his wife, as he makes clear in his diary. But he neither remarried, nor did he sink into grief. Probably he tried to and succeeded in drowning his grief in public work; yet during his private moments, he could not help reminiscing about her. He knew innumerable people, as a politician is apt to do, but none outside his family can claim to have become his confidante or special favourite. There were a few close people of course, like Dr Sarvepalli Radhakrishnan and Surendra Nath Sen, but it does not appear that he discussed matters of the state with them—or if he did, no one else knew what they talked about. Even within his family, only his *boudi*, his sister-in-law Tara Devi, could be said to be his real confidante—neither his brothers nor his children, after they grew up, could be said to have taken that place.

He liked the company of children and was fond of playing games with them. He was also fond of playing cards and reading detective novels for indoor recreation. His sense of humour and propensity for practical jokes have been described in the next chapter. In this regard, he was different from his elder brother Rama Prasad who was a very reserved and religious person.

Syama Prasad was also essentially a person with a very deep and abiding belief in the omnipotent, the universal God, as has been described earlier. When he was lying ill or convalescing in his Madhupur house in 1945–46, with a lot of time on his hands, the diary entries that he made give one some insight into his religiosity: 'One song from *Sakta Padavali*[7] which I have liked and committed to memory is: Mother Kali should be worshipped with the nectar of one's ardent devotion. Ostentatious worship is wholly unnecessary since it makes one proud. Nor are traditional offerings, candles, lamps or chandeliers at all necessary. Ramprasad[8] says, one should simply light up the lamp of devotion in one's mind and let it blaze day and night. The evil passions will be consumed by the fire of such a burning devotion.'

And another entry which lays bare the depth of his feelings: 'For some nights, I have been praying, pouring forth my soul, my eyes filled with tears: "Give me shelter. If You want to take me, take me today itself. I will not even feel a twinge of remorse. I will gladly extinguish the lamp of my life. But if You want me to stay on for some time more, give me peace; allow me to regain my faith in You; let me believe that You are mine, that You are the refuge of the homeless, the king of the beggars, the friend of the friendless; You are the beacon light of the lost traveller; the vision of the blind; wisdom for the ignorant and the friend of the poor." These thoughts fill my heart to the brim.'

On a mundane level, it can be said with certainty that he was a very kind and humane person, and despite being in the thick of politics, he was always prepared to go to great lengths to undo an injustice at the micro-level, a quality that he had inherited in ample measure from the great man who was his father. His worst detractor could not have accused him of the cynicism that infects most Indian politicians. In his diary, he mentions the case of a person, a lowly retired government servant getting a pension of around Rs 30 or 40, who had suffered a cut in his pension because of breaks in service, and had applied for a condonation of the breaks, which would give him an advantage of the princely sum of Rs 6 per month. His secretary wrote a voluminous note, advising him against it, as all precedents were against such condonation. He overruled his advice (no mean task in the Indian bureaucratic set-up) and managed to get the breaks condoned and his meagre pension restored. When his secretary insisted on his stating reasons for breaking away from the precedent, he said that he had found from the application that the poor ex-government servant had to carry on his shoulder the burden of a large family. He therefore wrote on the file that, if in some foreign countries, large additions to families were specially rewarded by the state, there was no reason why the Bengal government should not liberally interpret pension rules so as to help the family to some extent.

His brother Uma Prasad mentions the case of one person (whom he did not name) who was a sworn enemy of Syama Prasad on the floor of the Legislative Assembly. Uma Prasad was therefore surprised to see that the gentleman had come to see Syama Prasad with a request and a companion in tow. To his further surprise, Syama Prasad obliged. The man, while leaving his house bragged to his companion, when he thought no one else was listening, 'See how easily I can get Syama Prasad to do a job?' Uma Prasad went back to Syama Prasad and reported the incident. Syama Prasad smiled and said, 'Don't I know what sort of a person this man is? But the other man really needed the job done.' The help and hospitality he extended to the poet Kazi Nazrul Islam, described in detail in Chapter 5, tell the same story.

A comparison with his celebrated father would be relevant at this point. Dhirendra Nath Sen, a contemporary, has remarked,[9] 'It was Asutosh's habit to make all feel at home in his presence, and at the same time to put the insolent ones in their proper place. Asutosh admonished and rebuked, but he admired and loved as well. Syama Prasad was more tolerant, if I may say so with respect, than his father. Asutosh never forgave a foe till he was humbled and made to know where he actually stood. By contrast, there was absolutely no bitterness in Syama Prasad's dealings with his opponents and critics.' According to his nephew, Justice Chittatosh Mookerjee, Syama Prasad had an incredible capacity for convincing and befriending people. Other people have also spoken of his 'sweet reasonableness' when negotiating. As opposed to this, Sir Asutosh used to overawe people with his powerful personality.

On a different level altogether, Syama Prasad, in his youth, was fond of dressing well. In the happy photographs that we see him in with his beloved wife of only eleven years, he appears very well dressed, almost foppishly so, in a *merzai* and dhoti, smiling broadly through his ample moustache. His photographs of his sojourn in England also show him very nicely turned out in a three-piece suit and a handlebar moustache. In the fashion of the times, he also liked to carry a swagger stick, called a *chhari*, and it had to be of very good quality. In his later years, he appears to have become indifferent to clothes, as often happens to widowers.

His niece Amita Roy Choudhury, daughter of his sister Amala and Pramatha Nath Banerjee, however, recalled that Syama Prasad was conservative in matters of women's dress and once told her not to wear sleeveless blouses. As opposed to this, her family was a lot

more liberal. Between Syama Prasad's two daughters, the elder—
Sabita—was brought up in a conservative manner, according
to Amita. If given the chance, she might have blossomed into a
prominent woman in her own right, may have entered politics
even. Arati, the younger one, on the other hand, was treated
much more liberally. Syama Prasad had a special concern for this
younger daughter of his, who never knew a mother's love and,
moreover, had suffered from tuberculosis.

But we shall see, throughout the book, how Syama Prasad
developed as a man, as an administrator and as a political leader.
Let us for the moment, return to his childhood and focus on a
place that had played a cardinal part in his life—a little-known
place called Madhupur.

The district of Santhal Parganas in south Bihar (now
Jharkhand) abuts a part of the south-western flank of Bengal. It
is a picturesque area, full of wooded low hills, swift rivers and
rolling country covered by sal trees, and is inhabited largely by
tribal people known as Santhals, whence it gets its name. The
small railway junction town of Madhupur in the district lay
on the Howrah-Patna-Mughal Sarai main line of the then East
Indian Railway, some five hours' train journey from Howrah,
the rail terminus serving Calcutta. A branch line took off from
Madhupur to serve the collieries in nearby Giridih. In this town
of Madhupur, Sir Asutosh purchased a tract of sal tree-covered
land, and completed the building of a large two-storeyed mansion
there in 1912. He named it 'Ganga Prasad House' after his late
father, to serve as a getaway from busy Calcutta. This mansion at
Madhupur, as we shall see, was witness to many historic events
involving Syama Prasad and his family and associates—such as his
convalescence in 1939 and 1945–46 and the stay of the celebrated
Bengali poet Kazi Nazrul Islam and his wife in 1942.

Syama Prasad was inordinately fond of this house, and hence
of Madhupur. Many years and many personal tragedies later, he

spent a full month in 'change' and convalescence following a heart attack, between December 1945 and January 1946. During this stay, on 16 January 1946, he would lovingly reminisce about his days at Madhupur, and write about in his diary in Bengali, 'How happy we were when the new house was built! Everything was so novel—the rooms, the furniture, the lights, the garden, the trees—all were new. My grandmother, father and elder sister were still alive.' He goes on to describe the antics of a very fat Brahmin and a voracious eater called Bahuballabh Shastri who always accompanied them, and how the man once fell from his bed in his sleep and everyone thought it was an earthquake! In fact, the Mookerjees had started frequenting Madhupur even before 'Ganga Prasad House' was fully constructed, and during those days, they stayed in the house of Bijoy Narayan Kundu, a friend, and that is where the supposed 'earthquake' struck. Syama Prasad also recalled their griha pravesh. One requirement of the ceremony was that the owner had to enter the house after a cow, holding on to its tail, and Syama Prasad observes, 'This was assigned to my grandmother. It was not easy to find a cow sufficiently docile that would not run away or charge back when its tail was held.'

He wrote:

That was the beginning of my association with this house. For thirty-four years, it has sheltered and comforted me through the ups and downs of my life. We used to come here so often those days—during the summer holidays, Christmas holidays and Puja holidays. It was the newness of the place that had a charm of its own. With what alacrity and care we laid out the garden! My father bought the best saplings from far and wide to plant fruit trees in the garden. We bought so many flowering plants and books. The whole house was fitted with water pipes and taps, although they could not be utilized for

want of a proper water pump. I remember our eagerness to
come here during the summer holidays. The first year, my
grandmother was still alive. She suffered from rheumatism, so
an *akanda* shrub was planted in the garden. Since she liked
to eat *chalta* [a sour fruit used in condiments], a chalta tree
was also planted. But she died before the tree could give fruit.
My mother was recounting this today while we were eating a
preparation of chalta. All our teachers used to come here—
Haren Babu, Mukunda Babu, Panditmashai, sometimes Satish
Babu, the headmaster and many others. In summer, the water
was as cold as ice. We used to store it in earthen jars so that we
could have a cold bath at noon. How joyous were those days!
In the afternoons, the wind would blow like a gale. We used to
read, and chat, and roam around.

The person in charge of the household was Kamala, Asutosh's
eldest and favourite child, and also, the most unfortunate.
Asutosh called her Rani-ma (queen mother), and doted on
her. Syama Prasad has remarked more than once in his diary
about how inexpensive and plentiful foodstuff was: 'In summer
one could get, for a rupee, 12 to 16 seers of milk. During the
Pujas it would escalate to 8 seers for a rupee [probably because
of demand shooting up, due to the influx of a large number
of people from Calcutta] . . . food was cheap and plentiful at
Madhupur . . . every morning we used to have a lump of butter
with *mishri* [crystallized lumps of sugar].' During the summer,
Puja and Christmas holidays, the Mookerjees used to invite
people down from Calcutta to spend some time with them.
Most of the boys' teachers had visited them at Madhupur.
Even when Asutosh had to spend time in Calcutta because of
exigencies of his work while the family was at Madhupur, he
would come over every weekend by Punjab Mail and leave by
the evening train on Sunday.

The solitude, clear air and pristine atmosphere of the Madhupur of those days never failed to transport Syama Prasad into a reflective mood. In his last diary entry, made at Madhupur on 27 January 1946, just before leaving for Calcutta after a month-long stay of 'change' and convalescence, he reflects:

> I have not been able to decide on any future course of action. I do not want to get involved in political factionalism. It can serve no purpose. I am sick and tired of all the disputes and quarrels. I want to do something that will give me peace. I do not aspire to glory any more, but I have the desire to do something constructive. I do not have the resources to enable me to do my duty to my family and still have enough left to give my dreams a concrete shape. I wish I could build an organization which could train at least twenty-five people every year, who would pledge their lives for the service of society. Where are the noble workers who would bravely take on the challenge of nation-building? The country cannot be redeemed by political wranglings. My organization would be a centre for the study of Sanskrit, not merely to learn the language, but to explore the vast resource of knowledge enshrined in it and spread it to the people and the world at large. Whatever is of abiding value in our culture is preserved in Sanskrit which is still inaccessible to the people. The erudite English and German scholars tried to kindle this lamp of wisdom for us but we, in our eagerness to imbibe western education, shied away from appreciating our own culture. What a shame! This nation can never come into its own if its search for an identity is not founded on its own culture.
>
> I will return home tomorrow. It seems as though I am returning after an eternity . . .

Another very popular getaway for wealthy Bengalis, then as well as now, is the seaside resort and pilgrimage town of Puri in Orissa, the abode of the Hindu deity Lord Jagannath whose magnificent temple adorns the place, and whose rath yatra (trip by chariot, to his aunt's house) once a year is a world-famous event. Madhupur, or its neighbouring towns of Simultala, Giridih or Karmatanr are no longer popular with Bengalis as resorts or getaways, but Puri continues to be just as popular as it used to be in Sir Asutosh's time. Puri is not as near as the Santhal Pargana towns, being an overnight journey away by train from Calcutta. Sir Asutosh had built a house in Puri also, on Chakratirtha Road, a little north of the B.N.R. Hotel, practically on the beach. This house, however, was much less popular and much less frequented than the Madhupur house, and the Puri house finds little mention in Syama Prasad's diary or any other chronicle. Syama Prasad has of course mentioned his occasional trips to Puri, of which one was memorable as a quasi-honeymoon (real honeymoons were unknown in those days), but nowhere has he described the Puri house with such love and nostalgia as he has in the case of the Madhupur house.

2

Student Days and a
Short Married Life, 1906–33

Syama Prasad began going to school at the age of five. Haridas Kar, his teacher, and later the headmaster of the school, remembered the exact date of his entry. It was on 23 July 1906 that he was admitted to Class II. Today, children from middle-class families start going to school from the age of two or even earlier, but in those days, five was too early for most boys. But he insisted on going because his elder brother Rama Prasad had already started going. His school, the Bhawanipur Mitra Institution, was a branch of the Mitra Institution (Main) of central Calcutta, but was by far the more famed of the two. Teaching had begun in a building in Kansari Para in Bhawanipur, not far from 77 Russa Road North, but later moved to a nearby and better location, next to Harish Park. This was on Harish Mukherjee Road, at its junction with Balaram Basu Ghat Road, where the primary section of the school still stands. The school was considered one of the best in Calcutta, indeed in the whole of Bengal, boasting one or two students almost every year among the top ten in the school-leaving examinations. It enjoyed this status till the 1970s, until the standard of all government-aided schools was deliberately, and by way of policy, diluted by the Left Front government of West Bengal. This was done principally through the abolition of the teaching of English language in the lower classes and lowering the standards in the upper classes.

A teacher of Syama Prasad at school, Harshanath Banerjee,[1] taught him between 1907 and 1910, and later became a successful lawyer at Alipore, remembered him as a very sunny child. According to Banerjee, he never tried to throw his weight around just because his father was such an important person, or because he and his brothers came to school in a horse-drawn carriage. He never used to quarrel with his classmates. One trait Banerjee had noticed was that he used to listen to stories about great men with a degree of interest unusual for his age—Banerjee remembered telling him about George Washington and Napoleon Bonaparte. Both Haridas Kar and Banerjee had written their reminiscences in a school publication after the death of Syama Prasad in 1953.

According to his brother Uma Prasad,[2] just one year younger than him, Syama Prasad was never particularly interested in sports, although he was quite fond of all the boyish fun. His interest outside his studies was principally in reading. Just as he was built bigger than most boys of his age, so was he also inclined to read and assimilate more, and mix with boys above his age. Although he was just one year older than Uma Prasad, he was three classes ahead of him in school. This, however, did him no good, because of a rule which required that one had to be at least sixteen to sit for the matriculation examination. So after finishing school, he went off to the family getaway at Madhupur to relax and enjoy himself. Meanwhile, it so happened that the question paper of matriculation was leaked out shortly before the examination, not once but twice, and the examination could not be held on time. The university then notified that those who would complete the age of sixteen before the delayed examination would be eligible for taking it. Syama Prasad fell in this category. He was promptly summoned from Madhupur by telegram and told to sit for the examination. He was not very well prepared, but went ahead anyway, and passed the matriculation examination of the Calcutta University in 1917, and became eligible for admission to college.

He also managed to get a scholarship besides a first division, although he would have done much better if he had gone about it in a better way.

In 1917, Syama Prasad, upon passing matriculation, entered Presidency College, the topmost degree college in all of Bengal. The pattern of education then in Bengal, which continued till 1960, was thus: ten years in high school from class one till ten; the matriculation examination, a public examination conducted by the Calcutta University (this was later renamed 'school final' after the Board of Secondary Education took the place of the university after Independence); two years of 'intermediate' studies in college (arts, science or commerce), followed by the intermediate examination in arts, science or commerce; two years of 'pass' or 'honours' course, leading to graduation and the bachelor's degree in arts, science or commerce; and two years of master's in a specific branch of arts, science or commerce, leading to the postgraduate or master's degree in that subject. Syama Prasad enrolled in the Intermediate Arts (IA) class, sat for the examination in 1919 and made it to the first position in IA.

Syama Prasad's reading habits had interesting sidelights. In his intermediate classes, he had finished the entire set of writings of Sir Arthur Conan Doyle, the creator of Sherlock Holmes, and was hugely impressed by them. He then wrote to Doyle asking for a signed photograph of him. Then, a few years later, when he went to England, he saw Doyle and had a long discussion with him about life after death, a thing that Doyle believed in and had studied. He later related this discussion to his brother Uma Prasad.

He was generally reserved in nature, but could, if provoked, give vent to his gift of repartee that found full expression against Prime Minister Jawaharlal Nehru in the Indian Parliament many years later. Uma Prasad recalled an incident in which a few boys, intending to make fun of his corpulence, crowded him on a staircase and started fondling his ample belly, pretending to be very familiar. Syama Prasad pretended even more familiarity and gave one of them a hefty punch on the back, apparently in jest. The boy, completely winded, gave up.

Syama Prasad's close friend Surendra Nath Sen,[3] the famous historian, recalled his liking for impish fun. For one thing, Sen said, he would not hesitate to demonstrate his skill in imitating other people's signatures. It would be difficult for anyone but a professional expert to find fault with some of these imitations, particularly the signatures of Sir Asutosh Mookerjee, J.R. Barrow and R.B. Ramsbotham. One morning, when Sen had gone to see him, he found him seated on his father's table with a solemn face surrounded by a few of his contemporaries. On a chair nearby was a middle-aged man with a bundle of much-handled papers. Syama Prasad gravely introduced Sen as one of the rising members of the Calcutta Bar to the man with the bundle and asked him to show Sen his papers. The old man, quite daft, was under the impression that Syama Prasad was really Sir Asutosh, and had come to him with a complaint, and Syama Prasad had done nothing to dispel that impression. The man seriously believed that he was God himself, and the Empire of India, therefore, belonged by right to him. But the British government had defrauded him of his dues and he wanted to sue them at the high court. He was, however, prepared to make an amicable settlement, provided the other party paid him one lakh rupees in full settlement of his claims! Strangely enough, this gentleman was still functioning as the headmaster of an English middle school in a neighbouring township. A harmless lunatic, he used to come to Calcutta on Sundays to seek the assistance of men of influence. Living within 12 miles of the city, he did not know yet that the Bengal Tiger was no more and encountered his son instead, who did not hesitate to join the fun.

On another occasion, as his nephew Purnendu Banerjee[4] recalled, the two of them were at Madhupur, walking by a bush, when Purnendu, then a child, bothered his uncle in some way. Syama Prasad picked up a couple of chillies from a shrub nearby and put them in his mouth and pretended he was hugely enjoying them. Purnendu did likewise, bit into one of the chillies and then let out a shriek—his mouth was burning. People from the house came running and Purnendu's burning mouth had to be cooled with water, sugar and ghee. Sir Asutosh admonished Syama Prasad, asking him not to do this to a small child again.

Purnendu's sister Amita Roy Choudhury recalled that once on April Fool's Day, Syama Prasad had poured loads of sugar into everybody's tea—with the result that they had to spit it out after the very first sip.

After passing his intermediate examination, Syama Prasad enrolled himself in the BA English honours class, and came first in the examination in 1921. In both IA and BA, he had topped the list in Bengali and was thus awarded the Bankim Chandra gold and silver medals. After this, however, instead of enrolling in the MA English class, he did so in Bengali, a department that had been started just a few years ago by his father against stiff opposition. He simultaneously enrolled in the evening law classes of the law faculty of the university. Here again, he topped the list in both and came out first in the class, in Master of Arts in 1923 and in Bachelor of Law (BL) the next year. In his MA class, he had opted for writing an original thesis on the social plays of Girish Chandra Ghosh, a famous Bengali actor and playwright of the nineteenth century and a disciple of Shri Ramakrishna Paramahansa.

Sir Asutosh enrolling Syama Prasad in the MA course in Bengali (instead of in English, which was the fashionable thing to do) is, incidentally, an example of his courage of conviction—he was never afraid to do what he believed to be true.

Syama Prasad's coming first at a stretch in the intermediate, graduation and postgraduate examinations while his father was the vice chancellor—and so powerful as to be practically synonymous with the university—inevitably gave rise to wagging tongues and rumours of nepotism on the part of Asutosh. The name of at least one of his contemporaries, later of the Indian Civil Service, have been heard by this biographer as having been deprived of their due places so that Syama Prasad could come first. Along with Syama Prasad, allegations of nepotism on the part of Sir Asutosh with respect to Pramatha Nath Banerjee, his son-in-law, have also done the rounds. No one had ever come forward to make these allegations seriously enough to provoke a formal inquiry. It has also to be regretfully admitted that spreading canards like these about people who have attained positions of eminence is an unfortunate trait present in many people. It had happened in the case of other luminaries too, such as Ishwar Chandra Vidyasagar and Rabindranath Tagore, among others. At any rate, no one has ever questioned the extraordinary academic merit of Syama Prasad.

Those years, when Syama Prasad was in Presidency College, were heady times when the world was changing very fast. Those were the days of the Russian Revolution in which a lot of middle-class Bengalis saw the coming of a new world order. The First World War, which had been raging since 1914, was coming to an end. Those were the days of the overthrow and murder of the Czar in Russia, Lenin's New Economic Policy, replacement of the Kaiser's rule by the Weimar Republic in Germany, the demise of the Ottoman and Austro-Hungarian Empires in Europe and the Middle East, the treaties of Versailles and of Sevres, the Khilafat movement followed by Kemal Ataturk's modernization of Turkey and the founding of the League of Nations. On the Indian scene, there was the dastardly massacre of 1516 unarmed people at a peaceful gathering by a British colonel called Reginald Dyer at Jallianwala Bagh in Amritsar, and Tagore's renouncing of his knighthood in protest thereof and the infamous Rowlatt

Act of 1919, which empowered the government to arrest Indians without trial. The Montagu-Chelmsford reforms were introduced in 1919 and ushered in a period of diarchy in the country, in which Indians were given some powers in respect of some less important departments of the government. A hitherto unheard-of Gujarati barrister by the name Mohandas Karamchand Gandhi, who had so far practised in South Africa, moved to India, joined the Congress and began to make his presence felt with his unusual brand of politics. There was a lot of action in Bengal also, when two young Bengali Hindu revolutionaries, Jatindra Nath Mukherjee (better known as 'Bagha Jatin' or Tiger Jatin) and Narendra Nath Bhattacharyya, collaborated with the German consul at Shanghai, and planned to import two shiploads of armaments and land them at Raimangal in the Sundarbans and at Balasore in Orissa. The plan did not work out. Mukherjee was killed in a gun battle with the police at Balasore in Orissa. Bhattacharyya escaped abroad, changed his name to Manabendra Nath Roy (better known as M.N. Roy) and became an associate of Lenin during and after the Russian revolution.

Was Syama Prasad, with the predilection towards politics that he would exhibit in later life, affected by any of these?

Apparently not at all, or else he could not have achieved the results that he did in his academic pursuits. He would also probably not have agreed to get married so early, which he did while in his MA class in 1922. Most Bengali revolutionaries were bachelors for life or at least till well past the age when, at the time, middle-class Bengali boys got married around twenty. In fact, at this stage he did not seem to be inclined towards politics at all. There is no record or recollection as to what he thought of the political developments at this time, but apparently a career in politics was not one of them. Very probably he had designs, following his father's footsteps, to become an educationist (which he did become for some time) and a lawyer (which he did not, in any serious measure). Anyway, for the moment his philosophy of life seemed to be contained in the oft-quoted Sanskrit saying *chhatranam adhyayanam tapah* (for a student, study is worship).

Another aspect, a very significant one, has also to be borne in mind, as this would be manifest time and again during Syama Prasad's later years. Though Syama Prasad had been a member of the Bengal Legislative Assembly since 1929 from the Registered Graduates' constituency, he entered full-time politics only some eight years later, in 1939. And then, he did not subscribe either to the dominant political line of the Hindus at that time, namely Gandhism, or to the violent politics of the Bengal revolutionaries, or to Marxism, or even to the pro-Axis, anti-British, militarist line of Subhas Chandra Bose based on the dictum, 'the enemy's enemy is my friend'. With respect to the last mentioned, he was categorical: in a letter[5] dated 12 August 1942, addressed to Lord Linlithgow, the viceroy of India, he said, 'No one genuinely interested in the welfare of India wants that the Axis powers should win the war, for their victory is a peril to the cause of world freedom and specially to Indian liberty.' In his statement on resignation from the post of finance minister in the Progressive Democratic Coalition cabinet (see Chapter 6) in November 1942, he had said,[6] 'The Indian public on the whole can possibly have no sympathy with any foreign aggressor. We do not want a change of masters.' Syama Prasad Mookerjee's basic beliefs, ideology and political methods were distinctly, fundamentally and decidedly right wing, Indocentric and constitutional. He was a constitutional politician at heart, the very antithesis of a revolutionary. As would be apparent from his reflections at Madhupur, he had a deep attachment to the rich past of India, and chose to draw ideological sustenance from Indian traditions, not from Marx, Mill or Webb. And in what would seem to be a somewhat un-Bengali trait, he had no taste for insurrectionist or violent or even left-of-centre, social democratic politics. Leftist tendencies in Bengali politics had already started with the Russian Revolution and the founding of the Communist Party of India in Tashkent in 1920. But these did not interest Syama Prasad in the least. The early Bengali violent revolutionaries of the *agni-yuga* (pronounced *Ogni-jug* in Bengali) genre, such as Aurobindo Ghose (before he turned to spiritualism), Khudiram Bose, Bagha Jatin, Surya Sen, Kanai Lal Datta, the Binoy-Badal-Dinesh trio and others were all Hindus almost to a man, and used to take oath upon the Bhagavad Gita. By the 1930s, quite a few of them had turned to communism, or were dwelling in the halfway house called the Congress Socialist Party. No person could be further from any of these than Syama Prasad. Neither their jargon-laden Marxist-Leninist doctrine, nor their agitative and revolutionary methods, nor their blind toeing of the Soviet line attracted him in the least.

At the same time, he did not develop any taste for Gandhian politics, with its pacifism and turn-the-other-cheek philosophy, as most politicians of the Congress genre did by and by, many of them probably without believing in it. The Congress had a typical bend-over-backwards policy of appeasement, allegedly propagated and internalized by the party, during the Khilafat movement and forever thereafter. Syama Prasad's distaste for this was not manifest at this stage, however, and was a later development. This was later encapsulated in his famous diary entry, 'Force must, in the last analysis, be met by force. An internal policy of non-resistance to armed violence would ultimately condemn any society to dissolution.' Much more on this later.

He sincerely believed that whatever power was given to one through a constitutional route ought to be grabbed by one and made use of to extract more power. Refusing to share any power unless power was given to the desired extent was, in his view, justifiable only if one was sure of winning one's case in the end. He had said this repeatedly in his diaries, and subsequent events

mostly proved him right. In a diary entry made on 5 January
1946, he observed:

> During the promulgation of reforms in India [meaning the
> Morley-Minto reforms, the Montagu-Chelmsford reforms and
> the Government of India Act 1935] Bengal was never under
> the influence of ministers who were truly responsive to public
> opinion . . . During the days of C.R. Das, the battle cry was
> 'down with dyarchy', and the Congress thought that the greatest
> achievement was to render the Constitution unworkable. Non-
> cooperation was the order of the day and it was not thought
> desirable or necessary that people's representatives should
> undertake the burden of office . . . What happened was that
> third-rate men were found available who could indulge in all
> fashions of intrigue and corruption . . . Another disastrous
> consequence was . . . that if Hindus deliberately chose to
> remain aloof, the King's government could be carried on with
> the help of Muslims mainly.

As we shall see later, this attachment of Syama Prasad to
parliamentary and constitutional politics manifested itself again in
his attitude during the Quit India movement of 1942 (which was
far from being wholly non-violent) and his reactions to Subhas
Chandra Bose's politics. While fully sympathizing with the cause,
and entreating the viceroy not to meet the presumed threat with
repression, he was never afraid to differ with them regarding the
methods used. He did not join the movement or try to prevail
upon his party, the Hindu Mahasabha, to support the movement.
There were some instances, like in 1945, when a boy had died in
a police firing in Calcutta, or when he courted arrest at the Ravi
bridge in Jammu and Kashmir in 1953 (which led to his death),
or when he did take to the streets against governmental tyranny or
by popular demand. But these seem to be exceptions.

As for his attitude towards Netaji Subhas Chandra Bose and his politics, it is clear that the two thought very, very differently, and steered very, very different courses. But they both aimed at liberating the country from the yoke of the British rule, and thereafter developing it into a strong and healthy nation. Syama Prasad's unalloyed opposition to the pro-Axis stand of Subhas has already been dealt with earlier. The two had considerable interaction, and there was some friction too. For example, in the Calcutta Municipal Corporation election in 1940 (dealt with later, in Chapter 4). This interaction was, however, over a very limited period, because Syama Prasad entered politics in full scale in 1939, and Subhas left India for Germany in January 1941, less than two years later. Some parallels between the two are, however, quite striking. They lived less than a mile apart in Bhawanipur, then a southern suburb of Calcutta—the Boses at 38/2 Elgin Road, the Mookerjees at 77 Asutosh Mookerjee Road. Both were from large, established, affluent families— Subhas and his siblings counted fourteen, Syama Prasad and his, half of that. Subhas Bose's father, Janaki Nath Bose, was an established advocate in Cuttack and Syama Prasad's father was, of course, Sir Asutosh. They were very close in age, Subhas having been born in 1897 and Syama Prasad in 1901. And the death or disappearance of both is shrouded in mystery, though the hue and cry raised in respect of Syama Prasad's death has been minuscule compared to that of Subhas's. According to the official version, Subhas was killed in an air crash immediately after taking off from Taihoku (Taipei), Formosa (now Taiwan), but millions of people do not believe this. In fact, there is some evidence to show that he was taken prisoner by the Soviets and died or was killed in captivity, and not much evidence has been made public, or even revealed before investigating commissions. A tiny number of people believe, or say they believe, that he is still alive, though he would be 120 now. As for Syama Prasad's mysterious death in captivity in Kashmir, a full chapter in this book has been devoted to the subject.

Syama Prasad's elder brother, Rama Prasad, got married in 1920. His wife, Tara Devi[7] (Bengali Brahmin women in those days generally used the ubiquitous surname Devi rather than their family names), remained a beacon in Syama Prasad's life—it is doubtful if Syama Prasad could have immersed himself in public life the way he did had this dutiful and affectionate sister-in-law not taken charge of his motherless children after his wife had died. She was his confidante in all family matters and a lot of public matters too—quite a few letters from Syama Prasad during his last days in captivity in Kashmir were addressed to her.

Wedding bells for Syama Prasad himself rang in 1922 while he was studying for his MA. The bride was Sudha Chakravarty, daughter of Beni Madhab Chakravarty and granddaughter of Bihari Lal Chakravarty, an important Bengali poet of the nineteenth century, settled in Muzaffarpur, north Bihar. Sarat Kumar Chakravarty, another son of Bihari Lal had married Madhuri Lata, the eldest child and daughter of the poet Rabindranath Tagore, but she died early from tuberculosis. The wedding was on 16 April, in a house in Nimtala, and the bride's side had arranged for a specially reserved tramcar to take the bridegroom's party (*borjatri* or *baraat*) from Bhawanipur to Nimtala. Sir Asutosh rode in this tramcar with the rest of the party, possibly the only time he rode on public transport. Almost exactly two years later, on 15 April 1924, Syama Prasad's eldest son and Asutosh's first grandson—Anutosh (Santu)—was born.

Syama Prasad apparently, had toyed with the idea of becoming a journalist or a columnist at some point of time during his studies and had mentioned this to Sir Asutosh, who, ever full of encouragement for all worthy pursuits, sent his son to Pat Lovett, a respected journalist and the editor of the then popular weekly *Capital*. They had a pleasant tête-à-tête and Lovett wrote a very warm letter[8] to Sir Asutosh, complimenting Syama Prasad as a 'charming young fellow who immediately conquered my sympathy. He has a worthy journalistic ambition which I shall do my best to encourage.' Later in life, Syama Prasad had founded an English daily called *Nationalist* and a Bengali one called *Hindusthan* in 1944. However, these were basically adjuncts to his politics and not independent journalistic ventures.

While in his MA class, Syama Prasad and his elder brother Rama Prasad had also started a monthly Bengali literary journal called *Bangabani* (Voice of Bengal) from their residence. This journal immediately shot into a prominence that was quite unexpected, considering the young age and inexperience of the editors. Several poems and prose compositions of Rabindranath Tagore were published in this magazine for the first time. It continued to be published for about six years, during which quite a few of Tagore's compositions appeared in it. Among other prominent Bengali littérateurs who contributed to it were Jyotirindra Nath Tagore (the poet's elder brother), Achintya Kumar Sengupta, Kumud Ranjan Mallik, Surendra Nath Sen, Kabishekhar Kalidas Ray, Chapala Bala Basu, Narendra Deb, and others. Binoy Kumar Sarkar, a prominent and controversial professor of economics of the time, wrote an essay on the composition of a Hindu *rashtra* (state). But the most interesting thing about this journal was that it serialized the immortal Bengali novelist Sarat Chandra Chatterjee's (author of the popular novella *Devdas*) highly controversial *Pather Dabi*. It was stridently anti-British and was proscribed and banned by the government as soon as it appeared in book form. It is not known why the government had permitted it as a serial—probably there were legal difficulties in banning it just then. *Bangabani* ceased publication in 1928. By then the brothers had become too busy in other pursuits and had no time to edit the journal.

Having passed the Bachelor of Law (BL) examination of the Calcutta University in 1924, Syama Prasad was eligible to practise as an advocate in the Calcutta High Court. However, he had apparently already decided that he would not be satisfied with this and would go to England to become a barrister. Sir Asutosh was not happy with his sons or sons-in-law going to England, which used to be the invariable destination of successful Indians in those days, either to compete in the Indian Civil Service (ICS) examination or to become a barrister.

The 1920s and the years immediately following were not a good time for the Mookerjees at all. The family was devastated by deaths of its members, all of them untimely, one after another. The first to go, in 1923, was Asutosh's pet, his eldest daughter and child, the singularly unfortunate Kamala, at the age of only twenty-eight. The family was returning from Madhupur to Calcutta in January 1923 after the Christmas holidays, with Syama Prasad's younger sister Amala (Bura) down with a fever. Suddenly, halfway through, somewhere near Asansol, Kamala also started complaining of severe abdominal pain, which got progressively worse. She had had a history of intermittent intestinal trouble for quite some time, and probably had a serious case of peritonitis while on the train. At that time, there was no cure for acute peritonitis. She did not live long after reaching Calcutta, and before dying, on 5 January, asked that the doors be opened, because 'she wanted to go'. She was quite conscious when she touched Asutosh's feet and said, 'I have made you suffer all my life. I could not make you happy', and was gone a short while after that. From that year on, there were no more Durga Pujas at the Mookerjee household. Her death affected Syama Prasad profoundly, and he has recounted each one of these deaths in his Bengali diary, written at Madhupur in 1945, in poignant language. Only a Hindu knows what a disaster widowhood is for a woman and her parents—it was many times worse then compared to now—and Kamala had been twice widowed, both times within a year or so of her marriage. Her misfortune is something that tormented Asutosh all the time, and her death wrecked him from inside. His family members often observed him awake at night, pacing the long corridors of his house. He could not have taken it much longer.

The next to go, therefore, was the grand patriarch, Sir Asutosh himself, the very next year in 1924. He had just turned sixty. And the last was Sudha, Syama Prasad's dear wife of only eleven years, aged only twenty-four, in the year 1933.

Asutosh, who had retired from his post of judge in the Calcutta High Court in January 1924, rejoined the bar, but rules forbade him to practise in the same high court. He had accepted the brief in the Dumraon (a major zamindari estate in Bihar) case and was to go to Patna to appear before the Patna High Court. Syama Prasad was already being groomed for the university by Sir Asutosh, and had been made a fellow of the university senate in the faculty of arts. He was due to go to Simla for the Universities' Conference. On the day of his departure and on the day before, Asutosh had a long talk with Syama Prasad on the balcony of no. 77 about university affairs and the former's expectations of Syama Prasad. The two of them then drove to the railway station and Asutosh talked all the while, rather uncharacteristically for him, as his son observed later. Syama Prasad left for Simla, and shortly afterwards, Asutosh left for Patna. That was the last time the son saw the father. While in Simla, he received a telegram to proceed post-haste to Patna. He was met at the station, among others, by Sir Hasan Imam, who looked grim and said, 'My boy, he is seriously ill.' Syama Prasad rushed to where he was staying to find his father dead. The next day his body was taken on a special train to Howrah. Jogomaya, his just-widowed wife, boarded the train in Jhajha and was beside herself with grief. A huge crowd had gathered at Howrah station to receive them. That was the end of the great man.

Syama Prasad had just eleven years of married life, and
not much is known about their conjugal relationship, except
that it was generally very happy. There had been a long period
of separation when he had gone away to England to study for
the bar between 1926 and 1927. This was usual in upper-class
Bengali families of the time, because no one was considered up
to the mark unless one was *bilat-pherat* (one who has been to
England). England was to Indians then the seat of their colonial
power and therefore the centre of the world. In his Bengali diary,
written during his convalescence at Madhupur in 1945, he had
recounted once that in Madhupur, during the Christmas holidays
in 1922–23, he and Sudha used to sleep in a particular room, and
those few days had been spent in heavenly bliss. This was the stay
at Madhupur during the return from which Kamala fell fatally
ill. And for a second time, in the same diary, he had recounted
the trip to Puri, during the Puja holidays the same year (October
1923) when his elder brother had taken his grieving mother on
a tour of pilgrimage. This was the time when he noted he had
become intimate with his wife for the first time (perhaps not in
the physical sense—that must have happened earlier). They used
to take long walks on the magnificent beach of Puri and had a
long stay together, away from Calcutta. He also recalled that this
was the time when she conceived Anutosh (Santu), her first born.
These two recollections are all that is known about the conjugal
life of the man. Of course, in the still-Victorian Bengal of the
1940s, no one could be expected to write much more than this.

Not much is known about Sudha Devi, Syama Prasad's
beloved wife of only eleven years. Her photographs, mostly faded
now, show her as a pretty woman of very fair complexion with
a round face, chubby cheeks and the rounded features usually
associated with upper-class Bengalis. Her elder daughter Sabita
remembered her very vaguely, for she was only seven when she
died. By all accounts (mostly Syama Prasad's diaries, written many

years later), they had a very happy married life and she completely surrendered herself to her husband, letting him attend to his public duties unhindered by the requirements of domesticity. She bore Syama Prasad five children, of whom the last one, a four-month-old son, died from diphtheria. She was heartbroken after this and contracted double pneumonia shortly afterwards. Antibiotics had not been discovered and there was no cure for the disease then. Her father took her away to his house on nearby Townshend Road and there, she breathed her last. One day, the children, of whom the eldest was only nine, were told, '*Tomader ma tomader chhere chole gechhen* (Your mother has left you and gone).' The children could not follow what it all meant. They all trotted to their grandfather's house to find their mother in her eternal sleep.

It was not the norm then for men to publicly mourn the death of one's wife. All that Syama Prasad is said to have remarked, while standing by the side of his wife's burning pyre, is '*Ki shorbonash-i na hoye gelo* (What a terrible, terrible disaster)!' His brother Uma Prasad has described this heart-rending scene in very poignant language in his book (in Bengali) on Syama Prasad's diary and his death.

Much later, in his diary on 4 January 1946, he fondly reminisced about his dear wife whom he had lost thirteen years earlier:

I loved her deeply and had infinite faith in her. Whatever she had to offer, she showered upon me unhesitatingly. I cannot express in words the joy and happiness that I felt in the eleven years that she was with me. She was not very familiar with the world outside and I was so immersed in university affairs that I had little time for much else. I still have not got over the grief of losing Sudha . . . The loss affected me more emotionally than physically. I am emotionally so dependent that I don't find any stability unless I have someone by my side to lend me strength. I did not consider marrying again, not only because of my intense love for Sudha but because I had my children's welfare at heart . . . It would not only have hurt their feelings to see a stranger usurp their mother's place, but the other person's presence would perhaps have created other complications too. I have never hankered for physical pleasures so I didn't miss them. But I did need a person who would understand me and wish me well; a person who would inspire me, empathize with me and respect my innermost sentiments.

Syama Prasad also described Sudha's unbearable agony after the loss of their four-month-old boy in a private diary. However, his surviving niece who has the custody of that diary, and who has otherwise been the soul of cooperation and support in the writing of this biography, declined to reveal the contents of that diary for reasons of family privacy.

After Sudha died, Jogomaya had indeed asked Syama Prasad to marry again—she said someone was needed to take care of the children. Syama Prasad flatly refused and said that a stepmother could not possibly do it. Then his elder brother's wife Tara Devi stepped in and said she would take care of the children. Syama Prasad's elder daughter Sabita recalled that after this, whenever asked how many children she had, Tara Devi always used to answer, 'Eight', meaning her own four and Syama Prasad's four. Syama Prasad's children had very few occasions to miss the love of their mother.

In his diary, Syama Prasad recalled how his two sons and two daughters were all brought up by his dear boudi, Tara Devi, like her own children. In the same diary entry, he expresses his gratefulness to her too, for what she had done for his children after they lost their mother:

Boudi took my children to her bosom and gave them a lot of affection . . . I do believe that my children understand how much they owe their aunt . . . When the tragedy struck, she willingly took charge of my children and I was grateful to her. On that dreadful night, my five-year-old daughter, Hasi, had wept near her mother's body and had clung to her aunt, crying 'Let us go home, auntie'. Soon after, when Santu [Anutosh, his eldest son] had an attack of typhoid [a disease with a high mortality rate then] . . . she nursed him with a mother's tender care. Quite amazingly, Santu came back from the jaws of death and recovered. Since then, over the years, I have found strength in the rare brand of fond affection that Boudi has showered on me.

Syama Prasad was a very loving father and used to absolutely dote on his motherless children. They called him by the endearing name Bapi, instead of the usual Baba, but in the manner of the times used to address him with the honorific *aapni* (Bengali for the Hindi word *aap*) and not as *tumi*, as would be done today. Sabita or Bua, the eldest daughter, when interviewed in 2010, did not remember any occasion when he had beaten them or yelled at them, which was rather unusual for the times, for it used to be said then, 'Spare the rod and spoil the child.' Sabita grew up to be a bit of a tomboy and used to play cricket with her brothers and cousins. Once she fell and cut her leg so badly that she had to be given several stitches. When the doctor was putting in the stitches and she was crying in pain, Syama Prasad promised her a huge doll. Being the big sister, she was a shadow of the mother to her younger siblings, especially Ontu, the youngest, who was very attached to her and used to cry a lot when she had to leave her father's house for her husband's. Anutosh (Santu) and Debtosh (Ontu) were also outgoing by nature, but Arati (Hasi) was rather withdrawn and introverted.

Syama Prasad used to tell the children that they should tell him of any mischief that they did and not hide it from him. He was extremely busy and had little time for his children, but he used that little time to shower his love on them. He used to talk to them about their mother (whom Sabita and Anutosh remembered only vaguely and Arati and Debtosh almost not at all), what she was like and so on.

Asutosh was against his children going abroad, and it is doubtful if Syama Prasad could have gone to England to study for the bar if he had been alive. After his death, however, there was no problem and Syama Prasad left for England in 1925, leaving behind his wife of three years, his one-year-old son Santu (Anutosh) and his entire huge extended family. He reached England in due time and took up residence at 112 Gower Street in London and joined the Lincoln's Inn. He shared this accommodation with Surendra Nath Sen, the historian, and Jatindra Mohan Majumdar, another old friend.

Sen recalls this association and their days together in London in a short article thus:

It is necessary to explain here that the main object of Syama Prasad's visit to England was not legal distinction. He wanted to acquire first-hand knowledge of British and French Universities . . . He sat for the Preliminary Bar Examination within a few weeks of his arrival at London. Naturally he did not do well. There was no question of a good class but he passed in all the subjects except one. Under ordinary circumstances the result would be considered satisfactory if not creditable; but the tongue of calumny soon got busy and made much of Syama Prasad's failure. As it seems mean-minded jealousy fed by hereditary hatred later sublimated it into a theme for a Convocation Address!

Sen is clearly referring here to something that Sir Jadunath Sarkar must have said in his convocation address. The latter was another famous historian, but a bête noire of Sir Asutosh, and naturally of Syama Prasad and also of Sen, Radhakrishnan, and all the people close to Sir Asutosh. The matter of this animosity of Sir Jadunath is corroborated by S. Gopal, yet another historian, and Radhakrishnan's son and biographer.

Syama Prasad earned his title as a barrister-at-law in 1927, and came back the same year. Just as with his studentship in India, he pursued his studies single-mindedly, and did not indulge in the other pastimes that Indian students used to—such as soapbox oratory at Hyde Park Corner, being an India League activist or flirting with Englishwomen. It was as uneventful as that. All that he apparently did, apart from pursuing his studies for the bar, was to represent Calcutta University at the Conference of Universities of the British Empire, held in London in 1926. He also grew a huge handlebar moustache.

However, as Sen recalls, he indulged in an odd diversion. He took part in theosophical exercises like playing the planchette with Sir Arthur Conan Doyle, of whom he had been an admirer for a long time.

Syama Prasad's stay in England was, however, remarkable for some of the friendships he made with other outstanding personalities. Among them, easily the most prominent was Dr Sarvepalli Radhakrishnan, the great philosopher and the second President of India. It is not as if they did not know each other earlier. In fact, before leaving for England, Radhakrishnan was already a resident of Calcutta, and on the George V Chair of Professorship of Mental and Moral Sciences of Calcutta University. He was installed in this chair by none other than Sir Asutosh, who wanted the 'best man in India' for the post. In Radhakrishnan's biography, written by his son Sarvepalli Gopal, he has observed that 'though Syama Prasad was much younger in years, they met

frequently. From this time grew a friendship which deepened
with the years.' In fact, although Syama Prasad's public duties
did not permit him to practise seriously at the bar, he was, much
later, one of the lawyers who represented Radhakrishnan free of
cost in a libel suit that Radhakrishnan filed against Ramananda
Chatterjee, a prominent Bengali man of letters and editor of the
then-formidable literary magazines *Prabasi* and *Modern Review*.
According to Gopal, Radhakrishnan had also suffered at the
hands of Sir Jadunath Sarkar, the vice chancellor of the university
who regarded all friends of the Mookerjee family as his enemies.

Radhakrishnan never dabbled in active politics, but had
definite political views, and Gopal has remarked[9] of him that 'he
found himself more in sympathy [barring Gandhi] with Syama
Prasad Mookerjee, even though the latter had joined the Hindu
Mahasabha, than with Rajagopalachari who was prepared to
sacrifice national interests in an effort to reach a compromise with
Jinnah'. Their friendship extended to social interaction too, and
the Radhakrishnans often visited the Mookerjees, and Gopal used
to play with other children of the household in the long corridors
of no. 77.

The identity of views on the role of religion in everyday
life between Radhakrishnan and Syama Prasad and the distance
between those of Radhakrishnan and Jawaharlal Nehru would
make this aspect clearer. In *The Discovery of India*, Nehru wrote,
'India must break with much of her past and not allow it to
dominate the present. Our lives are encumbered with the dead
wood of this past . . . India must, therefore, lessen her religiosity
and turn to science.' Radhakrishnan on the other hand, in an article
titled *Vivekananda and Young India*, published in the magazine
Prabuddha Bharata, by the Ramakrishna Mission, wrote:

Whatever may be your social programme, whatever revolutions
you may bring about in the economic and political world, unless

you have the dynamic inspiration of religion, you will never succeed in the enterprise. Even if you are radically minded, ask yourself the question whether you are going to reduce human beings to mere political or social creatures or would you give them some inner sanctity which nothing outward can touch?

This is perfectly in tune with Syama Prasad's religiosity which has already been described in the previous chapter.

Further, in the foreword to *Educational Speeches of Dr Syama Prasad Mookerjee*, Radhakrishnan wrote:

> His religion was not of the narrow kind. He was catholic in his sympathies and broad-minded in his outlook. Patriotism is not merely love of the land in which we are born; it is respect for the ideals by which we are sustained. That man has a spiritual dimension, that its development can take place in various ways, that we should have respect for all these ways are some of the cardinal features of Indian tradition. It is Indian and not merely Hindu. Syama Prasad Mookerjee was an ardent advocate of these great ideals.

Much later, in April 1943, Syama Prasad's elder daughter Sabita was leaving for Jamshedpur with her husband after her wedding and her family had come to bid her goodbye at Howrah station. She was crying her heart out as all Indian women do when they leave their parents' homes after marriage. Radhakrishnan too had accompanied the party to the station. On finding his dear friend Syama Prasad distraught and tearful, he decided to travel to Kharagpur (halfway to Jamshedpur on the same line) by the same train where he had some work to do, and consoled both father and daughter by saying that he would be with Sabita till Kharagpur. He visited Sabita more than once at Jamshedpur, without any invitation, so fond he was of the Mookerjees.

Also, when Radhakrishnan was the Vice President of India, and quite some time after Syama Prasad's death, Sabita asked him to suggest or arrange some practical training for her younger sister Arati (Hasi), who had just passed her intermediate examination after recovering from a serious bout of tuberculosis (see Chapter 10). He promptly got her admitted into a course on librarianship in Delhi, after which she got a job as a librarian in the Ministry of External Affairs. This proved to be very fortuitous because in Delhi she took up residence in a small flat in a building where a young civil engineer called Paresh Bhattacharji also used to live. They met, fell in love and married. Their wedding was held in Delhi and was attended by Radhakrishnan and several cabinet ministers, among others. They later emigrated to the United States. Arati lived till her end in the Queens area of New York City with her son, Sandip (see Epilogue).

Syama Prasad's fondness for Madhupur and 'Ganga Prasad House' remained unchanged through the years. Probably because he had spent some of his best days of childhood and boyhood here, he absolutely loved the house, and arrival at Madhupur always filled him at once with joy and reflections. In the last entry made by him in his English diary on 27 January 1946, he expressed his love thus in poignant language: 'Farewell Madhupur! I have spent one month here in this house . . . Let me end by expressing my gratitude to you, Madhupur, for whatever I have gained by my stay.'

3

University Years, 1924–38

Syama Prasad took to working for the Calcutta University as a duck takes to water. Sir Asutosh, multifaceted genius that he was, apparently chose his first son to succeed him principally at the High Court, and the second one at the university. It is interesting that he made both his sons wear both hats—Rama Prasad was also a member of the university syndicate, while Syama Prasad studied for the bar in India and England and became a barrister. Quite definitely, Sir Asutosh had no inkling (nor, for that matter, did Syama Prasad himself) that his second son was eventually consigned for a different level of leadership altogether. Had he known, it is doubtful that he would have been pleased. He had groomed Syama Prasad, trained him and made him his understudy specifically for making him step into his shoes at the Calcutta University, which he had turned into a truly great institution. And he could see, with his insight, that Syama Prasad was more than equal to the task. In fact, in a letter to Pat Lovett, the editor of *Capital* referred to earlier, he had written[1] about his son, 'He has the making of a man in him.'

The Calcutta University, the oldest university in the Indian subcontinent, was founded in 1857. It is the only university in India which as many as four Nobel laureates—Ronald Ross, Rabindranath Tagore, Chandrasekhara Venkata Raman and Amartya Sen were associated with. It has ranked consistently among the first 500 universities in the world, and was taken to these dizzy heights to a large extent through the efforts of Sir Asutosh Mookerjee (some of which have been described in Chapter 1). It is another matter that under the communist rule in West Bengal, the university had become a hotbed of petty politics—so much so that a duly appointed vice chancellor, Dr Santosh Bhattacharyya, had not been allowed to attend work because of opposition by the communist-affiliated employees' union.

The university has generally functioned as an autonomous body with varying degrees of control of the state government over it, and the de jure control has lessened with the years, though during recent times, especially from 1977 to 2011 during the communist rule in the state, the de facto control of the ruling party has been all-pervading. During Syama Prasad's time, however, there was little difference between de facto and de jure control. The university was and is nominally headed by the chancellor, and this post is held ex officio by the Governor of the state. The function of the chancellor, however, is confined to the appointment of the vice chancellor and presiding over the convocation function, and it is the vice chancellor who effectively runs the university with the help of a body of a small number of associates known as the 'syndicate'. The syndicate is responsible to the 'senate' of the university, which is a much larger body and consists of academic as well as non-academic persons involved with the university.

Upon Sir Asutosh's death, Syama Prasad was elected to the university syndicate, and thus, at the age of only twenty-three, was catapulted into one of the most powerful positions in India in the field of education. It is quite true that he had the advantage of succeeding his father to a post (as the Nehru–Gandhis have done in independent India many years later) where one ought not to be placed by hereditary succession, and it can very well be argued that this is unfair. But the way he conducted himself upon being so appointed blunts this argument to a great extent. He had been well coached and trained in the affairs of the university, and plunged into his work with such vigour and enthusiasm that it prompted Acharya Prafulla Chandra Ray[2] (also known as Sir P.C. Ray, which he did not like) to write[3] to him within a year of his taking over, 'You seem to have emerged as a real *bap ka beta* in the university! No one is prepared to work so hard and so selflessly as you are now doing.'

Syama Prasad had developed an excellent rapport with Acharya Ray despite being forty years his junior—so much so that Acharya used to treat him like a favoured equal in conducting affairs of the university. Acharya had completed sixty years of age in 1922 and was due for retirement. But Sir Asutosh knew his worth and extended his tenure by a special resolution by five years. By the time this period expired, Sir Asutosh was gone, but the university extended his term by another ten years to a total of fifteen years. Acharya did not accept any money towards his salary during these fifteen years, donating the entire proceeds to the university. Even after his attaining the age of seventy-five in 1937, when Syama Prasad was the vice chancellor, the university refused to let him go, and appointed him professor emeritus. The only favour he took from the institution was to be allowed to live in a tiny cubicle in the University College of Science, surrounded by his laboratory instruments and his students and researchers who looked upon him as no less than their father.

In truth, Syama Prasad refused to consider his youth a handicap, and had no problem interacting with people many years his senior, no mean task in Indian society where grey hairs are held at a very high premium. His brother Uma Prasad has written that he had the charming capacity of combining respect for elders with equality in official position. In 1926, Cambridge University hosted a Congress of Universities of the British Empire in London. Syama Prasad wanted Acharya to represent the university at the Congress, but Acharya was disinclined, mainly because of his age and state of health. But upon Syama Prasad's insistence he wrote[4] back, 'Very well. I leave the matter to your judgment. If you think it will do good, I am ready.' By the time this Congress was held, Syama Prasad had arrived in London to study to become a barrister, and he was also among the representatives. Right through his involvement with the university, he had always got the unstinted cooperation of Acharya, so impressed was the older man with the ability of the younger.

During his period of apprenticeship under his father, as well as during his early years of independent functioning as a member of the syndicate, he thought about what he wanted out of education—the basic changes that he wanted to bring about in the field. He had already formed some ideas while studying in England to become a barrister. His principal objective was, as his friend Dr Surendra Nath Sen had observed, not excelling in the field of law but studying the workings of British universities. And he did intend to bring about fundamental changes, and as we shall see, succeeded in this effort to a large extent.

One great achievement of Syama Prasad was involving the poet Rabindranath Tagore intimately in the working of the university. Of course, this happened much later, when Syama Prasad became the vice chancellor. Tagore then was already seventy-three, not in particularly good health and had moreover, in the years immediately preceding, imposed upon himself a difficult schedule of travelling all over the world—he visited Europe and the USA in 1930, Persia (now Iran) by aircraft in 1932 and Ceylon (now Sri Lanka) in 1933. Despite all this, he could not but respond to Syama Prasad's call. However, even earlier, on behalf of the university, Sir Asutosh had, during his lifetime, forged a relationship not only with the poet but also the Tagore clan, many of whose members were talented in their individual fields. He frequently invited the poet to lecture at the university and decorated him with medals and honours of various descriptions. He also appointed the poet to the board of management of the Khaira bequest to the university. He appointed Abanindranath Tagore, the celebrated artist and nephew of the poet, to the post of Vageshvari Professor of Fine Arts. He also appointed Nagendranath Ganguly, the poet's son-in-law, to the Khaira chair of agricultural sciences. On a personal level, the poet was in touch with the Mookerjees—the journal *Bangabani*, started and run by the brothers Rama Prasad and Syama Prasad featured a number of Tagore's lyrics, as has been mentioned in Chapter 2. The poet and Sir Asutosh also thought alike on many important issues. During Sir Asutosh's second spell of vice chancellorship (1921–23), Gandhiji's call of non-cooperation had touched the hearts of students and many of them had left formal studies and plunged themselves into the movement. In fact, some used to believe so much in their new-found romanticism that they believed just spinning the charkha would get them Swaraj, complete independence, in just six months. Sir Asutosh was totally against this kind of adventurism and said so in so many words, urging them to ignore the call and get back to their studies, something that did not make him popular among students in those charged times. However, Tagore was steadfastly by his side in supporting him in this view. In fact, on 14 August 1924, during the condolence meeting following Sir Asutosh's death, chaired by the poet, there were catcalls by some students which made the poet leave the meeting.

After Sir Asutosh's death, the complexion of the administration changed and with it, its attitude; the new university administration was in no mood to pursue his worship of excellence and spend money in order to invite eminent professors to serve in or lecture at the university. Shortly after his death, Tagore had sent requests to the university to accommodate the Norwegian orientalist Sten Konow and the Russian fugitive linguist and philologist

L. Bogdanov, who were with Visva-Bharati earlier, but who could not be kept there any longer owing to a serious shortage of funds. The syndicate declined both requests. Likewise, a request from Professor James Cousins to invite the Japanese poet Yone Noguchi was similarly declined. Syama Prasad was too young and too much of a newcomer to the syndicate to influence decisions at this stage, and moreover was away in England during 1926–27 studying for the bar. But when he took up the reins as vice chancellor, he ushered in another era of enlightened running of the university.

Meanwhile, Syama Prasad had decided to run for the Bengal Legislative Council seat on a Congress ticket from the university constituency as he considered this to be essential for influencing government policy on education and acting as watchdog on the government's actions relating to education. As expected, he sailed through, and became possibly the youngest council member ever in the province. However, the same year, the Congress gave a call for boycotting of councils in tune with its objective of complete independence which it was then pushing. Syama Prasad was in the council not for politics but for education, and he totally disagreed with the approach being applied to education. But he had been elected on a party ticket. So he dutifully resigned, and ran again as an independent candidate, and once again sailed through. Thereafter, right through his membership of the council or assembly, he continued to espouse the cause of education even when he was in the thick of politics.

Sir Asutosh's second stint as vice chancellor was followed by Bhupendra Nath Bose, the lawyer and freedom fighter, who had been the president of the Indian National Congress in 1914. Bose in turn was followed by William Ewart Greaves, Sir Jadunath Sarkar, the famous historian, and W.S. Urquhart. None of these people, however, had a fraction of the vision, energy and courage of Sir Asutosh. Moreover, Sir Jadunath, the eminent and outstanding historian that he was, was said to bear animosity towards Sir Asutosh and took it out in petty ways on his son Syama Prasad and his friend Dr Sarvepalli Radhakrishnan, as has been described by Surendra Nath Sen in Chapter 2.

Urquhart was followed by Dr Hassan Suhrawardy, a surgeon who had served for long as a medical officer with the East Indian Railway. Suhrawardy had never had anything at all to do with education earlier, and his appointment was obviously a ploy of the British government to placate the Muslims. In fact, he was the very first Muslim to be appointed to the post of vice chancellor. He served from 1930 to 1934. One remarkable event during his tenure was the appointment in 1932 of his cousin Hasan Shaheed Suhrawardy (usually referred to as Professor Suhrawardy to avoid confusion) as the Vageshvari Professor of Comparative Arts. He was the elder brother of Huseyn Shaheed Suhrawardy, the premier of Bengal during 1945–47, the civil supplies minister for the province during the famine and the engineer of the Great Calcutta Killings (see Chapter 8). Professor Suhrawardy, however, was a very different kettle of fish from his infamous brother. He was an established connoisseur of art and had studied in Oxford, Russia and France.

It was during this phase of his life, however, that the greatest of personal tragedies befell Syama Prasad. He lost his four-month-old infant son, his fifth child, from diphtheria, and then his beloved wife of only eleven years, Sudha Devi, from pneumonia (see Chapter 2). Becoming a widower affects most men profoundly, and Syama Prasad was no exception. Outwardly there was very little manifestation. He must have carried on with his university work as he would otherwise have, but he was shaken to his core, as his diary entries during his convalescence at Madhupur (1945–46, see Chapter 7) reveal. He was always an introvert by nature, and with the departure of his wife, he lost one of his closest confidantes. The only person left, in whom he could still confide, was his sister-in-law Tara Devi, who took care of his motherless minor children and brought them up with all the care of a mother. It appears that he also became careless about his appearance—photographs of the dapper Syama Prasad of his youth, in his merzai (an upper garment), with chhari (swagger stick) in hand, or the Syama Prasad in England in his three-piece suit, sporting a formidable handlebar moustache, are quite a contrast to the person of later years, sartorially very uncaring, a very simply dressed Bengali gentleman of the times in just a *bandhgalla* or a punjabi (which, used in the sartorial sense in Bengali, means a kurta) and dhoti, with his *koncha* (pleated end of his dhoti) hanging short of the ground. He wore trousers only in cold weather, and that too with a bandhgalla. Neither of the two fitted him well and he did not seem to care.

Tagore sent him a very touching condolence message in Bengali following his wife's death. In the message,[5] written in the poet's usual lyrical prose, he said, 'I know you have a very strong mind, and will be able to get over this sorrow in time. Death is the ultimate experience in life . . . I pray that you receive that message of renunciation which serves as the bridge between this world and the next.' Only Tagore, who had to suffer the unbearable sorrows of the untimely deaths of so many of his near and dear ones—his dear sister-in-law Kadambari, his wife Mrinalini, two of his daughters Madhurilata and Renuka, and his dearest child, his younger son Shami—knew what death meant up-close, and could write about it with such feeling.

By this time, Syama Prasad had more than got the hang of running the university. Vice chancellor Suhrawardy, who knew next to nothing about educational administration, had the good sense to defer to Syama Prasad and almost always submitted to his better judgement. Syama Prasad, in his turn, always extended his unstinted cooperation to him. By this time, he had totally plunged himself into university administration and there was no doubt in anyone's mind as to who was running the university.

It was no wonder therefore that Syama Prasad would succeed him in 1934 as vice chancellor, the youngest person ever to be so appointed. He was so appointed, not once but twice, by the formidable Governor of Bengal Sir John Anderson.

Dr M. Ishaque, a noted scholar of Persian and the founder of the Iran Society in Calcutta, and a member of the senate, threw a party in his honour at the zoological gardens.

Vice chancellorship of Calcutta University, the premier university in the whole of India in many ways, elevated Syama Prasad at the age of just thirty-three to the rarefied heights at the top of a very rigid hierarchy that was always a feature of British India. By being elevated to this honorary office, he became one among the foremost 'non-officials', as they were then called, and earned the right to talk on just a little less than equal terms to the Governor, who also doubled as his immediate superior as the chancellor of the university. It is difficult to conceive today, in these relatively egalitarian modern times, what this meant in terms of prestige for a thirty-three-year-old Indian man at that time when a premium used to be placed on grey hairs on the one hand and British blood on the other. Yet all this power neither went to the man's head nor did it make him think that he could now rest on his laurels. Instead, it made him, if anything, humbler; and with all the energy of his young body he toiled on indefatigably, to make the university better, and yet better. Vice chancellors before him used to spend at most a couple of hours at the university on weekdays. Syama Prasad used to spend the whole day at the university and received people at his home in connection with university work on all days, including Sundays.

Syama Prasad's achievements in the field of education were mostly during the years of his vice chancellorship (1934–38), and some of them brought about fundamental changes. He was clearly critical, without articulating it in so many words, of the scheme hatched by that arch-colonialist Thomas Babington

Macaulay, one on which the educational system of the country was based, and planned to set it right. Macaulay had written with disdain, rare even in that heyday of colonialism, in his famous (or infamous) 1835 'Minute on Indian Education':

> [A] single shelf of a good European library was worth the whole native literature of India and Arabia . . . I certainly never met with any Orientalist who ventured to maintain that the Arabic and Sanskrit poetry could be compared to that of the great European nations . . . It is, I believe, no exaggeration to say, that all the historical information which has been collected from all the books written in the Sanskrit language is less valuable than what may be found in the most paltry abridgments used at preparatory schools in England . . . [and finally] We must at present do our best to form a class who may be interpreters between us and the millions whom we govern; *a class of persons, Indian in blood and colour, but English in taste, in opinions, in morals, and in intellect* [emphasis added].

In other words, the educational system was directed at producing a group of English-educated Indians whose gamut would stretch from the so-called 'brown sahibs', the Indian barristers, civil servants and college professors, all the way down to the lowly clerk in the office of a British jute merchant in some godforsaken corner of the country. This class would consider itself superior to those who did not know English and gradually, proficiency in a foreign language would emerge as the criterion for respectability in society. Sadly enough, this position holds true to this day.

Consider what Syama Prasad had to say about this. In the All-Bengal University and College Teachers' Conference held on 22 February 1933, just eight months before he was appointed vice chancellor, he said,[6] 'The students that we are turning out do not have the capacity to fight life's struggle . . . we have to bear in mind that following the education that we give them they should be made able to earn a living through a profession or business. The system of education that we have right now is singularly unsuitable for this purpose.' Again, in his presidential speech at the All-India Educational Conference at Nagpur in 1935 he said:

> It is incorrect to look upon educational institutions as factories to produce potential clerks and low-paid staff. We have to turn out students who are capable of providing leadership to our self-governing institutions, such as municipal corporations, provincial and central legislatures and also of directing the affairs in various fields of life such as financial, commercial and industrial ones. India today badly needs people who are imbued with the spirit of service and also innovative, courageous and liberal in outlook . . . It is also for you not only to inculcate in the minds of youth the passion for knowledge and truth and spirit of reverence but also to foster in them the love of their motherland—that real patriotism—which impels one to sacrifice everything for the good of one's country.

Note the last few sentences—they are in direct contradiction of what Macaulay intended. They are also in consonance with what Sir Asutosh had declared, referring of course to the field of education, 'Freedom first, freedom second, freedom always.' In fact, Macaulay's teaching had quite a few unintended consequences. The students receiving education in English not only learnt about the glory of the British Empire, Pax Britannica, and the 'white man's burden' described by Kipling, they also learnt about the French and American Revolutions, and about Irish patriots like Emmet, Parnell and McSwiney who fought British imperialism. So much so that the revolutionaries Surya Sen (better known as Masterda), Pritilata Ohdedar and others who staged a daring raid on the Chittagong Armoury in 1930 had modelled themselves on the Irish revolutionaries and had called themselves the Indian Republican Army after their Irish counterpart. But that is another story. In any case, no one in the field of education had so far been so forthcoming as Syama Prasad about the need to reform the system.

However, as we shall see from the next chapter, Syama Prasad did not believe in confrontation, except as a last resort. Therefore, even if he had a clear idea of de-Macaulay-ization in his mind, he never uttered it and went about the whole task in a very quiet, orderly, constitutional way, as was his style. He carried this out mostly during the period of his vice chancellorship.

One of the most colourful events introduced by him during his period was the celebration of the university foundation day on 24 January. The university had no tradition of any such celebration before Syama Prasad. He probably saw the need for injecting some pomp and pageantry into the otherwise humdrum life of the university. For this purpose, he also changed the seal and emblem of the university and got designed a university crest or emblem which was placed at the centre of a flag in deep blue. Earlier, the university emblem had the seal of British India with a few embellishments, followed by one with three elephants holding up a book, with the words 'Advancement of Learning' written inside the circumference. Syama Prasad got it completely changed into one with a full-blown lotus, with the word 'Shri' in Bengali letters at the centre. Shri is a Sanskrit word also found in most modern Indian languages, one of whose meanings is 'eternal beauty'. During the foundation day celebrations, some 3000 boys and girls from different affiliated colleges would march with a band with their individual college symbols and uniforms in a colourful procession in the pleasant winter sun. The poet Tagore himself had composed the marching song, *'Cholo Jai, Cholo Jai (Let's Go, Let's Go)'*. At the head, there would be boys with the university flag designed by Syama Prasad. The march would start from Presidency College at 7.30 a.m. and end at the Calcutta Maidan where the vice chancellor and syndicate members would be present on a rostrum, taking the salute from the students. The senate members would also be present. There would be an exhibition of gymnastics and callisthenics from the students. Then the vice chancellor would address the gathering. In his first address, Syama Prasad laid bare what he expected from the students and his scheme for the same. He said that he wanted to develop students 'into men, strong and self-reliant, hard-working and fearless, proud of their national culture but not narrow in their outlook, anxious to promote peace and happiness, filled with lofty idealism but not swayed by class hatred or unthinking emotion—men who will be the worthy leaders of a new Bengal, who will carry the torch of learning and freedom to the lasting glory of their beloved motherland'. Of course, as was common practice then, he used the masculine gender alone throughout. Besides, the number of girls must have been very small.

Syama Prasad later had serious trouble with this emblem. The Muslims, with their numerical majority in the province of Bengal and consequent political power, objected saying that the 'Shri' and the lotus were both Hindu symbols and smacked of idolatry, which had hurt Muslim religious feelings. Some called for a boycott of the university and some went to the extent of demanding an Islamic university. The convocation of 1937 was a landmark one in which Rabindranath Tagore delivered an address in Bengali, which had so far not been done. But no Muslim student was present at the function. Muslim ministers of the cabinet such as Fazlul Haq, Huseyn Suhrawardy, Nazimuddin and Azizul Haque also stayed away from the convocation. Ultimately, Syama Prasad was forced to make a compromise. He dropped the 'Shri' and replaced it with a sun and the lotus bud at the centre. The full-blown lotus remained, together with the motto, 'Advancement of

Learning'. Later the lotus bud was also dropped in favour of a bed of lotus pollen.

The most significant function of the university was of course its convocation, during which the university ceremonially conferred degrees on its students. In his second convocation address in 1936, he declared[7] his objectives for the university in clear terms, which Dr Dinesh Chandra Sinha, a commentator and researcher on his educational achievements, has termed his *panch sheela* for education. He said:

> Our ideal is to provide extensive facilities for education from the lowest grade to the highest, to mould our educational purpose and to draw out the best qualities that be hidden in our youth, and to train them intellectually and physically for devoted services in all spheres of national activities, in villages, in towns and in cities. Our ideal is to make the widest provision for a sound liberal education, to find the correct synthesis between cultural and vocational and technical training, remembering always that no nation can ever achieve greatness by turning its youth into a mere machine-made product with nothing but a material end in view. Our ideal is to afford the amplest facilities and privileges to our teachers so that they may be endowed with learning and character and freedom and regard themselves not only as torchbearers and interpreters of knowledge and conquerors of new realms of thought, but also as makers of men and women, of leaders and workers, true and brave, upright and patriotic. Our ideal is to link up education with the best elements of our culture and civilization, drawing strength, wherever necessary from western skill and knowledge. Our ideal is to make our universities and educational institutions the home of liberty and sane and progressive thoughts—generously assisted by the state and the public—where teachers and students will

meet and work in an atmosphere of harmony and mutual understanding, where none will suffer on grounds of caste, sex, creed or religious or political belief.

In his address[8] delivered at the Nagpur University, to the convocation of which he had been invited in 1936, he raised his pitch a little, and spoke a little more stridently in favour of freedom in education. Not only that, he also linked it to the country's yearning for freedom. 'First and foremost', he said, 'a system of education consistent with the genius of the people of India and suited to modern life and conditions, cannot be achieved unless and until India enjoys the political status which will give her the liberty to decide for herself what constitutes her national needs and how best they can be satisfied.'

It is doubtful if anyone else in India, particularly among Indians, had preceded the father–son duo of Sir Asutosh and Syama Prasad in bringing about such fundamental reforms in the educational framework imposed on the country by Macaulay. Through the speeches quoted above, Syama Prasad put forth his ideas on such reforms. First, his abiding pride in the glory of ancient India and second, his exhortation to students to be proud of it effectively rubbished Macaulay's theory of a single shelf of a good European library being worth the whole native literature of India. And yet, he was not chauvinistic or doctrinaire in his approach—he asked students to be 'proud of their national culture but not narrow in their outlook', thus emphasizing the need for the correct balance between Indian and western values. This may seem somewhat inane by today's standards, but few had spoken in these tones before him, especially in the field of education. And finally, he reiterated his basic beliefs as a right-wing person, as a constitutionalist and as the very antithesis of the then-fashionable Marxist revolutionary by asking the students not to be 'swayed by class hatred or unthinking emotion'. These beliefs found greater expression during the political phase of his life in his attitude towards the Quit India movement (see Chapter 5).

Syama Prasad, during his four years of vice chancellorship, had implemented an array of measures that bore witness to his original thinking and untiring work. Today, these measures may seem run-of-the-mill, but in the pre-war British times, some of them were nothing less than revolutionary. A short description of some of the measures are given in the following paragraphs.

Syama Prasad introduced teaching and examination using the mother tongue as the medium of instruction till the matriculation stage. Macaulay had laid down in his minute, in very strong language, that no language other than English could possibly be the vehicle of education among the 'natives' for any kind of education. He discussed how and why English was preferred to Sanskrit and Arabic. He did not even mention, let alone consider, the modern Indian languages. It lay on Syama Prasad to undo this mischief, and he did it.

Among a few more of the tasks that he took upon himself were: (a) standardizing spellings in Bengali; (b) coining and compiling Bengali terminology for official, scientific and technical words; (c) establishing the Asutosh Museum for preservation and research on artefacts of ancient civilizations; (d) introducing a course in domestic science for women out of Vihari Lal Mitra funds; (e) introducing education in social welfare, to which business management was added later and the Institute of Social Welfare and Business Management was set up; (f) setting up an Information and Employment Board in the university to make students aware of their employment opportunities; (g) introducing teachers' training courses; (h) revamping and strengthening of the University Training Corps to enthuse students to take up military studies and a career in the armed forces of the country—a pet subject of his in which he probably saw the possibility of instilling discipline, courage and method in Bengali boys; (i) setting up a Students' Welfare Board for looking after the health of the students; (j) publishing booklets on different subjects of literary and scientific interest in Bengali for general education of the public; (k) expanding the confines of the library and reading room—he erected an extra floor on the Asutosh Building and decorated the library with frescoes on the walls, depicting the development of India and the contribution of Bengal in such development; (l) setting up the University Rowing Club at Dhakuria Lake (now Rabindra Sarobar); (m) setting apart an area in the Calcutta Maidan for university athletic activities; (n) introducing the communication engineering special paper in the applied physics course, which later blossomed into a separate department known as radiophysics and electronics; (o) introducing research facilities in Chinese and Tibetan languages and culture; (p) introducing geography as a subject from matriculation till masters; (q) introducing courses in agricultural sciences; (r) removing the age bar for appearing in the matriculation examination; (s) introducing a course in Islamic history and culture; and (t) permitting PhD theses to be submitted in Bengali.

A rather unfortunate incident in Syama Prasad's otherwise glorious innings at the university was the exit of the Nobel laureate physicist Sir C.V. Raman. Although at this point of time it was Hassan Suhrawardy and not Syama Prasad who was the vice chancellor, everyone knew who was running the university.

Raman had joined the Indian finance department as an assistant accountant general after a brilliant academic career, but had pursued, on the side, his studies in physics—which was his first love. Sir Asutosh, forever in search of talent, saw the brilliance of the man and invited him to join the university. In response, in 1917, Raman resigned from his government service and took up the newly created Palit professorship in physics at the University of Calcutta. At the same time, he continued doing research at the Indian Association for the Cultivation of Science, Calcutta, where he became the honorary secretary. The Indian Association for the Cultivation of Science (IACS) was a private institution for promoting scientific research, founded by Dr Mahendra Lal Sircar, a product of the nineteenth-century Bengal renaissance. Raman used to refer to this period as the golden era of his career. Many talented students gathered around him at the IACS and the University of Calcutta. On 28 February 1928, through his experiments on the scattering of light, he discovered the Raman Effect.

He eventually won the 1930 Nobel Prize in Physics 'for his work on the scattering of light and for the discovery of the effect named after him'. He was the first Asian and first non-White to receive any Nobel Prize in the sciences.

Calcutta University heaped honours on him and even faraway Glasgow University honoured him with an honoris causa doctorate. But by 1933, he had made up his mind to leave Calcutta for Bangalore, probably in view of the political disturbances in Bengal. However, instead of resigning his post as Palit professor, he applied for 'leave without pay' for fourteen months. Raman was granted the leave he asked for and left for Bangalore, but retained his honorary secretaryship of the IACS and for this purpose, got amended the articles of the association.

It is as a result of this last-mentioned move that some acrimony developed between him and his Calcutta-based peers, many of whom were also associated with the university. Ultimately, in view of his stature, the university decided to waive all objections, but meanwhile relations with his erstwhile colleagues had soured. The university did not give him a grand farewell as it ought to have done, but just passed a resolution recording its appreciation of his signal achievements in science. Raman, on his part, did not set foot in Calcutta ever again. It was a rather unsatisfactory end to a glorious innings of an outstanding scientist who had brought the greatest of honours to the country, to the university and to himself. Sir Asutosh Mookerjee, who had seen the promise in the nameless bureaucrat and persuaded him to join the university, would have been indeed very saddened.

The proximity of Syama Prasad to the great poet Tagore has been mentioned earlier in this chapter. Syama Prasad now proceeded to add a new dimension to that proximity, which was earlier at a personal level through Tagore's writing in the Mookerjee brothers' literary magazine *Bangabani*. During the immediate post-Asutosh period, the university had turned down Tagore's requests for employing Professors Sten Konow and L. Bogdanov, but after Hassan Suhrawardy became vice chancellor, Syama Prasad could get the university to invite Dr Anna Selig at the request of the poet. Dr Selig was the executive secretary of the International University Service of Germany, and the university offered her a readership for delivering certain lectures after she finished a similar series of lectures in Visva-Bharati. In fact, at this stage the persecution of Jews (many of whom had occupied leading faculty positions in German universities) in Germany at the hands of the Nazis had begun, and this was taken advantage of. According to Justice Chittatosh Mookerjee, even Einstein had considered coming to Calcutta.

With a view to increasing contact and interaction between Tagore and the university, in 1932, Syama Prasad got the university senate to pass a resolution to invite the poet to deliver a course of lectures connected with Bengali language and literature at the postgraduate level. For this purpose, the poet would be given the status of a professor, but the ordinary rules of the university would not be applicable to him. The seventy-one-year-old poet listened to the man who was forty years his junior, despite some resistance, and accepted the offer. The poet thereafter began to take an active interest in the university and kept in constant touch with Syama Prasad. In 1934, he inaugurated an 'International Club' established in the university, out of funds donated by the

American philanthropist Andrew Carnegie for promoting world peace. The University Cultural Association gave a felicitation to the poet on this occasion. The poet in turn delivered a lecture on human values across national divides. On 29 June 1935, the birthday of Sir Asutosh, a memorial to him, in the form of an undergraduate college, a hall and library, was inaugurated next to Hazra Park (now Jatin Das Park) in south Calcutta, and Tagore sent a poem specially composed for this occasion.

The provincial minister-in-charge of education at this time was Azizul Haque, a Muslim leader from Santipur in the district of Nadia, who had regard for the poet. He also succeeded Syama Prasad to the vice chancellor's post in 1938. He took the cue from Syama Prasad with regard to involving the poet in educational activities, and launched a scheme of 'Education Week' under the auspices of the provincial government. Tagore delivered the inaugural address for launching the scheme of 'Education Week' under the auspices of the provincial government on 8 February 1936. In his lecture, the poet proposed publishing a set of books for popular education. This scheme did not find much favour with the subsequent provincial governments, and as a result, very few such books got published. One such book was by Tagore himself.

In 1936, Syama Prasad as vice chancellor wrote to the poet requesting him to deliver the address at the annual convocation of the university. This was unprecedented, for so far no 'outsider' had been invited to address the convocation. The poet declined, because at that time he would be on tour elsewhere, but accepted it the next year, subject to a condition:[9] 'If you are going to break a tradition,' wrote the poet, 'by asking me, an outsider, to address the convocation you will have to break yet another convention and permit me to address in Bengali.' And the university accepted this, and Tagore delivered his address in Bengali! This was unthinkable at the time, not only because there would be several among the dignitaries present who would not understand the language, but also because it was the general feeling that 'anything important' had to be done in English. Remember, Macaulay's successors, following his minute, had successfully created the class which was 'Indian in blood and colour, but English in taste, in opinions, in morals, and in intellect'. Sir John Anderson, the powerful Governor of Bengal and the chancellor of the university, was present at the function and had obviously given his consent, equally obviously at Syama Prasad's persuasion. However, no Muslim student or Muslim minister was present. This was 1937, and the Muslim League-led government had already come to power in Bengal.

The controversy regarding the 'Shri' and the lotus on the university emblem, referred to earlier, was raging at the time, and the Muslim League-led provincial government saw in this a good opportunity to spread communal poison all around. Not only that, the League government also had no qualms about dubbing some of the poet's compositions as 'idolatrous' and 'anti-Muslim'. It ought to be said here that the multitude of Bengali Muslims have reversed their position on Tagore by adopting Tagore's song 'Amar Sonar Bangla' as the national anthem of Bangladesh. Thus, Tagore remains possibly the only poet in the world whose writing serves as the national anthems of two countries, Bangladesh and India.[10] However, Kazi Nazrul Islam, a poet from West Bengal, whom Syama Prasad had saved from the clutches of penury and death (see Chapter 5), is also equally revered in both countries.

The last meeting between Syama Prasad and Tagore took place in August 1940 when the University of Oxford decided to confer on the poet a honoris causa DLitt degree in a special convocation organized at Santiniketan. There is a background to this. After Tagore received the Nobel Prize in 1913, the British government conferred knighthood on him in 1915. But the poet himself refused to continue as a knight, and renounced his title after the British butchery at Jallianwala Bagh in Amritsar in

1919. The British were aghast, but could do nothing against the only Nobel laureate from Asia and from their Empire. However, thereafter, although the whole world stretching from Japan to Argentina decorated him with honours of various descriptions, the British strictly refrained from doing any such thing. Finally, Oxford relented, probably at the insistence of Dr Sarvepalli Radhakrishnan.

After Syama Prasad demitted the office of the vice chancellor, the university conferred an honoris causa doctorate degree on him. The prefix of 'Dr' somehow fitted him well, and gradually, he came to be universally known as Dr Mookerjee. Only in Bengal, he continued to be referred to as Syama Prasad, sometimes with the honorific suffix 'babu' attached—Syama Prasad Babu (not Syama Babu, as some erroneously call him). In this book, therefore, he will henceforth be called and referred to as Dr Mookerjee.

Dr Mookerjee was followed in his chair by Azizul Haque, a mention of whom has been made earlier. He was a pleader in a district court who never had anything to do with education in the past, but had been appointed the minister in charge of education in the Muslim League–Krishak Praja Party cabinet headed by Fazlul Haq and later the Speaker of the Bengal Legislative Assembly. He had been appointed to take care of the Muslim League's agenda, and he tried to do just that. Dr Mookerjee wrote in his diary on 23 January 1939, 'It is amazing how utterly indifferent he is to the work and needs of the university—except in so far as Muslims are concerned.'

Even after he handed over his charges to Azizul Haque, Dr Mookerjee remained the most influential member of the senate and the syndicate, and continued to serve the university as a member of the Postgraduate Council of Arts till 1947 when he moved to New Delhi.

Two events of enormous political importance took place during this phase of Dr Mookerjee's life. These must be mentioned in any discussion on this period. They did not affect Dr Mookerjee the educationist in any significant way, but had a profound effect on his life and work when he stepped into the arena of politics in 1939. The first of these was the Communal Award of 1932; and the second was a virtually new Constitution for British India, the Government of India Act of 1935. A reference to these two events is therefore necessary.

When the Indian leadership failed to come up with a constitutional solution to the communal issue after two round-table conferences, the British Prime Minister Ramsay MacDonald announced his own formula for solving the problem on 16 August 1932. He said that he was not only a Prime Minister of Britain but was also a friend of the Indians and thus wanted to solve the problems of his friends. According to the award, the right of a separate electorate was not only given to the Muslims of India but also to all the minority communities in the country. The award also declared untouchables as a minority and thus the Hindu depressed classes were given several special seats, to be filled from special depressed class electorates in the area where their voters were concentrated. Under the Communal Award, the principle of weightage was also maintained with some modifications in the Muslim-minority provinces. Principle of weightage was also applied for Europeans in Bengal and Assam, Sikhs in the Punjab and the North-West Frontier Province, and Hindus in Sindh and the North-West Frontier Province.

The Muslim League rather reluctantly accepted the award. In its annual session held in November 1933, the All India Muslim League passed a resolution[11] that read: 'Though the decision falls far short of the Muslim demands, the Muslims have accepted it in the best interest of the country, reserving to themselves the right to press for the acceptance of all their demands.' The Congress on the other hand followed a strange policy of 'non-commitment'— which really meant that they neither accepted nor rejected it.

Now, that is a strange position for a national party to take, but take it they did, and this created endless trouble later.

The aspect of the award which affected Dr Mookerjee later in his political life was not so much the separate electorate for Muslims as the disproportionate weightage given to 'Europeans', that is expatriate Britishers. Their total number in India at any point of time never exceeded 10,000—Bengal possibly had less than 2000 of them. Even this was a large number, mainly due to the concentration of industries in the region and the cultivation of jute and tea in the province and the resultant commerce. Yet the number of seats they had in the Bengal Legislative Assembly was twenty-five, in a house of 242. As we shall see in Chapters 5 and 6, John Arthur Herbert, the Governor of Bengal, played untold mischief in the province with the help of this group.

The Communal Award paved the way for the Government of India Act, 1935, which did away with the diarchy era of the Montagu–Chelmsford reforms and ushered in an era of supposedly greater autonomy for the provinces and greater participation of Indians in the administration. However, in the context of Bengal, it also meant the political emasculation of the Hindus which brought Dr Mookerjee from the arena of education to that of politics. That is the subject of the next chapter.

4

Entry into Politics, 1939–41

D r Mookerjee's political career had begun in a small way.
When he entered the Bengal Legislative Council in 1929 as
a Congress candidate from the Calcutta University constituency,
it was a projection of his growing reputation as an educationist. In
a sense, this was not really a political move, because his intention
behind entering the council was to act as a watchdog for the
interests of the university in the legislature. When the Congress
gave a call for boycott of councils in 1930, Dr Mookerjee duly
obeyed and resigned from the council. Perhaps he was confident
that he could walk into the council any time he wanted to. As a
matter of fact, he was re-elected to the council as an independent
candidate from the same university constituency.

The primary reason behind Dr Mookerjee's entry into full-
time realpolitik lay in the treatment meted out to the minority
Bengali Hindus by the rabidly communal Muslim League–
Krishak Praja Party coalition government of Bengal.[1] It was a
coalition for namesake, with the Muslim League calling all the
shots, and the Krishak Party (including the Prime Minister and
the Hindu ministers) meekly following. As always, the Congress,
which was roundly supported by the Hindus of Bengal, chose not
to take up their case for fear of losing the vote of a particular
community, and Dr Mookerjee was persuaded that he, of all
persons, could not stand and idly watch the situation. Those who

blame Dr Mookerjee today for not doing 'inclusive politics' are
rather unaware of the political realities of that time. It is important
to recontextualize his life in the context of the political realities of
that time.[2]

The Government of India Act of 1935 came into effect in
1937, and in the same year, Dr Mookerjee was again elected to the
Bengal assembly. So he had the opportunity to study the working
of provincial autonomy from close quarters. Nevertheless, since
his tendencies lay in the sphere of educational administration, Dr
Mookerjee did not feel attracted to the 'noisy and dusty career
of a politician'. Rather, he felt that the best way for him to serve
his country would be through the path of education. The major
factor that drove him into politics was the political situation,
particularly the aftermath of the Government of India Act of
1935. The minority Hindus of Bengal (about 47 per cent) had
already been crushed under Ramsay Macdonald's Communal
Award of 1932, which reduced Hindus to political impotence.
The Congress's reaction to the Communal Award was of 'non-
commitment'—they neither supported it nor opposed it. It is
difficult to see how the premier political party of India refused
to take a position on an important pronouncement by the British
Prime Minister. This refusal turned out to be a grave blunder.[3] In
the 1935 Act a separate electorate was provided 'with a vengeance'
for giving special protection to the majority Muslim community
in Bengal.

In his diary written much later (1944), Dr Mookerjee records
some of the glaring instances of Hindu suffering, such as the ratio of
communal representation in respect of the services, the defilement
of Hindu images, the suppression and supersession of better
qualifications in respect of Hindus, and preferential treatment of
Muslims in educational and other technical services, the passing
of laws specially jeopardizing Hindus, the encouragement of riots
and attacks on Hindu women. Almost identical sentiments were

expressed by Nirad C. Chaudhuri,[4] who trod a very different path from Dr Mookerjee.

The Muslim League–Krishak Praja Party coalition was brought to power, which paved the way for the communalization of the Muslims. The 1937 elections brought the Congress back as the single-largest party in Bengal, but it was unable to form a government without the cooperation of at least Abul Kashem Fazlul Haq's Krishak Praja Party. About Haq at this stage, Dr Mookerjee had observed, 'Fazlul Haq, lovable and emotional as he is, was dying for power.' Abul Mansur Ahmad, a close political associate of Haq, had in his memoirs, dubbed Haq a stunt-master, and had commented that while he was a moving speaker in both English and Bengali, he could say quite foolish things in extempore speeches. Disinclined to fall into the arms of the Nazimuddin-led Muslim League, Haq implored the Congress to form a coalition ministry in Bengal with himself as Prime Minister. Dr Mookerjee regrets that, '[i]f this had been done, Bengal would never have gone under the heels of League-cum-British conspiracy' and 'India's political history would have been different.' But the Bengal Congress disagreed on some inconsequential points with the Krishak Praja Party, the reason for which is suspected to be instructions by the Congress high command. As a result, Haq was literally driven into the arms of the Muslim League. The reason behind this political stupidity is not clear—it was certainly not based on any principle, for in neighbouring Assam, the Congress had been allowed to form a coalition. This one single act of the Congress may be considered, in my opinion, to be one of the causes of the miseries of millions of Bengali Hindus, especially those from East Bengal who were rendered refugees some years later.

Thus Haq became the premier of Bengal and the leader of the Krishak Praja Party–Muslim League coalition. But neither any of the Hindu ministers, nor the sensible and moderate,

though irresolute, Haq, could exercise any restraining influence
on the League diehards in framing and executing the government
policies. Fanatic zeal was let loose on the province. He was made
to dance as the clever Leaguers like Suhrawardy, Shahabuddin and
Nazimuddin wanted him to. Using him as their cloak, the League
effectively and ruthlessly carried on their campaign of denuding
Hindus of their rights, on which alone they thought they could
build their Islamic structure. Legislative and administrative
measures were either adopted or advocated by the communal
Haq–League ministry, which aimed at a deliberate curtailment of
Hindu rights. The pollution of Hindu temples and defilement of
Hindu idols, attacks on Hindu women and the encouragement
of communal riots were some of the instances of such suffering in
the social and religious spheres.[5]

The Hindus, as it was apparent from their circumstances,
were hurt by the Haq ministry in other areas, too.[6] In the case
of employment in government services, merit and ability were
disregarded, and by the miracle of communal favouritism, the door
to government employment was practically closed for Hindus. In
1938, the Fazlul Haq ministry changed the rules regarding police
recruitment such that while enlisting Bengali constables, the
superintendent of police must see that not less than 50 per cent of
the recruits are Muslims. In the same year, vigorously applying the
policy of offering Muslims preferential treatment in the field of
employment pursued by Viceroy Mayo and Lieutenant Governors
Fuller and Hare, the ministry passed a legislation which stipulated
that 60 per cent of all government appointments must be reserved
for Muslims.[7] Some Hindu leaders, headed by the maharaja of
Burdwan and including Dr Mookerjee who represented no
political party yet and were merely a combination of individuals
and minor interests, waited on deputation on the acting Governor
of Bengal Sir John Reid regarding the communal ratio in services.
Their request went up to the viceroy and the secretary of state

but they got no protection as a minority community and their interpretations of the act were brushed aside. Next year, the government decided that the basic percentage of reservation for Muslims in all cases of direct recruitment would be fifty, and in cases of promotion there would be additional reservation over and above 50 per cent direct recruitment. In 1940, a special officer called the communal ratio officer was appointed to implement this decision. The policy of recruiting Muslims from outside the province or even outside India was adopted to fill up the quota of 50 per cent if Bengali Muslims with minimum qualifications were not available.

As the competition for control of local bodies became fierce, the tension between Hindus and Muslims grew more acute. Further, the Muslim League government brought under its control the Dacca University, which had been established to promote higher education among Muslims. And in 1938, it appointed Azizul Haque, Speaker of the Bengal Legislative Assembly, as vice chancellor of Calcutta University where Hindus were in control. While the Muslim League wanted to bring under its control the entire system of education from schools to universities, the loss of control over educational institutions was particularly intolerable for bhadralok Hindus who were so far largely responsible for Bengal's intellectual and cultural heritage, including the celebrated Bengal Renaissance of the nineteenth century.

In a 1944 diary entry at Madhupur, Dr Mookerjee laments that while 1939 continued to be a year of Hindu oppression at the hands of the communal Haq ministry, who 'had steadily gone on with its well-planned activities for crushing the legitimate rights of the Hindus', the Congress betrayed the interests of the Hindus whose position had become desperate and helpless. Then came two black bills, the Calcutta Municipal Bill and the Secondary Education Bill. The visit of Vinayak Damodar Savarkar to Bengal in March 1939 with his new ideology of

the Hindu Mahasabha coincided with the introduction in
the Bengal assembly of the Calcutta Municipal Bill. This
gave a separate electorate and increased seats to Muslims and
was intended to foist the Muslim League's control over the
Calcutta corporation. This was to be achieved by reducing the
Hindus—who were in a predominant majority in Calcutta
in population, voting strength, and rates and taxes—to a
permanent minority in the corporation. In terms of numbers,
the Hindus constituted roughly 70 per cent of the population
of Calcutta, but the bill sought to reduce their representation
to about 46 per cent, and moreover, divided the Hindu seats
between caste Hindus and scheduled castes. An editorial in
the *Calcutta Municipal Gazette*[8] said, '[T]he nation is made
to drink . . . [from] the poison cup of communalism.' In the
course of the debate in the assembly, Dr Mookerjee pleaded
for throwing out altogether the bill which marked the climax
of the Haq government's discreditable policy, pursued for the
last two years, of ruthlessly dividing, weakening and crushing
the Hindus of Bengal, who had been the chief torchbearers in
the fight for India's progress and freedom.

As apprehended, the Hindu ministers in the cabinet, Nalini
Ranjan Sarker and Sir Bijoy Prasad Singh Roy, refused to criticize
the bill in the legislature, despite pressure from Dr Mookerjee,
among others.

The unkindest cut of all came in 1940, when the Haq
ministry introduced the Secondary Education Bill, taking
control of secondary education in the province. This had been,
till then, controlled by Calcutta University, which was, in turn,
controlled by Hindus. Now it would be vested instead in a
nominated secondary education board in which Muslims were to
be given a greater say. Apart from its political effects, this move
had serious financial repercussions for the university. The fees
for the matriculation examination were an important source of

revenue for the university, and being deprived of that would mean curtailment of many functions.

Dr Mookerjee could be said to have been finally forced out of his academic seclusion by these bills, which constituted total communal usurpation of control over higher education and municipal politics. In his own words, higher education 'was made the plaything of party and communal politics' and he realized that he would not be able to do his duty as an educationist if he did not also handle the associated politics. Meanwhile, retirement from vice chancellorship left him free to enter politics. Politics demanded his alignment with an active political party whose platform he could utilize for rousing public opinion outside the legislature. The party which naturally evoked his sympathy and support was the Congress, the most powerful political organization in the country. He had been passively associated with it since his entry into public life and it still enjoyed the overwhelming support of the Hindus. But he had become thoroughly disillusioned, indeed disgusted, with the Congress's policy of compromise with the Muslim League, even at the cost of vital national interests which 'lamentably betrayed the interests of the Hindus'.

Meanwhile, Dr Mookerjee, and for that matter the people of the province of Bengal, lost a good friend and well-wisher in the untimely death of Lord Brabourne, the benign and gentle Governor of Bengal, in February 1939. Lord Brabourne, more properly Michael Knatchbull, 5th Baron Brabourne, had been posted as Governor only in 1937 after the despotic rule of Sir John Anderson, and had, in the course of conducting the affairs of the university, struck up a good relationship with Dr Mookerjee based on mutual respect. The latter made a poignant speech in the assembly, paying tributes to the memory of the departed Governor.

The person chosen by the British to replace Lord Brabourne was Sir John Arthur Herbert, after a short stint by Sir John Reid, the acting Governor. According to several top ICS[9] officers who served under him, including one who was his private secretary, 'he did not have the talents necessary for the job'. The last sentence, as we shall see, could perhaps qualify as one of the greatest understatements of the century.

By the middle of the year 1939, it was clear that the Congress in Bengal could not be expected to take up the cause of the Hindus against the oppression of the Haq–League ministry. Even then, Dr Mookerjee had long discussions with both Subhas and Sarat Bose on the political situation in Bengal. He requested them to take up the Hindu cause, not by way of any communal favouritism but in order to fight oppression and injustice. This would have rendered it unnecessary for him to organize a separate political body. But the Bose brothers were reluctant to do so—first, because they thought it might still further rouse the Muslims, and secondly, because their non-communal image might be tarnished if they openly stood by the Hindu cause.[10]

Sadly enough, this obsession with 'secular image' and so-called 'non-communal credentials' persists to this day all over India (but probably nowhere more than in West Bengal). And that is why these nefarious activities of the Muslim League government in Bengal during 1937–40 and 1942–47, and the anti-Hindu pogroms of 1950, 1964 and 1971 in erstwhile East Pakistan, and of 1992 and 2001 in Bangladesh seldom find mention in the history books.

Then came the fateful Congress session at Tripuri (near Jabalpur) in 1939. Subhas Chandra Bose had been re-elected president, defeating Gandhi's candidate Pattabhi Sitaramayya. But Subhas failed to carry the Congress with him on account of the immensely superior politicking skills of Gandhi, and finally had no option but to resign at the Calcutta Session of the AICC on 29 April, and the staunch Gandhian right-winger Rajendra Prasad was elected to succeed him.

Dr Mookerjee, while observing this tussle within the Congress from a distance, was aware that at least in Bengal, neither the Forward Bloc, nor the so-called 'Khadi Group' owing allegiance to Gandhi, would lift a finger to help the beleaguered Hindus of the province. He also recognized the need for an organization in Bengal which would back his efforts and was on the lookout for a guide. This he found in the Maharashtrian freedom fighter Vinayak Damodar 'Veer' Savarkar, a close disciple of Lokmanya Tilak. He had just been freed from his internment in Ratnagiri by the Congress government of Bombay and had come to Calcutta to reorganize the Hindu Mahasabha movement in Bengal. The Hindu Mahasabha was a sociopolitical organization dedicated to the welfare and upliftment of the Hindus, and centred mainly in Maharashtra. The other all-India organization dedicated to Hindu welfare was the Rashtriya Swayamsevak Sangha (RSS), with which Dr Mookerjee would come in intimate contact much later. The RSS was also founded by another Maharashtrian, Dr Keshav Baliram Hedgewar, in 1925, and had no direct connection with the Mahasabha. It functioned purely as a social movement and steered strictly clear of politics.

Convinced that the Congress had fallen from the high pedestal of nationalism by its policy of appeasement with the Muslim League, Veer Savarkar sought to infuse new life into the Mahasabha within a few months by building it as a true instrument of the national will based on the ideal of Hindutva, on patriotism and its age-old culture. In his presidential address at the twentieth session of the All-India Hindu Mahasabha held at Nagpur in December 1938, Savarkar called upon Hindu *Sanghatanists* (Mahasabha adherents) to boycott the Congress, refrain from paying them a single farthing, not voting for the Congress ticket and to vote only for a confirmed Hindu nationalist with a view to chastise the Congress's anti-Hindu policy and to cure it of 'intolerable hypocrisy'. In March 1939, Savarkar himself formally relaunched the Mahasabha's caste consolidation programme in Bengal which underlined the importance the party placed on caste unity and was part of a broader campaign to create a united and self-conscious Hindu political community in Bengal.

Meanwhile, another important personality, a fiery Hindu monk, had entered the political fray in Bengal and had become instrumental to a great extent in Dr Mookerjee's entry into mass politics. He was Swami Pranavananda, earlier known as 'Binod Sadhu', from the village of Bajitpur in the district of Faridpur in East Bengal. He founded the Hindu monastic and philanthropic order Bharat Sevashram Sangha (known outside India as Pranav Math) which today stands side by side with the Ramakrishna Math and Mission, founded by Swami Vivekananda, as two of the biggest organized Hindu monastic orders of India, both based in West Bengal. However, unlike the Ramakrishna Math and Mission which strictly steers clear of politics, the Bharat Sevashram Sangha and its founder were always active in Hindu consolidation and empowerment. To this end, Swami Pranavananda undertook a programme of setting up 'Hindu Milan Mandirs' all over Bengal, especially in Muslim-majority East Bengal, as a forum for congregation of Hindus, regardless of caste. It is worth noting that during this time the RSS, though professedly non-political, under the stewardship of Dr Hedgewar and later Guruji Golwalkar, was quietly going about the same task all over India.

In December 1939, a huge Hindu conference was held in Deshbandhu Park, Calcutta, in which Dr Mookerjee presided and Swami Pranavananda played a major part. Among the attendees were important Bengali Hindu leaders and other distinguished Bengali Hindus of the time who had become concerned about the atrocities on Hindus and the anti-Hindu, rabidly communal policies of the Haq–Muslim League ministry. Among them were Sir Manmatha Nath Mukherjee, a retired judge of the Calcutta High Court and the law member in the viceroy's executive council;

Sir Nil Ratan Sircar, a famous physician; Sir U.N. Brahmachari, the medical researcher who invented urea stibamine, the first remedy for the fatal tropical disease Kala-azar (visceral leishmaniasis); Bijoy Chandra (B.C.) Chatterjee, a barrister; Hirendra Nath Datta, a philosopher; Dinesh Chandra Sen, a celebrated literary person; Hemendra Prasad Ghosh, a journalist and critic; Kumar Pramatha Nath Roy, a zamindar and philanthropist; Ramananda Chatterjee, editor of the respected Bengali literary journal *Prabasi*; S.N. Banerjee; Mrinal Kanti Ghosh; Jatindra Nath Roy Choudhury; Sanat Kumar Roy Chaudhury; Nisith Chandra Sen; and several others. Among the prominent absentees were Congressmen, including the Bose brothers, and the Hindu participants in the Haq–Muslim League ministry such as Nalini Ranjan Sarker and Sir Bijoy Prasad Singh Roy. This was probably the first such conference in which Bengali Hindus, so far in a self-denial mode under the 'secular' Congress leadership, brought to public attention the dangers that the community was facing from aggressive Muslim communalism.

Veer Savarkar came to Bengal again in August/September 1939 and Dr Mookerjee was brought in close contact with him. Dr Mookerjee toured different parts of Bengal in September 1939 and was greatly perturbed at the helpless position of Bengali Hindus, whom the Congress, in my opinion, failed to rouse and protect. While touring eastern Bengal, he realized how desperate the position of Hindus had become and how the spirit of resistance against an outrageously communal aggression was dying out— slowly but surely. This was how Dr Mookerjee, along with some others, were drawn to Savarkar's influence that gradually took root. Nirmal Chandra Chatterjee, a renowned barrister of the Calcutta High Court and Veer Savarkar's host in Calcutta, invited several prominent men of the city, including Dr Mookerjee, to meet him. Incidentally, Chatterjee was also the father of Somnath Chatterjee, the erstwhile leader of the Communist Party of India

(Marxist) and the Speaker of the Lok Sabha during 2004–09. Dr Mookerjee, who was deeply impressed by Savarkar's analysis of the Indian political situation and his gospel of unalloyed nationalism to checkmate the anti-national policies of the League and the 'cowardly passivity' of the Congress party, was pressed to join the Mahasabha by Nirmal Chatterjee, S.N. Banerjee, Asutosh Lahiri and others. Thus, circumstances inevitably led him to the Hindu Mahasabha, which took up precisely those issues that worried the bhadralok, many of whom despaired of any effective remedies from a Congress party led by the Bose brothers. His entry into the Mahasabha and his quick rise to the position of its working president marked the beginning of his active political career.

Dr Mookerjee's entry was welcomed by Gandhi, who was greatly impressed by his thoroughly nationalistic outlook and told him,[11] 'Somebody was needed to lead the Hindus after Malviyaji [Pandit Madan Mohan Malviya] . . . Patel is a Congressman with a Hindu mind, you be a Hindu Sabhaite with a Congress mind.' Dr Mookerjee had quipped, 'But then you will dub me as communal.' Gandhi had replied, 'Like Shiva who drank the poison after churning the sea, somebody must be there to drink the poison of Indian politics. It can be you.' In fact, Gandhi, without ever saying so in so many words except as above, appears to have had a deep appreciation of Dr Mookerjee's abilities. It was at his insistence that Nehru was induced to include him as the minister for industries in the first Indian cabinet in 1947.

At that time, there were two Hindu *sabhas* in Bengal, one that owed allegiance to the all-India body, and the other which functioned under B.C. Chatterjee's leadership. An agreement was reached between the two sabhas and they came together under the presidency of Sir Manmatha Nath Mukherjee. On 27 December 1939, Veer Savarkar launched the Mahasabha conference in Calcutta, flying its saffron flag over Deshbandhu Park. Nalini Ranjan Sarker, the astute but unprincipled politician who had engineered the Haq–Muslim League coalition, claimed that the Mahasabha leaders had been 'attempting to win him over' for some time. According to Dr Mookerjee, 'This was a great beginning of a great struggle.' This also heralded a new stage in his career. He came out of 'academic seclusion' and became an active political leader, although he continued to give much of his time and attention to university affairs.

Dr Mookerjee found formidable obstacles when he started organizing the Hindu Mahasabha. Any nationalist Hindu consolidation was bound to be disliked by the British. He and his associates also had to encounter bitter opposition from the fanatical elements gradually gaining force under the banner of the Muslim League. Additionally, they had to meet resistance from the three important elements within the Hindu community— one being the Congress. Dr Mookerjee's diary says, 'Subhas [Bose] once warned me in a friendly spirit, adding significantly, that if we proceeded to create a rival political body in Bengal he would see to it, *by force* [emphasis added] if need be, that it was broken before it was really born. This I considered to be a most unfair and unreasonable attitude to take up.' The second element was the Communist Party which would brazenly support the Muslim League but dub the Hindu Sabha as 'communal and reactionary'. Gangadhar Adhikari, an important theoretician of the Communist Party and author of the infamous Adhikari Thesis,[12] declared, 'Wherever people of the Muslim faith living together in a territorial unit form a nationality . . . they certainly have the right to autonomous state existence.' The third element was a section of the scheduled castes who, having secured thirty seats in the Legislative Assembly through the Poona Pact,[13] were being made to demand a separate political entity, antagonistic to Hindus.[14] The scarcity of the true fighting type of men, able to rouse popular enthusiasm, added to their difficulty in organizing the Hindu Sabha in the different parts of Bengal; this was in

contrast to the ways of the Congress, which by reason of its long
career of service had secured the loyalty of many a brave and selfless
worker. But the Mahasabha knew that what they had proposed to
do was very near the heart of the vast majority of Bengali Hindus
who would soon be able to march ahead. All felt great wrongs
were being done, but they did not know what to do, largely due
to a sense of defeatism.

Dr Mookerjee toured Bengal extensively and did his best
to stir up public opinion in favour of the Mahasabha, which
asked the Hindus to organize themselves and sink all their petty
differences. They gradually tore away the embarrassment felt
by the Hindus to call themselves so, lest they be branded as
'communal'. Dr Mookerjee's entry galvanized the Bengal Hindu
Mahasabha into a dynamic organization that started to attract
the Hindu intelligentsia and began to be looked upon as a force
in Bengal politics. His bold but rational presentation of the
Mahasabha ideology and his frontal attack on the Congress policy
of appeasement of and compromise with the Muslim League at
the cost of the Hindus created a stir all over Bengal and India.

Dr Mookerjee's appointment as working president of
the All-India Hindu Mahasabha early in 1940 due to the
continued ill health of Veer Savarkar gave him a wider stage for
the presentation of the Mahasabha ideals by touring the whole
of India and addressing mammoth meetings. Balraj Madhok,[15]
who was studying for his degree in Lahore at that time, heard
him delivering to a packed hall in the winter of 1940. It was an
extremely forceful, methodical and convincing exposition of the
aims and ideals of the Mahasabha and its differences with the
Congress, which set all his listeners thinking. In the course of his
short stay in Lahore, he addressed a rally of Rashtriya Swayamsevak
Sangha (RSS) as well and said: 'I see in this organization the one
silver lining in the cloudy sky of India.' It was this admiration
for the RSS which continued to draw him closer to it in his later

years. His whirlwind tour took the country by storm. It was felt everywhere that a powerful star was rising on the Indian horizon. His personality gave the Mahasabha a new status and prestige and he himself steadily rose to prominence as a national figure due to his political courage, organizational skill and oratory. It has been said that for the first and the last time, the Hindus of Bengal found a spokesman who did not care at all for political expediency or personal interest. In 1940 and 1941, outside the assembly in Bengal, the Mahasabha 'kept the public fully alive to the dangers lying ahead' under Dr Mookerjee's strong leadership and carried on its work of consolidation.

Meanwhile, conflicts within the Congress in Bengal, in the wake of Subhas Chandra Bose's revolt against Gandhi, helped the Hindu Sabha to grow into prominence in the province. In the legislature, the disciplined Congress party was at last split into two groups—one under Sarat Chandra Bose (who did not, however, formally leave the Congress and join the Forward Bloc), the other under Kiran Sankar Roy, representing the official Congress party. Dr Mookerjee's diary says: 'In these circumstances, the Bengal Hindu Mahasabha was going ahead. We had friendly relations with both sections and tried to preserve a united front whenever occasion demanded it.'

However, Lord Linlithgow's efforts to get support for the war from the political parties failed and the Congress withdrew its ministries from the provinces on 29–30 October 1940. Thereupon, Jinnah became more aggressive than before, called upon Muslims to celebrate a 'Day of Deliverance' throughout India, and widely circulated wild stories of Muslim oppression, while the oppression of Hindus by the Muslim League ministries was never given any publicity. The grievances of the Muslim minorities against the Congress governments began with Jinnah's resentment at Nehru's refusal to enter into a coalition in UP;[16] the grievances culminated in unreasonable fears that the Congress high command would completely undermine the federal principle. But even then, there was no talk of Pakistan or the partition of India.

On 24 March 1940, the Muslim League passed in Lahore its fateful and momentous resolution on Pakistan. Ironically, it was moved by Fazlul Haq, the essentially non-communal (but forever vacillating) Muslim leader of Bengal, an erstwhile junior to Sir Asutosh Mookerjee, who had just joined the League and left it shortly afterwards. The League demanded, for the first time, that India must be partitioned, since Muslims were a separate nation and they must have a separate homeland of their own in India where the green, crescent and star flag of Islam would fly in all its glory. This was the Pakistan demand. All responsible men, especially those belonging to the Congress, laughed at the idea, saying that it was a mere stunt. In fact, few Muslim leaders initially took Pakistan very seriously, and even for Jinnah probably, it began as a bargaining counter, useful to block possible British constitutional concessions to the Congress. Very soon, however, the idea spread and was fanned by the fanatical zeal of Muslims almost all over India. In provinces where the League was in power, it received full support from officials and Muslim consolidation went on in full swing. In provinces where the Congress ministers resigned, officials joined the League to deprive Hindus of their lawful rights. Thus, the Hindu point of view as such had practically no one to support it. While the Congress uttered no word against the Pakistan scheme, the Mahasabha alone agitated against it, impelling Secretary of State Leopold Amery to wash his hands clean of the Pakistan proposal (December 1940). This was how the Hindu Mahasabha was steadily gaining influence, thanks to the League's activities and the failure of the Congress to stand up for the rights of Hindus.

The Congress had done untold mischief by boycotting the census of 1931, thus making the entries hardly dependable; although, as noted in Dr Mookerjee's diary, '[O]n the Census figure however our political fate depended, and the loss we thus suffered was incalculable.' The Mahasabha wanted Hindu solidarity to grow and for caste prejudices to disappear. As part of its caste consolidation programme, Dr Mookerjee visited Chandpur in Tipperah in eastern Bengal in late 1939 to have the local temple opened to all Hindu castes. In 1940, the Mahasabha sponsored a well-organized agitation in Bengal as soon as the operations related to the census of 1941 got under way, creating much distrust between the two communities. The Mahasabha wanted to check the growing tendency among the scheduled castes to regard themselves outside the Hindu fold due to the enmity of caste Hindus. A section of scheduled castes bitterly opposed the Mahasabha's declaration that they call themselves Hindus only in their census returns. Ultimately, those who belonged to the scheduled castes were recorded as Hindus all over Bengal. The Mahasabha made an effort to get the Santhals, a tribal people inhabiting different parts of Bengal, counted as Hindus in Bankura. This prompted counter-efforts by the Muslim League to use money to make some Santhals record their religion as 'aboriginal'. In early 1941, Dr Mookerjee took a personal interest in that campaign in Bankura. The Mahasabha's publicity campaign had great educative value, providing impetus to all Hindus to take an active interest in the census and uniting them to a great extent. Premier Haq, who discovered, in Dr Mookerjee's activities, 'a sinister design to reduce the Muslims of Bengal to a minority',[17] carried on a most bitter propaganda campaign against Hindus. A huge protest meeting held at the Town Hall in Calcutta, presided over by Sir N.N. Sircar, former law member of the viceroy's executive council, demanded Haq's dismissal.

Dr Mookerjee had meanwhile been impelled to enter the political arena to save Bengali Hindus from their miserable plight as a result of being systematically humiliated and persecuted by the Muslim League with the connivance of the British. The task that faced him in Bengal was twofold. He had to establish his position vis-à-vis the Congress leadership which had come to regard the Hindus as their own flock who could be fleeced by them at will. He also had to meet the challenge of the Muslim League. The main figure on the Congress side in Bengal at that time was Subhas Chandra Bose, whose stand against Gandhi at the Tripuri Congress and subsequent exit from the Congress presidency had made him a hero in Bengal. He was planning to hold Bengal, and particularly Calcutta, as his own citadel, to demonstrate his strength to the Congress high command by winning its corporation election that was scheduled to be held in March 1940. While the official Congressmen found themselves totally unprepared to fight against Subhas, the Bengal Hindu Mahasabha, which wanted a strong Hindu Sabha party in the Calcutta corporation, decided to contest the elections.

This pitted the two stalwarts directly against each other in their bid to win the loyalties of Bengali Hindus. The Mahasabha was prepared to work with Subhas and run elections jointly, provided they also worked as a team in the corporation later on. Subhas agreed to this but the situation soon made him realize that in a tripartite contest between the Hindu Mahasabha, the Muslim League and his men in the name of the Congress, the League might secure a majority. Dr Mookerjee and Bose then agreed that the Mahasabha and Subhas's Congress should contest an agreed number of seats to be determined by mutual consultation. A selection board was formed, Subhas, Sarat Bose and Rajendra Chandra Deb representing Subhas's Congress, and Dr Mookerjee, S.N. Banerjee and Sanat Kumar Roy Chaudhury representing the Hindu Sabha.

Then began an unfortunate mutual game of attrition. Constituencies were accordingly selected and candidates approved, but in respect of just two constituencies, the two groups could not arrive at any agreed decision about the candidates to be set up.

One night after a long and heated discussion, Sarat Bose broke the joint front.

Thereafter, Dr Mookerjee himself was attacked and abused by some Congressmen and women and got injured while addressing a meeting. This brought about public criticism, and Subhas suggested to him that there should be no attempt at disturbing the meetings of the rival parties. This incident proved the mettle of Dr Mookerjee as a political leader, who was not worried about his personal safety, and created a salutary effect on his opponents. In the elections that followed, the Mahasabha stood its ground very well, winning about 50 per cent of the seats and gaining tremendous prestige. Through the efforts of mutual friends, it started negotiations again for forgetting the past and putting up a united stand for serving the corporation. Here again, there was a break-up due to Subhas's tactics. He wanted to come in as an alderman and asked Dr Mookerjee also to come. The latter told Subhas that it was a mistake for a leader of Subhas's stature to try to grab power everywhere, and that they must divide work among able followers. Bose, who had his own likes and dislikes, ultimately again broke away from the Mahasabha.

Dr Mookerjee had meanwhile refused the offer of working with the Muslim League because he held that a patched-up agreement, for some immediate narrow gain, between diametrically opposed parties could never work. The Mahasabha thought that fighting hard to get rid of the Muslim League ministry, while working closely with it for sharing power and patronage in the corporation, would be bad for the party and would send a totally wrong message to the populace. Subhas, however, had different ideas on these questions. In order to have the corporation under his control, he came to terms with the Muslim League and installed a League mayor, a Sindhi Muslim businessman called A.R. Siddiqui, as soon as he failed to negotiate with the Mahasabha on his terms. He was out to wage a relentless

war on the League ministry in one breath; in another, he was a
warm and dear ally of the League while it ruled the corporation.
The Mahasabha, however, fully utilized Subhas's coalition with
the League to openly attack it with the indirect support of the
official Congress group, who knew that the former could openly
fight with Subhas, whom they regarded as their great enemy.
Among the media (then limited to newspapers), the Mahasabha
was supported by the English daily *Amrita Bazar Patrika* and
Bengali *Jugantor*, while the highly influential English *Hindustan
Standard* and Bengali *Anandabazar Patrika* were controlled by
Subhas and Sarat Bose.

The fight gradually took on bitter overtones. A public meeting,
called at the Town Hall in Calcutta, under the presidency of
Ramananda Chatterjee, the famous journalist and editor of the
premier Bengali periodical *Prabasi*, was broken up by the hired
agents of Subhas led by Hemaprabha Majumdar and Lila Roy,
injuring Nirmal Chandra Chatterjee and others. Next, Subhas
and his men played on the emotions of Bijoy Chandra Chatterjee,
a prominent Mahasabhaite, who had lost in the election by only
three votes, by making him feel that the Mahasabha was against
him, and set Chatterjee up as a Bose–League candidate for
aldermanship. The Mahasabha considered this betrayal a blow
to themselves and lost Chatterjee through disciplinary action.
Inside the corporation, the Sabha, though in minority, wielded
considerable power under the able leadership of N.C. Chatterjee.
During this period, the Mahasabha candidate Asutosh Lahiri
convincingly defeated the Bose group candidate in the election
of mid-1941, when the Dacca riots brought the Mahasabha into
great prominence. According to Dr Mookerjee's diary, Subhas
was so exposed to public criticism due to his short-sighted alliance
with the League that he soon came down in public estimation.

Viewed in a proper perspective, however, in the history of the
freedom struggle of India, as enacted in Bengal, these few cases of

friction between these two great leaders, and that too in municipal politics, appear to be minor aberrations. Dr Mookerjee was second to none in his appreciation of Subhas's epic struggle, stretching across his defiance against the mighty Mohandas Gandhi for Congress presidency, his escape to Germany, his perilous voyage in two submarines from Germany to Japan through enemy waters, including switching submarines in choppy seas, his organizing the Indian National Army, and his struggle in South East Asia followed by his mysterious disappearance. Dr Mookerjee recorded a moving tribute to Subhas's heroic role as a fighter for India's freedom in a diary entry on 21 October 1944, where he wrote, 'Today it must be admitted that taking him as he is, he is one of the foremost Indians of his time who regarded no means or method as bad if he felt he could thereby attain power to wrest the freedom of the country . . . A national hero in exile to serve his country's cause—that is how he appeals to many of his countrymen who may not agree with him always.'

Then again, in a dictation to Baridbaran, his stenographer at Madhupur, on 5 January 1946, Dr Mookerjee said:[18] 'Meanwhile, the part played by Subhas Bose became widely known and this staggered the whole of India. The Azad Hind Fauj (also known as the Indian National Army or I.N.A.) which he organised in Burma and in other parts of South Asia became known to the people of India, and everyone realised what an amazing act of daring, patriotism, and organisation it must have been. At one stage Pandit Jawaharlal Nehru announced that if Subhas Bose came to India with the help of Japan he would, if necessary, go out and fight with him single-handed with a sword in his hand. When however he realised what a stupendous part Subhas had played in organising the Indian National Army, Nehru slowly changed over and started admiring the activities of the I.N.A.' The question here is, whether this changeover was out of conviction or political expediency.

Regarding Gandhiji's opposition to Subhas's election in the Tripuri Congress and his subsequent ouster, he wrote in his diary on 2 February 1939, 'Read Gandhi's statement on Subhas Bose's election carefully. I cannot conceal my disappointment at its tone and content. Why should he be so upset at Subhas's victory? . . . Further, he [Gandhi] complains, Subhas's manifesto against the "seven pillars of wisdom" (Vallabhbhai & co.) was unjustifiable and unworthy. But what about the manifesto of these honourable gentlemen themselves; and what right had they to state that behind Subhas's back they (including Gandhi) had decided that it was unnecessary to re-elect him, and what is more, that S's election would be harmful to the interests of India?'

Leonard Gordon, the biographer of Sarat and Subhas Chandra Bose, has also observed that Dr Mookerjee was essentially a family friend of the Boses, though he differed from them on many political issues. He would fight to get them out of prison and press the government with questions about their health when they were in prison.

The problem presented by the Muslim League was, however, of a different kind. With the connivance of the British bureaucracy, the League–Praja Party ministry of Bengal was making a planned effort to communalize the life of Bengal. There were two major planks in its programmes. One was to *Muslimize* the administration and sap the sources of Hindu supremacy in the educational and cultural spheres by depriving them of their hold over the university and secondary education. The second was to engineer riots, particularly in East Bengal, to demoralize the Hindus into fleeing from their homes or getting converted to Islam.

Dr Mookerjee successfully foiled the League plans to dominate the sphere of secondary education through legislation. When the League found it very difficult to capture Calcutta University, they proposed to weaken it by depriving it of control over secondary education which had been under the academic jurisdiction of the university since 1857. Early in 1940, Premier Haq introduced in the assembly the Secondary Education Bill, which sought to take away control of secondary education from the university, in which Hindus were firmly entrenched, and entrust it to a nominated Muslim-majority secondary education board.

It is the espousal of this Secondary Education Bill by the Muslim League which is said to have really forced Dr Mookerjee out of his 'academic seclusion'. He led the opposition to the bill inside and outside the legislature with a stirring agitation. Months of sustained Mahasabha propaganda against the Secondary Education Bill followed. Meanwhile, he also kept up his efforts to get the Congress on to his side. Ultimately, most Congressmen, including Sarat Chandra Bose and Rai Harendra Nath Chowdhury, accepted Dr Mookerjee's ideas.

There were stormy debates on the Secondary Education Bill in the Bengal assembly from August 1940 to September 1941. Speaking on the bill on 28 August 1940, Dr Mookerjee recommended, on behalf of the Opposition, that secondary education should be directed to technical, agricultural, industrial and commercial channels. He wanted a system of education that would enable Muslims of Bengal to develop themselves according to their beliefs. Similarly, he wanted Hindus to develop their education according to their best traditions and ideals. In March 1941, in protest against the Secondary Education Bill, the official Congress party staged a walkout from the assembly. On 8 September 1941, Dr Mookerjee rose to support the motion for recommittal of the bill to the select committee. He placed the reasons why the government should not proceed with the bill as had been introduced into the house. He finally had the satisfaction of holding up the bill on the floor of the house, when all attempts at an honourable settlement failed.

Dr Mookerjee's successful resistance to the Secondary Education Bill purely through constitutional means, without once taking the fight to the streets, once again showed the quality of the man as a constitutional and parliamentary politician. Of course, he must have been shrewd enough to understand that on the streets the bhadralok Hindus would be no match for the riff-raff of the Muslim League, particularly with the British administration being totally on the side of the latter. This quality of Dr Mookerjee found further expression in the Parliament of free India when he criticized Jawaharlal Nehru for his weak-kneed policy towards Pakistan and his abandonment of the interests of the East Bengal refugees on the assurances of Liaquat Ali Khan.[19]

Later, when the Muslim League came back to power in 1943 after an interregnum, and Nazimuddin became Chief Minister, the matter was resurrected and debated again. Nothing appears to have resulted from the meeting (July 1944) of Dr Mookerjee and the Chief Minister to discuss possible changes in the Secondary Education Bill. It was in post-Independence West Bengal in the early 1950s that Calcutta University was divested of secondary education which was then entrusted to the West Bengal Board of Secondary Education, and the matriculation examination was rechristened 'school final'. Of course, the setting up of the University Grants Commission in 1956 took care of the financial losses that the university underwent as a result of being deprived of the examination fees.

Dr Mookerjee was equally successful in frustrating the League's other plans to communalize the polity in favour of Muslims. In 1940–41, there were serious allegations of oppression of Hindus, especially in Noakhali. Accordingly, on 22 March 1941, Governor Sir John Herbert called a conference of the party leaders to consider how communal relations could be improved. The Mahasabha asserted that so long as a single-party communal ministry remained in office, the real cause would remain untouched. A coalition ministry, enjoying the confidence of a large section of Hindus and Muslims, could alone help to inspire good feeling between the two communities.

While the conference was meeting at the Government House, the Dacca riots broke out. The whole city of Dacca was in flames. In the town, the Hindus were, more or less, prepared to resist the attack. Whether this major communal riot, which continued for over seven months, was pre-planned or had any connection with the Mahasabha agitation on the Secondary Education Bill, is still unclear. The press was forbidden to publish any news about it under the Defence of India Rules. But as soon as Dr Mookerjee came to know about it, he decided to visit Dacca, an act of extraordinary personal courage. He went there as the first Hindu non-official from outside. It was first suggested by the Governor that the Muslim ministers, against whom there were allegations of instigating the riots, would not go to Dacca nor should Dr Mookerjee, the situation being left in charge of the local officers. Fazlul Haq, the Nawab of Dacca and Shahabuddin, however, went to Dacca in a chartered plane. After obtaining the British chief secretary's permission, Dr Mookerjee requested the Governor for a seat in the plane. But the plane took off long before he reached the airport. Not a man to be daunted by such tactics, he risked his life travelling in a tiny private aircraft piloted by a friend of his, called Lohia, an extremely hazardous act in those early days of aviation. Before he got down, he could see the whole city in flames. Commissioner Blair at first did not allow Dr Mookerjee to enter Dacca on the grounds of safety. Further, Muslims would have become uncontrollable if he had remained there. However, when Dr Mookerjee told Blair that the Governor knew he was coming and he had no right to stop him, he was allowed to go. He went directly to the palace of the Nawab of Dacca, the president of the Bengal Muslim League, from where the entire carnage was being planned and organized. He stayed for four or five days at vice chancellor R.C. Majumdar's house. Although Hindus could not be beaten in the town, their condition in the rural areas was pitiable; Dr Mookerjee visited the riot-affected rural areas to inspire confidence in his suffering Hindu brethren by his personal courage and by systematic exposure of the League designs.

Early in April, an anti-Hindu pogrom took place in the rural areas of the Narayanganj subdivision of Dacca district. This resulted in the flight of about 3000 persons to the princely state of Tripura. It took days before the government could control the situation. The Mahasabha sent relief parties from Calcutta. Dr Mookerjee himself went a few weeks later to Agartala to thank the maharaja personally for his generosity. After his return to Calcutta, he wanted the public to know about the happenings in Dacca. But since the press was gagged under the Defence of India Rules, the only way to get the news published was to raise the matter in the assembly. He sent a wire to Congress president Maulana Abul Kalam Azad to ask Congress legislators to support him for moving an adjournment motion. When the Maulana refused to do anything about the matter just then, he wrote to Gandhi who directed Azad to send wires to Bengal legislators to support Dr Mookerjee's move. Thus, he was able to tell the country what had been done to the Hindus of Dacca. It was following his exposures in the assembly that the government was forced to restore calm and punish the guilty. 'These riots and disturbances opened the eyes of the Hindus considerably and the work of the Sabha received a great impetus.'

In the strained aftermath of the riot, the Mahasabha appeared to have gained ground at the expense of the Congress. In the electoral field, it secured some notable successes during the year 1940. It came out with flying colours in the hotly contested election to the Calcutta corporation, so that the Congress could not muster a majority in the corporation on their own. In Sind, the Mahasabha totally defeated the Congress and got a clear majority.

Further, while the Congress uttered no word against the Pakistan scheme, the Mahasabha alone agitated against it. Lastly, the 22nd session of the All-India Hindu Mahasabha, held at Madura in December 1940, passed a resolution advocating direct action if the demand of the people for a real transfer of power to them was not met. The Congress, while also making a similar demand, was not prepared to launch a struggle yet.

Dr Mookerjee, who had joined the Mahasabha in the belief that they would not hesitate to fight the government and thus pave the way themselves towards national freedom, welcomed his party's stand. However, in the middle of 1941, the party's All-India Committee met in Calcutta for a special session and decided to hold in abeyance the resolution passed at Madura on the pretext of the Dacca riots. According to Dr Mookerjee,[20] '[T]he withdrawal of the Madura resolution was a severe blow on the prestige of the Mahasabha, and made people feel that we could only talk big but ran away from the field of action. This had a very disheartening effect on my mind.'

Such disappointment notwithstanding, Dr Mookerjee's zeal for struggle was not affected. He toured the Punjab and found a new awakening among Hindus. His entry into politics infused new vigour and vitality into the Hindu Mahasabha movement in Bengal and the rest of India. Not only that, it also forced or induced the Congress, forever chary of taking up Hindu causes for fear of being dubbed 'communal', to work in the interest of the persecuted Hindus of Bengal.

5

Finance Minister of Bengal, 1941–42

By 1941, Abul Kashem Fazlul Haq had been in power as Chief Minister for more than three years, but as it appears he was far from happy, or even comfortable. Dr Mookerjee, in a diary entry, observed his state as follows: 'Haq discovered towards the latter half of 1941 how dangerous his position had become. Left to himself he is one of the most lovable personalities one may think of. He indeed shines in the company he keeps. A good batch of friends and followers may help him to do enormous good to his people and country. A bad lot may lead him to hell. As I said of him once, he is at once an asset and a liability of no mean order.'

Haq had in fact played, much against his better judgement, into the hands of persons who posed as his friends but were really his arch-enemies. This was bound to be because his Krishak Praja Party was basically a party of peasants who happened to be largely Muslim. It had little to do with Islam. At the same time, the Muslim League was first and last a Muslim communal party, manned by big landowners of the community. It was not entirely his fault that he had been catapulted into such an unenviable state. It is quite true that, as Dr Mookerjee had put it, he was 'dying for power', but he was pushed into the lap of the Muslim League by the Congress refusing to form a coalition with him in 1937 in

Bengal. In order to become Chief Minister, he had betrayed his party and joined hands with Nazimuddin and Suhrawardy under the banner of the League. The League stalwarts, who never liked Haq, fully utilized him as their convenient tool for stabilizing their position, and that of the League as defenders of Islam, and even made him move the Pakistan Resolution at the League's Lahore session in March 1940. Haq was also forced or induced to openly justify all the anti-Hindu misdeeds of the ministry committed through the dishonest machinations of the communal Leaguers.

Dr Mookerjee records in a diary entry, dated 6 December 1945 (when he was lying ill in Calcutta after the election trip to Barrackpore—see Chapter 8), 'We wanted to check the growing tendency among the Scheduled Castes people to regard themselves outside the Hindu fold—their antagonism to Caste Hindus was being slowly nurtured on political consideration—Caste Hindus were the enemies of the Scheduled Castes' progress etc. We wanted that Hindu solidarity must grow; we wanted that caste prejudices should disappear. We therefore declared that we should not indicate our castes but call ourselves Hindus in our census returns. This was bitterly opposed by a section of Scheduled Castes people. Still our propaganda had great educative value. We not only got all Hindus to take an active interest in the census but united them as far as possible.' Premier Haq, egged on by the Leaguers, discovered in the Mahasabha's work in the census operations 'a sinister design to reduce the Muslims of Bengal to a minority'[1] and carried on a very bitter propaganda campaign against it.

As soon as Haq discovered that he was going to be stabbed in the back by his colleagues and some co-workers, he began machinations to get out of the ministry, but in a way which would reinstall him as premier. Dr Mookerjee, on the other hand, thought it necessary in Bengal's wider interests, as that of India's, to keep the League out of power by befriending and strengthening Haq and mustering together all the non-Congress Hindu forces in the legislature. In Dr Mookerjee's diary, he records that Sarat Bose was, at that time, a Congress rebel and the master of his own group. He was also trusted by the Muslims. He was therefore free to take a decision irrespective of the dictates of their central leadership, and it was mainly through his efforts that Haq decided to bring about the breakdown of his own ministry. Probably both factors, namely Dr Mookerjee's efforts and Haq's eagerness to get rid of the Leaguers were responsible for the ultimate downfall of the League ministry.

Meanwhile, a definite majority of members, numbering about 127, had signed and declared their readiness to follow Haq. The official Congress party under Kiran Sankar Roy's leadership was also not in favour of the League. The anti-League legislators threw out a challenge to Sir John Herbert, the Governor of Bengal. Whatever his personal desire or the advice of the ICS clique might have been, Herbert did not dare flout the will of the majority of the legislature, and ultimately decided to ask Haq to form the ministry.

On 7 December, Haq submitted the resignation of his coalition ministry. Of the 127 legislators who had declared their readiness to follow Haq, the Nawab of Dacca was one. He was till then with the League and was not elected the party leader, and was nursing a grudge. Ispahani (of the 1943 famine notoriety— see Chapter 6) called Fazlul Haq 'the old fox . . . the black sheep of Barisal', and Jinnah expelled both Haq and the Nawab from the League, saying that they had been 'weeded out'. Herbert could no longer hold off the formation of a new cabinet under Haq. After a brief and abortive flirtation with the idea of an Azizul Haque-led 'War Cabinet', on or about 10 December, he decided to summon Haq to form the ministry and the latter accepted the invitation.

It was a foregone conclusion that Sarat Bose would be a leading member of the cabinet. Herbert, however, was not in favour of this and told Dr Mookerjee that Bose should be dissuaded and that the first batch of ministers should consist of Haq, the Nawab of Dacca and Dr Mookerjee. Meanwhile, on 7 December, Japan bombed Pearl Harbour, and the next day, the Allied powers declared war on Japan. On 11 December, there was a sudden bombshell when Sarat Bose was arrested on the orders of the Government of India under Regulation III 'due to suspicion regarding his contacts with Japan'. The progressive coalition ministry was sworn in on 12 December. Dr Mookerjee became finance minister, the only representative from his party. Upendranath Barman was the sole scheduled-caste minister (from the Rajbangshi community) and there was no agreement regarding the name of the second scheduled-caste member who had to be a Namasudra man.[2] The Bose group was represented by two ministers, Santosh Bose and Pramatha Banerjee. The Muslim names were chosen by agreement, though Dr Mookerjee could not discover the real reason for the selection of Abdul Karim, who, according to him,[3] was 'old but entirely honest. His brain often failed him.' The newspapers were out with information regarding the personnel of the ministry.

Fazlul Haq initially faced a lot of opposition from his party colleagues regarding the inclusion of Dr Mookerjee in the cabinet because of his pro-Hindu credentials and his trenchant criticism of Haq when he was blindly pursuing the anti-Hindu policies of the Muslim League. In reply to this opposition, Haq told Abul Mansur Ahmad,[4] one of his closest associates, 'Listen Abul Mansur, you do not know Dr Mookerjee, I do. He is the son of Sir Asutosh. It doesn't matter that he belongs to the Hindu Mahasabha. You will not find a more liberal person or a better well-wisher of Muslims among Hindus. If you trust me, you must trust him too.'

Abul Mansur Ahmad has remarked in his autobiography that once he got to know Dr Mookerjee during his interactions in the ministry, he found every word of what Haq said to be true.

Despite being a Mahasabha leader, Dr Mookerjee, according to Ahmad, was liberal towards Muslims. Driven by this impression, Ahmad wrote an editorial in his popular (among Muslims) journal *Nabajug*, asking Dr Mookerjee to embark on a political tour of the whole of Bengal, starting from his own district of Mymensingh. He said that he would ensure that there would be no upsets in the meetings, but Dr Mookerjee would have to ensure that he won the confidence of the Muslims. Ahmad had further observed that he was confident he could do it.

These were the circumstances under which the second Haq ministry was formed. And Dr Mookerjee, within just two years of his entering mainstream politics, belonging to a party that had hitherto practically no support in the province, became the finance minister of the Bengal Presidency. Not many have been able to match this achievement.

There was intense relief in the public mind, especially among Hindus, at the termination of the League ministry, which had caused immense injury to them between 1937 and 1941 and had also retarded the real progress of Bengal as a whole. For the first time, the ministry depended for its existence on the combined support of elected Hindu and Muslim members and was backed by Anglo-Indians and Indian Christians as well. The League party under Sir Nazimuddin had, as its allies, the European members of the house who never liked a strong Hindu–Muslim combination in the province.

Entry into the Bengal government at that crucial time was the beginning of a new and very significant chapter in Dr Mookerjee's life. Bengal had so far known him as an educationist. His association with the Hindu Mahasabha was frowned upon by many of the Congress-brand nationalists who doubted his wisdom in joining hands with Haq. However, the determined fight he put up against the hostile British government and unsympathetic bureaucracy not only silenced his critics but also raised his stature as a practical and far-seeing politician, a capable administrator and, above all, an arch-nationalist.

From the beginning Dr Mookerjee was aware of the plight of the coalition government. He realized that 'a difficult and rugged path full of obstacles' lay ahead. He doubted if he could really do any solid work. The absence of Sarat Bose, who would have brought a good deal of prestige and strength to the new government, was a real handicap. 'But even this,' says Dr Mookerjee, 'did not break our solidarity and we were determined to give the province a real choice to recover its lost position.' Disturbed by the fact that the ministers were interacting with Bose frequently in the Presidency Jail at Calcutta, Herbert, with the help of the Government of India, managed to get him transferred to Mercara in Coorg, a small Indian state in south India. Bose thereupon issued instructions that the ministers of his party should resign. The ministry could not remain in office for a day without the active support of the Bose group. The Nawab of Dacca and Santosh Bose, however, went to Mercara and persuaded Bose to suspend his judgement for the time being. Dr Mookerjee himself went to Delhi to meet the viceroy and home member Sir Reginald Maxwell about Bose's release, or trial, or transfer to Bengal but they were adamant and nothing could be done.

The second and major handicap of the new ministry was an unsympathetic bureaucracy, headed by a Governor—all open supporters of the Muslim League and terribly upset with their failure to have a League ministry. Their main grouse was that this ministry was capable of functioning without the support of the 'European Group', and thus that group could not influence the course of things as they could during the Haq-led League ministry. The British, moreover, fundamentally hated any cooperation between the Hindus and the Muslims and wanted the coalition government to fall. In matters affecting the economic and political welfare of the people, the ministry got little cooperation from

Herbert, who pressed them again and again to abandon Fazlul Haq and to settle with the League. The Defence of India Rules had made the position of the Governor, who had direct access to the secretaries and district officers over the heads of the ministers, exceptionally strong vis-à-vis the ministry, whose powers were greatly circumscribed and who had little voice regarding the all-important questions of defence of the province against the impending Japanese invasion. At a time when the political situation in Bengal was uneasy, the state unfortunately happened to get a group of short-sighted, reactionary, unsympathetic and unresponsive British ICS men who vainly thought that by repression alone they could govern the country and whose administration fanned the communal flame and bowed to the will of Clive Street. Dr Mookerjee made home minister Haq pass orders which they thought were just and rational. But in a 'regular tug of war', they were outmanoeuvred by the Secretariat or vetoed by the Governor. Herbert accused Dr Mookerjee of interfering with the affairs of the home department which was not his own. Haq and he both replied that it was perfectly constitutional for them to have acted together on the grounds of joint responsibility. It thus turned out that Dr Mookerjee was the only really strong man in the ministry.

Dr Mookerjee's stature as an educationist and leader of the intellectual elite of Bengal forced the Governor, hostile as he was, to show him respect. Haq had the highest regard for Dr Mookerjee not only because of his abilities but also because he held his father Sir Asutosh, from whom he had received his legal training, in the highest esteem. He looked upon the former as his *gurubhai* (disciples of the same guru or teacher). As a result, Dr Mookerjee soon began to be looked upon as the guiding spirit of the coalition ministry, and the ministry itself earned the sobriquet of 'Syama–Haq' ministry. Dr Mookerjee claimed that this ministry was indeed the first since the inception of British rule which had the solid backing of the people, including a considerable section of Muslims who were prepared to follow the leadership of Haq.

This claim, however, was only partially true. The League was undoubtedly the most important political force in the Muslim community. Haq, on the other hand, was definitely a leader with real mass appeal, but at the same time, he lacked the courage of his convictions. Because of this, he failed to organize Muslims under the banner of his own party. As for the Hindu ministers, apart from Dr Mookerjee, no one could really claim even minimum influence over his own community. In addition, the 'Khadi group' of the Congress, which had quite a following among Hindus, was not very friendly towards him and occasionally exhibited streaks of mischievousness towards the ministry.

Within a few days of his becoming a minister, another important event took place in 1941. The 23rd annual session of the Hindu Mahasabha was scheduled to be held in the end of December under the presidency of Veer Savarkar at Bhagalpur in Bihar, then under Governor's rule after the resignation of the Congress ministry in 1939. The Bihar Governor Sir Thomas Stewart started voicing his concern from 19 May. As the Id festival of Muslims fell sometime towards the end of December and Bhagalpur happened to be perhaps the most communally disturbed city in Bihar, the government was not prepared to allow the session to be held during that period. Apart from the risk of serious communal trouble, another factor that weighed with the government was the proximity of Bhagalpur to Nepal and the known attitude of the Mahasabha towards Nepal as a counterblast to Jinnah's Pakistan movement. The Mahasabha was prepared to shift the date by a few days so that the session and the Muslim festival might not clash with each other. But this gesture was misunderstood as a sign of weakness. On 26 September, the government issued a notification prohibiting the holding of the all–India conference in Bhagalpur between 1

December 1941 and 10 January 1942. On 3 October, president Savarkar requested the Bihar Governor to allow the Mahasabha to hold the session on any date from 1 January 1942 onwards but the Bihar government considered that 5 January was the earliest possible date on which the session could commence. At its meeting held in New Delhi on 11 October 1941, the All-India Working Committee of the Mahasabha considered all facts, and resolved that the session must be held at Bhagalpur from 24 to 27 December, three days in advance of the Id festival in spite of the ban and ordered arrangements accordingly. Savarkar then made a further representation to the viceroy to intervene so that they might be allowed to hold the session. The viceroy replied that the decision in the matter rested with the Governor of Bihar and that he was not prepared to interfere with his discretion on it.

Around 23 December 1941, Dr Mookerjee, then finance minister of Bengal, suggested to the viceroy the possibility of curtailment of the period and certain details of the session as a compromise. But Stewart was averse to this solution, which, in his judgement, would have represented only a nominal concession by the Mahasabha, whose presidential address had already been issued, and who had then left themselves no time in which to negotiate. The government took active steps to prevent defiance of the ban. Dr Mookerjee's diary says: '[E]nthusiasm was great in all parts of India and thousands flocked to Bhagalpur to attend the session in defiance of the ban. We made effective arrangements to give the movement a start from Bengal. Leaders like Moonje and Khaparde came to Calcutta and left for Bhagalpur from here. Savarkar the President-elect was arrested at Gaya. Other leaders were arrested in or near Bhagalpur. I had not disclosed what I was going to do.'

After Savarkar's arrest, Dr Mookerjee decided to leave for Bhagalpur and accordingly spoke to the Governor, offering to resign his ministership in case Sir John Herbert felt embarrassed.

In a commendable, though uncharacteristic, gesture the Governor did not ask for his resignation. Dr Mookerjee courted arrest at Colgong (now Kahalgaon, in the Bhagalpur district). While he was let off after four or five days, it was yet an 'unprecedented' act on the part of a minister in office 'to violate a ban which he regarded as unjust and improper' openly. Anyway, hundreds were arrested, and the enthusiasm was so tremendous that the greater the number of arrests, the more stubborn was the resistance offered.

The first task before Dr Mookerjee as a minister was to place the financial adjustment between Bengal and the central governments on a fair and reasonable basis. He was amazed to find that the main work of the finance department was to make elaborate rules for curtailing small items of expenditure, whereas many big items were swallowed easily, especially when they affected the interests of whites. His secretary, Walker, 'a man of ability but little imagination',[5] at first tried to be dictatorial but very soon discovered who the boss was. A landmark incident in this regard is described below.

In January 1942, Walker and Dr Mookerjee went to New Delhi to attend a conference of finance ministers and advisers of Indian provinces, mainly to decide how contributions made by the Government of India to the provinces for war purposes would be calculated and adjusted. It was agreed that if previous sanctions of the Government of India were to be obtained on every matter before incurring expenditure, work would suffer from delay. In order to solve this impasse, it was unanimously agreed that either the provincial government should go on spending, with the adjustments being made periodically later on, or some officer representing the Government of India should remain on the spot and give his opinion immediately without referring the matter to Delhi. After the plenary session of the conference was over, it was decided that the finance department of India would consult the respective secretaries of the provinces and put into shape schemes, which would finally be examined by the finance member, Sir Jeremy Raisman, and the provincial ministers or advisers concerned.

According to this arrangement, when Dr Mookerjee went the next morning to the room of the finance member at the Imperial Secretariat, he was greeted by Raisman and Walker who stated that the arrangements had been completed and were waiting for his approval. Raisman smilingly told Dr Mookerjee that to simplify matters, the Government of India would be prepared to entrust to Walker, the provincial finance secretary, as their representative, the very responsible duty of approving provincial expenditure for which the Centre was taking either full responsibility or advancing big loans. Thinking at first that the idea was to place Walker's services for the time being at the disposal of the Government of India, Dr Mookerjee inquired accordingly and was amazed to learn that the proposal was that Walker would discharge the dual function of continuing as his secretary and also scrutinizing and approving the relevant items of provincial expenditure for which the Centre was going to make payment. 'In other words,' so says his diary, 'it was quite conceivable that a scheme which I as Finance Minister would approve as necessary in Bengal's interest might be rejected or modified over my head by my own Secretary claiming to act as the representative of Delhi.' Dr Mookerjee congratulated Raisman for being prepared to trust somebody in the Bengal government to act on behalf of the Government of India, but he added firmly that if this somebody was to be taken from Bengal, it must be the finance minister and not anybody else, and further that he was not prepared to have his decision altered by anyone who would continue to be his subordinate in the Bengal secretariat.

Not prepared for 'this direct onslaught', Raisman and his companions said that it would involve enormous labour, to which

Dr Mookerjee replied that that was a matter to be judged by him. It was apparent that while Delhi was prepared to trust a European ICS man belonging to a province, there was no question of trusting an Indian provincial minister. Ultimately, it was decided that some officer like the accountant general of Bengal, who was unconnected with the Bengal secretariat, would be selected to do the work. Dr Mookerjee says in his diary: '[T]his small incident left a mark on my mind. This happened hardly a month after my assumption of office and I felt how hopeless the position was.'

This incident illustrates both the chicanery of the British in dealing with Indian ministers as well as Dr Mookerjee's insight into the ways of Indian officialdom and his firmness in dealing with it appropriately. It also shows that he could not be intimidated by any white-skinned man, ICS or not.

Dr Mookerjee got along very well with his secretarial staff, who knew that if they worked hard and honestly, they had nothing to be afraid of. Regarding interpretation of rules, Walker was amazed at his minister's determination to interpret them liberally, particularly to the advantage of the poorly paid staff. One pathetic case of a government pensioner who wanted his small pension of about Rs 30 or Rs 40 per month increased by Rs 6 or Rs 8 per month has already been described in Chapter 1. Dr Mookerjee did it despite the opposition of his entire officialdom.

Finally, he handled the provincial budget efficiently, overcoming serious handicaps that attended its framing. It had been only two months since the present ministry had taken office and it fell to his lot to prepare—in barely three weeks—its budget proposals for 1942–43. These were passed at the cabinet meeting held in the first week of January 1942 and presented to the Legislative Assembly on 16 February. In his opening speech, he said that in a limited sense, his budget was in the nature of a War Budget, dealing with civil defence schemes of considerable magnitude. 'Nation-saving' took the place of 'nation-building'.

He asked all the parties in the house to agree that as long as the existing emergency would continue, there could be no diversion of the inadequate resources of the province to purposes that could wait.

Dr Mookerjee finished his speech on 24 February by calling for communal harmony and sinking of all political differences, for if Japan came, even Jinnah's Pakistan scheme would pale into insignificance. One may conclude with the following extracts from his diary: '[M]y secretarial staff was full of admiration for the slashing remarks I made in my reply, completely silencing the opposition. The speech was more political than financial and was in reply to the general discussion on the budget of the year . . . I had to play with crores of rupees, borrowed from other sources . . . I was happy however that the financial adjustment between Bengal and India was on a fair and reasonable basis.'

Another task before the new ministry was to prepare Bengal to meet the danger of Japanese invasion, which was becoming more threatening after the declaration of war on Japan on 7 December 1941. The British government of India was then thinking of withdrawing and following a scorched earth policy instead of preparing the people to fight the enemy. 'The secret instructions as to what officials . . . were to do in case of invasion and failure of the military, practically indicated that the Government had given Bengal up for lost.'[6] Dr Mookerjee found in the enunciation by the Government of India of the Denial Policy—which included destruction of means of transport and communication and removal of rice and paddy from the dangerous zone—'a shocking proof of the nervous breakdown of British administration in India'. He pleaded earnestly that the means of communication in the so-called danger area should, instead of being destroyed or removed, be allowed to work and could be destroyed at the last moment in case of defeat and invasion by the enemy. In case the enemy never came (as they did not), the policy of destruction imposed by the government would cause a complete breakdown of the social and economic life of a large part of the province. His advice was, however, disregarded and he was told that but for the fact that he was himself a minister, his attitude would have been misinterpreted as indicative of sympathy with the enemy. It was this scorched earth policy, this invention called 'Denial and Evacuation' fashioned by the infamous trio of Leopold Amery, Lord Linlithgow and above all, Sir John Arthur Herbert, that gave rise to the infamous Bengal Famine of 1943. This famine, and Dr Mookerjee's role in first trying to prevent it and later arranging for relief, has been discussed in the next chapter.

There was yet another matter regarding which the ministry felt helpless. They were prevented by the existing army laws from mobilizing the people for the defence of their homeland. Dr Mookerjee decided to take up the matter directly with the Governor. Having learnt that the Governor was going to New Delhi to discuss the war situation with the viceroy, he addressed an important letter to him on 7 March 1942, pressing hard on the urgent need of raising a Bengal army for home defence in the face of imminent Japanese invasion. Herbert, of course, objected. First, he said that it was entirely against the Indian army policy to let Bengal have her own army. Dr Mookerjee countered by saying that man could undo the existing man-made regulation. Herbert's second objection was that sufficient arms and ammunition were not available. Dr Mookerjee said that arms and ammunition must be manufactured in increased quantity or imported from abroad. Countering Herbert's third objection of there being no military trainers, Dr Mookerjee said that trainers would have to be brought from other parts of India or of the Empire, if necessary. He felt that the real obstacle was distrust of Indians and Bengalis by the British. He appealed to the Governor and the viceroy to give Bengal the right to raise a special home army, consisting of an equal number of Hindus and Muslims, for the defence of Bengal.

The appeal failed and the situation in Bengal and elsewhere continued to deteriorate.

The reaction of the British, however, could not be said to be unexpected. The British had had their cupful of Bengali middle-class militarism, ranging from Khudiram Bose to Surya Sen and finally to Subhas Chandra Bose, and were in no mood to teach a large number of them how to handle modern armaments. Perhaps, with a Governor like Herbert, Dr Mookerjee need not have wasted the effort.

Meanwhile, in March 1942, the British government, in a bid to solve the Indian question for the efficient execution of war policies, and with a view to secure Indian political support for the war effort, sent to India Lord Privy Seal Sir Stafford Cripps. Cripps, a Labourite MP, had just returned from Russia after tremendous success and appeared almost as popular as Prime Minister Churchill. Dr Mookerjee had known Cripps when he had come to India earlier and he had two long discussions with him, first on 28 March as part of a Savarkar-led Hindu Mahasabha delegation and then on 30 March 1942 as minister of Bengal. Dr Mookerjee found him very conscious of his own importance. He boasted that India would either make him or mar him and if he could settle with India, there would be none to compete with him in the whole British Empire. Be that as it may, Dr Mookerjee records in his diary: 'Cripps made a genuine attempt to solve the Indian problem . . . Regarding the Scheduled Castes he was completely indifferent. From this point of view his failure was a matter of deep tragedy, for he was determined not to play with minority or rake up small parties in order to create artificial barriers.' Although there was much in Cripps's scheme that the Mahasabha liked, he said that the document had either to be accepted or rejected in toto so far as the fundamental parts were concerned and that the British regarded the right of non-accession (the right of individual provinces to remain in India or secede from it) as fundamental. Dr Mookerjee bluntly told Cripps that India was not such an easy problem that he could tell her either to take it or leave it. The Mahasabha then raised the question of defence minister and said that they would want to have two defence advisers, one Hindu and one Muslim, whose advice the viceroy would undertake to accept. Cripps said that it did not appear to him to be a very practical scheme.

Dr Mookerjee also intensely disliked the scheme for the possible partition of India and was very concerned regarding his non-accession provisions that empowered the provinces to secede from the Indian Union. He said, 'You are breaking with your own hand the one great achievement of the British in India—the political unity of India as a whole.' Aware of the weakness of his scheme, Cripps said this was the least His Majesty's Government could do to placate the Muslim League. Cripps pointed out to Dr Mookerjee what the alternatives were to the acceptance of the scheme and he fully realized the seriousness of the situation. Further, Dr Mookerjee was, according to Cripps, convinced that it was necessary for those who did not wholly agree with the scheme to accept it in order to solve some of the pending problems.

Dr Mookerjee's diary reveals that in later times he revised his opinion about the Cripps plan. It is true that the scheme on paper practically gave Indians nothing for the time being with regard to interim arrangements. Even then, looking at it from a distant point of time, Dr Mookerjee felt that Indians could have accepted the offer and grasped the power in 1942, however unsatisfactory in some respects the offer might have been. At that time, Japan was proceeding towards India at a terrific speed, everything was crumbling, and British prestige was at its lowest ebb. His Majesty's Government wanted to settle in its own interest, and without a willing India on her side, England could not win the Asiatic War. Indians could have then hastened the dawn of fuller freedom. Dr Mookerjee recorded that they could deliver the goods, only if

Congress, as the largest and most well-organized political party in
India, agreed to come to terms with His Majesty's Government,
not otherwise.

From the trend of things in Bengal up to about the middle of
1942, it appears that Dr Mookerjee had decided that there was no
longer any point in being 'nice' to Herbert—the man had chosen
to be his enemy, and was bent on overturning Haq's ministry and
installing a Muslim League-led coalition. In July 1942, therefore,
while away at New Delhi to see Viceroy Linlithgow, among
other chores, he wrote a very long letter on 26 July to Governor
Herbert, in which he gave vent to his entire dissatisfaction in the
manner Herbert was carrying on, and predicted that disaster was
bound to come if he did not mend his ways (it did come, in the
shape of the famine). Earlier, on 7 March, he had written another
important letter on the eve of Herbert's departure for Delhi, where
the latter was going to hold a conference with the viceroy and the
commander-in-chief regarding the war situation. In that letter,
he had pressed him hard to allow them to raise a Bengal army,
especially for home defence. Herbert, of course, did not oblige.

In the long letter[7] that he sent from New Delhi, dated 26
July 1942, he directly accused Herbert of wantonly harbouring
ill feeling towards the ministry and trying to subvert it. There
were solid reasons for this accusation, and Dr Mookerjee, while
remaining strictly parliamentary, was nothing short of brutal
in the language in which he lambasted Herbert, and together
with him, the British bureaucracy. He principally attacked him
for his machinations, while being at the head of the British
administration, to support the Muslim League. Consider some of
the language that he used—only Dr Mookerjee would have had
the guts to write to a British Governor in such language:

It is an open secret that the Hindu and Muslim combination in
Bengal under Mr Fazlul Haq's leadership was not welcomed by

a section of permanent officials . . . We are often told that India's future political advancement was being retarded because of the failure of leaders of Hindus and Muslims to work together in the sphere of State Administration. For the first time in the history of British India, whatever democratic constitution has been handed over to us, in spite of its manifold defects, was sought to be worked in Bengal by Hindu and Muslim representatives who wielded considerable influence over their own community. The success of this experiment naturally would give a lie direct to the plea of communal disharmony standing in the way of India's political advancement. It would be therefore to the interest of diehard officials to see that this experiment proved a failure . . . To speak frankly, your own attitude towards the ministry has been far from satisfactory from the very beginning . . . though the Muslim League for seven months carried on a relentless and vituperative campaign against the ministry and specially the Chief Minister, thus weakening the forces of law and order and rousing communal passions, you all along characterised them either as constitutional agitation by the Opposition or mere attacks on ministers individually which did not affect Government as such . . . You have allowed to function, in this province, a government within a government, where real power has been wielded by men who have very little responsibility in carrying on the constitutional Government of the province with the willing support of the people. This is a serious charge. But it is just as well that you should know that whether consciously or unconsciously, you have created this deep impression in the minds of your ministers, which is hardly consistent with the good administration of the province.

But together with the charges against Herbert and the bureaucracy, the letter also focused on the need for the British to look at Indians in a different way. Dr Mookerjee, unlike Subhas Chandra Bose, was no admirer of the Japanese, and did not unreservedly believe in the dictum, 'my enemy's enemy is my friend'. When he was writing this letter, the Congress Working Committee had already finalized the 'Quit India' phase, and Dr Mookerjee, in all probability, could foresee that this would bring about terrible reprisals from the British, and was trying to soften the blow that was coming. He tried to convince Herbert that while the Indians did want the British to go, it could wait till the end of the war, and they most certainly did not want the Japanese to take their place. We shall presently see how things turned out in practice.

When Dr Mookerjee met the viceroy in Delhi, he discovered that Linlithgow was fully prepared to sternly meet the political situation. He also realized that the Haq ministry would be expected to fight the Congress agitation. He concluded by saying that what he asked for was power for the chosen representatives of the people to be shared with the Governor, acting as the constitutional head, to deal with the vital problems during the war. Meanwhile, Herbert had complained to the viceroy that he was not very certain of the attitude of Haq (with respect to disciplining the Congress when they rebelled) who, under Dr Mookerjee's influence, showed signs of wobbling, with the result that the Bengal government might be reluctant to take necessary action. No trouble was apparently anticipated with ministers in the Punjab, Orissa or Sind.

On his way back to Calcutta, Dr Mookerjee halted at Allahabad for a few hours and had a long discussion with Pandit Jawaharlal Nehru. He gave Nehru copies of his letters to the Governor, which indicated how he was struggling against heavy odds while carrying on his duties as minister. When he returned to Calcutta, the stage was practically fully set for the Quit India movement to be launched. Gandhi had been authorized to give the final direction regarding the beginning of the movement.

But before we go to the momentous days of the 'Quit India' call, let us digress a bit to describe an incident which showed Dr Mookerjee as the intensely humane person that he essentially was. The incident concerned the famous Bengali poet Kazi Nazrul Islam who, like Rabindranath Tagore, straddles two countries— India and Bangladesh.

Nazrul was always rather carefree in matters of money. He had run up a debt of 7000 rupees (a huge sum in those days) because of the illness of his wife and the cost of her treatment, for which he had to borrow money from loan sharks. Just then he got an offer as a music director in a Bengali film and hoped that the money he got from it would get him out of the woods. At this stage Fazlul Haq, to whom he was close, asked him to take over the editorship of his party organ *Nobojug*, and said he would take care of his debts. However, after Nazrul let go of the music directorship, Haq began to drag his feet on this, and did not pay him any money for the next several months. Nazrul was in terrible straits and finally approached Dr Mookerjee in July 1942. The latter not only arranged for repayment of his debt but also sent him to Madhupur as a house guest in his own house for 'change' and recuperation. Nazrul stayed with his wife in the annex to Ganga Prasad House for nearly two months, and she recovered to a great extent. This made a world of difference to Nazrul. The letter he wrote to Dr Mookerjee in gratitude towards the end of his stay at Madhupur would wring anybody's heart.

Though he did not know it yet, around this time, Nazrul had begun to suffer from an unknown, but serious, neurological disorder (possibly Pick's disease, similar to Alzheimer's). This caused him eventually to lose his voice and memory. He lived on as a vegetable in Calcutta till 1972. Invited by the Government of Bangladesh, Nazrul and his family moved to Dacca in 1972, where he died four years later.

We can now return to the Quit India movement. Gandhi finally gave the call of 'Quit India' from the Gowalia Tank Maidan (now called August Kranti Maidan) in Bombay on 8 August 1942 when the All-India Congress Committee approved the resolution. The British almost instantly retaliated by throwing all the principal Congress leaders in jail the very next day and, as a result, the movement became a disjointed one, led mainly by second or third-rung leaders with local followings.

The other political parties also did not follow the Congress in the movement. The communists openly sided with the British and made efforts to derail the movement. The previous year Hitler had launched his Operation Barbarossa, or the attack on Soviet Russia. Until this point the Indian communists had dubbed the war an 'Imperialist War' and opposed it. With the attack on the Soviets, they changed their line overnight, and what was the Imperialist War now became the 'People's War'. From this point onwards, the Indian communists totally sided with the British and indulged in abject hypocrisy to whitewash the misdeeds of the British. The Muslim League and the Hindu Mahasabha both distanced themselves from the movement. Dr Mookerjee, a Hindu Mahasabhaite since 1939, toed his party line and continued with parliamentary politics. Dr B.R. Ambedkar, the leader of the scheduled castes, was also bitterly critical of the movement, saying that it was a mad venture which took the most diabolical form and proved to be a complete failure.

Haq told Dr Mookerjee upon his return to Calcutta that important secret instructions had arrived from the Government of India and he had requested the Governor to place the whole matter before a cabinet meeting. The Governor declined to do so and replied to Haq that the cabinet would meet later. Herbert expected any minister who disagreed with the Government of India's policy would forthwith resign. The ministers met to consider the unprecedented situation. Responsible ministers were to be treated with suspicion and refused access to important documents which were being secretly discussed with ICS officers—this was a real mockery of provincial autonomy. On the morning of 9 August, the Governor summoned the cabinet, but the meeting could not proceed and had to be adjourned. This is because all the ministers insisted that they would not proceed without seeing the documents. As the ministers were about to leave the Government House, Additional Home Secretary Porter came with the file and handed it over to the Chief Minister who gave it to Dr Mookerjee. He took the file home and read it very carefully. It was clear that long before the Congress could give any provocation, the government had decided to start its campaign of repression, and all the details for this purpose were elaborately outlined in the letter. It was tersely put that 'prevention was better than cure' and this time, the government was determined to anticipate a possible revolt and sternly deal with the situation from the beginning. The government appeared to have a clear foreknowledge of the phase of the freedom struggle, namely the 'Quit India' phase that was coming, and was quite adequately prepared for it. Or could it have been an insider who had passed on advance information on it? We shall never know.

It was clear that the government envisaged running Bengal through the Governor and the ICS coterie, keeping the ministers as figureheads. Dr Mookerjee felt very uneasy about the whole thing, as it was useless to function as a minister when they would become mere tools at the hands of the bureaucracy. The ministers met at the house of the Nawab of Dacca to decide a course of action, but the meeting broke up without a final decision. It was clear that none of the ministers was willing to resign. All of Dr Mookerjee's colleagues begged him to not resign and precipitate the matter. The Governor, on the other hand, felt that Dr Mookerjee would most likely quit office. Herbert reminded the ministers that the policy was that of the Government of India, and that was unchangeable. If any minister disagreed with it, he would be glad if he offered his resignation at a time when India was threatened with a dangerous war.

Dr Mookerjee's personal views on the Quit India resolution were, however, balanced and not completely in line with that of the Mahasabha. He was in complete agreement with the patriotic content of the resolution, but had serious reservations as to the technicalities, and these point to his eye for detail and his political foresight. Before the adoption of the resolution by the AICC it had been approved by the Congress Working Committee meeting at Wardha in July 1942, and about this Dr Mookerjee was wary and watchful. In the letter[8] dated 26 July 1942, addressed to Governor Herbert, he wrote:

> The announcement made by the working committee that the British is being asked to withdraw, followed by further explanations that such withdrawal will not interfere with the British or Allied troops remaining in India and fighting the enemy, discloses considerable loose thinking. The British withdraws. No constituted government is determined by the British in agreement with Indians or otherwise to whom power will be handed over at the time of withdrawal . . . and things go on merrily. If the Indian problem had been such an easy one, India would have attained freedom long ago.

And again, he unequivocally records in the letter that he wrote to Lord Linlithgow on 12 August 1942, just four days after the Congress adopted the resolution:

> The demand of the Congress as embodied in its last resolution [referring to the Quit India resolution of 8 August] virtually constitutes the national demand of India as a whole. It is regrettable that a campaign of misrepresentation is being carried on . . . characterising the Congress invitation as a virtual

invitation to Japan and a surrender to chaos and confusion . . . Just as the Congress has a duty not to do anything suddenly which is bound to lead to chaos and disorder, so also have you a similar duty to ensure that there can be no just cause for discontent and disaffection, resulting in chaos and disorder. Repression is not the remedy at this critical hour.

All this, however, fell on deaf ears. The British government in India was so much on the edge and so apprehensive of a Japanese attack that they jumped at the slightest noise and let loose a regime of total repression. It happened in many places, but the one that affected Dr Mookerjee personally was what happened in Tamluk, in the Midnapore district of Bengal. We shall look at this phase of the freedom struggle, and the subsequent tragedy with which Dr Mookerjee was deeply involved, in the next chapter. Let us for the present look at the total Bengal and India scenario.

In any case, the Quit India call put the whole country into a state of rebellion. And because the topmost leaders had been thrown in jail, the movement had no central control. Disturbances of an extraordinary nature took place. Destruction of railways, roads and other means of communication compelled the police and protectors of law to surrender to the will of the people. Bengal was set on fire and Calcutta witnessed scenes of unbelievable acts of repression and shooting. Many innocent lives were lost.

The Quit India movement had meanwhile placed the Hindu Mahasabha in a difficult position. The Mahasabha's Working Committee met in Delhi from 29 to 31 August 1942 and reviewed the political situation. It was emphatic in its condemnation of the repressive policy of the government and stated categorically that but for the bungling of the government and its hasty action, things would never have gone so badly. On his way to Delhi, Dr Mookerjee could see from the appearance of the railway stations and their adjoining localities how terrific the uprising had been. In fact, if it had continued for some more time the entire administration would have collapsed completely. The chief point of attack was the breaking of communications, and during a period of war, this obviously can have a disastrous effect on the administration. Still, there was no doubt that the situation had become acute on account of the perverseness of the government and its refusal to transfer power to the people of India.

While in Delhi, Dr Mookerjee had a long discussion with Sir Sikandar Hyat Khan, then premier of Punjab, and leader of the multi-religious Unionist Party. But Khan put him on his guard. He said that the key to the settlement lay with the viceroy. It was no use trying to come to an agreement with Muslims without the League, for the viceroy would not even care to look at it. He had made up his mind that he was going to recognize Jinnah as the only leader of the Muslims.

Dr Mookerjee on 8 September 1942 requested the viceroy for an interview, especially to obtain his permission to meet Gandhi at Poona. He was granted such an interview the next day. Among other things, Sikandar Hyat Khan was proved absolutely right. The interview did not go well for Dr Mookerjee who had to face a lot of uncomfortable questions which could not be answered— neither by him nor anyone else.

Linlithgow told Dr Mookerjee that he had ruined his chances of acting as a mediator by insisting on prior repudiation of Pakistan by His Majesty's Government as a condition of any settlement. He then asked him to explain what he meant by 'national government', to which Dr Mookerjee had to confess that he really had no clear idea. He said that national government was national only if it was really representative. Linlithgow asked if Dr Mookerjee expected to get the Congress and the League to support his national government, to which Dr Mookerjee had to reply that he had little hope of either. Secondly, Dr Mookerjee could give no answer to the question whether he expected that a government based essentially on the Mahasabha, without either Congress or the League, could be described as 'national' in a true sense. Thirdly, he admitted that the risk of severe communal trouble in the event of a completely Hindu political government at the Centre was not negligible. Finally, the viceroy added that any alternative to his existing executive council must be able to deliver the goods in terms of popular support and give full support to the war. Dr Mookerjee's argument was the usual one—that if the Muslim League would not play, and the Congress could not play, the British ought to give the vacant seats to the Mahasabha. Linlithgow warned him that if he was thinking of a government based essentially on the Mahasabha, with odd sections of the Muslims, he could hardly hope for much success if both Congress and the Muslim League were out in opposition.

Dr Mookerjee found the viceroy very bitter. He said that the Hindus were doomed, as Jinnah was made great not by the government but by the Congress who made the mistake of taking him seriously about Pakistan. He frankly admitted in his diary: 'However much I disagree with the viceroy on other matters, there was a good deal of truth in what he said.' Anyway, Linlithgow did not say that the door was closed to any constitutional progress. He clearly told Dr Mookerjee about the practical objections likely to operate against his scheme. When the latter asked if he could go and see Gandhi, the viceroy replied in the negative. He then asked if he could come back in a few days. The viceroy said not unless there were some really substantial changes in the position. Dr Mookerjee merely told the press that he had a 'full and frank' discussion with the viceroy but his diary records his disappointment: 'Thus our efforts failed. But we demonstrated that in spite of tremendous odds, an agreement between the Hindus and Muslims and also other communities . . . could [be reached] only if the British Government took a rational view of things.'

Then Dr Mookerjee met Jinnah. Here were two people, politically at two opposite poles, completely convinced of their positions, and not prepared to concede anything to the other without a real struggle, and without solid political logic behind. They met as resolute, self-respecting equals—no brotherly business here, no coaxing, no genuflections. This meeting was in Delhi and lasted for three hours. Dr Mookerjee records that they spoke very frankly to each other. According to V.P. Menon, the principal idea which he had put to Jinnah was that representatives of the two communities should meet and that each should explain in what respect it expects protection from the other. The Mahasabha would be willing to concede the fullest measure of autonomy to the provinces and would give the minorities the maximum protection in respect of their religion, language and customs. On the question of Pakistan, however, Jinnah was as adamant as Dr Mookerjee was against it and they could not discover a point of contact. Dr Mookerjee reminded Jinnah that before Cripps came out to India, all that Jinnah wanted was that his Pakistan should not be tabooed, but considered dispassionately at the time of constitution-making. Dr Mookerjee asked why on that basis should they not agree to demand from the viceroy the immediate establishment of an interim national government, followed by the release of Congress leaders. Jinnah's reply was immediate. He said that the situation had changed since Cripps gave him something like Pakistan, though it was not exactly what he wanted. His basis for settlement would now therefore be the acceptance of the principle of Pakistan here and now, and then only could he talk of an interim settlement. Dr Mookerjee exposed to him the utter fallacy of his Pakistan logic, but it made no impression on him. In any case, as Dr Mookerjee notes in his diary, there was no acrimony between the two and they agreed that they should not issue statements accusing each other, but would consider themselves happy that they had tried to explore each other's point of view, respecting each other's sentiments.

When Dr Mookerjee came back to his work in Bengal, he found the assembly in a state of great excitement. Herbert was not happy regarding the way in which the ministers were behaving. He complained that they were not sufficiently vocal in their condemnation of lawlessness and he wanted a suitable resolution to be passed on the floor of the assembly. The ugliest possible scenes followed. Shouts and counter-shouts, attacks and counter-attacks went to extreme lengths. Ultimately, the assembly had to be adjourned sine die.

It was clear to all that this demonstration was made possible only because of the Governor's instigation. The European party had by now decided to side with the Opposition. Till now it was acting as an independent party and hardly, if ever, voted against the ministry. Now, it had decided to join hands with the Opposition, which thus gained considerable numerical strength.

Dr Mookerjee told Herbert, when Herbert laid down the ironclad rule that all ministers must either abide by the Government of India's policy or resign, that he did not resign immediately for two reasons. He would like first to put the all-India issues before the viceroy and then His Majesty's Government, which was the constitutional way of conveying a minister's views to the highest British authorities regarding matters Indian. Secondly, since his colleagues were not going to follow him, he was anxious to have 'assurance' from Herbert that he would not take advantage of his resignation and instal the League into power again by threat or intrigue. Herbert assured Dr Mookerjee that he would not do anything of the kind. On 12 August 1942, Dr Mookerjee sent his letter to Linlithgow through Herbert himself. In this historic letter, he put forth the viewpoint of nationalist India and concrete suggestions for an immediate settlement between England and India.

Off and on, one hears of mischievous propaganda equating Dr Mookerjee with the communists with regard to the opposition to the Quit India Movement. This letter of Dr Mookerjee, addressed to the viceroy, written just three days after the launching of the movement, should set to rest all doubts in this regard. In the letter[9] he wrote:

> It is therefore essential that India's free status should be recognised immediately and the people of the country called upon to defend their own country in co-operation with the Allied Powers, and not merely look upon Britain to fight the impending aggression. The demand of the Congress, as embodied in its last resolution, virtually constitutes the national demand of India as a whole . . . you [have] a similar duty to ensure that there can be no just cause for discontent and disaffection resulting in chaos and disorder. Repression is not the remedy at this critical hour.

As said earlier, he was in complete agreement with the patriotic content of the resolution, but had serious reservations as to the technicalities, and was not afraid to speak out.

Not only this, but while Congressmen were languishing in jail, Dr Mookerjee took a keen interest in their welfare and arranged for Calcutta University to take their classes in jail. A relative recalled that when one Kushiprasun Chatterjee, an advocate and a Congress activist, felt insecure about keeping cash belonging to the Congress party at home, the person he thought of for keeping the cash with was Dr Mookerjee—and he cooperated.

Dr Mookerjee received the viceroy's reply to his letter towards the end of September. It was of course anticipated. The viceroy could not do anything at that stage and his first duty was to maintain law and order in the country. Dr Mookerjee made up his mind to tender his resignation and the question was when he would do so. Apart from the all-India issues, he fully realized that in the provincial sphere, he could hardly do any work leading to the good of the province in view of the hostile and unsympathetic attitude of the Governor and the coterie of officials who practically ruled over the province. The political situation also rendered his position extremely difficult. Whatever the cabinet recommended was practically turned down.

Everybody knew about Dr Mookerjee's letter to the viceroy dated 12 August 1942 and the viceroy's reply to it made his resignation inevitable. He, however, assured his colleagues of loyal support so as to keep the ministry in office, despite a determined assault from the League and the Europeans. Haq tried to have the matter reconsidered, but neither the Governor nor Dr Mookerjee himself was agreeable to any such course of action. His last interview with Herbert was on the evening of 19 November. The interview ended abruptly after there was a difference of opinion between Herbert and Dr Mookerjee on the issue of publication of the latter's correspondence. The Governor accepted Dr Mookerjee's resignation on 20 November in Calcutta. And thus ended the first spell of ministership of Dr Mookerjee, begun in December 1941, even before he had completed his first year.

Meanwhile, in response to numerous inquiries regarding the reasons for his resignation, Dr Mookerjee issued a statement on 21 November. He clarified that his resignation was not due to any difference of opinion between himself and the Chief Minister or any of his colleagues or any member of the Progressive Coalition party. Apart from Dr Mookerjee's general dissatisfaction with the interfering attitude of the Governor, there were two specific matters in which Dr Mookerjee failed to obtain even partial relief related to the imposition of collective fines and the handling of the Midnapore situation. Collective fines were imposed in Bengal in utter disregard of the ordinance itself and to terrorize Hindus. With regard to Midnapore, the legitimate measures taken by the government to check lawlessness were understandable but the repression that continued after the havoc caused by the cyclone and flood on 16 October, was staggering. Despite ministerial protests, repression and so-called relief went hand in hand. Dr Mookerjee called upon public opinion to immediately assert itself, both with regard to collective fines and the Midnapore situation. According to him, the office of a minister was not an end in itself but the means to an end, the end being service to the people. He resigned because he felt during the last few weeks that his capacity for doing good was being curbed more and more.

It was a great pity that the British government failed to utilize the gigantic energy and ability of a workaholic like Dr Mookerjee, due partly to the laws and constitution as prevalent then and also due to the pig-headedness of Herbert. One may conclude by saying that it was a tragic case of a right man in the wrong place and at the wrong time.

In between, however, there had been a cyclone-tsunami at Contai, in the district of Midnapore, and the concealment of the same from Dr Mookerjee had brought matters to head and also contributed to his resignation. This has been described in the next chapter.

6

The Great Bengal Famine, 1942–43

A branch of Hindu mythology has it that the temporal world is ruled by a series of fourteen kings called Manu, sons of Brahma, each of whom reigns for 43,20,000 years; and at the time of change of Manu, there is always some terrible disaster—flood, drought, pestilence, tsunami or whatever. A change of Manu is known as a Manvantar and in Bengali, the term has come exclusively to mean 'famine'. The Great Bengal Famine of 1943 is popularly known in Bengal as the Ponchasher Manvantar (the Famine of Fifty), because it took place in the year 1350 according to the Bengali calendar. In those days, ordinary Bengali Hindus used to consult the Bengali calendar (a solar calendar) for most purposes and the Christian calendar only for official work.

The famine, in which an estimated 3 million people died, was man-made. It was a direct result of the war, coupled with some horrible misdeeds committed by a few Britishers in the course of their panicky reaction to the war. A combination of a cyclone and tidal wave, presumably a tsunami, at Contai in the Midnapore district had the effect of triggering the famine, but it would have happened anyway. It was not the result of hoarding of foodgrains by Indian traders or rich farmers, as the British had cunningly canvassed and the Muslim League had endorsed, and as is believed by many. Dr Mookerjee, while not exactly predicting the famine, had observed that certain measures taken by the British administration were sure to cause a complete breakdown of the social and economic life in the province. He also played a cardinal role in organizing relief for the famine-affected, and thereafter in exposing the misdeeds mentioned. It is therefore necessary to recount in brief, for purposes of this biography, the situation in which India was placed in 1942–43 vis-à-vis the war, especially the one in the Eastern theatre being fought between the Allies on the one hand and the Japanese on the other.

The beginning of 1942 had seen Dr Mookerjee, belonging to the Hindu Mahasabha, comfortably ensconced as the finance minister in the Progressive Democratic coalition cabinet of Bengal, headed by A.K. Fazlul Haq. He was so involved that the cabinet had come to be called the Syama–Haq cabinet. There was just one big problem. At this point of time the British viceroy in New Delhi was Lord Linlithgow, and his boss at India House, London—the secretary of state for India—was the Rt Hon. Leopold Amery— neither of whom had any reason to be happy with the fact that Hindus and Muslims were happily cooperating in Bengal. And their man in Calcutta, Sir John Arthur Herbert, the Governor of Bengal, was ten times worse, if not more. Dr Mookerjee would later describe him as a 'cheaply clever, third-rate Governor', a person 'not competent to become a Head Clerk in Clive Street'.[1]

Herbert personally and the British generally hated the cabinet and wished it to fall. And fall it did, largely through the machinations of Herbert and the weaknesses of Haq, coupled with other circumstances. But why did they wish it ill? The reasons were stated with absolute clarity in Dr Mookerjee's statement of resignation on 16 November 1942:

[E]ven the combination that we had formed under the leadership of Mr A.K. Fazlul Haq proved something too bitter to be swallowed by a section of permanent officials in this province and by no less a person than the head of the provincial administration himself [meaning Herbert]. British rule thrives . . . on constant strife between Hindus and Muslims. And even a partial unity on the part of the members belonging to these two great communities served as a nightmare to those bureaucrats who held in their hands the real powers of administration.

Meanwhile, the Second World War raged on. Soon after Britain declared the war in 1939, Lord Linlithgow, the viceroy, unilaterally declared India a belligerent state on the side of the Allies without consulting Indian political leaders or the elected provincial representatives. Dr Mookerjee had observed, much later, in his diary:

[I]t [the Congress] could not make up its mind whether it would support or oppose the government. Its declared attitude against Fascism and its pro-China policy made it say things vehemently opposed to Germany. Indeed Gandhiji went to Linlithgow and expressed his profound grief at the prospect of Westminster Abbey being bombed . . . [but] Linlithgow's efforts to get the support of the political parties did not succeed. His Majesty's government was not prepared to offer anything substantial.

In the long letter that Dr Mookerjee sent Herbert from New Delhi, dated 26 July 1942, he directly accused him of wantonly harbouring ill feeling towards the ministry and trying to upset it. Apart from these charges against Herbert and the bureaucracy, the letter also focused on the need for the British to look at Indians in a different way. Dr Mookerjee, unlike Subhas Chandra Bose, was no admirer of the Japanese, and did not unreservedly believe in the dictum, 'my enemy's enemy is my friend'. When he was writing this letter, the Congress Working Committee had already finalized the Quit India phase, and Dr Mookerjee, in all probability, could foresee that this would bring about terrible reprisals from the British, and was trying to soften the blow that was coming. He tried to convince Herbert that while the Indians did want the British to go, it could wait till the end of the war, and they most certainly did not want the Japanese to take their place. We shall presently see how things turned out in practice.

Dr Mookerjee met the viceroy in Delhi towards the end of July 1942. He could gather that the latter knew Herbert's limitations very well but could not, or would not, go beyond the Constitution, no matter how many thousands died. He also discovered that he was fully prepared to meet the political situation with as much sternness as the British bayonets would allow him to. Meanwhile, on 8 August 1942, the Congress was meeting in Bombay to give its ultimatum its final shape. Then the 'Quit India' call was given, and the Congress leaders were promptly put behind bars. This prompted Dr Mookerjee to write the historical letter of 12 August 1942, dealt with at length in the previous chapter. He received the viceroy's reply to this letter towards the end of September, and after that his resignation was just a matter of time. What finally brought it about was the natural disaster in the district of Midnapore, and Herbert's concealment of the same from him while he was still minister.

Following the declaration of the Quit India movement, the people of the district of Midnapore rose in complete revolt which was by no means non-violent. Dr Mookerjee, at least on record, did not approve of the violence, or of the declaration of independence. In his statement[2] following his resignation on 16 November 1942, he used strong words against the freedom fighters, saying, 'I do not for a moment ignore that the political disturbances in some parts of this district [Midnapore] were of a serious character. One can well understand any legitimate steps taken to combat lawlessness and open defiance of authority . . . ' Earlier, in a letter[3] to Governor Herbert dated 26 July 1942 he had said in unequivocal terms, 'Anybody, who during the war, plans to stir up mass feelings resulting in internal disturbances or insecurity must be resisted by the government that may function for the time being.'

So what accounts for Dr Mookerjee's disapproval of these fearless acts of freedom fighters? Was it Dr Mookerjee the constitutional politician talking? Or was it Dr Mookerjee the humanist, who knew that the iron hand of British imperial power will in no time descend with all its terrible might on these foolhardy young men, and so was he trying to soften the blow by prevailing upon Herbert to act reasonably, sensibly, with a little mercy? Probably it was a mixture of both, and an exhibition of his political sagacity. That he was politically in sympathy with the movement is amply proved by his correspondence as discussed in the previous chapter. But he also knew that the freedom fighters of Tamluk would only be able to hold out for some time and, after that, British repression of the worst kind would hit them (it did, repression beyond all imagination). He probably had also factored in the presence of two Muslim ICS officers, District Magistrate Niaz Mohammed Khan and Subdivisional Officer Wazir Ali Shaikh, who, in the communally charged atmosphere of the times, were viewed by the Hindus as being eager to suppress what they saw as essentially a Hindu revolt.

As apprehended by Dr Mookerjee, the British retaliated brutally, most certainly not confining themselves to 'legitimate steps' as suggested by him. They deployed both the police and the military who took the law completely into their own hands. They made few arrests. Instead they killed, burnt, tortured, maimed and raped, all with a carte blanche issued by Governor Herbert. To give but one small example, on 29 September 1942, the Royal

Indian Air Force *bombed* parts of the area under Sutahata police station (near the present Haldia Port). At this point of time, the district magistrate of Midnapore was Niaz Mohammed Khan of the Indian Civil Service, a Punjabi Muslim, who later opted for Pakistan and became a very important civil servant there.

At this juncture, a terrible cyclone hit the Midnapore coast in the very same Tamluk and Contai subdivisions. This was on 16 October 1942, on the Ashtami day of Durga Puja, the biggest festival of Bengali Hindus, and the streets were full of people in Contai town. In no time, the town went under 5 feet of water. This was a time of year when no cyclone is normally expected, and the population was taken totally unawares. Some 30,000 people were said to have lost their lives in the first fifteen minutes.

It is not quite clear what exactly had happened. A cyclone alone, however severe, cannot cause this kind of sudden flooding and wholesale and instantaneous disaster so far inland (Contai town is separated by about 14 kilometres of dead-flat country from the sea). There were reports of a few river embankments being ruptured, but there were no dams in the vicinity whose bursting could cause this kind of flooding. Upon questioning an eyewitness, who spoke only Bengali, one got the answer, '*Shagor bhenge porechhilo* (The sea broke down upon us)'. The nature of the disaster, coupled with this description, suggests a tsunami caused by a seaquake which happened simultaneously with the cyclone. Tsunamis had not been studied in detail then, which accounts for the misdiagnosis.

Something else had happened in the meantime. On 27 January 1941, Subhas Chandra Bose, who was supposedly lying ill at his residence in Elgin Road, Calcutta, and was under close watch by the police, managed to slip away and eventually escape to Germany, and thence to Japan. The tsunami-cyclone of Contai, or whatever it was, combined with the turn the war had taken in the Eastern theatre and the disappearance of Bose had the effect of totally disorienting Herbert. On 19 January 1942, the Japanese had invaded the British colony of Burma. A few bombs were dropped in Bengal, especially in the Calcutta docks, and the Feni area of the Noakhali district near the Burma border. India was apparently the next stop, and Bengal the threshold.

All this made Herbert lose all sense of proportion. He, on his own, without even consulting the provincial government (at this time, A.K. Fazlul Haq's Progressive Democratic coalition cabinet, of which Dr Mookerjee was a minister) decided to launch a scorched earth policy of the type followed by the Russians in the wake of the Nazi invasion of Ukraine and Russia. Herbert called it the policy of 'denial and evacuation'. But there was a difference. In Ukraine and Russia, the Germans were a reality, not a threat; also, the Russians and Ukrainians were not fond of the Germans, to say the least. The scorched earth policy therefore had an element of spontaneity. As opposed to this, in Bengal, the Japanese were a mere distant threat. In fact, they never came to India. In all probability, they had no intention of coming to India—their occupation of Burma was probably directed towards cutting off the land route to China. Also, the people of Midnapore had no more hatred of the Japanese than they had of the British. Therefore, they had no intention to burn their own produce and run away from their own land. It appears that the extent of the revolt in Midnapore in August 1942 was prompted largely by these excesses of Herbert.

Herbert, in his fear-crazed state, had no time or inclination to consider these fine points. Also, later in the year, to his fear of the Japanese was probably added a desire to wreak vengeance on the *natives* of Midnapore for what they did during the Quit India phase. He carried out the twin policies of denial and evacuation in Midnapore under a veil of total secrecy and in a draconian manner, and in this he was assisted to no small degree by his like-minded lieutenant, District Magistrate N.M. Khan. Such was the secrecy that there was neither any reporting in the press nor did anything get recorded in the archives. As a result, it will never be known when exactly the policy was first put into implementation in Midnapore and when it was withdrawn. Most of this information is gleaned from the autobiography of Ashok Mitra[4] who, as an ICS officer himself, was privy to a lot of information never recorded or released to the media.

The denial policy had been adopted by the Government of India, but the facts that Bengal was a frontier province in the war and that it had a panicky and vindictive Governor such as Herbert had the effect of the policy being applied in a draconian manner in Bengal as nowhere else. Dr Mookerjee dubbed the policy as 'shocking proof of the nervous breakdown of the British administration in India'. The secret instructions as to what officials, civil and military, were to do in the event of invasion and failure of the military practically indicated that the government had given up Bengal for lost. Dr Mookerjee pleaded earnestly that boats, cycles and other means of communication should not be destroyed or removed in the so-called danger area but they should be allowed to work according to a rigorous timetable. In case of defeat or invasion by the enemy, they could be destroyed at the last moment by the government's own staff. In case the enemy never came (as they did not) the policy of destruction contemplated and imposed by the government would lead to a complete breakdown of the social and economic life of a large part of the province.

The government, of course, did not listen to Dr Mookerjee, and the apprehended breakdown of the social and economic life did indeed take place. The name of that breakdown was the Great Bengal Famine of 1943. This denial policy was the real reason behind the famine, not hoarding of foodgrain by Indian traders as has been cleverly canvassed by the British. This is corroborated by Ashok Mitra[5] of the ICS, who at that time was the subdivisional officer of Munshigunge in the district of Dacca in East Bengal.

Ashok Mitra, together with his colleague Madan Mohan Lal Hooja of the Imperial Police, did a surprise raid on one of the biggest rice warehouses in his area—and found practically nothing.

There is more. Not only did the government not listen to Dr Mookerjee regarding the destruction of the means of transport, he was also quietly told that but for the fact that he was himself a minister, his attitude would have been misinterpreted as indicative of sympathy with the enemy—a barely concealed threat to throw him into prison like Sarat Bose.

The 'denial and evacuation' policy, according to Ashok Mitra, roughly worked this way. First, government agents, together with the police, would raid all locations where major stocks of foodstuff could be expected. They would then throw away the rice or forcibly take it away, to be stocked in government warehouses. Anyone who resisted was not only beaten up severely, but was also not paid a farthing. How much rice or paddy was thrown away in this manner will never be known. What was stocked in warehouses began to be released from June 1944, when rationing was first introduced. Because of the total lack of any hygiene or care in these warehouses, the rice became putrid and foul-smelling and mixed with muck and tiny pieces of stone called *kankar*—inedible for all practical purposes.

The other aspect of Herbert's denial policy was the mass destruction of all indigenous means of transportation of foodstuff. This meant the sinking of thousands of country boats (some of them, such as the *balam nouka* of East Bengal, being as big as barges), and the breaking of tens of thousands of bullock carts everywhere. Even bicycles were not spared. This stopped movement of rice from and to the interior. Movement by rail, steamer or road was not stopped, but rail wagons manufactured in India were exported in large numbers, causing a serious shortage all over the Indian Railway system. As for roads, it must be remembered that at that time movement by road was insignificant because of the rudimentary state of the network. Even to reach Midnapore by road from Calcutta, a trans-shipment or ferrying was necessary at Kolaghat. Dr Mookerjee estimated that more than 10,000 bicycles and thousands of boats had been seized and destroyed in Midnapore alone.

In Midnapore, side by side with the excesses of the denial policy, the retributions continued. Dr Mookerjee came to know of the excesses committed by the police, military and government functionaries and confronted Governor Herbert. He asked him point-blank whether there were secret instructions to the police and the military about burning houses of ordinary people as a retaliatory measure. Herbert went on the defensive and replied that 'none in the headquarters knew of such instructions'. On 15 October, there was a conference at the Writers' Buildings, Calcutta, in which Dr Mookerjee, the chief secretary, the inspector-general of police (then the head of the provincial police force) and the deputy inspector-general in charge of the criminal investigation department were present. In this meeting, Dr Mookerjee was given to understand that immediate information would be sent to the officers concerned, telling them that it was against the policy of the government to take any retaliatory steps, such as burning and looting, and if such steps had been taken in the past, they must not be followed again. After this, on 16 October, he left for the hill resort town of Darjeeling for a week of rest with his family.

And on the very same day, Contai was struck by the tsunami-cyclone.

Dr Mookerjee received no news of the disaster for the first three days, such was the muzzling of the media and means of communication. He was in touch daily with the Governor, who also happened to be in Darjeeling at that time. It could not have been that the Governor was not told of the disaster and yet Dr Mookerjee came to know of it only on the fifth day when some people from Midnapore came to see him in Calcutta, and the news was passed on to him in Darjeeling. This can only mean that the Governor, unfazed by the loss of some 30,000 lives, had deliberately withheld the information from his own finance minister, and sat enjoying the cool climes of beautiful Darjeeling! Emperor Nero could hardly have done better. He did not even issue a message of sympathy to the people affected by the disaster, which subsequently even the viceroy did. Later, Dr Mookerjee came to know that the home department had stopped all publicity of the disaster lest the same should reach the enemy and be taken advantage of by them. It was a preposterous argument, bordering on the idiotic—the Japanese radio had broadcast news of the disaster only one day after it happened.

Dr Mookerjee hurried back to Calcutta and took stock of the situation based on available reports, which turned out to be meagre. He could reach Midnapore, with two other ministers of the government, as late as twelve days after the event. He stated in his subsequent speech of resignation that 'the sufferings of the people that we witnessed were beyond description. Relief was . . . in a hopeless state of confusion and people were denied the barest facilities for movement and work.' When Dr Mookerjee came back to Calcutta to take up the matter of adequate and orderly relief with the government, he met with an indifference that could only be the result of the policy followed by Herbert. He said in his statement of resignation afterwards, '[For] two days we discussed the situation with the High Command of the happy coterie at the Secretariat and I felt disgusted at the obstructive and unrealistic attitude of these so-called public servants.' He further expressed in characteristic strong language his extreme disapproval of the attitude of the government functionaries, especially the police, in the area, which ranged from apathy and indifference to cruelty and bestiality. While doing so, he made it clear that although some of the officers concerned were Muslims while the victims were mainly Hindus, he was not singling the Muslims out—indeed the number of Hindu officers against whom such allegations had been made were far greater in number.

While visiting Midnapore he found the attitude of N.M. Khan, the district magistrate, correct, but distinctly obstructive. Dr Mookerjee had visited political leaders then incarcerated in prison under the Defence of India regulations and planned to mobilize their support for relief operations. For this, they needed to be released. However, this was neither agreed to by the home department nor by Herbert. To top it, Khan also sent a confidential report to the home department about the meeting between the prisoners and Dr Mookerjee.

However, what Dr Mookerjee found to be most disgusting, depraved and revolting was the apathy, callousness, indifference, heartlessness and utter cruelty and bestiality that government functionaries exhibited towards the victims of the catastrophe. These functionaries were Indians, mostly Bengalis, most of them Hindus, many of them from Midnapore. The way they behaved with the victims upon the instigation of their British masters would put the Spanish conquistadores of South America to shame and make one want to throw up! It is hard to imagine today that an instruction had to be issued from Calcutta, at the instance and insistence of Dr Mookerjee, that it was not the policy of the government to burn and loot the houses of ordinary citizens in retaliation for their rebellious activities! And even after this, and even after the tsunami-cyclone had struck Contai, the government functionaries continued with their nefarious activities, especially at night! Dr Mookerjee himself recorded that in the presence of the district magistrate, complaints were received that boats were deliberately not made available on the fateful evening, or even later, to save the lives of people who were perilously resting for a brief while on the roofs of their *kutcha* houses which ultimately collapsed. One gentleman gave a harrowing description of how he and others had begged the officers to allow a boat, found by them, to ply for a couple of hours to rescue some men, women and children lying marooned in a nearby place. The request was not only summarily rejected, but the people who were using the boat were threatened with dire consequences. The people who were marooned and not rescued were ultimately washed away, never to be found again. Even after the catastrophe, curfew orders were not lifted even though the local people pleaded with the officials and offered every cooperation. Cows were requisitioned under the Defence of India regulations! The floods and the storm had destroyed an estimated 75–85 per cent of the livestock. Of the few that remained, many, including milch cows, were snatched away by the police and military ostensibly for feeding the troops. Bona fide private relief workers from Calcutta, even after they produced their credentials, were thrown into jails.

Moreover, the government imposed collective fines on the populace. But not on the entire population—only on Hindus! Dr Mookerjee, in his letter to Herbert following his resignation, likened it to the imposition of *jizya*, the poll tax imposed by the Muslim rulers of Delhi upon non-Muslims, abolished by Emperor Akbar, but reimposed by Aurangzeb.

Directly resulting from this, Dr Mookerjee resigned from the cabinet on 16 November 1942. He sent his resignation to the Chief Minister, requesting him to forward it to the Governor. Of course, the Midnapore affair in the aftermath of the tragedy at Contai was not the only reason for his resignation. It was just the proverbial straw that broke the camel's back. Together with his formal resignation sent through the Chief Minister to the Governor, he also wrote a separate letter to Herbert on the same day. In this letter and in his resignation speech made before the assembly, he recorded in detail the circumstances which led to his resignation. Among the other reasons he stated, the principal ones were the total disinclination of Herbert and his coterie of British civil servants to let the ministry do its work; the constant fomenting of Hindu–Muslim strife and differences, in which the Muslim League eagerly cooperated; the misapplication of the Defence of India regulations; the refusal to free political prisoners to do relief work in Midnapore; the imposition of collective fines on Hindus alone; and the defeatist policy of denial and evacuation.

The concluding paragraphs of Dr Mookerjee's resignation speech are as memorable in their directness and clarity as in revealing the intense patriotism and political insight of the man. He said:

> When we come here as members of the legislature we seek to reach the goal of our national freedom through the path of constitutional struggle. The history of the countries which still form part of the British Empire [he was referring to Canada and Australia] but which had to wring from unwilling hands the charter of their liberty afford glorious examples of constitutional struggle and victory . . . We have as much right to throw off the yoke of British domination as England is anxious to save herself from Hitler's profane hands . . . Today in the crisis that threatens us, not as Hindus or Muslims as such, but as Bengalis and Indians, let us demand the inauguration of an administration which will recognize our just and political rights. A Hindu and a Muslim may differ on many things but do they not equally detest slavery—and it is for ending the state of intolerable slavery that I am asking for your support and cooperation.

Dr Mookerjee's resignation was accepted by the Governor on 20 November 1942. The previous day, he had an interview with Governor Herbert who wanted an assurance from him that the letters he had written to the Governor should not be made public. Dr Mookerjee flatly refused to give any such assurance unless machinery was provided to sack an incompetent Governor such as

Herbert 'who was unfit to shoulder the great responsibility of his office during a grave emergency'. Thereafter, Dr Mookerjee has remarked, presumably tongue in cheek, 'He was greatly annoyed at this remark and our interview came to an abrupt end.'

Calcutta was bombed by the Japanese in December 1942, though compared to other theatres of the war it was a very tame affair. At that time, Dr Mookerjee was living in Madhupur. From there he proceeded to Cawnpore (now Kanpur) to attend the All-India Hindu Sabha session. This was his first appearance after his resignation and there was considerable enthusiasm about him. In the meeting, the leaders called upon the British government to pay heed to their proposals in this hour of crisis. Some people were in favour of direct action, but this was not implemented owing to the opposition of Savarkar and Dr Moonje.

Meanwhile, in Calcutta, things were going from bad to worse for the Progressive Democratic coalition ministry led by Fazlul Haq. The Muslim League and the European group had ganged up against them, and Muslim and scheduled-caste members were defecting. The Hindu Sabha was out of the ministry with Dr Mookerjee's exit, but continued to support them, as did the Congress. After Dr Mookerjee's resignation, Fazlul Haq had taken over the finance portfolio, but it was apprehended that he would not be able to get the budget passed easily. At this stage, Herbert sent for him and asked him to put in his resignation, unless he agreed to repudiate whatever Dr Mookerjee had said about the British administration. Haq was not prepared to do this and Herbert kept on pressuring him to sign the letter of resignation that he had already typed. Haq eventually capitulated and signed it. He told his colleagues, including Dr Mookerjee, of his resignation only the next morning, by which time the resignation had already been accepted. The budget had not been passed, so after some more pressurizing, which Dr Mookerjee successfully resisted, the Governor on 31 March 1943 declared Bengal to be a province under Section 93 of the Government of India Act, and a 'Governor's Budget' was passed.

There was a great uproar against this, and a huge demonstration was organized, which was addressed by Haq and Dr Mookerjee and attended by Hindus and Muslims alike. The theme of the demonstration was that the Governor had found the cabinet too independent for his tastes and had, by his machinations, got a perfectly legitimate government dismissed. But Herbert was not a person to be shamed by public uproar against him. He sent for Nazimuddin and got him to form a ministry in which three caste Hindu ministers and three of the scheduled castes were persuaded to join. Then there was a demonstration organized by the Muslim League welcoming the ministry, and the Hindu ministers joined the Leaguers in defending their action. Incidentally, at this stage, Suhrawardy (of whom much will be said later in this book) tried very hard for the premiership, but was passed over for the top post and given the portfolio of civil supplies.

It ought to be mentioned that Viceroy Linlithgow had a rather poor opinion of Herbert and was extremely critical of him regarding actions as have just been described. In a letter addressed to Amery, dated 2 April 1943, the secretary of state for India, Linlithgow, wrote:

> I am very disturbed about this business of Herbert and his ministry . . . I cannot imagine greater folly than to present someone of the type of Haq with a draft letter of resignation, head him off from consulting his colleagues . . . Other aspects that concern me very much are the suggestions that Haq at this time had a majority, and that Nazimuddin certainly had not, and has not. I am sure it is most dangerous for Governors to play politics, even if they are of outstanding capacity, and I fear that poor Herbert can hardly claim to be of the latter category.

However, on the grounds of administrative consistency, Linlithgow always backed Herbert.

Meanwhile the price of foodstuff, principally rice, kept on rising steeply and inexorably. Bengalis, like most Indians, are principally cereal-eaters, and the price of cereals (rice in their case) affects them more than that of any other commodity. The price of rice per maund (about 36 kilograms or 80 pounds) in February 1942 was about four rupees. It jumped to sixteen rupees per maund in December 1942, and to 100 rupees in September 1943. The little rice that was in the market therefore moved away to where the purchasing power was, namely to Calcutta. The countryside first tried to survive on inedible stuff, such as assorted roots, leaves and snails. Some died as a result, the rest just starved, and came over to Calcutta in search of any food that could be got by begging.

The bulk of these people were from nearby districts, chiefly Midnapore, where the tsunami-cyclone of October 1942 had killed off an astounding number of people, mostly men who were out of doors when the tsunami or cyclone surprised them. The womenfolk were then left to fend for themselves, and finding nothing at all to eat, they travelled to Calcutta. The people from faraway districts such as those in East Bengal found this difficult, and stayed on where they were, to die there.

In the meantime, the wedding of Dr Mookerjee's elder daughter Sabita was arranged to Nishith Banerjee, an engineer. But Dr Mookerjee at the time was so busy with famine relief that (according to Sabita herself) he could not be present during the wedding ceremony.

According to official estimates, 15,00,000 people died in the famine. Unofficial figures are much higher, and at the very least, double of the official estimate, that is to say not less than 30,00,000—some have even put it in the neighbourhood of 50,00,000. Whatever the figure is, the enormity of the tragedy is imaginable even from the official estimate. It is like all the people of a fair-sized town dying from starvation, no less.

The famine was an important landmark in the life of Dr Mookerjee for three reasons. First, he had shown remarkable foresight in trying to dissuade the Governor from impoverishing the countryside in the name of collection of foodstuff for military personnel, and had resigned when he found that the Governor would not listen to him. Secondly, when the famine became a reality, he had organized a massive relief effort, which saved innumerable lives—a task which should have been undertaken by the government, but was not done, or done properly. And thirdly, he had ruthlessly exposed the crimes of omission and commission by the British administration and the Muslim League ministry, the horrible acts which would have never come to light without Dr Mookerjee's initiative, mostly thorough speeches in the Legislative Assembly.

According to Dr Mookerjee, in Midnapore, a starving man fell unconscious from sheer excitement at the sight of a thali of rice in a *langarkhana* before he could put any in his mouth. He died shortly afterwards. Another man, found dead on the bank of a river, was found to have his stomach full of sand. Driven by hunger, he had swallowed sand.

Central to the genesis and mismanagement of this famine were four people. Among them Leopold Amery, the secretary of state for India, Viceroy Linlithgow and Governor Herbert have already been introduced to the reader. The fourth person was Herbert's minister in charge of civil supplies in Nazimuddin's cabinet, a sinister and at the same time flamboyant and colourful character called Huseyn Shaheed Suhrawardy, of whom more will be heard in this book. Scion of an aristocratic Muslim family from Midnapore, Suhrawardy used to drive his own Packard and frequent a nightclub of Calcutta called the Golden Slipper. He has been described by Larry Collins and Dominique Lapierre, in their bestseller *Freedom at Midnight*, as 'setting himself the prodigious task of bedding every cabaret dancer and high-class whore in Calcutta'. Ashok Mitra, who saw both at close range, contrasted them by saying that while Nazimuddin was a quiet and affable gentleman, Suhrawardy was nothing less than a 'rough, tough bully'.

It may be mentioned in passing that Madhusree Mukerjee, in her *Churchill's Secret War*, has put the principal blame for the famine on Churchill. In fairness, this is not so. Churchill had a World War on his hands. He couldn't be less bothered about the Bengal Famine—to that extent he is certainly culpable. But the principal villains of the piece were certainly Herbert, Suhrawardy, Linlithgow and Amery, in that order.

By the time Nazimuddin's cabinet had taken over in April 1943, with Suhrawardy in charge of civil supplies, the famine was already a reality, with the worst yet to come. As in Mao's China and Kim's North Korea, the first task of the new administration, ably assisted by the British bureaucracy under Herbert, appeared to be to pretend that that there was no famine, nor was there to be one. And in their eagerness to please Herbert who had so lovingly installed them in office, they made totally asinine statements, like Suhrawardy saying that there was no deficiency, rather a sufficiency of foodgrains, and he would, if necessary, himself look under the *taktaposh*es[6] of people to apprehend and recover hoarded foodgrains. This and similar statements were lambasted by Dr Mookerjee on the floor of the house, as described later, though unfortunately there was little else he could do.

It was therefore but natural that Herbert would address Viceroy Linlithgow in a secret report[7] saying, 'Since his resignation, Dr Mookerjee has devoted himself to exploiting the situation in Midnapore in a manner calculated to discredit His Excellency [Linlithgow], the Governor and Government officials.' Herbert's scheme was that this terrible tragedy or combination of tragedies should remain unknown to the rest of the world; and because Dr Mookerjee wanted the same to receive due publicity so that relief would be forthcoming, Herbert took it as Dr Mookerjee throwing a spanner in the works. One of Dr Mookerjee's statements was banned under the Defence of India Rules, and this was justified by the Government of India in the council of states. His statements were dubbed as 'over-dramatization of facts'.

After resigning, Dr Mookerjee plunged into relief work, initially for the cyclone-tsunami victims of Midnapore, and later for the famine victims as the famine became more and more of a reality. He set up the 'Bengal Relief Committee' for comprehensive famine relief throughout the province, and set about the task of collecting donations. He travelled to Bombay in July to give publicity to the famine so as to get funds from likely donors. The naming of the committee clearly indicated that he intended this committee to be a purely non-partisan affair. However, because of pressure from within his party, he had to yield to some extent and start a parallel organization called Bengal Provincial Hindu Mahasabha Relief Committee. He became the president of the latter while remaining a vice president of the former under the presidency of Sir Badridas Goenka. Meanwhile, under his stewardship, both the Bengal Relief Committee and the Bengal Provincial Hindu Mahasabha Relief Committee applied themselves to relief work among Hindus and Muslims alike—in fact, in eastern Bengal, the bulk of famine victims were poor Muslim cultivators, and Dr Mookerjee and his committees worked for their relief with as much verve and energy as they did for that of the Hindus of Midnapore. He also made an appeal to the Bengal Legislative Assembly members for donating a part of their daily allowance to famine relief, saying,[8] 'We now get Rs 40 per day. I do not know what it will be hereafter. Let us agree to a voluntary cut of Rs 10 and let us keep apart this sum for the purpose of opening homes where these women and children may be housed and fed.' Sadly enough, very few of the legislators responded to his call.

The famine gave rise to the politicking that is the inevitable result of the ugly trait of some Indian politicians to take advantage of calamities to further their own ends. A Muslim communal party called Khaksar Party started relief camps outside Bengal, and taking advantage of the situation, tried to convert Hindu destitute children to Islam in return for relief. Dr Mookerjee immediately contacted the leaders of the Khaksar Party in Calcutta. He demanded that such Hindu children be handed over to the Hindu Mahasabha and that the transporting of children outside the province be stopped forthwith. Eventually, he managed to put enough pressure on the government to stop this transportation altogether. Some rich Muslims from South Africa sent donations to the famine relief effort despite Jinnah's forbidding them to do so.

The setting up of the Bengal Relief Committee and the Hindu Mahasabha Relief Committee by Dr Mookerjee served as a catalyst and a beacon for other prominent people to come forward and either join his organization or found other organizations for famine relief. Among the organizations which were set up and the people who headed them were the following: Marwari Relief Society (Mangturam Jaipuria), Ramakrishna Mission (Swami Madhavananda), Arya Samaj Relief Society (Deepchandji Poddar), Stock Exchange Relief Committee (Govindlal Bangur), Gujarat Seva Samiti (Pranjivan Jaitha), Punjab Relief Committee (Lala Karamchand Thapar), Calcutta Relief Committee (Dr Bidhan Chandra Roy), Howrah Relief Society (Chiranjilal Bajoria), All-India Women's Conference Relief Committee (Vijaylakshmi Pandit), Bengal Women's Food Committee (Lady Ranu Mookerjee), All-Bengal Flood and Famine Relief Committee (G.L. Mehta), *Daridra Bandhab Bhandar* (Dr Radha Binode Pal). The premier business houses of Birla Brothers and

Soorajmal Nagurmal also sponsored their own relief work, as did quite a few zamindars in their respective areas. Some of these committees had affiliated organizations in the districts through whom they organized the distribution of relief. Dr Mookerjee also organized a Relief Coordination Committee of which he was one of the vice presidents, the other being Dr Bidhan Chandra Roy, the legendary physician and later Chief Minister of West Bengal. The Relief Coordination Committee was presided over by Sir Badridas Goenka.

The relief organizations carried out the following activities:

1. Free kitchens and free grain distribution centres for the totally destitute and starving
2. Cheap canteens and grain shops for those who could still pay something
3. Minimal housing for the destitute
4. Hospitals earmarked and equipped to treat the famine-affected
5. Supply of free clothing to the needy
6. Supply of free milk for destitute children and infants

The donations collected by the relief committees from all over India aggregated to about fifty lakhs or 5 million rupees, of which more than one-third was collected by the Bengal Relief Committee alone. With this money, all these organizations operated relief centres in Calcutta and all over rural Bengal, from Dantan in Midnapore to Jalpaiguri to Chittagong. The stamp of Dr Mookerjee's indefatigable energy was apparent behind each one of these efforts.

All that Dr Mookerjee, out of power, could do about the famine was to organize relief and chastise the government through whose panic, combined with unbelievable cynicism, the famine had been caused—and he did both in good measure. There was no forum to publicly criticize the principal villain Herbert, but Suhrawardy, his minister in charge of civil supplies, had made matters worse both for himself and the famine victims through his personal misdeeds, and he had to face the assembly. Dr Mookerjee proceeded to lambast and expose him in the assembly in the most parliamentary and civilized manner possible, and practically tanned his hide as far as possible with words. The assembly, at this time, had been based on the Communal Award of 1932 and the Government of India Act of 1935, and had separately elected Hindu members, scheduled-caste members, Muslim members, Indian Christian members and a disproportionately large number of 'European' (meaning British) members. The ruling coalition was largely of the Muslim League with a few Hindus, and they held power with the help and support of this European group.

Dr Mookerjee delivered two extremely hard-hitting speeches in the Bengal Legislative Assembly, one on 14 July 1943, and the other on 17 September 1943. In these, he condemned the Muslim League ministry and the British bureaucracy, and singled out Suhrawardy, the minister in charge of civil supplies at the time. Suhrawardy was condemned not only for the bungling of the famine relief arrangements, but also for the blatant partiality and disregard for norms of spending public money that he showed in respect of a known Muslim League benefactor called Ispahani. The speeches are memorable as much for their pungency and eloquence as for the recording of facts for posterity.

In his speech[9] in a debate on the food situation in Bengal, Dr Mookerjee said:

Now, Sir, in one of the statements issued by Mr Suhrawardy it was said that the worst feature of the last ministry's food policy [meaning Fazlul Haq's ministry] was its insistence on shortage. That was on 17th May [1943]. Then again, he said 'There is, in fact a sufficiency of foodgrains for the people of

Bengal.' I ask specially the members who are sitting opposite, anxious to give their support to the ministry, to demand an explanation from Mr Suhrawardy. What were the data before him which justified him to make that remark that there was in fact a sufficiency of foodgrains for the people of Bengal? Not satisfied with this bare statement, he proceeded to remark, 'Full statistical details, which will clearly demonstrate that there is a sufficiency, will soon be published.' Where are those statistics? Have they been collected, or are they being manufactured?

Dr Mookerjee went on to say:

Mr Amery declared [in the House of Commons]—'Yes, there is some trouble in India and in Bengal, but there is no shortage of foodstuff in the country; there is only hoarding and maldistribution . . . Now Sir, what happened next? Mr Suhrawardy declared that there was plenty of foodstuffs in Bengal. All that had to be done was to find out the foodstuff even from under the *taktaposhes*. After a tiring and busy day he seriously made a speech declaring that, if necessary, he would himself go under the taktaposhes of every householder and bring out the rice. I know that many householders got nervous. If Mr Suhrawardy really starts entering into the households and going under the taktaposh at night or even during daytime, heaven protect those householders from the after-effects of those ministerial attacks! Could there have been, I ask, a sillier approach to a problem vitally affecting the lives of millions of people?

It is true that that the famine was not Suhrawardy's or the Muslim League's creation—that credit must go to the Amery–Linlithgow–Herbert trio. His positive contribution to famine relief efforts—if it could be called that—was the appointment of M.M. Ispahani

Ltd, known benefactors of the Muslim League, as sole purchasing agents of the government of Bengal for the purchase of foodgrains from neighbouring provinces. In his speech before the Bengal assembly, Dr Mookerjee attacked Suhrawardy on this question as well. He said:

> What did Mr Suhrawardy do with regard to Orissa and Bihar? Why did he not negotiate with the governments of these provinces? . . . I have nothing personal against Mr Ispahani . . . it is a question of principle. It was nothing short of a scandal that the ministry should have appointed a particular firm as its sole agent, and what is more, advanced about two crores of rupees to that firm without a single scrap of document. Can Mr Suhrawardy produce a single contract entered upon between the Ispahanis and the Government of Bengal? It is a mockery.

Right through this speech, the flamboyant Suhrawardy and his Muslim League and European cronies mostly sat silently, because they had nothing to say in their defence.

Yet, the record reveals amusing sidelights at the few points when they tried to interject, because then they laid themselves bare to the barbs of Dr Mookerjee's acerbic wit. At one point, the record reveals, 'Mr Suhrawardy utters something.' And he promptly gets it back, 'It is no use coming here and speaking in a tone which befits the residents of the Zoological Gardens.' At another point Suhrawardy quipped, 'Nonsense.' Came the answer, 'Nonsense is an epithet which applies to the Civil Supplies Minister, because he is today totally devoid of sense, and if that means nonsense, he is nonsense personified.'

Dr Mookerjee began his speech on 17 September 1943, a time when the famine had reached its worst phase, by moving a resolution, the draft of which read as follows:

This Assembly is of the opinion that the statement of the Civil
Supplies ministry on the food situation is utterly disappointing
and unsatisfactory . . . Its latest action in promulgating the
price control of rice without making suitable provisions for
supply has intensely aggravated the misery of the people. The
ministry has failed to discharge the elementary responsibility of
any civilized government by its failure to save human lives and
to procure for the people essential commodities for their bare
existence.

In graphic language, Dr Mookerjee described the indescribable
misery of people in the Bengal countryside, while members on the
government benches, purporting to represent such countryside,
sat and listened silently:

Let me however emphasize that the death roll mainly due to
starvation, and diseases following such starvation, is rapidly
increasing. Reports of suicides, desertion of families and
children, of dead bodies lying uncared for are pouring in from
different parts of Bengal . . . Only last week I was in Midnapore.
In my presence there was the case of a person who came to have
his food at a free kitchen and the very sight of food resulted
in such a state of excitement that before the food could reach
his mouth he lay there unconscious and never woke again . . .
Now, Sir, in Contai jackals and dogs have been freely feeding
themselves on dead bodies.

Dr Mookerjee rounded off his speech by saying towards the end:

It is indeed amazing that the government has bungled
throughout. I am at a loss to understand what the policy of
the government is. Does Mr Amery still hold that the people
of Bengal are suffering because of overfeeding or deliberate

hoarding, especially by greedy agriculturists? Why are foodgrains not being rushed to Bengal from Australia and other parts of the world outside India?

Memorable speeches, all of them. But something more ought to be said about Dr Mookerjee's actions when viewed in the context of the present-day politics of West Bengal. Dr Mookerjee did not once dream of holding a rally (*janasabha*), calling a Bangla bandh (total immobilization of Bengal), blocking highways (*abarodh*) or smashing up furniture, ostensibly to draw the attention of the world to one of the worst tragedies ever to befall Bengal. Some or all of these surely would have been done today as a knee-jerk reaction in current-day West Bengal politics, if a tragedy a tenth of the size had hit the state. If somebody proposed calling a bandh to Dr Mookerjee, he would surely have looked at him in incredulity and said, 'But that is going to make matters worse for the people! That is going to make movement of foodgrains even more difficult!' No, Dr Mookerjee did not do any of these things, for he was not a Leftist. Instead, he went about organizing relief, visiting the districts, talking to people, keeping the government (many times more powerful and authoritarian than at present) literally on its toes.

The present idiom of political movement among Indian Bengalis, which begins with obstructing public arteries and otherwise disrupting public life, probably began with the burning of thirteen tramcars by the communists in 1953, to protest a one-pice hike in tram fares—more on this in Chapter 15. Dr Mookerjee would have loathed and detested this idiom, something that has made West Bengal today notorious for shooting itself in the foot. But that is another story.

A caveat should be added. It has been said earlier that hoarding was not the *cause* of the famine. However, some hoarding took place as an *effect* of the famine.

Meanwhile, His Excellency the Governor John Arthur Herbert, principal author of the tragedy, already sick in mind and body, eventually fell so ill while the famine was raging that Sir Thomas Rutherford, the Governor of Bihar had to be asked to take additional charge of the Governorship of Bengal from 6 September 1943. Herbert died shortly thereafter, unlamented, on 11 December. Meanwhile, in October 1943, Lord Wavell replaced Herbert's patron, Lord Linlithgow, as viceroy. Things immediately began to take a turn for the better.

The famine gradually abated, and is today a speck in the history of a troubled province in especially troubled times. Presumably because of the apparent appeasement policies of the governments of West Bengal, one might like to believe that the historians did not dare to write anything critical about a particular community (in this case Suhrawardy). The famine gets just a one-line cursory reference in history books, and the present generation who have not seen it know almost nothing of it.

In retrospect, Dr Mookerjee, in a diary entry dictated to his stenographer Baridbaran at Madhupur on 5 January 1946, appreciated the part played by the ordinarily pro-British daily the *Statesman* in exposing the maladministration. It showed great courage of conviction, he said, and by its pictures and articles it staggered public opinion through the civilized world. The ministry was openly accused of helping profiteers and sharing ill-gotten gains. Dr Mookerjee further recounts:

While millions died for want of food, an equal number followed to the grave on account of illness and malnutrition. Then came want of cloth, and people died in thousands during winter for want of shelter and protection. The whole atmosphere was nauseating. A Government that claimed itself to be civilized was carrying on its administration smoothly, and was even running a war, and allowed millions of its subjects to wither away for want of food, medicine and raiment. If it had been in other countries, such a Government would have been blown to pieces in no time. There would have been food riots and rebellion in the land. But our men being what they were and our country being what it was, everything was attributed to fate and people quietly died without raising even a murmur. I was specially charged with having made political use of a situation that was so serious. My whole energy and attention were employed for organizing relief, irrespective of party and communal considerations, and I often wished that instead of making a hopeless attempt to save lives against tremendous odds and difficulties, we should have organized resistance so that the machinery of the Government might have been uprooted.

Today's generation may know nothing of the famine, but it is too deeply etched in the minds of the still-surviving few, like the lady who wrote to this biographer describing how she had to traipse her way among emaciated, twisted corpses on the streets of Calcutta, just to reach a tram stop en route to her college. Or those, who had heard the lonesome wail of the starving voices, sometimes breaking, sometimes croaking, '*Ektu phan dao go, ma* (O mother, please give me some *phan*[10])', fading away into the gas-lit Calcutta night. No way these people will forget the famine, as long as they live. Or, for that matter, forget Dr Syama Prasad Mookerjee.

7

Difficult Years, 1944–46

The year 1944 dawned with the prospects of Allied victory in the war brightening. The tide had not quite turned on the Burma front—it would be June or July before the Japanese would abandon all plans they might have had of invading India and begin withdrawing. However, their supply lines were becoming impossibly stretched, and the supply bases were being relentlessly bombed by the Americans. The famine had abated, but there was little else that made the new year any different from the past one. The bomb scare continued in Calcutta, and hordes of people fled the city for the countryside to escape being bombed. In the parts of India other than Bengal and Assam, the war was something far away that the people just read about in the morning papers and heard over the radio. Meanwhile in Bengal, after the illness and death of Herbert, R.G. Casey, an engineer and businessman, took over as Governor in January 1944.

The abating of the famine freed Dr Mookerjee from his relief duties, with the result that he could have a breather. In the Amritsar session of the Hindu Mahasabha in December 1943, he explained[1] in detail his rationale behind joining the Mahasabha and not the Congress. He said:

So long as communal considerations loom large in the field of Indian administration and the Anglo–Muslim conspiracy continues, the Hindu Mahasabha must function as an active and fearless political organization which can both achieve the rights of Hindus and of India as a whole. So long as a third party remains in India and an aggressive anti-national anti-Hindu Muslim League party holds its sway over the Muslim masses, enjoying the favours of the British Govt and planning to veto the elementary rights of the majority, Hindus for their sheer existence must have their own political organization to fight for their own rights and liberties. The political goal of Hindu Mahasabha is complete independence of India. It stands for joint electorate, if necessary with reservation of seats. It asks for no special favours for Hindus in any part of the country. Its aim and policy are consistent with the welfare of India as a whole.

The remarkable similarity between these political goals as espoused by Dr Mookerjee and as subsequently enshrined in the Indian Constitution some six years later cannot be missed, and points to the foresight of the man.

At the beginning of the year, he made some very important entries in his diary, beginning on 2 January 1944. These entries, though long and detailed, were far from continuous—the next entry in his English diary is found on 21 October 1944 and the next one on 6 December 1945. These were not about contemporary events; they chronicled his entry into politics in 1939 and the years thereafter—the despotic and highly communal rule of the Muslim League–Krishak Praja coalition nominally led by Fazlul Haq, followed by the subsequent Progressive Coalition led by the selfsame Fazlul Haq, in which Dr Mookerjee was the finance minister, and the antics of Governor Herbert.

The Muslim League had adopted its Pakistan Resolution, based on Jinnah's two-nation theory, at its Lahore session in 1940. No one had the foggiest idea of what this Pakistan would be like.

The Mahasabha was the only organization to expressly protest the resolution. Here they were up against not only the Muslim League but also the ambivalence of the Congress who suffered from the grand delusion that they represented Hindus and Muslims alike. Those who have seen the telefilm based on Bhisham Sahni's *Tamas*, produced and screened more than fifty years later, would have noted how the Muslim League man was forcefully declaring that the Muslim League represents the Muslims and the Congress the Hindus; and how the popular character actor A.K. Hangal, playing the part of a Congressman, was pathetically whining, trying to convince him that the Congress was for Hindus and Muslims alike. In fact, the Muslim League man was speaking the truth, or at least what then was the truth. Now the tragedy was that the Congress rode almost exclusively on Hindu support, and Hindus supported them without reservation; but the Congress would not lift a little finger to help the Hindus when they were faced with a Muslim fundamentalist (the term was not current then) onslaught. In fact, much earlier the Congress had adopted, inwardly of course, the maxims as articles of basic belief, 'A Muslim can do no wrong,' and even if he does, 'Thou shalt not speak ill of Muslims lest thou be called communal.' The Congress, therefore, could not or did not take a resolute stand against Pakistan, although Nehru had earlier dubbed the idea 'fantastic nonsense'.

Dr Mookerjee, as a Mahasabha leader, was among the first to protest the idea and take his struggle to the streets. Even earlier, at his behest an 'Anti-Communal Award Day' was observed by the Mahasabha. This was against the 1932 Communal Award made by the British Prime Minister Ramsay Macdonald, regarding which the Congress had taken the inexplicable stand of 'neither accepting nor rejecting'. The worst features of the award were that it gave separate blocks of seats to Hindus and scheduled castes (while no such separation was made between Sunni and Shia Muslims), and reserved a disproportionately large number of seats for 'Europeans'. The idea was to let Europeans act as the balancing group between the Hindus and the Muslims. It is with the support of this European bloc that Governor Herbert did the mischief of installing a Muslim League ministry in Bengal in 1943.

In a huge rally held at the Corporation Park in Dacca, Dr Mookerjee called upon Hindus to unite against the communal politics of the League and the shameful capitulation of the Congress before the unfair demands of the League. In the 1942 Lucknow session of the Mahasabha, Dr Mookerjee had declared that the country will fight till the last drop of blood against the kowtowing to the Muslims by the Congress. Then again, in the 1943 Amritsar session of the Mahasabha, he declared that no discussion with the League, which premised on their Lahore resolution, was possible.

In the political firmament of Bengal, there was no Hindu leader at this time to match Dr Mookerjee in stature, despite the fact that he had entered active politics just five years ago. Subhas Chandra Bose had left India in 1941, and Sarat Chandra Bose was incarcerated in faraway Coonoor. His constitutional politics, his refusal to kowtow to unreasonable demands of the Muslim League and his right-wing views were making an impression on the people.

Meanwhile, something sinister was happening within the Congress. Chakravarthi Rajagopalachari, better known as C.R. or Rajaji, a Tamil Brahmin, was the most prominent leader in the Congress from south India, which was then almost synonymous with the Madras Presidency. In a meeting of the Congress legislators of the suspended assembly of Madras Presidency held in April 1942, he came out with a suggestion that the party accept the principle of partition as the basis for an understanding with the Muslim League. This suggestion was roundly criticized and summarily rejected in the AICC meeting at Allahabad later in the same month.

Rajaji resigned from the Congress Working Committee and his seat in the suspended Madras assembly, and declared that he would henceforth propagate these views of his as an independent political worker. Shortly thereafter, Gandhi's Quit India movement started and all the first-rung leaders of the Congress, including Gandhi, were herded into jail, and the C.R. formula entered cold storage. Rajaji, however, was not sent to jail because of his resignations and his opposition to the Quit India proposal.

Gandhi, with the other Congress leaders, remained incarcerated in jail right through 1943 and into 1944. The British released him on 6 May 1944, principally because his health was deteriorating and the British wanted no part of the responsibility for anything untoward happening. Meanwhile, Rajaji had been busy canvassing support for his pet formula, and had time to work on Gandhi after his release. In July 1944, he advanced a refined version of his offer of 1942 so that the League's claim for separation might be accepted to secure the 'installation of a national government'.

This C.R. formula proposed a settlement with the League in return for its cooperation with the Congress in the 'formation of a provisional interim government'. The basis of the formula was Rajaji's belief, not altogether mistaken, that firstly the Congress's opposition to the war effort was wrong; and secondly, the Muslim League could not be ignored any longer as being the voice of the majority of the Muslims of India (as the Congress had sought to do through Nehru's famous 'fall in line' theory of 1937). C.R.'s advocacy of his formula ultimately resulted in Gandhi finally accepting the modified formula, and on this basis, he proceeded to start a round of talks with Jinnah. Accepting a political theory, which happened to have elements of truth, from a party colleague like Rajaji is one thing, but publicly trying to convince a determined and formidable adversary like Muhammad Ali Jinnah was a totally different kettle of fish.

Meanwhile, Dr Mookerjee and other Mahasabha leaders had heard rumours that Gandhi, who had since been released, was going to surrender to Jinnah on the issue of Pakistan. They had a meeting of the All-India Working Committee in Delhi and Savarkar expressed his definite view that such a move would soon take place. Soon after Gandhiji's release, Sir Badridas Goenka and Nalini Ranjan Sarker went to see him in Bombay. Dr Mookerjee specially asked them to tell Gandhi that there should be no attempt to appease the Muslim League, and no commitment of any kind should be made before the Congress leaders were released, particularly without consulting the Hindu Sabha regarding Bengal. Both came back to Calcutta and said that they were definitely given to understand that there would be no talk of any compromise, and Gandhi asked everyone to remain fully assured on this point. When Savarkar raised his doubts at the meeting of the All-India Working Committee, Dr Mookerjee, based on what he had learnt from Goenka and Sarker, told him that there was no possibility of any such commitment at all. Before Dr Mookerjee left Delhi, however, he was startled to find an announcement that the famous C.R. formula conceding the principle of Pakistan was secretly approved by Gandhi while he was undergoing his fast at Poona in 1942, and negotiations with Jinnah had started on that basis.

Dr Mookerjee issued a statement[2] from Allahabad on 10 July, strongly protesting this act of surrender and betrayal. 'The real surprise, painful indeed,' he said, 'is that Gandhiji should have allowed his name to be dragged into this amazing offer which is a virtual acceptance of Pakistan.' Dr B.R. Ambedkar, the leader of the scheduled castes, was also strongly critical[3] of the formula. 'Rajaji's plan mingles political issues with religious issues. There is a trap which asks for help in the struggle for independence, baited with thoughts about creating Pakistan. The ancient kings had marriage alliances with neighbouring states to get help in case of an attack by a foreign country. In the bargain the bridegroom was never nice and there was no money in it either.'

After Dr Mookerjee returned to Calcutta he tried to organize public opinion but found a great change in the minds of those who were responsible for moulding public opinion. The Communist Party which all along had played a shameless role in attacking the foundation of Indian nationalism was applauding the move taken by Rajagopalachari. The Mahasabha's first meeting at the Calcutta University Institute was broken by the communists in an act of abject goondaism.

Dr Mookerjee went to Poona in August 1944 to deliver the inaugural address at the Tilak anniversary. There was a record attendance at the public meeting which he addressed, and he criticized Gandhi's new move as being highly detrimental to the interests of Hindus and also to the country as a whole. He met Gandhi at Wardha on his way back to Calcutta and had a long talk with him in the presence of Rajagopalachari. He warned him that Jinnah would never agree to what he had offered and he would merely lower the cause of Indian unity and nationalism by his proposed surrender.

Gandhi was not able to offer any convincing reply, except to take refuge in mysticism and answer[4] that, 'at momentous periods of his life he had acted according to his inner voice which made him understand what was right and proper'.

On 17 July 1944 Gandhi wrote to Jinnah asking for a meeting. Jinnah wrote back informing him that he would be glad to receive Gandhi at his residence in Bombay sometime in the middle of August. Dr Mookerjee, by way of a last-ditch attempt to stall these talks, sent Manoranjan Chaudhuri, a party colleague, as an emissary to Gandhi with a letter dated 19 July 1944, together with supporting papers. In the letter, he emphasized how undesirable any partition of the country would be and entreated Gandhi to stand up to Jinnah and oppose him. He said he was sure that neither the British government nor the Muslim League would accept Gandhi's proposal of transfer of power, but Jinnah would later use these proposals as a handle to extract further concessions. Dr Mookerjee also reminded Gandhi of the strong opinion against partition that the latter had expressed in an issue of the periodical *Harijan* of 1943, and requested him to adhere to that stand; and also that many Muslims in India still considered Pakistan to be a ridiculous, unacceptable, impracticable idea. In such circumstances if Gandhi sat in talks with Jinnah as the representative of Muslims in India, then that would provide an indelible stamp of approval on the man and sadden and disappoint all nationalist Muslims.

Gandhi, however, seemed to pay no attention to the letter. The talks took place for eighteen days, beginning on 9 September 1944 at Jinnah's palatial residence on Mount Pleasant Road, Malabar Hill, Bombay, and predictably failed. Gandhi's apparent wooing and Rajaji's near-capitulation bent before the iron will of Jinnah. He pretended to just rubbish it, but must have been secretly pleased that Gandhi and Rajaji had come so close to accepting his dream. In short, Jinnah would not budge an inch, but the Congress had meanwhile walked quite a few miles to meet him, and there was no way it could backtrack. The Congress and Gandhi had very nearly conceded Pakistan, and they would take another three years to do it wholly. In Lord Linlithgow's words, 'The Hindus were doomed because Jinnah was made great . . . by the Congress.'[5]

Gandhi's overture to Jinnah not only made Jinnah great but also did great harm to Bengal in particular, in that it drove a large number of Muslim leaders who were still resisting League domination, towards the League, as Dr Mookerjee had correctly predicted. This happened not only in Bengal but in other provinces as well. But its effect in League-ruled Muslim-majority Bengal was most detrimental. In fact, after Herbert's misadventure of dismissing the Haq ministry and installing Nazimuddin, things were going very badly for Nazimuddin. Suhrawardy's mishandling of the famine and Dr Mookerjee's exposure of the same before the whole world made matters worse for them—so much so that Wavell wanted to dismiss the cabinet and impose direct Governor's rule under Section 93. When things were going so badly for the League, Gandhi's concessions to Jinnah gave them a sudden shot in the arm, a burst of oxygen. The opposition coalition party had with them about fifty Muslims who were opposing the Muslim League and sat with them in the Opposition, all determined to oust the League. When these Muslim members found that Gandhi himself was going to make a compromise with Jinnah and recognize the League as the most powerful champion of Muslim interests, 'they thought it wise and prudent'—so says Dr Mookerjee's diary—'to desert us and join the League. Thus, member after member ran away from us and our opposition Coalition Party stood the chance of being disintegrated.'

Dr Mookerjee also found that many of the newspapers which had for so long opposed the Muslim League and had worked with the 'nationalist elements'—meaning the anti-League Muslims—were now faced with the fact that Gandhi (which meant the Congress) was going to compromise with Jinnah. As a result, they thought it wise and prudent to join the League. Thus, the Gandhi–Jinnah talks strengthened the Muslim League in Bengal, and the success achieved by Dr Mookerjee in consolidating all such nationalist elements was largely ruined.

In December 1944, Dr Mookerjee presided over the Mahasabha session at Bilaspur. He was fully aware of the political, social and economic aspects of the problem before the country, as also of the urgency of establishing direct contact with the masses. But he failed to collect a band of enthusiastic workers who would accept the task of carrying out the Mahasabha's policy and programme as 'the mission of their lives'. Moreover, many undesirable persons had taken hold of the organization in different parts of India, as we shall see later in this chapter. In fact, in a letter[6] addressed to Leopold Amery on 1 July 1945, Lord Wavell, the viceroy who had succeeded Linlithgow, observed, 'The Mahasabha is a curious body. Many of its rank and file seem to be Congressmen, and on big political issues will follow Gandhi rather than S.P. Mookerjee or Savarkar.' Wavell was right—as was proved in the elections to the Bengal assembly held later in December 1945. Wavell was also critical of Dr Mookerjee personally, and called him 'bitterly communal'—but by all accounts, he was a poor judge of character; and for that and other reasons he eventually jockeyed himself into such a position that both the Congress and the Muslim League wanted him out. Attlee, the new British Prime Minister, had remarked about him, 'A great man in many ways, you know, but a curious silent bird, and I don't think silent people get on very well with Indians who are very loquacious.' Eventually he was sent home in a letter which made Wavell, upon reading, remark to his aide Abell, 'They have sacked me, George.'

Around this time, Dr Mookerjee added two significant achievements to his list. First, he founded two daily newspapers, one called *Nationalist* in English and the other *Hindusthan* in Bengali, towards the end of 1944. Dr Mookerjee's strong words used in the *Nationalist* caused Governor Casey to write to Viceroy Wavell that Dr Mookerjee's articles were anti-British and anti-Allies. Around this time (December 1944), he brought out a volume titled 'Awake Hindusthan', which was a collection of his speeches delivered at various places all over India, from Shillong to Lyallpur (now in Pakistani Punjab) and from Ludhiana to Madura.

By June 1945, Lord Wavell had unfolded a plan and the Congress leaders were released from jail one by one to enable them to participate in the discussions on the plan. Dr Mookerjee observes in his diary that after being released, the Congress leaders

made a few positive and strident utterances that projected them
as pro-Hindu leaders (which Patel, among them, truly was, but
very few of the others). Nehru and Patel completely identified
themselves with the events of 1942. Unlike Gandhi, they did
not raise the question of whether the people were in favour of
non-violence or whether they advocated violence. The defenceless
common people had not revolted thus for independence since the
First War of Independence of 1857. The leaders extolled the people
for their heroism and sacrifice and sympathized with their trials
and tribulations. This approach evoked a new response among the
Hindu masses. They protested vociferously against Pakistan and
the Muslim League. The strong terms they used—especially Patel
and Nehru—to criticize Jinnah and the League made many feel
that the Congress had, at long last, really abandoned its policy of
pampering the Muslims and indulging Jinnah. Actions and words
like these would later prompt front-ranking Mahasabha leaders
like Gokul Chand Narang of Punjab, Mehr Chand Khanna of
NWFP, Dr Tripathi of Bihar and a few more to defect to the
Congress.

Dr Mookerjee watched with great regret the phenomenon
of this shift of almost the total support base of the Mahasabha
to the Congress as a result of this clever move by the Congress
leaders. He succinctly analyses the same in a diary entry which
he wrote during his illness at Madhupur in January 1946. He
also observes that although the Congress leaders proclaimed that
they were against the formation of Pakistan, they were in reality
evading the decision regarding the partition of the country under
the garb of self-determination. As to the role of the press, they
not only refrained from bringing this inconsistency out into the
open, they also tried to misinform the people in many ways. The
people of the country, particularly the Hindus, who had become
almost obsessed with the idea of gaining independence at any
cost, failed to analyse this issue in depth. Since the Congress

leaders repeatedly proclaimed that there would be no compromise on Pakistan, the people felt that the Congress had accepted the tenets of the Mahasabha, and did not see any need for a separate existence of the same.

How wrong they were! Dr Mookerjee, in his diary entry on 10 January 1946, gives vent to his frustration at this abandonment by the Hindus of the Mahasabha which, under his leadership, had worked indefatigably for the Hindu cause. He minces no words and writes completely without any concern for political correctness. How could, he asks himself referring to the Congress, an organization which was built on Hindu support, consider it a sin to uphold Hindu interests and fight another organization (referring obviously to the League) which was dedicated to establishing Muslim dominance? What could be more tragic than the fact that Hindus failed to understand this simple truth despite their intellectual and financial resources?

During all this, on 21 August 1945, the central government announced central and provincial elections in the coming winter. It appears from a secret India Office document dated 11 January 1946 that there had already been a decisive swing towards the Muslim League in Bengal, which Jinnah had virtually won over, and that accordingly the League was poised to emerge from the elections with greatly enhanced strength and prestige. The provincial elections of 1946 predictably resulted in a resounding success for the League, which increased its seats from thirty-nine in 1937 to 115 in a house of 250. Suhrawardy, who was unanimously elected the Muslim League party leader in the assembly, formed a ministry and became the new Prime Minister of Bengal on 24 April 1946.

The League had, of course, meanwhile further consolidated its position among the Muslims, and made the Hindu–Muslim polarization even stronger. The group known as 'nationalist Muslims' had begun to dwindle after Gandhi and C.R.'s ill-fated overture to Jinnah in 1944, and by this time the polarization was almost complete, barring a few like Maulana Azad or Syed Nausher Ali of Bengal. Its line was totally and stridently communal, anti-Hindu and pro-Pakistan, and there was no hypocrisy about their communalism. Abul Hashim, the general secretary of the Bengal unit of the League, a left-inclined Muslim leader from Burdwan, one of the westernmost districts of Bengal, had put forth his views in a fiery pamphlet titled 'Let Us Go to War'. In this task, he had help from his communist colleagues, among whom he particularly mentioned Nikhil Chakravartti[7] in his memoirs. The absence of Congress leaders during the war (they were all in jail), the death of Sir Sikandar Hayat Khan of Punjab and the weak-kneed, wavering politics of Fazlul Haq in Bengal helped the Muslim League in this regard. Sir Sikandar, the powerful and charismatic leader of the Unionist Party (basically a pro-British, trans-religious party of rural landlords), was very popular in Punjab. As for Haq, he constantly vacillated between stridently anti-League and pro-League positions and finally reapplied to join the Muslim League in 1945. As Dr Mookerjee had said of him once, 'Haq was at once an asset and a liability of no mean order.'

Now we come to a short but tumultuous phase of Dr Mookerjee's life, the closing months of 1945, which were as hectic as they were frustrating, and which finally took a physical toll on him. This was the period of Dr Mookerjee's election campaign of 1945 for the Central Assembly elections, interspersed with the incidents in Calcutta connected with the Indian National Army (INA) trials.

The Mahasabha was relatively more powerful in Bengal than elsewhere, so everyone expected it to fare better there. But events took a different turn. Apart from the loss of the support base, Dr Mookerjee's Mahasabha colleagues had started to waver. After Sarat Bose's release from jail, Dr Mookerjee had tried very hard with him to work out an arrangement of seat-sharing in order to avoid the division of Hindu votes in the coming elections. This, however, did not work out. Dr Mookerjee started the election campaign for his party in late October 1945 after the seat-sharing talks with Sarat Bose broke down. The Hindu electorate, however, answered decisively against any splitting of their votes, by casting *all* their votes in favour of the Congress. So much so that a complete nonentity called Nagendra Nath Mukhopadhyay from the Hooghly district, fighting on a Congress ticket from the Calcutta Suburbs constituency, trounced Dr Mookerjee securing 10,216 votes to Dr Mookerjee's mere 346. The Congress swept the non-Muslim constituencies, and the Muslim League the Muslim ones. Total communalization of the electorate thus took place and the former's grand delusion of representing Hindus and Muslims alike was shattered. Their few remaining nationalist Muslims drew almost a complete blank in the Muslim constituencies. The circumstances relating to this election and its campaign have been dealt with in detail later in this chapter.

Dr Mookerjee observed with great bitterness in his diary two aspects of this period: Sarat Bose's intransigence and ultimate refusal in the matter of seat-sharing with the Mahasabha for the Bengal Provincial Assembly election due in 1945; and the manner in which his Mahasabha colleagues and people supposedly politically close to it had behaved in the run-up to and the aftermath of the election and defected to the Congress. His brief friction with the younger of the Bose brothers, Subhas, in 1940 during the elections to the Calcutta Municipal Corporation was far exceeded by his frustration with the elder, Sarat, five years later in 1945. Sarat Bose had been incarcerated in far-off Coonoor in Madras Presidency for nearly four years, and was released from captivity on 14 September 1945. There had been no certainty about his release—Casey, the Governor of Bengal, opposed it till the end—and Dr Mookerjee had already started talks about seat-sharing with Kiran Sankar Ray and his faction of the Congress.

Sarat Bose's release, however, altered the picture and Dr Mookerjee had to start talks afresh with him. In this he found the former quite an egotist and 'fond only of talking'. Apparently, Sarat Bose called Jawaharlal Nehru all kinds of names.[8] These remarks, as Dr Mookerjee had rightly observed, were both rude and irrelevant.

As to seat-sharing between the Mahasabha and the Congress, Dr Mookerjee appears to have been really fed up with Sarat Bose. He records in his diary that the tumultuous welcome that the latter received in Bombay after being released from prison had apparently gone to his head, and he had started comparing himself to Gandhi.[9] He acted strangely regarding seat-sharing, having first said that he would leave two seats out of the six general seats for the Mahasabha, then backtracking from the statement and using sarcastic and critical words about Dr Mookerjee in a speech at Deshbandhu Park. Leonard Gordon, biographer of the Bose brothers, also agrees that he could not make up his mind about seat-sharing and had vacillated in this regard. However, once it was certain that there would be no seat-sharing between the Congress and the Mahasabha, Sarat Bose became consumed with defeating Dr Mookerjee, and filed nomination papers from both Burdwan Division and Calcutta when he came to know that the latter might run from either of these two constituencies. He called the election to the Calcutta Suburbs constituency, from which Dr Mookerjee finally contested, the 'Key Fight' in India. He managed to do the defeating and upstaging, as the Hindu electorate en masse chose him and the Congress over the Mahasabha to prevent the splitting of Hindu votes, but he totally failed in respect of the so-called nationalist Muslim voters who, together with the communal Muslims, en bloc voted for the League. Gordon rightly observes that 'the results of the December election must have brought Sarat Bose some joy and a lot of tears'.

Regarding the perfidy of his colleagues and political friends, Dr Mookerjee quotes quite a few examples in his Bengali diary.

He specially mentions Kshitish Chandra Neogy, Debendranath Mukherjee, Sanat Kumar Roy Chaudhury and Ananda Mohan Poddar of Bengal, Gokul Chand Narang of Punjab, Mehr Chand Khanna of the Frontier Province, Maheswar Dayal Seth of Awadh, Roy Saheb Arora, Dr Tripathi of Bihar, Panchanathan, Reddy and Dr Naidu of Madras Presidency among those who deserted the Mahasabha as soon as they perceived that the Congress was growing in strength.

In Bengal, Dr Mookerjee's own constituency, Calcutta Suburbs, comprised forty-four municipalities and an electorate of 36,000 spread over the districts of 24 Parganas, Hooghly and Howrah. He had been told that it would be easy to handle this constituency. Things, however, turned out quite differently. To begin with, the Mahasabha was not very strong in any part of the constituency. Second, a sizeable section of the press was very hostile. Besides, two fairly popular news dailies—one Bengali and the other English—from the same house, both traditionally pro-Congress, as it seemed, appeared to be spreading false propaganda and canards against him, surpassing all limits of decency and all tenets of ethical journalism. Dr Mookerjee observes that while such things are bound to happen during elections, there ought to be a limit to deceitful propaganda, and the two newspapers exceeded this limit. They began spreading rumours, that he was a traitor and had vested interests; that the Mahasabha could do nothing good for Bengal since, like the League, it was also an enemy of the country; that during the struggle of 1942, the Mahasabha had helped the government, and so on. Personal animosity against him came to the forefront.

His opponent was the Hooghly Congress leader Nagendra Nath Mukhopadhyay, a political pygmy compared to him. The Congress started proclaiming that it did not matter who the better candidate was, but to maintain the predominance of the Congress as an organization, Dr Mookerjee should be defeated at all costs.

Dr Mookerjee in his Bengali diary rues the fact that while he did not expect any reward for what he had done for the Hindus and for Bengal during the last six years, he never thought that the Congress would make it their main objective to annihilate him. The Congress neither had the courage nor capacity to put up a candidate against Jinnah, and yet that very Congress, the prestige of whose leaders he had tried his utmost to uphold over the last three or four years during their captivity, was now going all out to defeat him.

He also records that while he could not find much support for the Mahasabha, he did get some support as an individual because of his contribution to society. Those who were comparatively elderly and understood the problems of Bengal were surprised at the hostility of the Congress towards him. The younger, new enthusiasts, who fervently supported the Congress, were dead against him.

Then the INA trials started in Delhi. Netaji Subhas Chandra Bose, after his escape from India in January 1941 had travelled to Nazi Germany and thence to Japan in two submarines. Then he travelled to South East Asia with the victorious advancing Japanese army and mobilized the Indian POWs in the Japanese POW camps into an army which he named the Azad Hind Fauj or the Indian National Army (INA). The British called it the traitor army and, after the British victory, decided to court-martial them. Now, the Congress did a neat volte-face with them. In 1939, Gandhi had told Subhas that they must sail in different boats, and in 1943 Jawaharlal Nehru had declared that if Subhas Bose entered India with the Japanese he would fight him with sword in hand. Now, sensing the mood of the populace, the Congress completely sided with the accused of the INA, and threw itself into the trial in their support. Sir Tej Bahadur Sapru, the renowned barrister, was engaged to defend the accused, whom the British seemed determined to hang. Nehru, who was a qualified barrister but had never practised, and by then had presumably forgotten all the law that he learnt in the Inns of Court, donned his gown and stood by the side of Sir Tej Bahadur and drew enormous applause by this gesture. However, he did not really argue on their behalf. As Leonard Gordon wryly remarks, 'Among Indian nationalists, Mahatma Gandhi and Jawaharlal Nehru, who had been extremely critical of Subhas Bose from 1939 to 1945, found it easier to deal with him in death [as Gordon had presumed] than in life.'

The trials invoked an enormous response all over India and, expectedly, particularly in Bengal which the Congress was quick to take advantage of. Dr Mookerjee opposed this and pointed out the inconsistencies in their stand. In a large meeting held in Calcutta in which the issue of the INA was raised, Dr Mookerjee spoke on the contradictions between the ideals of the INA and the Congress's stand on non-violence. Everyone lauded his speech. The election meeting was attended by about 40,000–50,000 people. He expressed his views, taking care to steer clear of personal accusations and spoke about how those who had joined the Congress out of opportunism and were deriding him for being a traitor had in 1942, either made themselves scarce or had managed to get released from jail by signing bonds. He told the people that both Sarat Babu and he could work for the country simultaneously. If Bengal had no need for Dr Mookerjee and the Hindus did not need his services any longer, he could divert his energies in some other direction. He said he did not believe that he was indispensable for the country. He had rendered whatever he was capable of and he had done it selflessly and willingly without expectations of any reward. If his services were no longer required, he would gracefully accept it because there was not an iota of self-interest in whatever he did. He got a big round of applause for the speech.

On 22 November 1945, Dr Mookerjee had been out campaigning in the eastern suburbs of Calcutta for election to the Central Legislative Assembly. He addressed a few important meetings in Barasat, Basirhat, Baduria and Taki and returned home at about 9 p.m., very tired after a full day of electioneering. He had heard that there had been a lot of violence in Calcutta and that the police had opened fire. Upon his return he came to know that a lot of people had been looking for him since late afternoon. Some youths had held meetings and had taken out a procession. The police had stopped the procession while it was passing through Dharamtala Street (now Lenin Sarani). It had been planned that the procession would pass through Lalbazar (the location of the Calcutta Police headquarters) and Dalhousie Square (now Binoy-Badal-Dinesh Bagh). The police had tried to stop them, claiming that it was a prohibited area, but the processionists, not having known about this earlier, refused to obey. Lathi charging and firing followed, resulting in the death of a few, and injury to many. All kinds of stories started circulating, but nobody knew exactly what had happened.

Dr Mookerjee rang up Dr Radha Binod Pal[10] and told him that they should be present at the scene of the disturbance and stand beside the students in their moment of crisis. Dr Pal in turn informed Dr Bidhan Chandra Roy.[11] Dr Mookerjee did not even get time to wash after a whole day of strenuous work and running around, and rushed to Dr Pal's house at about 9.30 p.m. The latter meanwhile had gone over to Dr Bidhan Roy's house. Dr Mookerjee then went to the Medical College Hospital. The gate was blocked by a crowd of people, who made way to let him in. He went to meet Principal Dr Lindon, who assured him that everything possible was being done to treat the injured. Meanwhile, Dr Pal and Dr Roy arrived. They took the situation in and went to make a telephone call to the Government House. Dr Roy spoke to Tyson, the police commissioner. Meanwhile Dr Mookerjee came to know that the situation at Dharamtala Street (now Lenin Sarani) was still quite grave. Thousands of students were squatting on the road, and the police were barricading them with lathis and arms in hand. Everyone requested them to go there. Dr Roy, meanwhile, had to leave to attend a serious patient. Dr Pal and Dr Mookerjee went to Dharamtala Street. Their car was stopped by the police when they reached the crossing, but on recognizing them, let them go. When they neared Wachel Mollah's shop, they saw a fully armed posse of policemen. The students were squatting on the road facing them and shouting slogans. Meanwhile, the Governor had arrived at the spot and requested Dr Mookerjee and Dr Pal to tell the boys to go back home. Dr Mookerjee went up to the boys, who started shouting even louder. They said that since the evening they had been telling the police to inform Sarat Bose and him about the situation.

The situation had, in fact, been exacerbated by Sarat Bose's refusal to come.

Be that as it may, the result of Sarat Bose's refusal was that the boys refused to budge. They were determined at any cost to follow the route they had already decided upon. They were not willing to let down their comrades who had willingly sacrificed their lives for the cause. They were determined to go ahead. They calmly assured Dr Mookerjee that they did not intend to indulge in violence and create trouble. The police were equally adamant, and it became a prestige fight. The boys and some policemen requested Dr Mookerjee not to leave as they thought his presence would at least prevent further loss of lives. Mrs Jyotirmayee Ganguli, the Congress leader, was restlessly pacing up and down. She, too, expressed the same view—who knew then that she would be killed the very next day in a car accident!

Dr Mookerjee, tired beyond belief after the harrowing experience of the day, on his feet since early morning without a minute's rest, eventually managed to reach home at 3 a.m. The next morning, at 10 a.m., he went to the university to talk to Dr Pal to ensure that schools and colleges remained closed for a few days. He feared that there might be more trouble if this was not done. After that he went to the Medical College Hospital. He met all the injured and inquired after their welfare. The college and hospital compound was filled with people. One gentleman came forward. His nephew, Rameswar Banerjee, was among the first to be shot dead. The police had still not handed his body over to his relatives. Dr Mookerjee went to the university with the gentleman and two of his companions. He returned home to have a bite of lunch, but had to rush back on hearing that a huge crowd, about 1,00,000-strong, had again gathered at Wellington Square and the previous day's performance was about to be repeated. The police were determined to stop them, and the situation was getting more and more precarious every moment. Dr Mookerjee got on top of a police truck and addressed the crowd. Simultaneously, he managed to persuade the police commissioner not to open fire upon the crowd, and told him, 'Let them go the way they wish to. You can't stop them without machine guns, and then thousands of them will unhesitatingly sacrifice their lives. The casualties will be greater than at Jallianwala Bagh and they still won't move.' Eventually the crowd was allowed to proceed and there was no further firing. Later, he went with Rameswar's parents to the morgue to recover the body and arranged for the body to be decently attired and carried. An enormous crowd, nearly 2,00,000 strong, followed the body in silence. Meanwhile, there was a lot of commotion in the southern parts of the city. An African-American driver of a US army truck had run over a boy, and a mob had set fire to the truck and thrown the driver into the fire. There was widespread arson and indiscriminate firing by the panic-stricken and crazed police. In the midst of all this, Dr Mookerjee managed to guide the crowd to Keoratala Burning Ghat without incident, walking with them all the way, a distance of well over 6 kilometres.

Dr Mookerjee recalled that Sarat Babu had not turned up. He came late at night. Dr Mookerjee went home at about 11 p.m., after the pyre had been lit. On the way back, he called on a gentleman who had lost his only son in the police firing near Hazra Park in south Calcutta in the evening's commotion. The mother was sitting with her son's body in her lap. The father was pacing about as if in a stupor. There, too, recalled Dr Mookerjee in his diary, he witnessed that strange forbearance. No one cried openly or showed his grief. 'My son has sacrificed his life to the British. Let him stay in my arms for the night. You can take him away in the morning.' These were the words of an uneducated, ordinary, middle-class mother! Dr Mookerjee wrote in his diary, 'This brought home to me the heightened awareness among the people and I realized that a revolution was brewing. If such a fearless consciousness could be disciplined and channelized in the right direction how longer could the British remain?' Ultimately, Dr Mookerjee returned home and went to bed, dead beat, around midnight. The nagging pain that he had in his feet for a long time had got worse. He would have to go on a tour from Kanchrapara to Barrackpore by car the next day according to a prior arrangement.

Dr Mookerjee left in a car with Sushil Chattopadhyay of Asutosh College, who was in charge of his personal campaign in the area between Barrackpore and Kanchrapara. Though he should have rested that day, he decided to go because the visit had been fixed and he thought that work would be disrupted if he did not go.

It was not easy to drive through the roads of Calcutta. Fires could still be seen here and there, even though it was only morning. Trams and buses were not plying and it was hazardous to travel by car. Dr Mookerjee's party was stopped at several points but was allowed to proceed on being recognized. He was out the whole day, making speeches and holding discussions. He received a warm welcome at Kanchrapara, Halisahar, Bhatpara, Naihati,

Jagatdal, Shyamnagar and Ichapur. The progress at Naihati was not too encouraging. The morning's editions of *Anandabazar Patrika* and *Hindustan Standard* made no mention of his role in the events of the past two days. Those who had been eyewitnesses to what he had done were appalled by this deception and shameless suppression of facts.

Dr Mookerjee had by then almost completed his campaigning for the elections. There was a huge meeting at Ichapur. Soon after that he started feeling ill. He suddenly felt very light-headed and thought that he would fall. Sometime later, he felt a severe pain in the heart. He was in the car, on his way to Titagarh. The pain was excruciating, and he had never before experienced anything like it. He realized that the malady was severe this time. He was supposed to go to Rai Bahadur Taraknath Chatterjee's house, from where he was to proceed to a meeting. It was by then almost 9 p.m. and 2000–3000 people were waiting for him. He somehow reached Chatterjee's house, lay down and asked for a doctor. He was so unwell that he could hardly speak. He asked Sushil to ring up his house in Calcutta and convey the news without mentioning the seriousness of his condition. He told him to say that he would not be back home that night as he was not feeling well. Unable to ward off his eldest brother's probing questions, Sushil told him everything. There was quite a furore at home. Dr B.C. Roy and Dr Indu Madhab Basu, both prominent physicians, were informed.

There was a big commotion in Calcutta. All kinds of stories were floating around and somebody had even rung up a newspaper office to confirm whether he was dead or alive. A local doctor came over to treat him and gave him some medicines. The pain subsided a little, but he was still very weak. At about 11 p.m. all his brothers, namely Rama Prasad, Uma Prasad and Bama Prasad, with his boudi Tara Devi and Dr Basu arrived at Barrackpore. Dr Mookerjee, upon their advice, decided not to spend the night away from home. They drove slowly and reached home at about

1 a.m. He wrote in his diary that he was feeling very ill and had never felt so weak before.

The next day, all the doctors who visited the Mookerjee household told Dr Mookerjee that he should take complete rest if he wanted to survive. They said that if he heeded their advice he could still be saved. Otherwise, he might have to lead the life of a disabled person for as long as he survived. There was a great deal of arguing over what would be done about the elections. The doctors, especially Dr Roy, held that he should not do anything that would cause excitement and tension. The elections were scheduled to be held in early December. Elections or no elections, he would not be allowed to step out of the house for fifteen days. He had fallen ill on a Saturday. Many meetings had been scheduled for Sunday at Uttarpara, Serampore and so on. He just could not attend them. Nirmal Chandra Chatterjee, a prominent Mahasabha leader and father of Somnath Chatterjee, would have normally gone in his place, but he did not go either, because the week before, some Congress supporters had disrupted a meeting in Howrah and insulted him. Debendranath Mukherjee went to Serampore but did not face any trouble there. On hearing this, Chatterjee went to Uttarpara. It was not possible for Dr Mookerjee to do much, sitting in the house. He still attempted to do some work, but suddenly he had a relapse.

The doctors were furious. They said there was no point in being suicidal. They would not allow him to do any work. Judging from the symptoms that he had, plus his age, obesity, his food habits and the strain that he had taken during the last two days, according to Dr Shuvo Dutta, a leading cardiologist in Kolkata, it is highly probable that he had two consecutive attacks, either of myocardial infarction or of angina. In the first (generally known as a heart attack), a bit of the heart muscle dies as a result of being deprived of oxygen, and in the second there is acute chest pain for the same reason—and this deprivation of oxygen happens because the coronary artery or arteries supplying blood to the heart muscle get constricted due to deposition of fatty substances inside them and cannot deliver sufficient blood. Today, these symptoms would have called for emergency treatment, followed by total immobilization and probably angioplasty or bypass surgery. In 1945, however, cardiology, as we understand the term today, was in its infancy, not even a recognized discipline of medicine yet, and even the simple electrocardiogram (ECG) machine had not been invented. Symptomatic treatment, probably with digitalis syrup (extract of the foxglove flower), was the only known treatment, and 'change' of air—that is, change of location, preferably to a place with a salubrious climate—was considered one sure-fire panacea for many illnesses.

The other leaders were reluctant to take up the responsibility of electioneering. Dr Mookerjee told Nirmal Chatterjee and Deben Mukherjee that he would be very relieved if they took charge. It was not just a question of defeat or victory. He was then the president of the All-India Hindu Mahasabha. He himself was contesting the elections, and it would have been natural for him to hand over his responsibilities to someone else on account of his illness. But sadly enough, nobody came forward to bear the burden and he was weighed down by a sense of pessimism. He regretted in his diary that the ideals which he had striven for in the past few years were shattered in one blow. What treachery, deception and selfishness there was all around! He had never wanted, he wrote, to establish himself in the political arena. If people felt that he could be of no service to them, he did not wish to impose himself on them. At any rate, since he himself could not manage to carry on with the work in the state of health he was in, and no one else was willing to take charge, there was no other way out for him but to withdraw from the contest. He, of course, could not formally withdraw—by that time the last date for withdrawal must have been past. The inevitable defeat of himself and his party followed. His having put in such superhuman effort to manage the situation and prevent a bloodbath on 22 and 23 November and even having put himself at the risk of losing his life, made no difference, and he suffered the ultimate humiliation of an ignominious defeat in the hands of Sarat Bose's Congress and the nonentity called Nagendra Nath Mukhopadhyay.

His illness continued. In the meantime, Gandhi, Jawaharlal Nehru and Vallabhbhai Patel came to Calcutta. There was great excitement all around. Thousands of people assembled to see them. It was as if some floodgate had been opened. Nehru, Patel, Govind Ballabh Pant and Rafi Ahmed Kidwai came to see him. Many people pressed him to join the Congress. He regretted in his diary that they just did not understand that he could not join the Congress unless the differences between the Mahasabha and the Congress—mainly relating to appeasement of Muslims— were resolved. He was in politics for power all right, but with the intention of using the power according to his beliefs and convictions, something that would have been impossible if he had joined the Congress. He went on in his diary, 'Nobody seemed to understand my point! People usually tend to go with the tide and do whatever is the order of the day.'

He records in his diary that later in the month, his health had started improving marginally—meaning presumably that he did not have any recurrence of symptoms. Gandhi wrote to him in Hindi inquiring after his health and he wrote back in Bengali. Meanwhile, election results began pouring in from all over the country. Two features were clear: first, the Mahasabha did not win anywhere, and secondly, the Congress did not get even a single Muslim seat. The clear and simple conclusion was that the Hindus wanted the Congress and the Muslims the League. Yet the Congress would never term itself a Hindu organization or fight for Hindus' rights, and would persist in its grand delusion that it represented Hindus and Muslims alike. Meanwhile, Dr

Mookerjee observed, if the Mahasabha could manage to survive with the support of its genuine workers, it would certainly get a chance to forge ahead.

The terrible strain, the life-threatening illness, the pervasive frustration sapped his energy and were too much even for a person of Dr Mookerjee's calibre to bear. He wrote in his diary a month later, 'I had no longer the strength or desire to shoulder the responsibilities of a leader. I wanted to engage myself in such work that would keep me out of controversies and strife in the last few years of my life. I wanted to immerse myself in some constructive work to help the Hindus regain their lost glory.' There was a meeting with Patel, presumably because among the top Congress leaders he was the most sensitive to the problem of the Hindus; letters were exchanged, but no understanding could be reached. The Congress felt that the Mahasabha lacked popular support and the Central Assembly elections had proved this, so why would they want to work with the Mahasabha? Finally, Dr Mookerjee called a meeting of the All-India Hindu Mahasabha Working Committee in Calcutta. L.B. Bhopatkar was made the acting president in order to relieve him. It was decided that the Mahasabha would contest the elections according to its relative strength in the respective provinces.

In the meantime, he had also relinquished many of his duties in the university. Since 1924, for twenty-two years, he had worked tirelessly for the betterment of the university. Now he had withdrawn his name from the syndicate elections. Rama Prasad, his eldest brother, would replace him. He had also asked him to stand in his place in the assembly elections.

All this duty done, he proceeded for the 'change' that his doctors and his relatives had been so long pressing him for. And to where else but Madhupur, for which December–January was the best season! But before that he wanted to spend some time with his elder daughter Sabita and his granddaughter Manju (whom he called Didibhai). So he first went to Jamshedpur and thence to Madhupur. His son-in-law Nishith insisted that Sabita and Manju should accompany him and stay with him at least for some time at Madhupur. His mother, Jogomaya, together with a companion, and his younger son Debtosh also went and stayed for a fortnight. His elder son Anutosh used to visit him from time to time from Burnpur near Asansol where he was working with the Indian Iron and Steel Company.

Dr Mookerjee's month-long sojourn at Madhupur not only gave him a new lease of life but also proved invaluable for posterity. Especially so to his biographers including this one, since it is during this holiday that he made some of his most extensive and significant diary entries which proved later to be invaluable for an understanding of the politics of the times. He reached the place on Christmas day, 1945, and stayed there till 27 January 1946. He had taken his stenographer Baridbaran with him, and started writing on 5 January 1946. He started one account in English and two in Bengali. He succeeded in writing a fairly detailed account in English, of his experience as a minister in Bengal from 12 December 1941 to 20 November 1942. Of his two writings in Bengali, one is an account of his childhood till he was eight years old. In the other one he laid bare his heart and one feels that one sees the author face-to-face. Ashim Kumar Datta, the compiler of his diaries, comments that it may be that he was writing it as an aide-memoire, to be used on a future occasion when he would sit down to write a history for the public. Alas, that opportunity never came. Here he writes about his extreme loneliness—he had lost his wife when he was only thirty-one, and how he missed her. He talks about the anguish he felt when he saw the shameless egotism in some people while organizing the election campaign for the Mahasabha. Above all, he expresses his frustration to find that all his efforts to prevent the division of his dear motherland had so far come to nothing, and the country was on the way to that inevitable destiny. This account gives one an insight into his philosophy of life. He does not refer to any text or teacher, but one can see that the bedrock of his values lies in the doctrine of selfless work preached in the Bhagavad Gita.

Compared to the life that he had had during November–December 1945, the stay at Madhupur was truly restful and it rejuvenated him. It was also a phase that brought him close to his family. But it was not without its physically difficult times. His heart was apparently repairing itself, and he had shown wisdom in giving it the chance to do so. But there were ups and downs. More than once he has complained, in his diary, that he still was not feeling well. On the evening of 9 January he wrote in his Bengali diary:

[F]or the last two days I have been feeling unwell. I was fine for about eight days. Yesterday I had a transient pain in the morning, then again in the evening. The pain struck me as I was sitting on the bed, writing some letters. It lasted for about five minutes but for part of that time the pain was excruciating. I could not breathe at all. Why does it happen—is it gas? I eat very frugally and then have medicines for digestion too.

His uneasiness degenerated into something worse the next day, when he wrote:

Yesterday, I had to stop writing. The pain in my heart was very slight but suddenly I started shivering. This sort of thing has never happened before. I wrapped myself in a sheet and sat in the easy chair but I could not bear it any more and went to bed. I covered myself with sheets, blankets and a quilt. I wore woollen socks and took a hot water bag, but nothing helped. I called Dr Mazumdar and he diagnosed these symptoms as malaria. I have never before had malaria in spite of having travelled so much. There was no respite until 10.00 p.m. I did not feel like removing the blankets and the quilt. The fever subsided at around midnight, but I had a headache and my body ached all over throughout the night. I could not sleep till early morning. The doctor said that perhaps it had been caused by the high dose of Vitamin B injection. I was feeling very weak this morning. My head felt very heavy but I did not have fever. My appetite was poor. I lay in bed the whole day. The doctor came to see me twice. Yesterday, my pulse rate had gone up to eighty-five, but today it had come down to sixty-four. Now I am sitting at the table. The room is dark though there is moonlight outside. It is warmer today. I am quite comfortable today, but who knows how much longer I will have to suffer? Who knows what more lies in store for me?

In the opinion of Dr Shuvo Dutta, a leading present-day cardiologist of Kolkata, Dr Mookerjee's symptoms all suggest unstable angina. What he thought was 'gas' is one of the classic symptoms of such angina, and is very common among Bengalis because of their food habits.

But by 14 January, he recovered considerably, and wrote, 'I have been slightly better these last two days. I went out for a walk in the morning and in the evening too. My appetite has improved somewhat. The doctor sends me porridge every morning. A multi-course midday meal is sent to me from Jogesh Babu's house. Sweets are sent from Jnanbabu's residence. Every alternate day, I go to the doctor's house for dinner.' This recovery was not caused by any medication because no medication existed then. It was just his life force that pulled him out of his illness.

The idle days at Madhupur, where he spent a month from 25 December 1945 till 27 January 1946 not only helped him recover, but also brought out the reflective, introverted person in him. Having taken his stenographer along, he took to writing his diary again, which he had been doing in fits and starts over the last few years.

It is here, in a diary entry dated 4 January, that he penned a momentous statement of his belief that stands out as a direct antithesis of the prevailing (and still paid lip service to) Gandhian dogma of ahimsa, non-violence: 'Force must, in the last analysis, be met with force. An internal policy of non-resistance to armed violence would ultimately condemn any society to dissolution.'

Apparently, the statement stands quite out of context with the rest of the text in the diary entry, though very much in context considering the state of the country then. This was the first entry of the day, and in English, and the very next sentence in the diary entry in Bengali has nothing whatsoever to do with this. This seems to be in the nature of a revelation, something that hits one between one's eyes all of a sudden. Doubtless he had been thinking of the Hindu–Muslim face-off over the last few days, and it would have been plain as daylight that his defeat was the result of total polarization of the polity on Hindu–Muslim lines, something that every true patriot dreads. It must have disappointed and alarmed him further that the electorate, in the mood of 'winner takes all', had reposed their faith in the Congress, little realizing that the Congress would not lift a little finger to protect the Hindus from a Muslim onslaught, should such a thing take place, for fear of being dubbed 'anti-Muslim' or 'communal'. But just these thoughts could not have caused this revelation. He must have been able to see in his mind's eye, in a flash as it were, what was coming: the gradual hardening of attitude on the part of the Muslim League, the foretaste of victory on its tongue, and its final, diabolical gambits: 'Direct Action' or the Great Calcutta Killings, the Noakhali Carnage, the reaction in Bihar, and the eventual capitulation by the Congress, the acceptance of partition, the Punjab bloodbath.

This thought has again been echoed by him six days later. In a Bengali diary entry on 10 January, he wrote the unwritable and spoke the unspeakable:

> There could be no dispute if both groups [meaning Hindus and Muslims] worked unitedly to preserve the Indian culture and live amicably according to their respective beliefs. But the Hindus did not worry about how they would protect themselves if the Muslims became overzealous and attempted to dominate them. In that event, the Hindu–Muslim problem would never be solved without a *civil war* [emphasis added]. We did not want a civil war, but if the other party kept itself in readiness and we were caught off guard, then we would be the losers. The Congress had failed to solve the Hindu–Muslim problem, nor would it ever be able to do so. The problem could be solved either by a mutual understanding, a friendly reunion, or a trial of strength. If there was no compromise, the more powerful party would emerge victor. How could an organization, which was built on Hindu support, yet considered it a sin to uphold Hindu interests, fight another organization which was dedicated to establishing Muslim dominance? What could be more tragic than the fact that the Hindus failed to understand this simple truth despite their intellectual and financial resources? Islam had a singular spirit of unity and equality that Hinduism lacked. Differences along lines of caste, creed or religion kept one Hindu from empathizing with another. On the other hand, one Muslim invariably felt a bond with another, irrespective of where he was from, whether it was from another part of India or another part of the world.

These daring words appeared to be prophetic, as was proved by events in Bengal a mere seven months later. What Jinnah in fact waged by way of his 'Direct Action' in Calcutta on 16 August that very year, followed by the Noakhali Carnage of October, were nothing more or less than civil war. And he won that war, for he was prepared. The prize of his victory was his Pakistan.

Dr Mookerjee's reference to a civil war throws up interesting questions. What if there had indeed been a civil war? Could it have prevented Partition? If it could, should such a war have been waged? At least in one case it did prevent Partition, when Abraham Lincoln went to war and succeeded in keeping the United States united! There have been three partitions so far in the world on religious grounds—those of India into India and Pakistan, Palestine into Israel and West Bank/Gaza and Ireland into British-ruled, Protestant-majority Northern Ireland and Catholic-majority Eire or the Republic of Ireland. The first two, in either of which Islam was one of the religions involved, were followed and are still being followed by serious hostilities, degenerating sometimes to nothing less than all-out war between the partitioned countries. The third, which was between the largely Catholic Eire and largely Protestant Northern Ireland has been affected (particularly the latter) by severe religious strife until recently, though there has never been any serious hostility between Britain and Eire. In other words, Partition does not seem to have solved any problems. Considering the circumstances, would it have not been better to go for civil war, in which Hindus, who were against the partition, would definitely have won because of their overwhelming numbers? And the country would have stayed united!

But not all of Dr Mookerjee's thoughts were so analytical. In times of solitude and total quietness under a starlit sky, he was overwhelmed by the smallness of human efforts and felt himself to be merely a pawn in the hands of inexorable forces, and could find comfort only in total surrender to the Supreme. Consider the following:

Oh merciful God, let me glimpse You within me. I do not ask anything for myself. Only give me a place at Your feet. Lift

me up and take me in Your fold; give me the strength and the
yearning to invoke You . . . My mind yearns to see You but I am
trying my best to restrain it. I have realized the futility of this
world. Here today, gone tomorrow—this is the process of life.
Then why fuss over such trivial things? We are only travellers
in transit. What is the difference between us and beasts if we
spend the little time we have on this earth, steeped in a mire of
lust and greed. I have often observed the instinctual behaviour
of animals. If men, who have a soul and can recognize God,
forget everything and indulge in these base pursuits, what can
be more tragic?

Dr Mookerjee is here following his private religion, or his private
interpretation of Hinduism, which is largely *advaita-vada*, the
identity of the worshipper and the worshipped, invoking the God
within oneself, with shades of the Semitic religions which provide
for prayer to a singular God. Of course, in such religions there is
no scope of identifying oneself with God without blaspheming
seriously, but Hinduism is different. As explained in Chapter 1,
Hinduism has no bar to this kind of private interpretation or even
to symbiosis between two sets of beliefs in one's mind. But above
all, what shines through all this is the humanity of the man.

In the midst of all this Dr Mookerjee was swept off his feet
by his granddaughter Manju, his dear Didibhai, when she arrived
from Jamshedpur with her parents on 19 January. He could not
help admiring the way 'she had learnt to chew food with her
teeth—six in all' and observed that she had grown up to be 'a
lovely child, full of life . . . a bit choosy about people! She stared
hard at her two Didimonis' [her late grandmothers'] photographs,
picked them up, turned them over and caressed them.' And that
must have brought a tear to Dr Mookerjee's eyes, for he thought,
'I wish Sudha was here. How happy she would have been to see
her granddaughter!'

As he got better at Madhupur, he began to get restless too, and yearned for the busy world of politics. And the opportunity came soon enough, when it was announced that a British Parliamentary delegation sent by the British Prime Minister to visit India was coming to Calcutta. The delegation was led by Professor Robert Richards, earlier undersecretary of state for India. Then he received a telegram that the delegation had expressed the desire to see him, and he promptly gave them an appointment. And he left Madhupur for Calcutta on 27 January 1946 and arrived the same day, but not before bidding a touching adieu to Madhupur, mentioned earlier, 'Farewell Madhupur! I have spent one month here in this house . . . Let me end by expressing my gratitude to you, Madhupur, for whatever I have gained by my stay.'

8

The Great Calcutta
Killings and the Noakhali
Carnage, 1946

Meanwhile, another game was afoot in Bengal, the only province in India where the Muslim League held sway. Suhrawardy was made Premier of Bengal in 1946, having won an internal power struggle within the Muslim League, replacing Sir Nazimuddin. India was soon to see bestiality at a different level—called 'Direct Action' by Jinnah and his League, and the 'Great Calcutta Killings' by the rest of the world. Casey, the Australian Governor of Bengal, was replaced by Frederick Burrows, an ex-railway guard of the British Railways and a trade union leader, and he and Suhrawardy developed a very close relationship.

Although the programme of Direct Action was announced by Jinnah only in July 1946, he must have been planning it for a long time, because the run-up for this started much earlier, possibly sometime in late 1945, when Suhrawardy had proceeded to change the complexion of the Calcutta Police. Several posts were created in the police headquarters at Lalbazar, and Hindu officers-in-charge of the thanas (regional police stations) were transferred there, to be replaced by Muslim officers. The constables of the Calcutta Police were, as a rule, recruited according to what was known as the ABCD rule—which meant that they were all drawn from the districts of Arrah, Balia, Chhapra and Deoria of the Bhojpur region of UP and Bihar. They were all Hindus. Suhrawardy, with the help of Niaz Mohammed Khan, proceeded to Muslimize the Calcutta Police by importing ex-servicemen from western Punjab and the North Western Frontier Province. Why the Calcutta Police in particular? Because Calcutta must have already been secretly chosen by the Muslim League as the theatre of the bloodbath that had been scheduled for 16 August 1946, called Direct Action or the Great Calcutta Killings.

At the level of senior officers also, a significant change was made. A Muslim Imperial Police officer, and said to be a very communally partisan one at that, was posted as deputy commissioner (headquarters) of the Calcutta Police, a pivotal post that had hitherto been manned only by Britishers. Calcutta Police has two separate cadres of field-level police officers—investigative and non-investigative. The former, comprising sub-inspectors and inspectors, largely Bengali Hindu so far, had been systematically infiltrated by Muslim officers who were thereafter placed in charge of police stations. The non-investigative posts, mainly sergeants, were manned mostly by Anglo-Indians, and continued to be so.

Dr Mookerjee, though acutely aware of what was happening, was quite helpless in the matter. To begin with, he just did not have the support of most of the Hindus. His ignominious defeat by a nonentity of the Congress in the December 1945 elections to the Central Assembly has already been mentioned. He subsequently ran from the University constituency in 1946 and entered the Provincial Legislative Assembly. Unlike the Muslims who were solidly behind the Muslim League (113 out of 119 Muslim seats), the bulk of the Hindus supported the Congress which would never and did never take their side, even in the face of the grossest injustices perpetrated by the League government. A much smaller number supported the Mahasabha which was politically quite weak despite Dr Mookerjee's leadership. The Hindus, thus, as if by a collective suicidal will, short-changed themselves and the Muslims got the best of both worlds. Remember Dr Mookerjee's words of frustration, recorded in his diary and mentioned in the last chapter: 'How could the Congress, an organization which was built on Hindu support, yet considered it a sin to uphold Hindu interests, fight another organization like the League which was dedicated to establishing Muslim dominance?'

Cut to faraway London from Calcutta. In the first post-war British election, the Conservatives lost and Labourite Clement Attlee became the Prime Minister. Unlike his predecessor and successor Churchill, granting independence to India was very much on his mind—Churchill on the other hand had declared that he had not become His Majesty's Prime Minister to preside over the liquidation of the British Empire. One of Attlee's first steps regarding India was to send, early in 1946, an all-party parliamentary delegation to India led by professor Robert Richards, a member of the Labour Party and at one time (in 1924) undersecretary of state for India, to meet Indian leaders and convince them of the British desire for an early settlement of the Indian constitutional issue. It was this delegation that Dr Mookerjee hurried to meet when he left Madhupur on 27 January 1946, cutting short his restful stay which had given him a new lease of life.

Attlee followed this with dispatching a very high-ranking Cabinet Mission to India to negotiate the terms with the Congress and the Muslim League. The delegation consisted of Lord Pethick-Lawrence, the secretary of state for India, Sir Stafford Cripps of the 1942 Cripps Mission fame and then the chairman of the Board of Trade, and Viscount A.V. Alexander, the first lord of the admiralty. The Mission arrived in India on 23 March 1946 and held a number of meetings with different political parties, other organizations and selected individuals till May.

The discussions were principally with the Congress and the Muslim League, but they held discussions with the Hindu Mahasabha also, in which Dr Mookerjee was accompanied by L.B. Bhopatkar. They handed in a memorandum which urged that His Majesty's Government should immediately declare India free and independent, that the integrity and the indivisibility of the country should be maintained at any cost, and that partition would be economically unsound, disastrous, politically unwise and suicidal. The Mahasabha would not agree to any suggestion that Hindus and Muslims would be represented in the central government on the basis of equality. Dr Mookerjee stressed that the Mahasabha could not compromise on the Pakistan issue. His own idea, which he had put to Jinnah in 1943, was that representatives of the two communities should meet and that each should explain in what respect it expects protection from the other. The Mahasabha would be willing to concede the fullest measure of autonomy to the provinces and would give the minorities the maximum protection in respect of their religion, language and customs.

After hearing out all concerned parties, the Mission put forth a set of proposals, commonly known as the 'Grouping Plan', which fell short of partition of the country. The substance of the proposals was that the country would be constituted as a loose federal polity with residuary powers to the provinces, and the provinces would be classified into three groups, depending on their geographical location and the religious complexion of the population.

The Congress, somewhat readily, and the Muslim League, somewhat reluctantly, accepted the proposals. However, Jawaharlal Nehru, who was the president of the Congress at the time, in a press conference, held on 10 July in Bombay, resiled from this position and declared that the Congress would enter the Constituent Assembly 'completely unfettered by agreements and free to meet all situations as they arise'; and also, that grouping of provinces, as proposed by the mission, would not work. When further questioned as to whether this meant that the Cabinet Mission Plan could be modified, he replied emphatically that the Congress had agreed only to participate in the Constituent Assembly and regarded itself free to change or modify the Cabinet Mission Plan as it thought best. Consequent upon this, the Muslim League on 29 July withdrew their acceptance of the Cabinet Mission proposals and went back to their demand for Pakistan. Maulana Abul Kalam Azad, in his autobiography *India Wins Freedom*, has termed this act of Jawaharlal Nehru an 'astonishing statement' and one of those unfortunate events that changed the course of history.

Together with withdrawal of acceptance of the Cabinet Mission proposals, on 29 July the Muslim League adopted a resolution that 16 August 1946 will be a day of 'Direct Action' by the 'Muslim Nation' in support of Pakistan. No explanation was forthcoming as to what would constitute such 'Direct Action'. Jinnah declared, 'Today we bid goodbye to constitutional methods . . . today we have forged a pistol, and are in a position to use it.' When Jinnah was asked whether this 'Direct Action' was going to be violent or non-violent, his terse reply was, 'I am not going to discuss ethics.' In villages and towns across the country Muslim League volunteers raised the war cry, *'Ladke lenge Pakistan, lekar rahenge Pakistan* (We shall wrest Pakistan by force, we must get Pakistan).' Meanwhile, Jawaharlal Nehru tried to eat his words and work out a solution with Jinnah by presenting him with a fresh resolution of the Congress, reiterating its acceptance of the Cabinet Mission proposals. This time, however, Jinnah would not budge, and said that Nehru's statement on 10 July showed the 'real mind of the Congress'. Viceroy Wavell too asked Jawaharlal to call upon Jinnah at his house in Bombay and try to prevail upon him. Jawaharlal did so, and ran against a brick wall.

In fact, while on 15 August Jawaharlal was sitting with Jinnah at his house in Bombay, trying vainly to persuade him to withdraw the threat of Direct Action, Suhrawardy, the Muslim League premier of Bengal was applying the finishing touches to the plans for the morrow in Calcutta.

Meanwhile, Dr Mookerjee and his party, decimated in the 1945 elections, could do very little except watch this diabolical game from the wings. The party which had stolen the affection of the public from them, namely the Congress, was in an even worse predicament, helplessly watching the so-called nationalist Muslim support base wither away. A prominent Bengal Congress Muslim, Syed Nausher Ali, was subjected to considerable mental torture, with a demonstration in front of his house in the Park Circus area (an upper-class Muslim-majority area of Calcutta) every morning chanting, 'Down with Nausher Ali, enemy of Muslims.' One day, he was summarily driven out of the house with his family, and a signboard was hung in front of his house which said, 'Muslim League Party Office'. His peers could give him no protection and Nausher Ali had to withdraw from politics for all practical purposes. But the Congress, forever scared of hurting minority sentiments and with a view not to alienate their 'nationalist Muslim' support base (which by then had almost ceased to exist), kept silent.

Suhrawardy, meanwhile, was busy with the preparation of the killings. He declared a public holiday on Friday, 16 August. The Congress staged a walk out in the Bengal Legislative Assembly on 12 August in protest against declaring a public holiday in response to a call by a particular political party for hartal (general strike) without taking the assembly into confidence. On 15 August an adjournment motion demanding a debate on the same question was defeated in the Bengal Legislative Council (upper house of the provincial legislature).

Meanwhile, the broad game plan for that day had been carefully prepared and circulated among Muslims of the city, at least a substantial number of them, by word of mouth. The pro-League newspaper, *Dawn*, of Karachi on 16 August published an advertisement which gave a call to use of force as being the only way to achieve what the Muslims wanted. S.M. Usman, the mayor of Calcutta and the secretary of the Calcutta Muslim League, circulated a leaflet in Bangla which read,[1] '*Kafer! Toder dhongsher aar deri nei! Sarbik hotyakando ghotbe!* (Infidels! Your end is not far off! There will be a total massacre!)'. Another pro-League newspaper *Morning News* said in its editorial that hurting a Britisher was not only against the Bombay resolution of the League, it was also against the tenets of Islam—thus obliquely suggesting to its readers that hurting Hindus was quite permissible.

There were open and direct incitements to rioting by top Muslim League leaders. Liaquat Ali Khan told the Associated Press of America that Direct Action meant 'resorting to non-constitutional methods, and that can take any form and whatever form may suit the conditions under which we live . . . We cannot eliminate any method. Direct Action means any action against the law.' The supposedly gentle Nazimuddin made an announcement on 11 August, saying, 'Our plans have not yet been finalized. There are one hundred ways in which we can create difficulties, especially when we are not restricted to non-violence. The Muslim population of Bengal know very well what "Direct Action" would mean, and so we do not need to bother to give them any lead' (see below Dr Mookerjee's remarks on the subject in the Bengal Legislative Assembly after the riots). A pamphlet[2] circulated by S.M. Usman was, however, totally forthright, and read as follows, 'The call to the revolt comes to us from the *Qaid-e-Azam*. This is the policy for the nation of heroes [meaning Muslims] . . . The day for open fight, which is the greatest desire of the Muslim nation has arrived . . . by fighting you will go to heaven in this holy war . . . Let us all cry our victory to Pakistan, victory to the Muslim nation and victory to the army which has declared jihad.'

The Communist Party of India openly supported this call to 'Direct Action'. In their seminal work on the collaboration of the communists with the Muslim League in pre-independence India, titled 'The Sickle and the Crescent', Sunanda Sanyal and Soumya Basu have shown the extent to which this collaboration went. Several people, Hindu, Muslim and British, have given detailed, partly eyewitness, accounts of the shape 'Direct Action' took. Among them, in the opinion of this biographer, those of Ashok Mitra, ICS and Lieutenant General Sir Francis Tuker are particularly deserving of note and belief, principally because they were both high-ranking government officers, one civil and the other military, and had no reason to be biased. Ashok Mitra, despite being a Hindu, had taken extraordinary risks to drive through the city himself in order to take a Muslim colleague of his to the Medical College Hospital where the wife of the colleague was an inpatient. Apart from Mitra and Tuker, an American scholar called Richard D. Lambert of the University of Pennsylvania had extensively researched the riots and wrote one of the most credible accounts of it, which was made use of by Stanley Wolpert, the biographer of Jinnah, and Leonard Gordon, biographer of the Bose brothers, among others.

Among Muslim chroniclers, this author has come across the account given by Mizanur Rahaman, a literary person and a magazine editor from Dacca, Bangladesh, where the complicity of the League government was considerably watered down[3]—which is surprising, since Rahaman was anything but a supporter of the League. A contemporary historian, Joya Chatterji, has given a similar explanation, in which she has roundly placed the blame of the riots on Marwari businessmen of Calcutta. However, this view has been rubbished by three of her contemporaries, Amales Tripathi,[4] Bidyut Chakrabarty[5] and Partha Chatterjee,[6] the last of whom has remarked on her 'astonishingly naïve view' of things. Abul Mansur Ahmad, on the other hand, gives a different account altogether. He also says that the murder hysteria had been taken to such a pitch by the League leaders that he was once asked by a friend (ordinarily a sensible, humane person), 'How many . . . have you killed? All your love for Muslims seems to be just lip service'![7]

Suhrawardy is quoted by Stanley Wolpert as having said that he would see how the British could make Nehru rule Bengal. Direct Action Day would prove to be the first step towards the Muslim struggle for emancipation. He advised them to return home early and said that he had made all arrangements with the police and the military not to interfere. The last bit was ominous.

The people who had come to attend the meeting had also come prepared to kill and loot and were suitably armed with muskets, crowbars, huge daggers and swords, large pieces of stones, and of course, the Muslim League flag. They then spread out, howling their battle cries, '*Allaho Akbar* (God is Great)', '*Pakistan Zindabad, Muslim League Zindabad* (Long Live Pakistan, Long Live the Muslim League)', '*Lekar Rahenge Pakistan, Ladke Lenge Pakistan* (We shall surely take Pakistan, we shall take Pakistan by force)'.

The army boss of Calcutta, Lieutenant General Sir Francis Tuker, general officer commanding-in-chief of India's Eastern Army, and Mackinlay's superior, observed that Suhrawardy had been 'more critical than helpful during the riots'. Tuker also termed the killings 'unbridled savagery with homicidal maniacs let loose to kill and kill and maim and burn. The underworld was taking charge of the city . . . the police were not controlling it.' Major Livermore observed that Calcutta was the battlefield of a battle between mob rule and civilization and decency. When the 7th Worcesters and the Green Howards (both British troop formations) were called out, they found College Street ablaze and the few unburnt houses and shops completely sacked, in Amherst Street the litter of mass looting, in Upper Circular Road the rubble left by the firebugs, on Harrison Road the cries of wounded and terrorized residents.

The tide of the riots turned the next day, that is 18 August, and Suhrawardy's goons and compatriots (some of whom had nothing to do with the riots) began to get a taste of their own medicine. The lead was taken by the Hindu *kalwars* (ironmongers and scrap dealers) from Bihar and UP, who were then joined by Sikhs and Hindu Bengalis. Suhrawardy was probably not prepared for any reprisals from Hindus, whom he must have taken as followers of Gandhi, and therefore necessarily incapable of violence. It was primarily these reprisals that forced him to call a halt to the devilry that he had, by unspeakable abuse of state power, unleashed. Meanwhile the atrocities rolled on to 19 August. A senior Imperial Police officer told Ashok Mitra that on 18 August, Suhrawardy was found sitting forlornly at the Lalbazar control room table, mumbling to himself, 'My poor, innocent Muslims!'

No official estimate is available of how many people died in the killings. The number of dead is normally determined by a body count, and this would have been not only impossible but also misleading, because a large number of bodies had been thrown into the River Hooghly, or in the canals that pass through the city, or were pushed into manholes. It could be anything between 5000–25,000, with probably four times that number grievously injured.

Maulana Azad remarks[8] in his *India Wins Freedom*:

Sixteenth August 1946 was a black day not only for Calcutta, but for the whole of India. The turn that events had taken had made it almost impossible to expect a peaceful solution by agreement between the Congress and the Muslim League . . . This was one of the greatest tragedies of Indian history and I have to say with the deepest of regret that a large part of the responsibility for this development rests with Jawaharlal [Nehru].

Interestingly, he does not put the primary blame on Jinnah or Suhrawardy.

As an example of deliberate abuse of state power to cause mass murders it compares well in intensity, though not in breadth, with the Nazi Holocaust and the Killing Fields of Pol Pot in Cambodia. The killings were allowed to proceed unabated for the first day, and a part of the second, before Burrows decided to call the army in. The decision of Burrows that there was no need to bring in the army, or the orders of Brigadier Mackinlay, mentioned earlier, to confine British troops to their barracks, and Suhrawardy's assertion in his Maidan speech that the police or military would not interfere with what the Muslims did, unmistakably points to a nefarious conspiracy between Suhrawardy and Burrows, and of unspeakable cynicism. The British, as the sovereign power, were certainly guilty of standing by and amusing themselves while Suhrawardy's goons stabbed and torched.

Noakhali followed Calcutta in short order. The population of the district in the British days was overwhelmingly—more than 80 per cent—Muslim. Now it is around 95 per cent or so. The minority Hindus were largely schoolteachers, lawyers, moneylenders, doctors, shopkeepers, small businessmen, artisans and the like. A few were small zamindars. The Muslims were largely cultivators, most of them sharecroppers or landless agricultural labourers. On the whole, the Hindus were financially somewhat better off than the Muslims. It is this financial disparity that was made use of by the Hindu baiters in the run-up to the carnage. There was another disparity—not economic, not political, not social. It was the fact that Hindu women were considered prettier than their Muslim sisters, and being in the minority, and infidels at that, were considered fair game. This is not being facetious. Words to this effect were spoken by no less a person than Sir Frederick Burrows, Governor of Bengal, when the widespread incidents of molestation, kidnapping and rape of Hindu women in Noakhali were reported to him.[9]

Just as Suhrawardy was the brain behind the Great Calcutta Killings, it was a Muslim League leader called Ghulam Sarwar who plotted the carnage at Noakhali and parts of the adjoining district of Tipperah. Unlike in Calcutta, there was no fear in Noakhali of the tide of rioting turning against the Muslims. The overwhelming numerical majority of Muslims and the remoteness of the area would ensure that there would be no retaliation, nor any swift official action.

Just how provocative Ghulam Sarwar's speeches and exhortations to attack the Hindus were can be made out only by a person who understands the Noakhali dialect (a lot of Bengalis, even East Bengalis, do not). An English translation is given below, with the caveat that it can never capture the explosive potential and sheer poison of the words.

> Brothers, all the fine rice that you grow—who eats it?—Hindus!
> Brothers, all the fat bananas that you grow—who eats them?—Hindus!
> Brothers, when our women fall ill who paws and feels them all over?—Hindu doctors!
> Brothers, why are we Muslims thin and underfed?—because we do not get enough to eat!
> Brothers, why are the Hindus fat and greasy?—because they get all the best things to eat![10]

These are lies of course, however much one might want to see the struggle between the haves and have-nots in them. The 20 per cent Hindus of Noakhali could never eat up even a quarter of the rice and bananas that the 80 per cent Muslims grew. The bulk of the Hindus, who were mostly either in the white-collar professions or small tradesmen or artisans could be only marginally better off than their Muslim brethren. The third allegation is particularly provocative, for obvious reasons.

The full moon night of Kojagari Lokkhi (Lakshmi) Puja is the first full moon after Durga Puja, usually in October. On this night, Bengali Hindus traditionally worship Lakshmi, the goddess of wealth. Sarwar and other League leaders chose this day to start their pogrom. They had already created the necessary atmosphere by moving from village to village, making inflammatory speeches to the congregations at the daily prayers, describing in vivid detail what the Hindus had done to the Muslims during the Calcutta Killings, duly skipping the other part. There were qualitative differences with the Calcutta Killings. In Calcutta, the intention of the marauders appeared to be primarily to loot and kill, or at least maim. In Noakhali the objective seemed to be to kill selectively, but mainly to rape and convert forcibly and to desecrate Hindu places of worship.

The Noakhali Carnage came to be widely known because of Mahatma Gandhi's famous visit to the district. Gandhi arrived at Choumuhani on 7 November 1946, almost a month after the carnage began and stayed in Noakhali till February 1947. A number of leaders accompanied Gandhi, others came along to join him. Among the prominent people who congregated in remote Noakhali were Acharya J.B. Kripalani and his wife (and a prominent member of Congress in her own right) Sucheta, Sarat Chandra Bose, Surendra Mohan Ghosh, Muriel Lister, A.V. Thakkar Bapa, Ashoka Gupta, Nellie Sengupta and others. Jawaharlal Nehru and Ram Manohar Lohia had also visited the district and rendered themselves memorable by certain utterances that Nehru made and Lohia quoted. That comes a little later.

Another person who accompanied Gandhiji was Louis Fischer, an American journalist who wrote a biography of Gandhi. He describes the Noakhali Carnage thus:

> Mr Arthur Henderson told the House of Commons on Nov 4, 1946 that the dead in Noakhali and contiguous Tipperah districts had not yet been counted, but will, according to estimates, be low in the three figures category. The Bengal government put the number of casualties at 218 . . . In Tipperah 9,895 persons were forcibly converted to Islam; in Noakhali inexact data suggested that the number of converts was greater.[11]

What did Dr Mookerjee do to prevent this holocaust, and what did he do during the holocaust? To answer the last question first, while the riots were raging, human beings had lowered themselves to such a level of bestiality that there was nothing to do except shoot at the marauders—and this is precisely what the British had refused to do, and the Muslim League had disabled the state machinery from doing. Dr Anil Chandra Banerjee, an eminent historian, has remarked in a short monograph titled, 'A Phase in the Life of Dr Mookerjee, 1937–46', that: 'It was not possible for an individual, however able and eminent, to fight effectively against an organization (namely the Muslim League) which controlled the Ministry and was supported by the Governor and the British Civilians . . . It is impossible to recall now the atmosphere of mistrust, neurosis and threats of inter-racial and inter-communal strife which enveloped the country in those days.' This is pretty much in line with the utterance of Abul Mansur Ahmad's friend who asked him how many Hindus he had killed.

The situation the country was facing, in short, was like this: on the one hand, the party representing practically all the Muslims of the country was resolutely bent on achieving Pakistan by bloodshed

Sitting (L to R): Debtosh (Dr Mookerjee's younger son), Arati (younger daughter), Tara Devi (wife of Rama Prasad, his elder brother), Sabita (elder daughter), Chittatosh (Rama Prasad's youngest son)
Middle row (L to R): Uma Prasad (Dr Mookerjee's third brother), Rama Prasad, Dr Mookerjee, Lalit Kumar Chatterjee (Tara Devi's father)
Top row (L to R): Anutosh (Dr Mookerjee's elder son), Manotosh (Rama Prasad's eldest son), Shibtosh (Rama Prasad's second son)

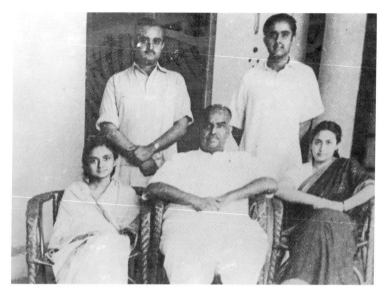

Sitting (L to R): Sabita, Dr Mookerjee, Arati
Standing (L to R): Anutosh, Debtosh

Dr Mookerjee with his lifelong friend Dr Sarvepalli Radhakrishnan,
holding a replica of the Sanchi Stupa

Huseyn S. Suhrawardy

Liaquat Ali Khan

Dr Mookerjee at Howrah station after resigning from the cabinet

The sub-jail where Dr Mookerjee was incarcerated

His funeral procession in Calcutta

and mayhem. On the other hand, the party representing almost all the Hindus of the country was caught in its own web of delusion, equivocation and fear of losing the support (which did not exist) of Muslims. In such circumstances, Dr Mookerjee, belonging to a fringe party such as the Hindu Mahasabha, could do nothing to prevent or stop the holocaust, for the simple reason that the bulk of the Hindus of Bengal had chosen not to vote for his party—and thereby brought disaster on themselves. All that he could do was to provide relief to the victims and lambast the perpetrators of the holocaust with words. And he did both in ample measure.

A no-confidence motion was moved (and duly defeated) in the Bengal Legislative Assembly after the killings. In the debate that followed, he again made a memorable speech, lambasting Suhrawardy and his cohorts for their open incitement to mass murder, at the same time emphasizing the irresponsible self-centredness exhibited by the resident whites (then called Europeans) of the city. Excerpts from his speech:[12]

Mr Speaker Sir, since yesterday we have been discussing the motion of no-confidence under circumstances which perhaps have no parallel in the deliberations of any Legislature in any part of the civilised world. What happened in Calcutta is perhaps without a parallel in modern history. St Bartholomew's Day[13] of which history records some grim events of murder and butchery pales into insignificance compared to the brutalities that were committed in the streets, lanes and bye-lanes of this first city of British India . . . What did actually the Cabinet Mission do? The Muslim League, the spoilt and pampered child of the British Imperialists for the last thirty years, was disowned for the first time by the British Labour Government . . . [Loud noise from the Government benches] . . . When Mr Jinnah was confronted at a press conference in Bombay on the 31st

July and was asked whether direct action meant violence
or non-violence, his cryptic reply was 'I am not going to
discuss ethics'. [The Hon. Mr Mohammed Ali: Good.] But
Khwaja Nazimuddin was not so good. He came out very
bluntly in Bengal and said that Muslims did not believe in
non-violence at all. Now Sir, speeches like these were made
by responsible League leaders . . . All this was followed by
a series of articles and statements which appeared in the
columns of Newspapers—the *Morning News*, the *Star of
India* and the *Azad*. Sir, there is one point I would like to
say with regard to the Britishers in this house. My friends
are remaining neutral. I cannot understand this attitude at
all. If the Ministry was right [then] support them, and if the
Ministry was wrong you should say so boldly and not remain
neutral. Merely sitting on the fence shows signs of abject
impotence. [Laughter]. My friend Mr Gladding [a leader of
the European group in the house] says luckily none of his
people were injured. It is true Sir, but that is a statement
that makes me extremely sorry. If a single Britisher, man, or
woman, or a child had been struck, they would have thrown
the Ministry out of office without hesitation but because no
Britisher was touched they can take an impartial and neutral
view! . . . It is therefore vitally necessary that this false and
foolish idea of Pakistan or Islamic rule has to be banished for
ever from your head. In Bengal we have got to live together.

But of course, reality turned out to be quite different. Pakistan
was born, to be broken up a quarter of a century later. In Hindu-
majority West Bengal, Hindus and Muslims learnt to live together,
as Dr Mookerjee had wanted. Muslim-majority East Bengal,
however, was a different story altogether.

Dr Mookerjee's role in Noakhali was, however, qualitatively
different, principally because of the huge number of rapes,

molestations and other forms of brutalization committed by the local Muslim men on Hindu women. This was one time when Dr Mookerjee came out not as an educationist, nor as a politician, but as a social reformer. The social custom of Bengali Hindus of the times had it that anyone who had been forced to eat beef would cease to be a Hindu. Of the various suicidal traits that Hindu society has had over the ages, this was one of the worst, and one that caused the thinning of its ranks. Likewise, any Hindu woman, who had been so much as touched by a Muslim, quite against her will, would lose her position in Hindu society, and either would have to become a Muslim or go into prostitution or commit suicide. It is this trait that was taken advantage of by Sarwar's goons. This is the state in which their rescuers, such as Sucheta Kripalani and Ashoka Gupta found them. When told that they had come to protect them, the Hindus would say with immeasurable sadness and resignation that it was no use, they were no longer Hindus, no Hindu would drink water touched by them.

It is this state of affairs that Dr Mookerjee set about to correct, by radically altering the dicta by which society had run its suicidal course so far. He approached the Ramakrishna Math and Mission, established by Swami Vivekananda, who were already doing relief work in the area and proposed that as one of the guardians of the Hindu religion they ought to come forward in this regard. The Ramakrishna Mission readily agreed and a booklet was published under their auspices under the signature of Swami Madhavananda, general secretary of the Mission. The booklet also contained endorsements by pandits of leading Hindu religious schools, such as those of the Nabadwip Samaj, Bhattapalli Samaj, Bakla Samaj, Kotalipara Samaj, Bikrampur Samaj and other religious luminaries such as Mahamahopadhyay Vidhushekhar Shastri and Bijan Kumar Mukherjea, a judge of the Calcutta High Court and president of the Sanskrit Samaj.

Dr Mookerjee also got leading Sanskrit scholars and religious gurus from all over India to issue dicta to the effect that none of these Hindus should consider themselves converted, nor should the women consider themselves violated. Among these scholars and gurus were the Shankaracharya of Kanchi Kamakoti Peetham, Jagadguru Swami Yogeshwar Ananda Tirtha of Goverdhan Math, Puri, Kashi (Benares), Pandit Sabha and the like. All these dicta were appended to the discourse by Swami Madhavananda and included in the booklet.

Dr Mookerjee also toured the affected areas of Noakhali and Tipperah districts and made a statement[14] in Bangla which is demonstrative of the pain he felt. A freely translated version of the same is given below.

What happened in Noakhali and Tipperah have certain features which have no parallels in the history of communal riots in India. The carnage at Noakhali was, of course, not a communal riot in any sense. It was a planned and concerted attack by the majority on the minority [the name for this in eastern Europe, when practised against the Jews, was 'pogrom']. The central purpose of this attack was to effect mass looting, conversion and total desecration of Hindu temples and deities. Killing was mainly for the influential Hindus and for those who resisted the rampage. Rape and kidnapping of Hindu women was an essential part of the plan . . . It is not a fact that this pogrom was the act of a few hoodlums or that they had all come from somewhere far away. Practically all the atrocities were committed by local Muslims and the Muslim population of the district was generally sympathetic to what they were doing. There were a few exceptions among the Muslims who had managed to save Hindu lives. Their number is negligible. The Hindus who had been saved in this manner but who had not been able to run away have all been forcibly converted. Those who have run away have been looted of all their belongings. That such a carnage was in the offing had been brought to the notice of the district administration repeatedly and well in time, but the administration took no steps against the persons who were inciting hatred . . . Thousands of people have run away from their homes with only the clothes on their backs. They are now housed at camps at Comilla, Chandpur, Agartala and a few other places. The total number of such destitutes would be somewhere between 50,000 and 75,000.

Apart from these people another 50,000 or so are still marooned in areas where the administration has no say. These people need to be rescued immediately. They have all been forcibly converted. Their belongings have been looted, their spirit is broken. They are hardly human beings any more. Their names have been changed, their women have been ravished. They are being forced to wear Muslim clothes. The men have to attend mosques. The women are given religious instruction at home by the Islamic religious leaders. All steps are being taken to ensure that they are totally cut off from their moorings and made to surrender completely to their tormentors.

They have lost the courage to even protest. They dare not meet any Hindus from outside who come to visit them unless they are with armed guards. Handbills are being printed in the names of influential Hindus in both their Hindu and Muslim names which say that they have willingly embraced Islam. They are being forced to write to the subdivisional officers to that effect. They can leave their villages only with the written permission of the local Muslim leaders. A few of them managed to meet me at Choumuhani near Noakhali and told their heart-rending tales.

The immediate task at hand is to rescue the minorities who are still marooned, and completely in the clutches of the majority community. Until recently the rioters had kept the villages inaccessible by cutting off the means of communication. This has now partially been set right by the military, but just access is not enough. Our volunteers will have to visit the villages to restore the morale and confidence of the thousands of Hindus . . .

I do not accept that so many brothers and sisters of ours who had been forced out of the Hindu fold have left that fold. They were born Hindus, they are still Hindus, and they shall die Hindus. I have said this to all and sundry: there cannot be any question of any *prayashchitta* (atonement for sins)[15] for them to come back to the Hindu fold. There shall be absolutely no talk of any prayashchitta.

Any woman rescued from a disturbed area and found to have been forcibly married to a Muslim shall go back to her family. All unmarried women and girls should be given in marriage as far as possible. Hindu society must get out of this horror with a clear sight and a view of the future. Else, its future is dark . . .

In this hour of its peril Hindu society will have to realize something very important: it must stand unified, or else it will perish. It is perhaps God's will that from this destruction the reawakening of Hindus will begin.

We are not to forget, at this hour of darkness, that we are 30 million Hindus living in Bengal. If we organize ourselves, and if at least some of us dare to brave all odds with resolution and without fear then we shall be able to vanquish our enemies and restore our rightful position in our motherland.

After returning to Calcutta from Noakhali, Dr Mookerjee formed a volunteer group called the Hindusthan National Guard. At this time, a similar group called the Muslim National Guards was already in existence, and among its tasks was to threaten anti-

League Muslims into capitulation. Today the 'secular' brigade would lose no time in dubbing the setting up of such a group as sheer fascism, or worse, but in the embattled, League-ruled, riot-stricken Calcutta of 1946 this worked wonders in instilling confidence among Hindus. Also, apart from touring the districts of Noakhali and Tipperah, restoring the confidence and morale of the Hindus, and embarking on his memorable task of social reform, Dr Mookerjee did the only other thing he could do and he was good at: he horsewhipped Suhrawardy's government on the floor of the council. Parts of the speech:[16]

> What has happened in Noakhali and Chandpur is without a parallel in the history of any civilised Government. My charge, Sir, is that not only have the people of Noakhali and Chandpur who belong to the majority community failed to give the protection that was due from them to the minority community and oppressed it . . . all this could have been stopped . . . my demand before the Government is that the Government should follow strictly the principles which have been laid down by the All-India Working Committee of the Muslim League with regard to the protection of the Muslim minority . . .

While discussing Noakhali it might be of profit to compare Gandhi and Dr Mookerjee's response to the carnage. Gandhi stayed away from Calcutta after Direct Action, but visited Noakhali shortly afterwards, in November 1946, and stayed there till February 1947. He did not make public statements condemning either holocaust, as Dr Mookerjee did. Gandhi's trip to Noakhali brought the obscure area to the front page of every newspaper of the country, and indeed to the attention of the world. Gandhi's mission apparently was to restore confidence in the Hindus so that they could come back to their villages and his method was abiding, endless love for one's fellow men. He chalked up a very punishing schedule for himself in visiting remote villages to hold prayer meetings there and kept it, moving over the very difficult terrain on foot at an incredible speed from strangely named hamlets like Toomchar and Qazirkhil to Atakhora and Lamchar. He had told Ashoka Gupta, one of the people who had come forward to assist him, and others at the very beginning of their project: 'Bear no ill will towards anyone. Work without fear, mix intimately with the villagers. Success will come your way only if you remain completely fearless, stay on the path of truth, inspire confidence in the weak. The rioters will respect you only when they see true fearlessness in you, not any fake bravado.'

According to Louis Fischer, the American journalist who accompanied Gandhi in Noakhali, his journey was a pilgrimage of penance, in which the pilgrim wears no shoes. Hostile elements, obviously Muslim Leaguers, strewed broken glass, brambles and filth in his path. He was once sitting on the floor of a hut in the midst of Muslims and discoursing on the beauties of non-violence.[17]

Gandhi, it must be acknowledged, had totally failed to achieve his central purpose of getting the Hindus back to their villages where they would live happily ever after in perfect harmony with the majority community, the Muslims. This just did not happen, the good intentions and deeds of a number, not very large, of sensible Muslims notwithstanding. The historian Mushirul Hasan has remarked, 'Never before did so earnest an effort achieve so little.' Today, in 2010, sixty-three years after Partition, and thirty-nine years after the formation of independent Bangladesh, there are very few Hindus (around 3 per cent, down from 18 per cent in 1946) in what used to be the district of Noakhali in British India. The proportion of Hindus in the whole of Bangladesh is currently around 9 per cent, down from 29 per cent in 1947.

An interesting sidelight of Noakhali was something Nehru said to Ram Manohar Lohia by way of a private conversation while visiting the place during Gandhi's stay there. To quote Lohia,[18] 'Mr Nehru spoke of the water, slime, bush and tree that he found everywhere in East Bengal. He said that that was not the India he or I knew and wanted with some vehemence to cut East Bengal away from the mainland of India. That was an extraordinary observation.' As for Lohia's own view, he has said,[19] 'I found the gay laughter of East Bengal women unparalleled in all the world.'

Did Gandhi understand what people like Jinnah, Suhrawardy and Sarwar were trying to do through the Great Calcutta Killings and the Noakhali Carnage? It is difficult to imagine that a person like Gandhi, with his razor-sharp intelligence and after a lifetime in politics, did not—but if he did, he never gave anyone any indication. What they were trying to do was to wage a civil war. And it did not end with Calcutta and Noakhali. What happened in Punjab in the wake of Partition and later in erstwhile East Pakistan in 1950, 1964 and 1971 were nothing less than a civil war. Worse still, an inconclusive variant of a civil war is still in progress in Kashmir, and continually spills over to mainstream India in the form of terrorism, like 26/11 in Mumbai.

As the succeeding seventy years would show, Partition did not solve a single problem, neither for India, nor for Pakistan, neither for Hindus nor for Muslims. On the other hand, it created insurmountable problems for both countries and communities. India has somehow muddled through these problems, remained one, and prospered, but Pakistan has broken up. It is today acknowledged to be a failed state, and Bangladesh used to be called an international basket case, though lately it has shown some encouraging signs of recovery. In fact, Mountbatten knew beforehand that it was going to be a disaster. He wrote in his diary,[20] 'Partition is sheer madness, and no one would ever induce me to agree to it were it not for this fantastic communal madness that has seized everybody and leaves no other course open. The responsibility for this mad decision must be placed squarely on

Indian shoulders in the eyes of the world, for one day they will bitterly regret the decision they are about to make.'

A look at the dramatis personae on the two sides in this civil war and another one that happened nearly a century earlier between the American north and south, also on the question of partition, reveals interesting facts. Gandhi conceded partition, Jinnah emerged victorious with his Pakistan. Lincoln resisted partition, went to civil war and emerged victorious too, with his United States intact. Jinnah was suffering from incurable tuberculosis at the time of Partition and died a natural death about a year later, but his second-in-command Liaquat Ali Khan was assassinated. So was Gandhi, so was Lincoln. And so, in all probability, was Dr Mookerjee, however much his death is sought to be passed off as natural (see Chapter 15).

Now as to the civil war: recall what Dr Mookerjee had written in his diary (in Bengali), on 10 January 1946 while convalescing at Madhupur (see Chapter 15):

> If Hindus and Muslims unitedly try to maintain Indian culture and traditions, and live side by side according to their own beliefs then there should be no problem. But if Muslims show overmuch devotion to their own religion and try to dominate the Hindus, then should the Hindus not think how they can defend themselves? *The Hindu–Muslim problem will not be solved without a Civil War* [emphasis added]. We do not want a Civil War—but if the other side prepare themselves for it, and we do not do so, we shall lose the war.

Earlier, on 4 January he wrote (in English), 'Force must, in the last analysis, be met with force. An internal policy of non-resistance to armed violence would eventually condemn any society to dissolution.'

The sheer sagacity, the outstanding perspicacity of the man shines through. These words, it must be remembered, were written when no Hindu believed that the country would be partitioned, when neither the Great Calcutta Killings nor the Noakhali Carnage had taken place. Nobody listened to him. His own party, the Hindu Mahasabha, had been decimated in the elections, and Hindu consciousness in the country was dominated by the Congress led by Gandhi. The Hindus listened to what the Congress told them and the result is today well known. According to a saying attributed to John Maynard Keynes, human beings will do the sensible thing, but only after all alternatives have been exhausted.

9

The Architect of
West Bengal, 1947

The city of Calcutta, now known as Kolkata, is the capital of the Indian state of West Bengal and the third largest metropolitan centre in India today. Till 1911, it was the capital of India, and at the time of Independence, it was the first city of the country, the second city in the British Empire. But for Dr Mookerjee, the city would have begun its journey post 1947 as the capital, not of West Bengal but either of the independent sovereign state of Bengal or of East Pakistan. Then, in the first case in all probability, very soon united sovereign Bengal would either have merged into Pakistan or declared itself an Islamic Republic, and the non-Muslims of that Republic would have been consigned to hell, or something pretty near it, as the bulk of the East Pakistani Hindus were (see Chapter 11). It was because of Dr Mookerjee that today it is part of India, and the capital of a state where its 73 per cent Hindus and 27 per cent Muslims live holding their heads high and in reasonable amity.

By the early 1940s, Jinnah had completely polarized the Muslims in the name of religion. According to the eminent historian R.C. Majumdar:[1]

His [Jinnah's] clarion call to the Muslims went home and changed the Muslim political outlook almost overnight. He touched the chord of religious feelings of Muslims which have always proved a potent factor in Muslim politics. The Muslim clergies in the countryside were soon up in arms against the Congress propagandists. The Congress made frantic attacks to counteract Jinnah's propaganda and passed resolutions guaranteeing full rights to the minorities, assuring them of the widest possible scope for developing in the fullest measure their political, economic and cultural life . . . for the common good and the advancement of the people of India. But all these fell on deaf ears.

Little by little, Jinnah's Pakistan had taken shape in his mind. When in 1933 Rahmat Ali in Cambridge, England, conceived Pakistan, he had just Punjab, the North-West Frontier Province, British Balochistan (the word 'Afghan' wrapping up the two) and Kashmir in mind, with which he had coined the acronym 'PAKistan', which also meant 'the land of the pure'. It was the vaguest of thoughts, and according to Lapierre and Collins, the authors of the bestseller *Freedom at Midnight*, was pooh-poohed by Jinnah as 'an impossible dream'. When Jinnah got the Pakistan Resolution passed in Lahore in 1940, he did not have any idea what it would consist of—but by that time the existence of a Muslim League government in Muslim-majority Bengal (thanks to the 1937 gaffe by the Congress of not forming a coalition with Haq) had definitely put Bengal within the ambit of his dreams. Then, while he had passed through the stages of demanding a 40-mile-wide corridor linking East and West Pakistan, cribbing about a 'moth-eaten Pakistan', and demanding the whole of Bengal and Assam to be included in East Pakistan, he and his sidekick Suhrawardy had launched Direct Action, in which an estimated 17,000 people had died within four days in Calcutta.

As it appeared in retrospect, Direct Action had several objectives. The primary objective, of course, was to prove that free, united India was an impossibility, by showing the Congress and the British that all the Muslims were with the League, and all that the Muslims were capable of, if pushed to the wall. A second objective was to ensure that the prize catch, Calcutta, had to be included in Pakistan. How was it to be done in a city where some 70 per cent of the population was Hindu and which was surrounded by a predominantly Hindu countryside? Of course, if the whole of Bengal was to become part of Pakistan then there would be no problem, but there was no certainty of that. One way was to scare the Hindus into leaving the city and that seems to have been one of the objectives behind launching the killings. Possibly, this idea had come from observing the way Bengali Hindus had fled the city after a couple of Japanese bombs dropped on Bengal.

What people like Jinnah and Suhrawardy had in effect done was to wage a civil war. Also, Lord Mountbatten told Collins and Lapierre that his aide George Abell had told him in early 1947 that the country was heading for a civil war. This civil war is exactly what Dr Mookerjee, with his remarkable political foresight, had predicted some eight months back, in a diary entry dated 10 January 1946 (as explained in the last chapter), when none of these carnages were anywhere on the horizon.

The plan of Suhrawardy and Jinnah, of course, worked only partly. India was eventually divided, but in Calcutta, not only did the Hindus offer resistance, but they also fought back with great vigour. As a result, more Muslims died in the fight and Hindus could not be scared into fleeing the city. The Noakhali Carnage, in a district that was 80 per cent Muslim, was only staged with the intention of furthering the political prospects of Ghulam Sarwar. Apart from killing a few thousand, raping a few thousand more Hindu women and forcibly converting more than a lakh Hindus (practically all of whom were reconverted to Hinduism), the carnage served no purpose—on the other hand, it brought on, by way of retaliation, the Bihar pogrom.

Then Suhrawardy, with a few other Muslim Leaguers, hatched a novel scheme. Suhrawardy would claim to be an ardent Bengali first, then a Muslim, and with a few gullible Hindu associates clamour for a 'sovereign independent undivided Bengal'. He would shout from the rooftops that Bengal and Bengalis were one, no matter what religion they followed, and they just could not be divided. He would, of course, have to sweep under the carpet the fact that only a few months ago he had tried mass murder on fellow Bengalis who happened to be Hindu. If he managed to get independent Bengal, with Calcutta of course, the Muslims would always have the power to decide policy because of their numerical superiority. After that, joining Pakistan (if he preferred that it remained sovereign) would merely be a matter of time. In fact, Suhrawardy had this gambit up his sleeve quite early, even before his Direct Action was launched. In a very significant public statement on 9 August 1946, he threatened to declare Bengal's complete independence from the Centre which the Hindu press interpreted as a threat to 'Pakistanize' the whole of Bengal forthwith. His personal focus was all along very strongly on Calcutta, for a variety of reasons, ranging from his West Bengali origin to his love for the city that had given him so many pleasures, not excluding those of the flesh. However, there are strong grounds to believe that he allegedly owned a huge lot of *benami*[2] property in the city. This is the reason why the person who had fought so hard for Pakistan was not in Dacca or Karachi on 14 August 1947, but in Calcutta, hanging on to the tail of Mahatma Gandhi's shawl for dear life, not leaving the city. He was trying to dispose of the property before going to Pakistan, and he eventually moved only in 1948.

Dr Mookerjee, who had so long campaigned so indefatigably to prevent the partition of the country, by this time realized that that dreaded partition was inevitable, a certainty. He had no doubt in his mind that if the whole of Bengal went to Pakistan then the condition of the 47 per cent Hindus of the undivided province would be worse than miserable (as was proved to be true from the treatment the Hindus of East Pakistan got—see Chapter 11). He therefore decided to make partition of the province a necessary corollary to partition of the country, presumably following the ancient Sanskrit maxim, *sarvanashe samutpanne ardham tyajati panditah* (when total disaster is imminent, a wise man relinquishes half). He therefore started mobilizing Bengali Hindus across party lines in support of partition of the province.

The partition movement was already well under way before the end of 1946, with the establishment of the 'Bengal Partition League'. Its declared object was to demand a separate province to safeguard Hindu interests in the Hindu-majority districts of western Bengal. The promoters of the Bengal Partition League were the Hindu bhadralok, who were determined to be once again masters in their own house and formed the core of the movement. In the months that followed the Calcutta Killings, Bengali Hindus of Calcutta and the surrounding districts were mobilized by being asked not to forget Direct Action Day, and demand partition of the province to create a separate 'West Bengal Province' within the independent Indian federation to save them from the unacceptable humiliations of living under Muslim raj. Zamindars, professionals, respectable white-collar clerks and business groups dominated the movement, and the petitions were addressed to either Congress President J.B. Kripalani or sent to Dr Mookerjee and the Mahasabha. After giving him a humiliating election defeat less than two years back, the Bengali Hindus suddenly realized who their best hope for emancipation from League rule was.

As soon as Dr Mookerjee realized that the only way of saving Bengali Hindus from certain and sure annihilation under perpetual Muslim rule was to divide Bengal, he put in all his resources to educate and mobilize public opinion accordingly. As this move gained momentum, there was criticism that the creation of the new province would support the cause of Pakistan. He replied by issuing a detailed statement on 9 March 1947. In this, he asserted that the move was meant to save one area of Bengal from Pakistan, which was repugnant in any shape or form, and not to support its cause. Referring to the criticism that his scheme would be stoutly opposed by the Muslim League, he said that he expected that because if the scheme succeeded 'Eastern Pakistan would virtually finish'. It was all the more reason why all Hindus in Bengal should look at this great issue with complete realism instead of emotion and stand united. He concluded his momentous statement with an appeal to the Congress party in Bengal to support his move in the wider interest of nationalist Bengal and India.

Dr Mookerjee's well-reasoned and forceful advocacy of the scheme for partition of Bengal succeeded in winning many Congressmen over to his side. At a meeting in Delhi on 9 March 1947, Bengali Hindu members of the Central Assembly adopted, with the approval of N.C. Chatterjee of the Mahasabha and General A.C. Chatterji of the INA, a resolution demanding partition. This was followed by a well-attended two-day conference of Hindu representatives from all parts of Bengal that started in Calcutta on 15 March 1947 under the auspices of the Bengal Provincial Hindu Mahasabha with Dr Mookerjee as president. The large number of invitees, apart from the Mahasabha members, included prominent persons like Lord Sinha,[3] Dr R.C. Majumdar,[4] Dr Suniti Kumar Chatterji,[5] Bhabatosh Ghatak, Iswardas Jalan[6] and Hemendra Prasad Ghosh.[7] The conference unanimously resolved that a separate province must be created comprising the Hindu-majority areas in Bengal and appointed a committee to frame a memorandum to be placed before the next scheduled conference.

In a statement on 19 March Dr Mookerjee asserted that their current proposal for Hindu Bengal was aimed at saving Bengali Hindus and also the cause of nationalism, which was their lifeblood. It had absolutely no similarity to Curzon's Partition Plan of 1905 that was aimed at giving a death blow to the 'seditionist' Bengali Hindus. Even then, Hindu (Congress) opinion was very divided. On the one hand, on 10 March Nehru was telling Wavell in private[8] that though 'the Cabinet Mission Plan was the best solution if it could be carried through, the only real alternative was the partition of the Punjab and Bengal'. On the other hand, Sarat Bose condemned and Gandhiji did not approve of the Bengal partition movement, though he did not seem to have very strong feelings on the matter, and had many other things to worry about. Bose had lost the bulk of his credibility after he had refused to lead the students' movement on 22 November 1945.

Meanwhile Dr Mookerjee, through his adroit stewardship of the partition movement managed to bring about what he had tried for so long—to make the Congress work for Hindu interests in tandem with the Mahasabha. When the Working Committee of the Mahasabha decided on 17 April to observe a one-day strike to protest the misbehaviour of Punjabi Muslim policemen, the Mahasabha leaders consulted the Congress leaders to chalk out a joint plan of action. While the demand for the creation of a separate province of West Bengal was endorsed by the provincial Congress and the Mahasabha, in the opinion poll held by the *Amrita Bazar Patrika* on 22 April 1947, partition gained a virtually unanimous vote of confidence, 98.6 per cent voting yea, with only 0.6 per cent favouring a united Bengal. Dr Mookerjee held a 'top secret' interview with Viceroy Mountbatten on 23 April, in which he explained that the main purpose of his visit was to convince the viceroy of the necessity for partitioning Bengal, if the Cabinet Mission Plan were to fail. He went into matters at great length using many plans and papers, which were left with the viceroy's chief of staff Lord Ismay. A mammoth public meeting, jointly convened by the Mahasabha and the Congress in Calcutta, was held in May

1947 to press for partition. It was presided over by the historian Sir Jadunath Sarkar, by no means a friend of the Mookerjees, but now an ardent supporter of the cause. The meeting set the pattern for as many as seventy-six subsequent public meetings that were organized by the two parties working closely together for the cause of partition until it became clear in July that Bengal would, indeed, be partitioned.

In a long letter addressed to Mountbatten on 2 May 1947, Dr Mookerjee, as the spokesman of a very large section of Hindus in Bengal and other parts of India, said that the Muslim League's attitude of negation and obstruction would alter if the British announced it was not going to depart from the main principles of the Cabinet Mission Plan. Around this time, however, the Cabinet Mission Plan was as good as dead, and partition of the country was almost an inevitability. Therefore, while opposing Pakistan, both from the Hindu viewpoint and in India's larger interest, he explained why, irrespective of whether India's division took place or not, it was essential that Punjab and Bengal should be partitioned. It is the quality of this advocacy of his that simultaneously made the Hindus of Bengal support partition and convinced the British about the inevitability of the partition of Bengal and the rejection of the dangerous (for Bengali Hindus) pipe dream of united sovereign Bengal.

The first reason, he argued, why Bengal, having an area of about 78,000 square miles and a population exceeding 60 million, and being one of the worst-administered provinces in British India, needed to be partitioned was purely administrative. The creation of two provinces out of Bengal's existing boundaries was both possible and eminently desirable. Secondly, during the last ten years, Bengali Hindus had suffered not only on account of communal riots and disturbances but in every sphere of national activity, be it educational, economic, political or even religious. Despite their immense contribution towards Bengal's development, they had no voice in its administration. Thirdly, a separation of Bengal would cause minimal displacement because the two major communities lived in two compact zones. Hindu Bengal would have about 35,000 square miles with a population of about 24 million, making it equal to and even larger than some of the existing provinces in India and some states in Europe and America. Fourthly, more than two-thirds of the Hindu population, including about 4.5 million out of 7.6 million of the scheduled castes, would live within Hindu Bengal. This would give an opportunity to both the major communities in the two provinces, which should remain within the Indian Union, to develop themselves according to their best ability and tradition. It would help to gradually eliminate the constant rancour and strife between them and eventually learn that the minority community in their respective provinces must be duly protected in their own interest.

If, on the other hand, he further argued, India was to be divided on communal consideration, the partition of Bengal would become an immediate necessity for several reasons. First, since Jinnah's claim for Pakistan was based on the theory that Hindus and Muslims were two separate nations and Muslims must have their own homeland and state, Hindus in Bengal might well demand that they must not be compelled to live within the Muslim state and the area where they predominated should be cut off and formed into a province that might link itself up with the Hindustan Union. Jinnah could never resist this demand for, as the Cabinet Mission pointed out in its scheme of 16 May 1946, the same logic and arguments applicable to Pakistan also applied to the partition of Bengal. Secondly, if Muslims being 24 per cent of India's population constituted such a formidable minority that their demand for a separate homeland and state became irresistible, surely 45 per cent of Bengal's Hindu population was a sufficiently large minority which could not be coerced into living within the Pakistan state against the will of the people. Thirdly, Dr Mookerjee called 'purely academic' the argument that if Bengal and Punjab were partitioned, the other portions of India also had to be partitioned on similar consideration. If there were other areas in India which were large enough to be constituted into separate provinces on communal consideration, their claim had to be justified on merits. Surely the existence of small pockets here and there—in East Bengal there were numerous towns with a majority Hindu population and also several Hindu pockets— could not justify the creation of new provinces. It was only because the Hindu-majority areas, contiguous in character, were large enough to form a separate province that the Mahasabha was justified in putting forward their claim for partition.

Fourthly, referring to Jinnah's talk of transfer of population and property, Dr Mookerjee said that clubbing an undivided Bengal with Pakistan would involve the transfer of about 26 million Hindus, which was next to impossible. On the other hand, if Bengal was partitioned, the question of transfer, affecting 9 million Hindus in Muslim Bengal and 6 million Muslims in Hindu Bengal, would be comparatively easier. Finally, referring to 'some loose talk' of a sovereign undivided Bengal that would be 'a virtual Pakistan' and would give Hindus no relief whatsoever, Dr Mookerjee said that the Mahasabha neither understood its significance at all nor supported it in any way. The framing of the Constitution of a sovereign Bengal would mainly be left in the hands of Muslim Leaguers, who would be guided by fanatical notions of a separate nationhood. So, the Mahasabha was not prepared to trust the fate of Bengali Hindus to them, nor did they want them to be cut off from the rest of India on any consideration whatsoever. They told Mountbatten that because the rule of law in Bengal had been substituted by the rule of gangsterism, the suffering of Hindus was indescribable. Dr Mookerjee implored the viceroy to fully consider his arguments and decide the partition question either himself or set up the machinery to facilitate the expression of people's views. The viceroy was also requested to dissolve the Bengal ministry as soon as the partition question was announced so as to prevent disastrous consequences. In conclusion, Dr Mookerjee stated that Bengali Hindus, who constituted a significant number among the Indian people and whose contributions to the growth of India's progress had been considerable, had the right to demand that in the free India to come, they must have their territory wherein they could live without fear and enjoy the fruits of peace and freedom, without depriving the majority community of its rightful interests in the area in which it predominated.

Governor Burrows, who was personally against the partition, was initially not sure that there was a general demand among the Bengali Hindus as a whole for the partition of Bengal. He had agreed by 1 May that the partition agitation must indeed be taken seriously and that Dr Mookerjee had made a dent in the minds of Bengali Hindus. Even Suhrawardy, who put forth the scheme for a united sovereign Bengal mainly to counteract the move of Dr Mookerjee, admitted on 15 May that the Mahasabha had 'captured the imagination of the Hindus on the score of partition'. The *Statesman*, a British-owned, pro-British newspaper of Calcutta, commented under the heading 'Twilight of Bengal' on 24 April 1947:

During the last ten weeks or so the movement for repartition of Bengal has grown from a cloud no bigger than a man's hand into a storm which blows all over the province and outside its borders, though the centre remains Calcutta. Fostered initially by the Hindu Mahasabha, which has not lost its influence with its seats in the legislatures, it received strong impetus from the . . . Congress Working Committee's resolution of March 8 on partition of The Punjab.

After Mountbatten took over as viceroy in March 1947, his initial attempts were to sell a united India to Jinnah. Among other ways, he argued that the very logic that Jinnah was putting forth to justify Pakistan would inevitably lead to the partition of the provinces of Punjab and Bengal, something that Mountbatten knew Jinnah dreaded, and by doing this, he hoped to get Jinnah to back off with his demand for Pakistan. Lapierre and Collins have described how the arguments used to go: Jinnah would counter Mountbatten by saying, 'Ah, but Your Excellency does not understand. A man is a Punjabi or a Bengali before he is a Hindu or Muslim. They share a common history, language, culture and economy. You must not divide them. You will cause endless bloodshed and trouble.' And Mountbatten would say, 'Mr Jinnah, I entirely agree.' Taken by surprise, Jinnah would say, 'You do?' Mountbatten would continue, 'Of course. A man is not only a Punjabi or a Bengali before he is a Hindu or Muslim, he is an Indian before all else. You have presented the unanswerable argument for Indian unity.' And then Jinnah would counter, 'But you don't understand at all,' and the discussions would start around the mulberry bush again.

Jinnah and Suhrawardy were understandably aghast at the idea of the partition of Bengal, because it would deprive their Pakistan of the prize catch called Calcutta, and would also take away the industrial half of Bengal. In addition, Suhrawardy had his personal reasons as detailed earlier. Jinnah issued a statement that the proposal for partition of the provinces of Punjab and Bengal was 'a sinister move actuated by spite and bitterness'. Suhrawardy, meanwhile, had to snare some gullible Hindu leader to collaborate with him It is surprising that supposedly sagacious and experienced Hindu leaders had not the slightest difficulty in reposing their faith on a person like Suhrawardy who had less than a year ago unleashed such unspeakable atrocities on the Hindus of Calcutta through his Direct Action.

The idea of a united sovereign Bengal was primarily Suhrawardy's, but from the alacrity with which Jinnah and Liaquat Ali Khan welcomed the idea, it would not be unreasonable to assume that they were also parties to the hatching of the plan. Stanley Wolpert, Jinnah's biographer, has quoted Jinnah that when Viceroy Mountbatten informed Jinnah of Suhrawardy's recently expressed hope that 'he might be able to keep a united Bengal on condition that it joined neither Pakistan nor Hindusthan', Jinnah said without hesitation, 'I should be delighted. What is the use of Bengal without Calcutta; they had much better remained united and independent. I am sure they would be on friendly terms with us.' Wolpert also quotes Liaquat Ali having told Sir Eric Mieville that he was in no way worried about Bengal as he was convinced in his own mind that the province would never divide. Suhrawardy drew a golden picture of his united Bengal, stating that 'it would be a great country, the richest and the most prosperous in India . . . a land that would be truly plentiful' and placed it before the press on 27 April 1947. The press, unimpressed by all the hype, asked him pointedly that if in the undivided Bengal Hindus and Muslims could live in such amity, why could they not do so in undivided India? And Suhrawardy, of course, had no answer.

Meanwhile, Sarat Bose had teamed up with Abul Hashim. Hashim was a West Bengali Muslim League leader from Burdwan and the provincial secretary of the League. He had advocated the killing of Hindus in very direct language on the eve of the riots. Together Bose and Hashim were going full steam ahead with their scheme and had taken upon themselves the task of drafting a 'Constitution' for their proposed united sovereign Bengal. However, Sardar Patel was extremely critical of the effort and wrote to Bose the same day he announced the plan, 'I am sorry to find that you have isolated yourself so completely from all-India politics and even in provincial politics, you have not kept in touch with us. In these critical times, we cannot afford to be stand-offish.' Sarat Bose replied to this note, trying to convince Patel of the correctness of his stand but, predictably, it cut no ice.

In order to forestall the efforts of the Suhrawardy–Bose–Hashim trio, on 11 May 1947, Dr Mookerjee conveyed to Pandit Nehru and Sardar Patel the Mahasabha's extreme anxiety about the final developments. Stating that Sarat Bose, who had 'no support whatsoever from the Hindus' and 'dared not address one single public meeting', was doing enormous mischief by trying to negotiate with Suhrawardy the possible contours of the sovereign Bengal, Dr Mookerjee expressed the hope that Nehru and Patel would not allow this idea of a sovereign Bengal to be considered seriously by anybody. Even if a loose Centre, as contemplated under the Cabinet Mission Plan, was established at the last stage, Hindus would have no safety whatsoever in Bengal. So Dr Mookerjee implored them not to allow the question of the partition of Bengal to be dismissed and demanded the creation of two provinces out of the existing boundaries of Bengal, Pakistan or no Pakistan. Finally, he considered it of utmost importance that the new declaration should also include an announcement for the immediate dissolution of the Bengal ministry that would otherwise 'play havoc with the province and particularly Calcutta'. He offered to come to Delhi, if his presence there was needed. On 13 May, Dr Mookerjee met Gandhi at Sodepur, near Calcutta to ascertain his views on the Suhrawardy scheme of united sovereign Bengal. Gandhi said he had not yet made up his mind but was trying to ascertain what the proposal really meant. When asked, Dr Mookerjee replied that the scheme, though apparently authored by Suhrawardy, was really being sponsored by British commercial interests and that Mountbatten had asked him to carefully consider the proposal. But Dr Mookerjee feared that Suhrawardy could surely manipulate the united sovereign Bengal idea to seek voluntary alliance with Pakistan with the help of the majority Muslim votes. Gandhi had no reply when Dr Mookerjee asked him whether he could contemplate Bengal as separate from the rest of India.

Nehru's reply to Dr Mookerjee was vague and evasive. However, Patel was totally direct and in his reply, assured Dr Mookerjee (see Chapter 11 for more on the relationship between the two leaders) that he need not worry at all and could depend on them to deal with the situation effectively and fittingly. The future of Hindus in Bengal was quite safe, as long as they stood firm and continued to give them such support as only they could. Describing the cry for sovereign Bengal as 'a trap to induce the unwary and the unwise to enter the parlour of the Muslim League' and asserting that Bengal could not be isolated from the Indian union, Patel, the party disciplinarian, coldly advised Sarat Bose and Kiran Sankar Ray to stand united on the official policy of the Congress, which insisted upon the division of Bengal and Punjab for the survival of the non-Muslim population. Even as Gandhi was in favour of avoiding partition, he wrote to Sarat Bose on 24 May that he was forced to change his stance, since his colleagues on the Working Committee had 'taken him to task for supporting Sarat Babu's move'.

There were a few others opposing partition of the province. The editorial in the *Statesman* has already been mentioned—it was probably echoing the sentiments of the British trading class, the *boxwallahs*, of Calcutta. Notable among the political leaders was Jogendra Nath Mandal, a leader of the scheduled castes from Barisal in East Bengal who had joined the Muslim League, having been enticed by the offer of being the law member in the interim government. He opined that the communal trouble would not be solved by partition. He also said that the Hindus of East Bengal would lose all their property and would be forced to migrate. Regarding this last issue, he was proved absolutely right, and it stretched to his own self. He became the central minister for law and labour in the Pakistan cabinet. Then, during the terrible anti-Hindu pogrom of 1950 (see Chapter 11) he visited his home district, and went back to Karachi and reported back to Liaquat Ali Khan. Liaquat told him to shut up or risk being thrown into prison. Mandal kept quiet, travelled and defected to India sometime later in the year, and sent in his resignation from India.

Leonard Gordon, biographer of the Bose brothers, pays the ultimate compliment to Dr Mookerjee by saying, 'Sarat Bose and [Abul] Hashim continued in their efforts into June [1947] but the veto by Nehru and Patel was crucial, as was the pro-partition coalition forged by Dr Syama Prasad Mookerjee.' A widely noted survey of Hindu public opinion by the *Amrita Bazar Patrika* in early May found an overwhelming majority, 97 per cent, supported partition. These findings were presented in an article 'Homeland for Bengali Hindus'.[9]

Apologists for the Muslim League and the whitewashing crew for the Calcutta Killings have even much later, persisted in criticizing Dr Mookerjee for spearheading the partition movement. Christophe Jaffrelot, for example, has made a travesty of historiography by saying that Dr Mookerjee (whom he calls *Shyam* Prasad) had 'resigned himself' to the partition of Bengal, when actually he was the proactive leader of that movement. He also supports Joya Chatterji, famous for her theory of absolving the Muslim League of responsibility for the Calcutta Killings, and says that she 'convincingly considers' Dr Mookerjee's advocacy of partition to be '*Bhadralok* concern with Hindu culture', which he equates with 'upper castes' high tradition', whatever that means. Joya Chatterji's stand has been effectively rubbished by contemporary historians Amales Tripathi, Bidyut Chakrabarty and Partha Chatterjee.[10]

All doubts and uncertainties were finally laid to rest when, on 3 June 1947, the Prime Minister of Great Britain, the Rt Hon. Clement Attlee, rose in the House of Commons to announce the acceptance by His Majesty's Government of the scheme to partition the country, and to table a statement by His Majesty's Government to that effect. The scheme provided, in somewhat convoluted language, for a partition of the provinces of Punjab and Bengal, subject to their respective legislative assemblies voting accordingly, and for a referendum in the district of Sylhet in the province of Assam. On 20 June 1947, members of the Bengal Legislative Assembly voted for partition of their province by a large majority.

About this triumph of having achieved the partition of Bengal, Dr Mookerjee is said to have remarked to Nehru, when the latter accused him of concurring in the partition proposal, '. . . I partitioned Pakistan.' Phani Bhushan Chakravartti, later the chief justice of the Calcutta High Court and sometime temporary Governor of West Bengal, observed, 'Dr Syama Prasad Mookerjee intervened and harnessed all the mighty powers he possessed to an organized and determined opposition to that plan [of united sovereign Bengal] and he forced a partition within a partition.'

The only jobs that now remained were to carry out the referendum in Sylhet and draw the line of partition.

When the electoral rolls for the Sylhet referendum were to be drawn up, a controversy arose as to whether voters in the Labour and the Trade and Commerce constituencies—meaning mainly the tea estate labour—should be allowed to vote. These labourers were all non-Muslim, imported from the areas that comprise the present-day state of Jharkhand and adjoining areas of Orissa. Eventually, they were excluded and the referendum took place from the general, Mahomedan and Indian Christian constituencies. Sylhet went to Pakistan, with a relatively thin majority, 2,39,619 to 1,84,041. Only three police station areas, namely Ratabari, Patharkandi, Badarpur and a part of Karimganj remained in India. To this day, a controversy persists regarding the role of the Assam Congress in this referendum which, it is alleged, made no effort to win the referendum or to oppose the disenfranchisement of the tea estate labourers. The Mahasabha had practically no strength in Assam, and the Hindus—of which there were two major linguistic groups, Assamese and Bengali—were solidly behind the Congress. The leader of the Bengali group, Basanta Das, a very wealthy zamindar from Sylhet, must bear considerable personal responsibility in this regard. In fact, after Partition he remained in Sylhet and tried to enter politics there, and even became a central minister in Pakistan. He was eventually EBDO-ed,[11] hounded out of East Pakistan like most Hindu politicians, and died in Calcutta.

The indefatigable Dr Mookerjee was active here too. He toured the district and persuaded Hindu Sylhetis all over Bengal to travel to Sylhet and vote at the referendum. Some of them came from as far away as Delhi and Burma. It is believed that because of their different culture, a section of the Muslim population also voted for India; and had there been a little effort on the part of the Assam Congress, perhaps the district would not have been lost to India.

Bengal (as also the Punjab) was eventually partitioned at the hands of an English barrister of distinction, Sir Cyril (later Lord) Radcliffe, the reason for whose choice was his lack of any connection with India. Sir Cyril was assisted by four other members of the Boundary Commission, namely Bijon Mukherjee, C.C. Biswas, M.A. Rahman and M.M. Akram, all of them lawyers, for the partition of Bengal. As the names tell, the first two were Hindus, the last two Muslims, and there was practically nothing that they agreed upon, with the result that the award, eventually published on 17 August 1947, two days after Independence, was entirely the handiwork of Sir Cyril alone. One point is to be noted with respect to the terms of reference of the Commission: the Commission was required to partition the province on the basis of Muslim-majority and non-Muslim-majority areas, not on the basis of Muslim-majority and Hindu-majority areas.

Even here, Dr Mookerjee intervened and convinced Radcliffe that while deciding the population balance for deciding whether to award a particular unit of area to India or Pakistan, the unit to be considered should be the thana, the police station area, and not the district or subdivision. It is on this basis that a number of districts themselves came to be partitioned; and the Krishnanagar and Ranaghat subdivisions of the Nadia district, the bulk of Malda district, the Balurghat and Raiganj subdivisions of Dinajpur district, the Bongaon subdivision of Jessore district and many other parts came to India.

As was to be expected, neither the Congress (meaning the Hindus) nor the League (meaning the Muslims) were happy with the award. West Bengal got 36 per cent of the land area and 35 per cent of the population. Only 16 per cent of the total Muslim population was left in West Bengal, but a whopping 42 per cent of the Hindu population was left in East Bengal, numbering some 13 million. Non-Muslim-majority, mostly Buddhist, Chittagong Hill Tracts was given to Pakistan on the grounds that its approach was only through Muslim-majority Chittagong. Muslim-majority Murshidabad district was awarded to India on the grounds that it contains the headwaters of the River Bhagirathi, which further downstream becomes the Hooghly and flows by Calcutta; in exchange, the much larger Hindu-majority Khulna district was given to Pakistan. The population of East Bengal, according to the 1941 census, was 28 per cent Hindu, 70 per cent Muslim and 2 per cent others, mainly Buddhists in the Chittagong Hill Tracts and a handful of Christians in the coastal districts and among the Garo tribesmen in the foothills of Mymensingh. As opposed to this, according to the 2001 census, the population of present-day Bangladesh is 10 per cent Hindu and 88 per cent Muslim. And it is in these figures that the terrible injustice done to the Bengali Hindus, quite a bit of it by themselves, lies. The part of this story, so far as is relevant to this biography has been told in Chapter 11.

Along with his task of partitioning Bengal, Dr Mookerjee had also started attending the sessions of the Constituent Assembly set up on 9 December 1946 in consequence of the Cabinet Mission proposals. That body soon got a taste of his persuasive oratory. In one of the very first speeches in the assembly on 17 December 1946, Dr Mookerjee opposed an amendment moved by Dr Jayakar that the resolution concerning the very object of the assembly, namely deciding the general shape the Constitution would take, should be effectively postponed till the representation of the Muslim League and the Indian states in the assembly was assured. It is surprising that such an amendment was proposed at all, because by then it was fairly certain that Jinnah would get his Pakistan, and that is why the League was not participating in the assembly. The future of the Indian states was even more uncertain, and their champion, Sir Conrad Corfield, was trying very hard to retain their status to the extent he could. Winston Churchill, then leader of the Opposition in the British Parliament, had remarked that the absence of the Muslim League in the Constituent Assembly was something like the absence of the bride in the church where the marriage was going to take place.

In reply, Dr Mookerjee lambasted the British as only he could:

I would say, Sir, that we should say to the British people once and for all, 'We want to remain friendly with you. You started your career as traders. You came here as supplicants before the Great Mughal. You wanted to exploit the wealth of the country. Luck was in your favour. By forgery, fraud and force you succeeded in establishing—these are all matters of history— your government in this country but not with the willing cooperation of people of this land. You introduced separate electorates, you introduced religion into Indian politics. That was not done by Indians. You did it only to perpetuate your rule in this country.'

And finally, on 15 August 1947, was born the Dominion of the Union of India, which eventually became the Republic of India, with West Bengal as one of its states, and Calcutta as the capital of that state. Two days later, on 17 August, the Radcliffe award was announced. In between, with the lowering of the Union Jack, the Indian flag had been unfurled at the collectorate at Khulna and Rangamati (Chittagong Hill Tracts) and the Pakistani flag at Krishnanagar, Malda and Berhampore. These were duly reversed.

And Bengali Hindus, having got their homeland, heaved a sigh of relief. And Dr Syama Prasad Mookerjee emerged successful against incredible odds. How right he was about snatching West Bengal from the mouth of Jinnah was proved by the subsequent events in East Bengal.

10

Central Minister of Industry and Supply, 1947–50

D r Mookerjee's inclusion in the central cabinet following Independence was no surprise. Having achieved the partition of Bengal and snatched away West Bengal, including the prize of Calcutta, from Jinnah's teeth, his position as the foremost leader from Bengal was unassailable. The only other leader of comparable stature was Sarat Bose, who had been discredited in the Rameswar Banerjee incident of 1945, and was moreover in a precarious state of health. Meanwhile, in the process, Dr Mookerjee had also achieved a remarkable degree of understanding with the Congress. On 10 July 1947, the Bengal legislature elected him as the Congress nominee to the Constituent Assembly of India for framing a new Constitution for India. Dr Mookerjee's performance in the Constituent Assembly, his political acumen, oratorical skill and mastery of parliamentary procedure won new laurels for him. His position as one of the topmost public figures, whose record of service in the cause of the country's independence was outstanding, was also universally recognized. He had become Bengal's undisputed leader and spokesman. It was, therefore, no wonder that his name readily occurred to the Congress leaders, who were then engaged in selecting capable people for the national government to be formed on 15 August 1947.

Gandhi's voice, however, was very material in his selection. He was always kindly disposed towards Dr Mookerjee, and had once remarked that he wished Dr Mookerjee to be a 'Hindu leader with a Congress bent of mind' after the late Pandit Madan Mohan Malviya, just as 'Patel was a Congress leader with a Hindu mind'. Prashanto Chatterji has commented in his treatise on Dr Mookerjee that Gandhi had realized that freedom had been achieved by the combined efforts of all the nationalist forces in the country and not by the Congress alone.[1] He, therefore, wanted the first government of free India to be a truly national government, capable of inspiring confidence and creating enthusiasm in the whole nation. He had insisted that the first cabinet be broad-based. It was at his insistence that a number of non-Congressmen, eminent in different spheres of national life, were invited to join the cabinet. They included, besides Dr Mookerjee, Sir John Mathai, the noted economist and business magnate, Sir Shanmukham Chetty, the well-known financial expert and B.R. Ambedkar, the noted jurist and scheduled-caste leader. Whatever little hesitation Dr Mookerjee had in his having to work with Congressmen was removed by his Hindu Mahasabha colleagues, particularly Savarkar, who strongly advised him to join.

Dr Mookerjee was given the important portfolio of industry and supply. He would probably have personally preferred education which had been his special field since his early youth. That would have been in the best interests of the country as well. He could have laid a sound foundation for a truly national education policy and moulded the new generation of the country constructively, while also preparing them for an intellectual revolution which must precede any social and economic revolution. 'But that was not to be. Maulana Azad,' wrote Madhok,[2] '[who] knew little about education, Indian culture or heritage, was determined to keep [the] education ministry within his grip with a set purpose.' Syama Prasad's experience as finance minister of undivided Bengal and his general grasp of things were also determining factors. This assignment gave Dr Mookerjee an opportunity to lay the foundation of India's industrial policy and prepare the ground for the nation's industrial development in the years to come. Madhok says, 'The loss to education and cultural life was thus a gain to the economy and industry.'

His record as minister for industry and supply for the two and a half years he remained in office amply justified the faith and trust that had been put in him. He brought his solid intellectual grasp and realistic understanding of the problems of industrialization in a predominantly agricultural country to bear upon the task entrusted to him. His experience, first as a chief executive of Calcutta University, the biggest employer of top intellectuals and scientists at the time, and then as finance minister of undivided Bengal, stood him in good stead. He carried no major ideological baggage and, therefore, could handle the task entrusted to him with refreshing realism. His intellectual prowess, mental alertness and rocklike integrity evoked spontaneous respect and fullest cooperation from the British-trained civilians. Even his political opponents praised the way he handled the industrial problems and formulated policies in independent India's most formative years.

Before we look at his performance in governance as a minister in the very first central cabinet of independent India, we have to look at two serious problems in other fields that beset him around this time. One of these was purely political—it involved his relationship with his party, the Hindu Mahasabha, that he had been associated with for the last nine years. The other problem was intensely personal. It involved a serious illness of his youngest child and daughter Arati, also called Hasi.

According to Dr Mookerjee's perception of the political scenario that followed Independence and Partition, the Mahasabha could no longer play the part of a staunchly Hindu political party that it did before Partition. For, its role before Partition was dictated to a great extent by its obligation to oppose and expose the misdeeds of the Muslim League and carry on a political struggle for the protection of Hindus from the onslaughts of the League, something the Congress did not or would not do. Moreover, the electorate was communally divided by an unjust award, and the Muslims in some cases got an improper advantage. Now that the antagonist, namely the Muslim League, was gone, the communal electorate was gone, and the party had been unsuccessful in preventing the partition of the country that was its principal objective, although it had succeeded in achieving the partition of Punjab and Bengal, which was its fallback position, Dr Mookerjee wanted the Mahasabha not to be restricted to Hindus alone and to work as a political body for the service of the masses. Savarkar did not agree, and the distance between them grew.

Then came the tragic day of 30 January 1948 when Nathuram Godse, a terribly misguided youth, incensed by what according to his perception was a treachery on the part of Gandhi on the country during the Kashmir hostilities, shot him dead during a prayer meeting. The country was struck dumb by pain. Although Godse was a Hindu Mahasabha member and close to Savarkar, there was no reason to believe that the leadership of the Mahasabha had anything to do with the assassination. Yet, the government had to be seen to be doing something drastic—so the party was banned and Savarkar prosecuted. Likewise, a Hindu social reform movement called the Rashtriya Swayamsevak Sangh (RSS),[3] which had nothing whatsoever to do with Godse or the assassination, was also banned. Nothing of course could be found against either Savarkar or the RSS and the government was forced to release Savarkar and lift the ban on the latter. Godse and one of his associates were hanged and a few others jailed. Dr Mookerjee unequivocally condemned the assassination.

After the banning of the party and the imprisonment of Savarkar and other leaders, those leaders of the Mahasabha who were outside prison resolved to take Dr Mookerjee's advice to transform the party and take non-Hindus. However, in August 1949, after the release of Savarkar and the lifting of the ban on the Mahasabha, the party went back on their resolution and decided that they would continue to remain in politics. Disagreeing strongly on this stand of the Mahasabha, Dr Mookerjee resigned from all his positions in the party. He was now a leader without a party, but a cabinet minister of the Union government nevertheless.

Now on to his personal problems. While Dr Mookerjee was in New Delhi trying to grapple with his new responsibilities as a central minister, his youngest child and daughter Arati (Hasi) was suffering from frequent onsets of low fever. She had grown up to be a very pretty girl, but rather introverted and withdrawn, quite unlike her elder sister Sabita (Bua) who was a tomboy and an extrovert. Dr Mookerjee doted on the motherless child in the little time that he could find for her, but that time was very little. She must have hidden the matter of her fever from her aunt and other relatives, because when the illness was diagnosed as tuberculosis it was quite advanced, and moreover of the 'galloping' type, the one that becomes fatal very quickly unless treated. This was towards the end of February 1948, and Streptomycin, the 'wonder drug' of Dr Waksman, had not come to India as a regularly available drug—it was probably still at a trial stage.

Dr Mookerjee on being informed consulted Dr Benjamin, who was then the adviser to the Government of India on tuberculosis, then a serious and countrywide health problem. Dr Benjamin advised him to take her, without any loss of time, to the sanatorium at Kasauli (Himachal Pradesh) run by Dr Joseph which was then the best place for treating the disease in India. Dr Mookerjee air-dashed to Calcutta and telephoned Captain V. Sundaram, the pilot who used to fly the Mysore maharaja's Dakota aircraft. Sundaram agreed, arrived at Calcutta with his wife and co-pilot Usha, and Dr Mookerjee put them up in the Grand Hotel. He also told Sundaram that he could spend the evening at an industrial exhibition that was on in the city. Sundaram says that they were accompanied to the exhibition from the hotel by a gentleman who simply introduced himself as Dr Mookerjee's brother. When they went to the exhibition, they found that their guide was being treated with unusual deference by the organizers. He asked around and came to know that the brother was a judge of the Calcutta High Court, none other than Rama Prasad. Sundaram has written in his autobiography, *An Airman's Saga*, that 'Usha and I had never met such an unpretentious man before.'

Arati was brought in very early in the morning while still on oxygen. They made the flight to New Delhi without any problems, although there were thunderclouds on the way, and Sundaram had to climb to 4000 feet for some distance. Usha acted both as co-pilot and nurse during the flight and reported that the patient was doing quite well. Arati was whisked away by ambulance to Kasauli from Safdarjung airport. Sundaram writes further, 'Dr Mookerjee thanked us, noting how touched he was by the attention and concern Usha had shown throughout the flight. "Usha is not only a good co-pilot, she is also a kind and gentle person," adding that he would be paying from his personal funds for the trip, and asking us to convey his thanks to the maharaja for the loan of this beautiful plane.'

Dr Mookerjee rented a bungalow in Kasauli for his relatives to stay close to Arati, and after some months got her removed to Davos and then Leysin in Switzerland which at that time had probably the best arrangement in the world for treating tuberculosis. Meanwhile, Streptomycin came on the market and reached her. In one year, she had completely recovered from her illness and resumed a normal life. Ironically, this Streptomycin *might* have contributed to Dr Mookerjee's premature death, just five years later.

Now we can return to Dr Mookerjee's public life. Dr Mookerjee had very clear ideas on the role of private capital in India's industrial development as also on the relationship between capital and labour. He was in favour of giving full scope to private enterprise under suitable government regulation and control, to play its part in India's industrialization. He wanted the state to utilize its meagre resources for developing that sector of industry whose growth was essential for the defence of the country but for which private capital was not readily forthcoming. In formulating this policy, he was guided solely by a realistic assessment of the needs and circumstances of the country and not by abstract theories or dogmas, to which he had no attachment.

Apart from the basic objections to total nationalization, he was convinced that India lacked the requisite resources, experience and trained personnel to nationalize all industries and still run them efficiently. He was, therefore, opposed to loose talk about nationalization of all industries which antagonized private capital. He also knew by experience that state-managed industries had been generally working less efficiently because of lack of incentive and initiative on the part of government employees who managed them, excessive use of government rules and formalities, and top-heavy administration. He, therefore, initiated the policy of managing the state-controlled industries through corporations, organized on the lines of joint stock companies, with the government supplying the major portion or the whole of the share capital and having some of its nominees on the board of directors, together with a number of private industrialists. Over the years this became the general pattern for running public undertakings in India.

He had made his ideas on industry quite clear in a speech he delivered in Calcutta on 21 April 1948 at the annual general meeting of the Eastern Chamber of Commerce at the Grand Hotel. He was very clear that the profit motive would have to remain and play a major part in the development of the country. He rubbished the classical Marxist theory of continual class struggle by stating that for the development of industry, cooperation between capital and labour was essential, and an atmosphere would have to be created where the two camps could play complementary roles.

Dr Mookerjee's ideas were reflected in the Government of India's declaration of industrial policy through a resolution dated 6 April 1948. This resolution envisaged a mixed economy, with overall responsibility of ensuring planned development and regulation of industries in the national interest lying with the government. While it supported the right of the state to acquire an industrial undertaking in the public interest, it reserved an appropriate sphere for private enterprise. Industries were placed into three categories according to the part which the state was to play in their development. In the first category were arms and ammunitions, atomic energy, river valley projects and railways, which would be the exclusive responsibility of the state. In the second category were industries which would be progressively state-owned but in which private enterprises would supplement the effort of the state. These included coal, iron and steel, aircraft, telephone, telegraph, wireless, shipbuilding and mineral oils. The third category would include all remaining industries, for example, fertilizers, cotton and woollen textiles, paper and newsprint and so on, which were left open to private enterprise, subject to regulation and control by the government. The coordination of cottage and small-scale industries was also recognized to be a part of the central government's responsibility. Between 1948 and 1950, the All India Handicrafts Board, the All India Handloom Board and the Khadi and Village Industries Board were set up to supply the much-needed organization and finance required by cottage and small-scale industries to survive and develop. In July 1948 was established the Industrial Finance Corporation of India (IFCI) which was a government-sponsored institution acting as an investment banker, collecting private savings on government guarantee of repayment and distributing them in the form of advances and long-term loans to industrial borrowers.

In accordance with the government's industrial policy, the Chittaranjan Locomotive Works (at Chittaranjan, West Bengal), the Hindustan Aircraft Factory (Bangalore), the Sindri Fertilizer Factory (Sindri, Bihar) and the Damodar Valley Corporation, the four most successful and gigantic governmental ventures, were conceived and organized by Dr Mookerjee.

As part of a plan to achieve self-sufficiency in locomotives, early in 1948 the government started at a cost of Rs 15 crore a factory to manufacture steam locomotives at Chittaranjan in West Bengal. The first India-made locomotive from assembled parts, named Deshbandhu, was produced in 1950. The workshop was originally designed to produce 120 locomotives and fifty spare boilers a year.

Hindustan Aircraft Limited was promoted by Walchand Hirachand in December 1940 in association with the Government of Mysore at Bangalore. During 1947–48, the Board of Directors was reconstituted with the minister of industry and supply, Government of India, as the chairman and the dewan of Mysore as the vice chairman. The factory, which was reformed into a limited company, undertook the assembly and manufacture of Vampire Jet Fighters for the Indian Air Force, built HT 2 (a trainer aircraft for civilian and defence purposes) and manufactured all-steel rail coaches for the Indian Railways, and bus bodies for various state and private transport authorities.

Dr Mookerjee also conceived the plan of establishing a steel plant at Bhilai, 16 miles west of Raipur and 9 miles to the east of Durg in the Central Provinces (later renamed Madhya Pradesh). His dream was fulfilled in 1955 when an agreement for the Bhilai steel plant with Soviet assistance came up, preceded and followed respectively by the Rourkela and Durgapur plants in Orissa and

West Bengal. It was again during his tenure as industry minister that the first steps for the manufacture of newsprint were initiated by establishing National Newsprint and Paper Mills Ltd in Nepanagar, Central Provinces, which went into production in 1954.

The idea of establishing a large-scale fertilizer factory, in the context of the grave shortage of foodgrains and the expanding population, goes back to the twilight years of the British Raj in India. The idea came to fruition after Independence, particularly in view of a world shortage of chemical fertilizers. Sindri in Bihar, a small village situated on the banks of the River Damodar about 14 miles downstream from Dhanbad, was ultimately selected. To the plan to produce 3,50,000 tonnes of ammonium sulphate was added 1,05,000 tonnes of cement per annum from the by-product, calcium carbonate, and to build a thermal power plant, not only to feed the plant but also to supply 20,000 kW to the Bihar grid. It was largely due to Dr Mookerjee's dynamic leadership that this vast and most modern factory went into production in October 1951. This was in accordance with the starting date anticipated in December 1947, although by that time, Dr Mookerjee had resigned from the ministry. Because this was one of the very first factories set up by the government,[4] a lot of bureaucratic wrinkles had to be smoothed out by him. He did all this very well, exhibiting great innovativeness in the process.

The Tennessee Valley Authority (TVA) of the USA, set up during the depression years of the 1930s, provided to the world a model for governmental enterprise through public works. Another of its striking features was ensuring cooperation among the various states in the Tennessee valley in a country like the USA where every state guards its rights very zealously and where any venture by the government is looked upon askance. The multipurpose Damodar River Valley Project, which was modelled after, but was far more complicated than the TVA, is another outstanding achievement of Dr Mookerjee. Its need had been particularly felt after a devastating flood on the Damodar River in 1943. Besides creating other disasters like tremendous loss of life and property, it had severed the main line of the East Indian Railway which was essential for the war effort. A joint venture of the central government and the provincial governments of Bihar and West Bengal, it was an enterprise owned and managed by a public corporation. The Damodar Valley Corporation Act, which received the governor general's assent on 27 March 1948, established a corporation for the development of the Damodar Valley in Bihar and West Bengal. The objectives behind this act were quite a few: flood control, irrigation, hydel and thermal power, internal water transport, afforestation, prevention of soil erosion, optimizing use of land, resettlement of displaced population, sanitation and public health measures, and economic and social welfare of the people.

It was again during his ministership that the Hirakud Dam Project on the River Mahanadi near Sambalpur in Orissa was initiated in 1948 to harness the river and provide irrigation to 67,00,000 acres of land in Sambalpur and Balangir districts of western Orissa. Up to June 1950, only preliminary work relating to land, buildings, roads and railways, powerhouse and workshop was completed. The dam, completed in 1957, also supplied power to Rajgangpur cement factory and vast areas of backward western Orissa.

From 21 September to the third week of October 1948, he undertook a whirlwind tour of the USA, the UK, Switzerland, France, Belgium and the Netherlands to discuss matters relating to the fertilizer factory at Sindri and the projected new steelworks, to consider imports of American and British steel and the extent to which purchase by foreign agencies should be replaced by the local agents of foreign manufacturers and suppliers. Through the tour, Dr Mookerjee also meant to recruit superior personnel for Hindustan Aircraft Limited and a cotton textile expert in connection with the newly started Textile Research Institutes.

The same consideration of the wider national good, which prompted him to delve deep into the diverse aspects of his ministerial work and advocate a policy of cooperation and coordination between the private and public sectors, guided his approach to the question of industrial labour. One result of this was the Factories Act of 1948, which followed the suggestions of the Rege Committee appointed during the Second World War to inquire into the conditions of industrial labourers in India and was modelled on the British Factories Act of 1937. The new Act was the first to codify the old international principle that no worker should be employed on any industrial process without making elaborate provisions regarding his safety, health and welfare.

Dr Mookerjee addressed a letter to Sardar Vallabhbhai Patel, home member, central cabinet, in which he contended that although ordnance factories were vital links in India's defence system, European officers, many of them strongly reactionary and intensely prejudiced, were practically controlling the administration and management of these factories, which gave them the power to frustrate national interests of overriding importance. He called upon Patel to devise some means for dispensing with every temporary non-Indian war recruit as soon as possible so that the ordnance factories, then the only department where there was a preponderant strength of European personnel, might be saved in a manner conducive to India's interests. He also argued that the policy of orientation of ordnance factories to civilian production on a mass scale could best be carried out by men whose national interests were essentially bound up with the success of the scheme, not by men whose stake was nil and interest, at best, half-hearted.

Dr Mookerjee's work as industry and supply minister also included solving problems that an industry might face and ensuring its development. One such was that of the matches industry, which owed its origin in India in 1926 to Swedish enterprise. In addition to match-producing factories at Ambarnath, Madras, Bareilly, Calcutta and Dhubri, all owned and run by the Swedish combine called Wimco, there were about 200 small cottage factories making matches by hand, mostly in the Sivakasi area of Madras (now Tamil Nadu). With the major factories producing the bulk of the total output, the cottage factories complained about their critical condition on account of the severe competition from the former and the loss of West Pakistan markets due to Partition. The grievances put forward by the south Indian cottage match manufacturers were mostly redressed by giving considerable relief in excise duty on handmade matches, making sufficient provision for the import of the required raw materials like potassium chlorate, sulphur and phosphorus and facilitating transport for the small-scale producers to move their goods to reach all destinations.

Dr Mookerjee had, during his period of ministership, devoted great attention to the woollen handloom, cotton textile and cotton handloom industries. His objective was to make available all government assistance so that the industries could stand on their own feet and thereafter flourish on a commercial basis. With respect to the woollen handloom industry which, among other tasks, was producing blankets, carpets, tweeds, shawls, scarfs, socks, pullovers, jerseys and, in the process, serving the needs of the defence services and the export trade as well, he ensured that the largest possible number of their workers were brought under the umbrella of cooperative societies. The cotton handloom industry was also languishing. It employed some twenty-five lakh weavers, but had been plagued by shortage of yarn during the war. Additionally, after Independence, it lost the markets in the areas that had now become Pakistan and Burma. To gain some fresh export markets, Dr Mookerjee arranged for samples to be sent to the trade commissioners abroad. Provincial and state governments using cotton cloth were also prevailed upon to use handloom. The Railways were persuaded to give concessions in freight. The government also set up a Central Institute of Cottage Industries at Harduaganj, near Aligarh, for the training of instructors and master-weavers in better techniques of production and new designs.

The last memorable achievement of Dr Mookerjee as the industry and supply minister was the development of the cotton textile industry, which was more than 150 years old and occupied the foremost place among India's organized industries, generating an estimated Rs 127 crore in capital and providing employment for 7,00,000 workers in 1938–39. It produced about 4737 million yards of cloth and 1614 million pounds of yarn annually, valued at about Rs 450 crore. By November 1949, new mills were installed and twelve mills were under erection, following acceptance by the British Indian government of the report (November 1945) of a committee appointed to prepare a plan for the development of the Indian cotton textile industry, to have the total weaving capacity of 6437 million yards of cloth a year. However, the price of mill-made cloth was still unconscionably high. A new textile policy was announced by Dr Mookerjee at a press conference in New Delhi on 30 July 1948, which envisaged reimposition of control over the price, production and distribution of cloth so as to supply the public with adequate quantities of cloth at reasonable prices. It froze the stocks of some 400 textile mills, on which ad hoc prices were proposed to be stamped. Sale of unstamped cloth held by wholesalers and retailers was permitted up to 31 October. The central, provincial and state governments assumed powers to requisition cloth from wholesalers and dealers at prices considered fair by them.

While working as the minister of industries, Dr Mookerjee had also to contend with a most unfortunate trait present among Indians: that of regional chauvinism. In a secret letter to

Dr Mookerjee dated 1 December 1948, Prime Minister Jawaharlal Nehru said that there was considerable talk in the Constituent Assembly and among the general public about the former converting his ministry into a 'miniature' Bengal. He invited Dr Mookerjee's comments on the matter. Nehru forwarded a copy of a letter from a member of the Constituent Assembly regarding his ministry. It is important to note that the complaint was not that he was favouring West Bengal in regard to establishing industries there or creating more employment opportunities for the Bengalis, but merely that he was running his ministry mostly with Bengali officers. Petty-mindedness of sick minds can descend to unfathomable depths indeed.

In reply, in a similarly secret letter to Nehru dated 4 December 1948, Dr Mookerjee wrote that the letter made a general reference to the 'highly unsatisfactory administration' of his ministry and to the 'lack of achievement of anything tangible' by it, without mentioning anything specific or pointing at anything in particular by way of details. On the other hand, those who were in touch with his ministry—officials and non-officials coming from all parts of India and even abroad—had paid compliments regarding the work done by the ministry. The only specific matter which the writer referred to in the letter as 'sins of commission' on his part related to the appointment of Bengalis in his ministry. This was factually wrong. The statement that 'seven out of eight heads of Departments in his Ministry were Bengalis' since Dr Mookerjee took charge was 'amazingly incorrect', as Dr Mookerjee put it. The three most important offices in his ministry were those of Secretary and two Joint Secretaries, who practically controlled the entire administration—and all three were south Indians. The two next important posts of director general, industry and supply, and director general, disposals, were held respectively by Dr J.C. Ghosh, a Bengali who was selected with cabinet approval, and Sivasankar, a south Indian who was

selected by Dr Mookerjee. Of the next three important officials,
the textile commissioner was a Bengali who was promoted from
the office of joint textile commissioner, which he held with
great credit before Dr Mookerjee became a minister; the iron
and steel controller was a Parsee; and the coal commissioner
was S.K. Sinha, a retired ICS officer, who was also selected
with cabinet approval. He asserted that no partiality had been
shown to anyone merely because he happened to be a Bengali.
He enclosed a short note regarding the method of appointments
to officers' posts followed in his ministry, which was presumably
similar to the procedure followed in other ministries as well. He
had no occasion to reject any recommendation of the Federal
Public Service Commission (FPSC) and of the selection board
attached to the home ministry. It was with the concurrence of the
cabinet that the special appointments of Dr J.C. Ghosh and S.K.
Sinha (retired from the ICS) were made. In most other cases,
postings were made on the recommendations, based on seniority
as a rule, of a departmental promotions committee within the
ministry and the question of arbitrary provincial bias did not
arise. Temporary posts, which had to be filled in, on an ad hoc
basis, went almost invariably to refugees from West Pakistan,
whereas only a few refugees from East Pakistan were selected.
In fact, Dr Mookerjee had many complaints on this count from
Bengalis. He added that the selection board could draw upon the
West Bengal government to a larger extent than other provinces
because it came to have a surplus of non-Muslim officers after
the partition.

Dr Mookerjee also enclosed two separate notes relating to the
appointments of two Bengalis, D.N. Mukherjee as salt controller
and M.K. Sengupta as general manager of Hindustan Aircraft Ltd,
Bangalore, described as 'a first-rate scandal' in the letter forwarded
by Nehru. In both notes he totally rubbished the allegations which
were apparently based on hearsay and were contrary to facts. In the

notes, he explained how each appointment had been made from among competent officers, strictly in accordance with established procedure and after due consultations with related officers.

Now that the question of provincial bias on the part of ministers had been raised, Dr Mookerjee requested Nehru to immediately call for a statement showing a complete list of appointments to all higher posts made in all ministries since 15 August 1947, detailing the procedure adopted in each case and also the percentage of persons belonging to various provinces. In his utmost anxiety to fairly and equitably represent all the provinces within the ministry, he had specially requested provincial governments to spare the services of some competent officers, but in most cases they failed to oblige. Regarding his own ministry, Dr Mookerjee offered to meet such members of the Constituent Assembly and others who had approached Nehru over the matter and satisfy anyone, who kept an open mind, regarding both the method of recruitment and the qualifications of the candidate selected. When one of his colleagues was the victim of an unfair attack of this character that was injurious not only to the minister concerned but also to the government as a whole, he looked forward to getting full protection from his Prime Minister.

Barely a year after Dr Mookerjee rebutted this complaint to the effect that partiality was being shown in appointments in his ministry, he received another secret letter from Prime Minister Nehru, dated 13 February 1950, forwarding a statement regarding gazetted appointments made in the industry and supply ministry and its attached organizations from 15 August to 22 December 1949. According to Nehru, this statement indicated that the number of Bengalis appointed was very considerable in relation to the total figure and also that some of the senior appointments were of superannuated persons. While not interested in provincial or communal percentages, Nehru thought that, in view of repeated criticism, Dr Mookerjee

should be careful to keep a certain balance within the parameters
of merit, merit being the chief criterion. Replying to Nehru on
15 February 1950, Dr Mookerjee said he was sorry to find that
the question of alleged partiality shown towards Bengalis in his
ministry, effectively answered by him already, had been raised
again. He then proceeded to show, with reference to records,
that out of 605 gazetted appointments made between 15 July
1947 and 15 December 1949, 188 were from Bengal, 115 from
Madras and the rest from elsewhere, all over India. Dr Mookerjee
wanted this campaign of calumny to stop once and for all and
requested Nehru to collect complete information regarding
the distribution of provincial representatives under different
ministries and also the procedure adopted to select them.

On another occasion, a whisper campaign was started by some
interested persons about a sham transaction by some officers of
the stores section of the supply department, who were alleged to
have sold huge stocks of toothbrushes and combs for a paltry sum,
though they were worth much more. Questions on the subject
had been tabled in Parliament. Files about the whole affair, with
the usual notes which admitted that stocks consist of both good
and bad toothbrushes and the price fetched had been really very
low, were submitted to Dr Mookerjee by the office staff at about
9.30 a.m. At about 10.30 a.m. he went to Parliament and at once
began answering questions raised in connection to this. Replying
to three questions, he answered that a very small price had been
obtained for a large quantity of these articles, some of which were
in good condition but others were so bad that they could not fetch
a good price. And immediately, he produced from his pocket a
number of toothbrushes which had absolutely no bristles! The
members looked at these worthless articles and were at a loss to
comprehend how they could be offered for sale. Officers of his
own department were puzzled as to how he could equip himself
with such effective materials within such a short time.

During this period Dr Mookerjee also wore two other hats. For one, he was elected the president of the Calcutta-based Maha Bodhi Society, the principal organization of Buddhists in India. Balraj Madhok, who had seen Dr Mookerjee at very close range, has observed that it was his firm conviction that Buddhist thought and culture could bind together the Buddhist world, particularly the South East Asian and East Asian countries with India. This culture was an essentially Indian inspiration and constituted a departure from orthodox Hindu belief in India, by not accepting the Vedas but nevertheless working within the broad framework of Hindu beliefs such as reincarnation. Dr Mookerjee felt that awareness of the thought and culture of Lord Buddha would create an abiding unity between India and the other countries, transcending any difference in the economic and political sphere. He also noted that while Buddhism had all but disappeared from its country of origin, namely India, it had been assimilated by the age-old current of Hindu culture. The fact that Buddha has been accepted as one of the ten avatars or incarnations of Lord Vishnu by the Hindus was in his belief compensating refutation of the premise that India had moved away from Buddhism.

While acting as such, he discharged an important function. He received the relics of the Buddhist saints and disciples of Buddha, Sariputta and Mahamouggallana, from Prime Minister Jawaharlal Nehru in a colourful function organized by the society at the Calcutta Maidan in January 1949. These relics had been taken away from the ancient stupa at Sanchi, Madhya Pradesh, by one General Cunningham in 1851, sent to England and kept in the British Museum. After India's independence, they were returned to India. Prime Minister Nehru handed them over to Dr Mookerjee, the then president of the Maha Bodhi Society of India, on 14 January 1949.

He visited Burma and French Indochina with the sacred relics. This was followed by requests from Ceylon (now Sri Lanka) and Tibet (not yet annexed by the Chinese) for an opportunity to see the relics in their own land before they were re-enshrined at Sanchi. The final act of this phase of his life was in the re-enshrinement of the relics in the new vihara at Sanchi near Bhopal, capital of present-day Madhya Pradesh, in November 1952. The function was presided over by India's Vice President and Dr Mookerjee's old personal friend Dr Sarvepalli Radhakrishnan. Thakin Nu, the Premier of Burma, visited Sanchi to take part in the ceremonies and told Dr Mookerjee, 'You do not know what a great service you have rendered to my country. Your visit with the relics brought about a wonderful change in my people. They have found their soul.'

Finally, a description of this phase of Dr Mookerjee's life would not be complete without a reference to the work he did as a member of the Constituent Assembly. One of the most memorable speeches that he made in the assembly was regarding the adoption of Hindi as the official language of the country. Dr Mookerjee was a great advocate of Hindi—which is remarkable, because a substantial part of the social class he belonged to, namely that of the Bengali middle-class bhadralok, was one of staunch anglophiles, and looked down upon Hindi (a small part of them still do). It must, however, be said in mitigation that in Bengal there was no fanaticism or violence about this anti-Hindi attitude of the type that was subsequently seen in Tamil Nadu.

Dr Mookerjee's speech on Hindi is an example of what a balanced approach to the question should be. While advocating progressive adoption of Hindi in clear terms, he had cautioned Hindi enthusiasts not to come on too heavy and thereby damage their own cause. He had also demonstrated his keen eye for detail when advocating the use of international numerals in preference to Devanagari ones. Excerpts[5] from his speech in the assembly, delivered on 13 September 1949:

India has been a country of many languages . . . Some of my friends spoke eloquently that a day might come when India shall have one language and one language only. Frankly speaking, I do not share that view . . . If it is claimed by anyone that by passing an article in the Constitution of India, one language is going to be accepted by all, by a process of coercion, I say, that that will not be possible to achieve. Unity in diversity is India's keynote and must be achieved by a process of understanding and consent . . . Left to myself, I would certainly have preferred Sanskrit . . . Why do we accept Hindi? . . . It is for the main reason that that is the one language which is understood by the largest single majority in this country today. If 14 crores of people out of 32 today understand a particular language, and it is also capable of progressive development, we say, let us accept that language for the purposes of the whole of India, but do it in such a way that in the interim period it may not result in the deterioration of our official conduct of business or administration and at no time retard true advancement of India and her other great languages.

11

The Pogrom in East Bengal and Resignation from Cabinet, 1950

The period of January–March 1950 saw a horrendous anti-Hindu pogrom[1] in erstwhile East Bengal or East Pakistan that served as a watershed in the life of Dr Mookerjee. It is estimated that some 50,000 Hindus lost their lives, and tens of thousands of Hindu women were brutalized in the pogrom. It led him to have serious issues with Jawaharlal Nehru and ultimately to resign from the central cabinet led by him. Following this resignation he founded a brand-new party called the Bharatiya Jana Sangh that eventually, long after his death, transmuted itself into the Bharatiya Janata Party (BJP). This party led the ruling coalition in the Union government between 1999 and 2004, and returned to power in 2014 after a ten-year interregnum with an absolute majority; it also runs the state governments in several states. This pogrom and its aftermath are therefore required to be studied carefully in order to understand the subsequent turns that Dr Mookerjee's life took.

This pogrom is unique in the world in two ways. First, no pogrom of such dimensions has remained so well-concealed from the eyes of the world for so long; and secondly, in no pogrom have the very *victims*, not the perpetrators, shown such alacrity, such extraordinary eagerness, in *concealing* it. This was believed to be the Pakistani state-sponsored persecution of the

Hindu minority in erstwhile East Pakistan, then also known as East Bengal. Its primary objective appears to have been to drive the Hindu elite and intelligentsia out of the country, cleanse the country of their influence (which was enormous) and grab their property. In the process humble Hindu agriculturists, artisans and fishermen were also persecuted, murdered and driven out.

Till 1947, teachers, lawyers, doctors, civil administrators, clerks, journalists, traders and the like, in short, people engaged in intellectual pursuits in any manner in East Bengal, were overwhelmingly Hindu. They were 13.5 million in number, that is about 29 per cent of the population, but owned nearly 80 per cent of the national wealth and financed 95 per cent of the educational institutions. In Dacca city, they owned some 75 per cent of the land and property. The bulk of the zamindars—the feudal landlords created by Lord Cornwallis's Permanent Settlement—were also Hindu. Moreover, they also formed the majority in most towns and owned the major part of the land there. All this contributed to a feeling of superiority among the Hindus. The countryside, on the other hand, was overwhelmingly Muslim, populated mostly by poor agriculturists, though there were Hindu pockets all over the province.

The Pakistani state machinery, dominated on the other hand by Punjabi Muslims, was determined to undo this, and with the help of similarly inclined East Bengali Muslim leaders, set about their task with determination. The populace was deliberately inflamed in the name of religion and encouraged to participate in the murder-mayhem-rape game. Once started, this game gathered its own momentum, and became an intermittent process, sometimes rising to a crescendo (as in 1950, 1964, 1971, 1988, 1992 and 2001) and at other times settling down to a squeeze, the intensity of which varied from time to time. As the years given will indicate, the process has not stopped even after

East Pakistan became Bangladesh. Together with the Hindus a handful of other non-Muslims, namely Christians and Buddhists, and Ahmadiyyas, also known as Qadianis, were also affected to a degree.

The second aspect of the pogrom is most baffling, intriguing and inexplicable. As a result of this concealment very few books exist on this enormous human rights abuse, and even fewer in English. Those interested are referred to this biographer's book titled *My People, Uprooted: The Exodus of Hindus from East Pakistan and Bangladesh* (see Bibliography).

Unlike in Punjab, the partition of Bengal was not followed immediately by any major rioting on either side. By January 1948, in a matter of just five months following Independence and Partition the bilateral exodus in Punjab was nearly over, and practically no Muslim was left in East Punjab, and no Hindu or Sikh in West Punjab.

Jayanta Kumar Ray's seminal work *Democracy and Nationalism on Trial: A Study of East Pakistan* (see Bibliography) provides, arguably, the best possible insight into the near-holocaust that overtook the East Bengali Hindus during the fifties and the sixties. In particular, the motivation of the Pakistani government in exterminating and/or driving out a huge chunk of their own population, an act that finds parallels only in the Jewish, Armenian and Cambodian holocausts in recent times, has been masterfully analysed by this eminent scholar in this book, and those interested in the subject are referred to the same. He has also, incidentally, rubbished the attempts by writers like Keith Callard and Abul Mansur Ahmad to whitewash the misdeeds of the East Pakistani government and people. Some subsequent writers like Michael Brecher[2] have, with a very superficial understanding of the times, tried to show the pogrom as essentially a two-way movement and criticized Dr Mookerjee as 'communalist' (what else?) for having taken up the East Bengal refugees' cause.

It was a serial of looting, torching, rape and murder of the Hindus. The common Muslim who was so far living in relative harmony with his Hindu neighbour was driven to a frenzy by the calls of the fundamentalist Pakistani state such as through the Radio Pakistan announcements. Aided by state-sponsored volunteers called *ansars*, they bathed East Bengal in blood. Roving loot-rape-murder gangs,[3] many of them who had lately moved into East Pakistan from Bihar, pounced on fleeing Hindus and brutalized Hindu women and took away everything before killing them. On 12 February 1950,[4] all passenger trains crossing the wide Meghna River over the Bhairab or Anderson bridge were stopped by marauding gangs who had boarded the train from its last stop. These gangs then singled out the Hindus, slit their throats and threw them into the river below. The coastal district of Barisal saw one of the worst carnages. Barisal is literally a maze of perennial rivers, canals and watercourses, with the result that Hindus found it very difficult to escape from the place and had to suffer their fate with their backs to the wall. The sites of some of the most horrendous killings in the district were the villages of Muladi, Madhabpasha and Lakutia. Muladi, an important riverine port, was the home of several hundred Hindus. When torching of their houses started, all the Hindus flocked to the police station for shelter. They were then attacked and the whole lot of them was killed in the precincts of the station.[5]

The government of West Bengal, under the stewardship of Dr B.C. Roy, took extraordinary measures to ferry the Hindus safely to West Bengal. Fifteen large steamers, belonging to the Calcutta-based British India Steam Navigation Co. and the Rivers Steam Navigation Co. were pressed into service to pick up stranded and beleaguered Hindus from the riverine parts of East Bengal, especially from Khulna, Barisal and the southern part of Faridpur districts. These steamers came in through the Sunderban deltas and disgorged their miserable load at the Babu Ghat and

Shalimar Ghat, wharves on the two sides of the Hooghly. Special trains and aircraft were also arranged and pressed into service. Very few could afford air travel, yet some of those that came in with injuries sustained by them at the hands of Muslim goons on the way to Dacca airport had to be given emergency treatment. A medical centre had to be opened for them at Calcutta airport.

In March 1950, some Muslims from the rural areas of West Bengal, especially Tehatta and Karimpur areas of the Nadia district and Bagda and Bongaon areas of the 24 Parganas district, left for East Pakistan. These are border areas, and a large number of them crossed on foot while others went by train. Later in the same month there was serious rioting in Howrah town requiring deployment of the army, as a result of which also some Muslims from Howrah and adjoining districts moved out. These were the only known instances of Muslims in distress moving en masse to East Pakistan from West Bengal. Apart from these, the movement between the two Bengals, unlike the movement between the two Punjabs, was strictly unidirectional. And this is what Dr Mookerjee objected to, in so many words, on the floor of the Parliament.

In truth the bulk of the Hindus of East Bengal had failed to see the writing on the wall and were also taken in by the assurances of Congress leaders like Gandhi and Patel. Dr Mookerjee was also a party to such assurances (presumably hoping that the Congress leadership would learn lessons from the Partition and adopt a reciprocal and firm policy towards Pakistan), and the East Bengal Hindus looked upon his inclusion in the Indian cabinet as a guarantee for their security and welfare. But he soon realized that Nehru seemed determined to pursue the same policy of defeatism towards Pakistan that the Congress had allegedly pursued towards the Muslim League—a policy which was largely responsible for the Partition. In spite of two inter-dominion agreements (April and December 1948), about 2.3 million Hindus (not counting those who rehabilitated themselves in India, or those Hindus of

East Bengali origin who were in India at the time of Partition and never went back) were forced to leave their homes in East Bengal during the first two years of Pakistan's existence. But the worst came early in 1950, when the massacre of Hindus on a wide scale planned by Aziz Ahmed, Chief Secretary of East Bengal, and his cohorts was started by Muslims all over East Bengal with the direct connivance of the Pakistan government.[6]

Meanwhile, Dr Mookerjee, together with Sardar Patel, was exerting relentless pressure upon Nehru within the cabinet to take drastic measures—either to go to war with Pakistan or to declare a policy of exchange of population between the two Bengals on the Punjab model or demand a homeland for East Bengali Hindus. They could not, while being in the cabinet, make any kind of public statement. Also, reprisals on a limited scale had started in West Bengal, in Calcutta and the Muslim-majority Murshidabad district. As a result of this pressure, and unnerved by the Calcutta and Murshidabad incidents, Nehru issued a press statement on 10 February and wrote to Dr Roy on 15 February expressing his great concern about the plight of the refugees. He also stated in a long speech before the Rajya Sabha on 23 February that henceforth he would be personally looking after the East Bengal refugee matter.

The press statement[7] of 10 February has a very significant sentence that encapsulates the totality of Nehru's attitude towards Pakistan and its state-sponsored persecution of Hindus. Nehru expresses his rather pessimistic attitude when he says, 'It is obvious that we cannot control the happenings in East Bengal except by consultation with the Central Government of Pakistan and the Government of East Bengal.'[8] Is it so obvious? Dr Mookerjee and Patel, being part of Nehru's cabinet, could not have publicly retorted. Jayanta Kumar Ray of the Indian Institute of Advanced Studies, Simla, however, found out by research as late as in 1968[9] that the pogrom of 1950 was the handiwork of the East Bengal government, more particularly of its Chief Secretary Aziz Ahmed.[10] This became even more manifest some six months later when, in October 1950, Pakistan's central cabinet minister for law and labour, Jogendra Nath Mandal,[11] defected to India and sent his resignation, describing in graphic detail the different aspects of the persecution that he had seen with his own eyes and had come to know by reason of his position. What Ray could find out in 1968 Nehru certainly would have known in 1950 through his intelligence network; yet he persisted in this attitude due to his preset notions about respecting territorial sovereignty, and expected cooperation from the very government that had let loose the pogrom! This could qualify as the height of political naivety. Driven by this attitude he subsequently signed the infamous pact with Liaquat Ali, which caused Dr Mookerjee to resign his cabinet berth. The latter has lambasted this attitude in his resignation speech mentioned later in this chapter.

Nehru tries to say in his 23 February statement[12] before the Parliament that, 'A kind of iron curtain fell on East Bengal during these days and accurate information did not come through except in driblets.' Later on in his speech, he says: 'We have received a large number of telegrams, letters and other accounts from individuals who have come from various parts of East Bengal giving particulars of the ghastly occurrences.' He already had the experience of having signed two futile inter-dominion agreements, he most certainly had his intelligence inputs, and now he had eyewitness accounts, all of which he chose to ignore. This is not all. He goes on to say, in the same speech, that the deputy high commissioner in Dacca had been advised by the Pakistan authorities to stay put in his house, that Liaquat Ali rejected his offer to have a joint fact-finding mission as well as that of a joint tour of East Bengal by the two Prime Ministers, and that the government of East Bengal had rejected an offer by the Chief Minister of West Bengal to send a relief party to the camps in Dacca with medicines and other supplies. He rejects the suggestion to have an exchange of population on the Punjab model on the grounds that, 'both India and Pakistan *should* [emphasis added] have the strength and capacity to discharge their primary function of giving security and confidence to their people, whoever they might be'.[13] A classic example of wishful thinking, typical of the man.

Nehru so far had not visited West Bengal where all the refugees had been headed. Meanwhile feelings were running very high in the city. Posters had appeared saying 'Nehru, declare war on Pakistan or resign'. At last he decided to come to Calcutta to see the situation for himself, and arrived on 6 March evening along with his daughter Indira Gandhi and Mridula Sarabhai. By this date the pogrom had been continuing in East Pakistan for at least a month during which Dr Mookerjee and Sardar Patel were relentlessly pressurizing him to take action. He met the Congress members of the state assembly the same evening at the Raj Bhavan with Dr B.C. Roy and Atulya Ghosh, the state Congress president. He briefed them on what the Union government had done and planned to do in respect of the problem. As it seemed there was precious little that Nehru's government had so far done, except give support to the steps that Dr Roy had taken and pay lip service to the refugees. At this stage, according to the veteran journalist Sukharanjan Sengupta, some Congress legislators asked him if exchange of population on the Punjab model could be considered, of course without the violence. Nehru is said to have remarked that this was a very difficult task, and would have to be considered carefully in all its implications. He was accompanied at all stages by Dr Mookerjee, but apparently the latter, probably out of concern for proprieties, did not make any statements.

This observation of Nehru was a very interesting one because, if true, it shows that even he did not rule out this possibility of exchange of population even after having made statements to the contrary on the floor of the Parliament. There was a report to this effect in the *Statesman* on 7 March also. Before this, again according to Sengupta, in a letter addressed to Dr Roy he had rubbished the idea of exchange of population as impracticable. Again, only a few days later on 17 March, on the floor of the Parliament, he made it clear that he had made up his mind against it. Why this vacillation, and what caused him to finally make up his mind? This exchange is referred to and discussed later in this chapter. Meanwhile we can return to Nehru in Calcutta.

The next day Nehru met Dr P.C. Ghosh, the former and first Chief Minister of West Bengal. Dr Ghosh was a native of Dacca district and spoke Bengali with a distinct Dacca accent. Several of his own relatives had since fled Dacca or were in the process of doing so. Nehru also discussed the situation with Asutosh Lahiri of the Hindu Mahasabha. According to Sengupta, the discussions generated more heat than light. Then on 8 March, Nehru, accompanied by Dr Mookerjee and Dr B.C. Roy, visited the border town of Bongaon through which the refugees from Barisal, Khulna and Jessore were pouring in. All three districts were severely affected by the pogrom. A large number of the refugees were squatting on the two sides of Jessore Road, the highway that ran through Bongaon into Pakistan. Dr Mookerjee translated for them when Nehru questioned them. Nehru even picked up a baby boy, cuddled him and said, '*Zinda raho, beta* (Stay alive, child).' Meanwhile Indira and Mridula Sarabhai spoke to the women in the camps and asked them about the atrocities they had been subjected to. Nehru then addressed the refugees in a speech and expressed his apprehensions about the problem and his ways of tackling it—no concrete steps, just platitudes.

The next day, on 9 March, he flew back to New Delhi and on the 10th addressed a letter to Liaquat Ali Khan, addressing him as 'Nawabzada'.[14] Was this a throwback to Gandhi's addressing Jinnah as 'Qaid-e-Azam' six years ago,[15] in 1944, and writing in Gujarati, resulting in the abortive talks? Probably. The same futility is apparent in all his subsequent actions right through the month of March 1950—mere exchange of letters, trading accusations and counter-accusations, then entreaties, offering to visit East Pakistan together with Liaquat and the latter flatly refusing, which finally culminated in Liaquat Ali travelling to Delhi on 2 April, and the two Prime Ministers signing the fateful pact, called the Nehru–Liaquat or Delhi Pact, on 8 April.

It is very difficult for a rational mind to understand the psychological process through which Nehru had reached the conclusion that further atrocities on Hindus in Pakistan could be prevented by a pact with Liaquat Ali. A key to this mind is provided by Binoy Mukhopadhyay,[16] then chief press adviser and registrar of newspapers, Government of India, who had observed Nehru at very close range. Unfortunately, Mukhopadhyay wrote only in Bengali, and as a result the products of his extremely perceptive mind are available only to a few. In an interview to the Bengali fortnightly *Desh,*[17] he calls Nehru a 'political somnambulist', a person living in his own dreamland of political make-believe. Nehru imagined, indeed convinced himself, that Liaquat Ali was a person with honest intentions and so long as he observed the pact (which he did), Liaquat Ali would do the same too. Pretty much the same as what an ostrich does when pursued by a lion—burrow its head into the sand in the belief that since it cannot see the lion, the lion cannot see it either. As an example of political naivety it compares well with another one that Nehru committed in the immediate past, which was the calling of a unilateral ceasefire in Kashmir while in hot pursuit of Pakistani marauders and thereafter taking the issue to the United Nations. Durga Das, the veteran journalist, has almost an identical observation[18] about Nehru where he says, '. . . nor did he bother to face facts. He wove fantasies round his ideals and believed that somehow his preachings would make people do the things he wanted.'

It was necessary to provide this longish introduction to underscore the intensity of the pogrom of 1950 and to understand the background of Dr Mookerjee's resignation from the Union cabinet in April 1950. Till the beginning of 1950 he had busied himself totally with the running of his own ministry but had kept himself abreast of what was going on. Dr Mookerjee, then one of the two Bengali cabinet ministers, had never hesitated to take up the cause of Hindus in British India. He obviously could not remain unaffected by the goings-on in East Pakistan even during the relatively calm period of 1947–50 (even though during this period 2.3 million Hindus left East Pakistan and sought state rehabilitation), and repeatedly drew Nehru's and Patel's attention to the matter. Nehru's reply was in the two inter-dominion agreements, totally futile, referred to earlier. Then came the 1950 pogrom, and ultimately the Nehru–Liaquat Pact, and Dr Mookerjee just had to move.

On 17 March 1950, Dr Mookerjee was still in the cabinet, indefatigably trying to prevail upon Nehru to agree to exchange of population or go to war with Pakistan. However, because of the respect he had of the joint responsibility of the cabinet he was not in a position to publicly air his views on the subject. This role was taken by Pandit Lakshmi Kanta Maitra,[19] a Congress member and a renowned scholar from Santipur, Nadia. It is not on record anywhere, but quite plausible that Dr Mookerjee spoke to Maitra and persuaded him to take this role in the house.

Nehru had, during his visit to West Bengal, also visited a refugee camp at Ranaghat, an important railway junction town very close to the East Pakistan border. There he saw some families with a few suitcases and quite a few women with bangles on their wrists, and instantly jumped to the conclusion that things were getting better. On 17 March he said,[20] 'I think this [persecution of Hindus] is lessening greatly now. I visited day before yesterday a big camp at Ranaghat where these people are arriving daily . . . and I had found that many of them have been able to bring a fair quantity

of luggage with them . . . Obviously there had been a relaxation.'
Maitra immediately pointed out Nehru's naivety by saying:

> During the last few days when Pandit Jawaharlal Nehru visited
> Bengal, Pakistan became cautious. They knew quite well that
> the Prime Minister of India was sitting in Calcutta . . . and
> they took jolly good care to see that some people at least from
> some points were allowed to come over to India with some of
> their belongings . . . Letters are pouring in which describe these
> tales, which I have never known happening in the history of
> any country in the world; nowhere has there been such a large-
> scale dishonour of women, large-scale abduction of women,
> mass-rape and other indignities on womanhood. I do not know
> if the Honourable Prime Minister enquired about that.[21]

Maitra was fully echoing Dr Mookerjee's feelings when he went
on to say:

> He [Nehru] has gone out of the way to attack the [Indian] Press
> in not observing restraint. You very well know that Pakistan
> had put an iron curtain over that territory . . . He [Nehru] was
> referring to some sort of a statement which he and perhaps the
> Prime Minister of Pakistan would make to ease the immediate
> tension . . . but Pakistan said 'No' . . . Whatever the Prime
> Minister of India proposed to Pakistan has been turned down
> . . . after all Pakistan is a professedly theocratic Islamic State.
> How on earth can you rely on their sense of justice to protect
> the non-Muslim minorities?[22]

In reply to what Maitra had said, Nehru said:[23]

> Now, the whole line of my argument, if I may say so, was this. I
> pointed out that in recent months there had been a certain flow

of refugees . . . Now, in passing I tried to put before you what the present position was . . . that is the whole course of the last two and a half years' history, and I mentioned, if you will remember what happened in Sind after the Punjab occurrences and what happened in East Bengal during the last two years or more, there was a certain process of, shall we call it squeezing out which occurs and has occurred . . . And when there is this widespread sense of insecurity and any special occurrence takes place, then immediately it becomes much greater insecurity and danger, because they live in a certain atmosphere of suppression and it is because of this that it is transformed into a dangerous situation which otherwise it would not be—otherwise it would be a local incident. Now that is the problem . . . We owe it to those people in East Bengal who may be in danger, we owe it to them, to give them protection, to give them protection in our own territory or to give them protection in their territory, if there is no other way, if circumstances demand it.

Disjointed, confused rambling, quite a bit of it self-contradictory, and no answer to the points that Maitra had raised regarding the obvious insincerity of the Pakistan government, and above all, utter defeatism. Furthermore, a dogged refusal to accept the fact that the very government which had engineered this pogrom (which Nehru could not have been unaware of, iron curtain or whatever notwithstanding) could never be trusted now to save them. The idea that 'you have to function through that government' was an absurdity.

And from here to the pact of 8 April, the fateful Nehru–Liaquat Pact or Delhi Pact, was just a hop away. With it the remaining Hindus of East Bengal were consigned to a living hell.

Liaquat Ali, who had so far been resisting all attempts by Nehru towards all joint action, even a joint statement, found himself in deep trouble when the reprisals in West Bengal to the pogrom in East Bengal caused about half a million Muslims to cross over from West Bengal to Pakistan. He, therefore, finally accepted Nehru's invitation to come to Delhi, knowing that Nehru would lap it up, which he did. And thus came about the pact.

Dr Mookerjee, finally, came in direct conflict with Nehru over his pusillanimous approach to the problem. Up to this point, probably, he was hoping against hope that with the help of Patel he would be able to dissuade Nehru from pursuing his make-believe scheme. All his hopes were, however, dashed when he learnt of Nehru's invitation to Liaquat Ali for making yet another agreement on the welfare of minorities. He protested against this course of action, reminded Nehru of the fate of the previous agreements, and is reported to have demanded the insertion of a penal clause to provide for sanctions against whichever country failed to honour the agreement. Apart from such a demand being quite legitimate, considering the past conduct of the Pakistanis, Dr Mookerjee had sensed that it would almost certainly wreck the impending negotiations, and if it did, Pakistan's real intentions would be proved. But Nehru would not budge from his firm belief in the good intentions of Pakistan. Finally, confronted by Dr Mookerjee in a cabinet meeting on 1 April 1950 when he could not meet his arguments, he lost his temper and overruled the former, who had told him to his face that he was flouting all conventions of joint responsibility of the cabinet on vital national questions such as the one created by the situation in East Bengal.

From that time onwards, Dr Mookerjee felt that he could neither do any good to the country nor redeem his pledges to the minorities of East Bengal by continuing in the cabinet. The only honourable alternative open to him was to resign from the exalted position of cabinet minister, a position which he had accepted for the service of the motherland two and a half years ago. He communicated this to Nehru on the evening of 1 April before his talks with Liaquat Ali started on 2 April. Nehru readily agreed and did not ask him to reconsider his decision. Dr Mookerjee assured Nehru then that it was not his intention to embarrass him during the talks and his resignation might come into effect after Liaquat's departure. On the morning of 3 April, he stated to Nehru that it might be considered inappropriate for him to attend cabinet meetings pending his resignation but the latter asked him to continue to attend the meetings.

In a letter to Nehru dated 6 April 1950, Dr Mookerjee tendered his resignation and requested to be relieved of his duties as early as possible. The reasons for his resignation, he said, arose out of the policy pursued by the government regarding Indo-Pakistan relationship, specially relating to Bengal, which were bound to fail (they did fail, as evidenced by the subsequent carnages, such as the Assam Mail massacre at Santahar junction in February 1951). Under no circumstances could Dr Mookerjee be a party to the agreement which was likely to be finalized on 8 April as it did not address the crux of the problem, was unlikely to offer any solution, would bring little solace to the sufferers and was bound to give rise to fresh communal and political problems in India with unforeseen consequences. He concluded by thanking Nehru for the opportunity given to him in the first cabinet of free India for two and a half years. He enclosed a copy of his letter of resignation to Deputy Prime Minister Sardar Patel on 6 April and expressed his deep gratitude to him for the confidence and affection he had always received from him.

The extent to which the pact was a dismal failure and rang the death knell of Hindus in East Pakistan is proved by a single statistic: according to a report published in the *Hindustan Standard*[24] of 20 March 1951, the Government of India had admitted that since 7 February 1950, not less than 41,89,847 Hindus had left East Pakistan.

Meanwhile, Commerce Minister Kshitish Chandra Neogy, the only other minister in the cabinet from Bengal, wrote to Prime Minister Nehru on 6 April, saying he had given his most anxious consideration to the terms of the agreement the latter had drawn up with Liaquat Ali. No East Bengali (which Neogy was, but not Dr Mookerjee) could be expected to believe in the honesty of purpose of Pakistan after the terrible happenings there. The very appointment of a man like Malik Feroze Khan Noon, a known Hindu-baiter, as Governor of East Bengal just on the eve of the Nehru–Liaquat talks was additional proof of Pakistan's mala fide intentions. Neogy inferred from the Prime Minister's action that he had lost confidence in him and so had no option but to tender his resignation. Neogy requested to be relieved of his duties at the 'earliest possible moment'.

Sardar Patel, for one, was hugely unhappy at the turn of events culminating in Dr Mookerjee's resignation. These two men were not affected by what Binoy Mukhopadhyay termed Nehru's 'political somnambulism', and shared the same thoughts about the future of the Hindus of East Bengal, and the same apprehensions, even certainties, about Pakistan's real intentions. But it was not Patel's style to poke his nose into matters from which the Prime Minister had excluded him. He had, with consummate political dexterity, arranged for the integration of all the princely states into India save one, but had to watch from a distance the goings-on in the one state that Nehru kept to himself and botched up for all eternity, namely Jammu and Kashmir. In a 'Strictly Personal' letter to Dr Mookerjee on 6 April, he said that in view of Dr Mookerjee sparing no pains to serve the country during those trying and troublesome periods since the formation of the first cabinet, he felt very unhappy at the turn things had taken. He had had no discussion with Nehru on the subject yet and did not know what had prompted his decisions. While he was very afraid of the reaction Dr Mookerjee's exit might cause in the country at that time, he still hoped that they should be able to solve the Bengal problem before it was too late. Meanwhile, he was certain that Dr Mookerjee would see that no action of his would harm India and, more especially, their dear afflicted province of Bengal.

Such was the deep respect and mutual appreciation these two men had for each other that when on 13 April they met, Patel pressed him very hard and asked him to reconsider his decision. On the night of 14 April Patel again appealed to Dr Mookerjee to reconsider and the latter spent a sleepless night. In a personal letter[25] to Dr Mookerjee dated 15 April, Patel said he was 'much distressed' and 'very unhappy' to find that he was still adamant on his decision to resign. He was hoping that Dr Mookerjee would be able to accompany him to Calcutta and share with him 'a great burden and tremendous exertions in a most difficult task'; instead, he found that he would have to face the 'full blast' of the effect of the resignations of both him and Neogy. It was some consolation, however, that at Patel's request Dr Mookerjee postponed his statement in Parliament. Replying on the same day Dr Mookerjee said he was distressed to find that on this particular occasion, he could not act according to Patel's request and hoped he would appreciate his viewpoint and forgive him.

Meanwhile, Dr Mookerjee discussed the matter with Neogy who was also unwilling to withdraw his resignation. Apart from the reasons given by him already, the latter felt very strongly that the impending trade talks should not be finalized or implemented by the cabinet for a period of around two months, during which time the government should satisfy itself that the political agreement was actually being implemented by Pakistan, giving the highest priority to the recovery of abducted women. Telegrams circulated to Delhi from the deputy high commissioner, Dacca, indicated how serious disturbances were still continuing in some parts of East Bengal, including the interior of Dacca. Apart from the border incidents separately reported by the West Bengal government, there were reports of about fifty women having been abducted. The Chittagong Mail was attacked thrice on 12 April. Nehru was requested to consider how far this would be regarded as a breach of agreement.

In the end the inevitable happened. Nehru brushed aside all reports of wrongdoings by Pakistan and continued in his belief in Liaquat Ali's good intentions. On the early morning of 19 April 1950, Dr Mookerjee returned from Bombay, promptly acknowledged Nehru's letter of 15 April and proposed to make a statement before Parliament after question hour on the very day for which the Speaker's consent had been obtained previously. As previously agreed, his resignation would come into effect from the 19th and he would be leaving Delhi for Calcutta on the 20th.

Dr Mookerjee's resignation speech, delivered before a packed Lok Sabha on 19 April 1950, is one of his best and most moving speeches. It encapsulates his clear understanding of Pakistani motives, and gives clinching arguments in favour of this understanding, as opposed to Nehru's belief in Pakistan's sovereignty and presumed good intentions. It is a powerful speech in terms of political content, loaded with a political message; and yet, at the same time, poignant in showing his deep empathy for the unfortunate victims of the Islamic cleansing process. The salient parts of the speech[26] therefore, need to be quoted with comments as appropriate.

Dr Mookerjee began his speech with the following introduction:

Sir, in accordance with parliamentary convention I rise to make a statement explaining the reasons which have led to my resignation from the Cabinet. Let me assure the House that I have not taken the step on the spur of the moment but after deep and deliberate thought . . . There is nothing of a personal character which has prompted me to resign and I do hope that those with whom I have disagreed will appreciate the depth of my convictions just as I have unhesitatingly appreciated their own. My differences are fundamental and it is not fair or honourable for me to continue as a member of the Government whose policy I cannot approve of.

He went on to say:

> I have never felt happy about our attitude towards Pakistan.
> It has been weak, halting and inconsistent. Our goodness or
> inaction has been interpreted as weakness by Pakistan . . . the
> circumstances that have led to my resignation are primarily
> concerned with the treatment of minorities in Pakistan,
> especially in East Bengal. Let me say at once that the Bengal
> problem is not a provincial one. It raises issues of an all-India
> character and on its proper solution will depend the peace and
> prosperity, both economic and political, of the entire nation.

In the last sentence he was almost prophetic, as is evidenced by
the spate of terror attacks today, engineered by Pakistan on India,
targeting Hindus and Muslims alike. Then further:

> There is an important difference in the approach to the problem
> of minorities in India and Pakistan. The vast majority of Muslims
> in India wanted the partition of the country on a communal
> basis, although I gladly recognize there has been a small section
> of patriotic Muslims who consistently have identified themselves
> with national interests and suffered for it. The Hindus on the
> other hand were almost to a man definitely opposed to partition.

This last part would today perhaps be considered grossly
'politically incorrect'; but is it not the unvarnished truth? And is
not a foundation in truth necessary to author a sensible policy?
  He then describes his personal role in the partition process:

> When the partition of India became inevitable, I played a very
> large part in creating public opinion in favour of the partition of
> Bengal, for I felt that if that was not done, the whole of Bengal
> and also perhaps Assam would fall into Pakistan. At that time

little knowing that I would join the first Central Cabinet, I along with others, gave assurances to the Hindus of East Bengal, stating that if they suffered at the hands of the future Pakistan Government . . . free India would not remain an idle spectator and their just cause would be boldly taken up by the Government and people of India. During the last two and a half years their sufferings have been of a sufficiently tragic character. Today I have no hesitation in acknowledging that in spite of all efforts on my part, I have not been able to redeem my pledge and on this ground alone—if on no other—I have no moral right to be associated with Government any longer.

Now Dr Mookerjee comes to the pact itself, the utter futility of which is manifest to him:

The recent agreement, to my mind, offers no solution to the basic problem. The evil is far deeper and no patchwork can lead to peace . . . if anyone analyses the course of events in Pakistan since its creation, it will be manifest that there is no honourable place for Hindus within that State. The problem is not communal. It is essentially political. The agreement unfortunately tries to ignore the implications of an Islamic State. But anyone, who refers carefully to the Objectives Resolution passed by the Constituent Assembly of Pakistan and to the speech of its Prime Minister, will find that while talking in one place of protection of minority rights, the Resolution in another place emphatically declares 'that the principles of democracy, freedom, equality, tolerance and special justice as enunciated by Islam shall be fully observed'. The Prime Minister of Pakistan while moving the Resolution thus spoke: 'You would also notice that the State is not to play the part of a neutral observer wherein the Muslims may be merely free to profess and practise their religion, because such an attitude on the part of the State would be the very negation of the ideals which prompted the demand of Pakistan and it is these ideals which should be the cornerstone of the State which we want to build. The State will create such conditions as are conducive to the building up of a truly Islamic Society which means that the State will have to play a positive part in this effort. You would remember that the Qaid-e-Azam and other leaders of the Muslim League always made unequivocal declarations that the Muslim demand for Pakistan was based upon the fact that the Muslims had their own way of life and a code of conduct. Indeed, Islam lays down specific directions for social behaviour and seeks to guide society in its attitude towards the problems which confront it day to day. *Islam is not just a matter of private beliefs and conduct* [emphasis added].' In such a society, let me ask in all seriousness, can any Hindu expect to live with any sense of security in respect of his cultural, economic and political rights?

Dr Mookerjee then recounts the experience of the Hindus of East Pakistan since Partition, something that Nehru seemed to have conveniently chosen to ignore because, as Binoy Mukhopadhyay said, 'it did not fit in with his pre-set notions'.[27]

It is not the ideology preached by Pakistan that is the only disturbing factor. Its performances have been in full accord with its ideology and the minorities have had bitter experiences time without number of the true character and functioning of an Islamic State. The Agreement has totally failed to deal with this basic problem.

Public memory is sometimes very short. There is an impression in many quarters that the Agreement recently made is the first great attempt of its kind to solve the problem of minorities. I am leaving aside for the time being the disaster that took place in Punjab; in spite of all assurances and undertakings there was a complete collapse of the administration and the problem was solved in a most brutal fashion. Afterwards we saw the gradual extermination of Hindus from East Bengal. About 13 millions of Hindus were still living and their future had been a matter of the gravest concern to all of us in India. Between August, 1947 and March, 1948, as many as five lakhs of Hindus were squeezed out of East Bengal. There were no major incidents as such; but circumstances so shaped themselves that they got no protection from the Government of Pakistan and were forced to come away to West Bengal for shelter. During that period there was no question of any provocation given by India where normal conditions had settled down; there was no question of Muslims being coerced to go away from India to Pakistan. In April, 1948, the First Inter-Dominion Agreement was reached in Calcutta, dealing specially with the problems of Bengal. If anyone analyses and compares the provisions of that Agreement with the recent one it will appear that in all essential matters they are similar to each other. This Agreement, however, did not produce any effective result. India generally observed its terms but the exodus from East Bengal continued unabated. It was a one-way traffic, just as Pakistan wished for. There were exchanges of correspondence; there were meetings of officials and Chief Ministers; there were consultations between Dominion Ministers. But judged by actual results Pakistan's attitude continued unchanged. There was a second Inter-Dominion Conference in Delhi, in December, 1948, and another Agreement was signed, sealed and delivered. It dealt with the same problem—the rights of minorities specially in Bengal. This also was a virtual repetition of the first Agreement. In the course of 1949 we witnessed a further deterioration of conditions in East Bengal and an exodus of a far larger number of helpless people, who were uprooted from their hearth and home and were thrown into India in a most miserable condition. The fact thus remains that in spite of two Inter-Dominion

Agreements as many as 16 to 20 lakhs of Hindus were sent away to India from East Bengal. About a million of uprooted Hindus were sent away from Sind. During this period a large number of Muslims also came away from Pakistan mainly influenced by economic considerations. The economy of West Bengal received a rude shock and we continued as helpless spectators of a grim tragedy.

Today there is a general impression that there has been failure both on the part of India and Pakistan to protect their minorities. The fact however is just the reverse of it. A hostile propaganda has been also carried on in some sections of the foreign press. This is a libel of India and truth must be made known to all who desire to know it. The Indian Government—both at the Center and in the Provinces and States—generally maintained peace and security throughout the land after Punjab and Delhi disturbances had quieted down, in spite of grave and persistent provocations from Pakistan by reason of its failure to create conditions in Sind and East Bengal whereby minorities could live there peacefully and honourably. It should not be forgotten here that the people who came away from East Bengal or Sind were not those who had decided to migrate to India out of imaginary fear at the time of partition. These were people who were bent on staying in Pakistan, if only they were given a chance to live decent and peaceful lives.

Thereafter Dr Mookerjee pointed out the gross instances of persecution of Hindus that had taken place in East Bengal, and summarized his reasons for resignation.

I have found myself unable to be a party to the Agreement for the following main reasons:

First—we had two such Agreements since Partition for solving the Bengal problem and they were violated by Pakistan without any remedy open to us. Any Agreement which has no sanction will not offer any solution.

Secondly, the crux of the problem is Pakistan's concept of an Islamic State and the ultra-communal administration based on it. The Agreement side-tracks this cardinal issue and we are today exactly where we were previous to the Agreement.

Thirdly—India and Pakistan are made to appear equally guilty, while Pakistan was clearly the aggressor. The Agreement provides that no propaganda will be permitted against the territorial integrity of the two countries and there will be no incitement to war between them. This almost sounds farcical so long as Pakistan troops occupy a portion of our territory of Kashmir and warlike preparation on its part are in active operation.

Fourthly—events have proved that Hindus cannot live in East Bengal on the assurances of security given by Pakistan. We should accept this as a basic proposition. The present Agreement on the other hand calls upon minorities to look upon Pakistan Government for their safety and honour which is adding insult to injury and is contrary to assurances given by us previously.

Fifthly—there is no proposal to compensate those who have suffered nor will the guilty be ever punished, because no one will dare give evidence before a Pakistan Court. This is in accordance with bitter experience in the past.

Sixthly—Hindus will continue to come away in large numbers and those who have come will not be prepared to go back. On the other hand, Muslims who had gone away will now return and in our determination to implement the Agreement Muslims will not leave India. Our economy will thus be shattered and possible conflict within our country will be greater.

Seventhly—in the garb of protecting minorities in India, the Agreement has reopened the problem of Muslim minority in India, thus seeking to revive those disruptive forces that created Pakistan itself. This principle, carried to its logical

conclusions, will create fresh problems for us which, strictly
speaking, are against our very Constitution.

The sixth and seventh points once again would be considered
today as 'politically incorrect in the extreme' and 'rabidly
communal' on the one hand or 'prophetic' and 'ominous' on the
other, depending on the point of view. Nevertheless, they reflect
the situation that has now developed in parts of West Bengal and
Assam, where the Hindu–Muslim balance has drastically altered
in favour of the latter, both as a result of increased procreation
as also massive infiltration from Bangladesh. The proportion of
Muslims in West Bengal has increased from 20 per cent in 1951
to 27 per cent in 2011 and that in Assam from 25 per cent in
1951 to 34 per cent in 2011. Incidents caused by the 'disruptive
forces' that Dr Mookerjee had predicted in his 'seventhly' began
in the 1980s, and are increasingly being heard of now.[28]

Of these, the Assam incidents, such as the Nellie or Gohpur
massacres of 1983, are better known. What has been happening
in West Bengal is relatively low-key, but no less serious. In fact,
they are low-key because the media in West Bengal, as if by some
unsaid conspiracy, has decided to suppress all news of Muslim
atrocities, and this itself is a cause for worry, for a festering sore,
if just bandaged and hidden from view, will not only not cure
itself but will infect the whole body and ultimately cause death.
The issue of fatwas on, followed by the driving out of Bangladeshi
author Taslima Nasrin, for which the ruling Communist Party of
India (Marxist) engineered a sham riot in November 2007, is a case
in point. The attack on the office of the venerable English daily
the *Statesman* in Kolkata by Muslim fundamentalists in February
2009, following the printing of a lifted article written by Johann
Hari, a fighter for atheism, from the *Independent* of London, is
particularly worth mentioning, because in this case the editor
of the daily was arrested—and yet all his fellow media persons

chose to keep the thing under wraps. The attacks on Hindus at Deganga, North 24 Parganas (September 2010), Naliakhali, South 24 Parganas (February 2013), Hajinagar, North 24 Parganas (October 2016), Dhulagarh, Howrah (December 2016) and Basirhat, North 24 Parganas (July 2017) are also similar examples. The chickens seem to be coming home to roost.

12

The Bharatiya Jana Sangh
Is Born, 1951

D r Mookerjee's resignation from the cabinet and his launching himself into all-India mainstream opposition politics proved to be a watershed not only in his own life but also for the nation. Till Independence he was essentially a provincial politician, though he had adorned the chair of president of the all-India Hindu Mahasabha. His appointment as a central cabinet minister brought him into the limelight at the Centre all right, but more as an administrator than as a statesman or politician. Now his resignation changed all that. Had he not resigned, there would never have been a Bharatiya Jana Sangh, and no nationalist opposition to the Congress. But that opposition was formed and, as we know today, its mutant displaced the Congress to rule at the Centre for six years between 1999 and 2004 and was again elected in 2014 with an overwhelming majority.

Dr Mookerjee's arrival at Howrah railway station on the morning of 11 April 1950 by the Kalka Mail brought forth literally a deluge of humanity into the station and its environs. Not only the station platforms and premises but also the adjoining Howrah bridge across the Hooghly River was a sea of human heads. A substantial part of this crowd was refugees

from East Bengal, for whom Dr Mookerjee had fought and
thrown away his cabinet berth. He was now a leader with
the support of a multitude, but without a party and without
any official position, except for his membership of the
Lok Sabha.

On his return to Calcutta Dr Mookerjee immediately
plunged into public life and began a broadside on the Delhi
(Nehru–Liaquat) Pact and what he saw as the Government of
India's weakness in its dealings with Pakistan. Addressing a
public reception held in Calcutta on 21 May, he said that the
sufferings of Hindus in East Bengal were not the outcome of
a sudden outburst of communal frenzy or misrule that had
plagued Bengal for ten years or more. On the other hand it
was the result of careful planning and implementation of that
diabolical plan (this is exactly what Jayanta Kumar Ray had
unearthed later). The weak-kneed policy of the Government
of India and the wishful thinking of Jawaharlal Nehru about
the presumed intentions of Pakistan had landed the Hindus
of East Bengal in this terrible and helpless situation. He also
recounted in a public speech in Calcutta on 21 May 1950[1]
that there were 502 cases of oppression on Hindus in ten
districts of East Bengal after the pact till 30 April 1950,
including eighteen cases of abduction of Hindu women (and
even cases of married Hindu women being given in marriage
to Muslims), 292 cases of murder, arson, burglary and dacoity
in which Hindus were the invariable victims, and 140 cases of
oppression, humiliation, harassment and extortion of Hindus
by lower-rank Muslim officials and non-officials. There were
seventeen cases of forcible occupation of houses and twenty-
two cases of assault at the hands of the local people following
complaints with the police. Wrongful arrests and detention of
Hindus who had returned to East Bengal after the pact for

inquiring about their properties and defilement of Hindu
temples were also reported.

When he came back to Delhi to deliver his resignation
speech, he was accorded a rousing reception in Feroz Shah
Kotla. This biographer interviewed Balraj Madhok, who was
the convener of that reception and very close to Dr Mookerjee
till his death. Madhok, nearly ninety when he was interviewed,
was approached through Prafull Goradia, both of whom were
then with the Bharatiya Jana Sangh. The old man reminisced
about Dr Mookerjee, with whom he had an intimate association:

In fact, I owe everything to him. He was my guru, he was
my guide. He announced his intention to form a party after
he resigned from the cabinet on 8 April 1950. He gave his
statement in the Lok Sabha on 19 April. It was a wonderful
document, and after that, the citizens of Delhi gave him a
reception at Feroz Shah Kotla ground. I was the convener
of that reception. After that speeches were made, people had
appreciated him. Then when he spoke last, he gave out his
intention that he wanted to form a party, not a personal
thing. He said, 'We need a nationalist alternative to the
Congress.' It was very well-received and soon after he had
finished his speech, he called me. He was not well versed in
Hindi, and used to speak in English only. 'Better you write
the manifesto,' he said. I said, 'Doctor Sahib, you said that
you want to make a party, you had made yourself clear that
you want to make a party. Who are the people who will come
to this party? What kind of ideas will they have? What kind
of manifesto . . .?'

Then he told me, 'Balraj, you have been connected with
Arya Samaj since your childhood and Arya Samaj was a big
movement in the country, you know the Arya Samaj mind.

You have been connected with RSS since your college days, you know the RSS mind; and you know my mind.' That was stressed, 'you know my mind'. So what more do you want to know? But that feeling, his mind was the mind of Savarkar, his mind was the Hindu mind, he was a nationalist and he was a man, who when he roared in Parliament Nehru used to sink (sic). So then I decided to write down the manifesto and this small cottage was allotted to me. Then I wrote that manifesto here, it took me more than two months . . . So that was the faith he had in me . . . That was his feeling, his thoughts about the party that he had in mind. So after the manifesto was ready, then it was vetted by a number of people, we used to sit together. Therein, I had used the words, 'The new party will be for a Hindu India, to be a Hindu Rashtra'; the words 'Hindu Rashtra' were specifically used in that, and he approved it. Other people have approved it. Then, when no reply came from RSS he decided that there should be a party, so he went back to Calcutta and there he declared the Indian Peoples' Party.

This last bit is, of course, chronologically not quite correct, but it must be understood that Madhok, nearly ninety, was trying to recall events of nearly sixty years ago. In fact, Dr Mookerjee had first decided to call it the 'Young India Party', but later changed it to the All-India Peoples' Party.

On 11 June 1950, Dr Mookerjee presided over an All-Bengal Refugee Conference at the Calcutta University Institute. In this meeting, he placed before the house an account of instances of persecution of Hindus in East Bengal just for the calendar month of May 1950. The list he placed is given in the next page.

Murder	32
Kidnapping/Abduction	23
Rape	5
Disappearance of young women	4
Public dishonour	6
Dacoity	202
Robbery	35
Theft	15
Extortion	76
Torching	16
Stabbing	56
Trespass	123
Harassment	19
Wrongful confinement	2
Desecration of Hindu temple	16
Total	**630**

In his speech before the Parliament on 7 August 1950 Dr Mookerjee placed three alternative proposals before the Government of India for its consideration. He said that it was clear that the Government of Pakistan had failed to provide security to the Hindus of that country, and the basis of Partition (and the tall promises given by Jinnah at Karachi upon his assumption as governor general) was set at nought. India therefore must declare war against Pakistan in order to ensure the security of the Hindus. Alternatively, India must demand that Pakistan must cede one-third of its territory in its eastern wing so as to enable rehabilitation of Hindu refugees. The third alternative was that it must bring about a peaceful exchange of population between the two Bengals, as had been done between the two Punjabs. He quoted from a League of

Nations document titled 'European Population Transfer of 1930–45' to illustrate that such exchanges had been recognized in international law. In furthering his arguments in favour of these alternatives, he said, speaking of the first proposal, 'I know the danger of it. I know what it means. It means war. This is a method which was contemplated by Mahatma Gandhi himself in extreme circumstances.'

As we all know now, Nehru completely ignored these alternatives, and did nothing. As a result the Hindus of East Bengal (later renamed East Pakistan) were subjected to the worst possible plight, with no help from India forthcoming. In fact, the success of the Nehru–Liaquat Pact became a matter of prestige with Prime Minister Nehru, with the result that all government functionaries felt (or were instructed to feel) obliged to vindicate Nehru's stand, and this could be done only by pretending that the Pakistanis were taking good care of their Hindu minority, while they were doing quite the opposite. There was a steady squeeze, mainly brought about by abject discrimination, social boycott and arbitrary and repressive governmental action such as requisitioning of Hindu properties. In the middle of this constant squeeze were serious pogroms from time to time, brought about by taking advantage of some happening, such as the 1964 pogrom following the supposed disappearance of Prophet Mohammed's hair from the Hazratbal Shrine in Srinagar, Kashmir, India, and the ultimate, bestial, mass-murder pogrom preceding the Bangladesh liberation in 1971. By then Dr Mookerjee was long gone, and the Hindus of East Pakistan and Bangladesh were conveniently forgotten by the entire Indian populace, including their close cousins, the Bangals of West Bengal. But the pogroms continued into the Bangladesh era: 1988, 1992 and 2001 saw three distinct pogroms that brought down the Hindu percentage in Bangladesh from 29 per cent in 1947 to about 9 per cent in 2010.

Meanwhile other news of total failure of the Nehru–Liaquat Pact did not take long in coming. In February 1951, the Assam Mail, which used to run from Amingaon in Assam to Sealdah in Calcutta through East Bengal was waylaid by a group of Bihari Muslims (who had emigrated from Bihar to East Bengal) outside Santahar junction and practically all the Hindus on the train were slaughtered. An eyewitness account by a young man who had managed a providential escape has been described in *My People, Uprooted* by this author.

In a meeting in Calcutta on 3 September 1950, Dr Mookerjee said, 'The present policy of appeasement of Pakistan must cease. Whether we start with a definite plan of economic sanctions or we intensify military action is a matter of procedure and strategy.'

In an article he wrote in the 1952 Durga Puja (October) edition of the Bengali fortnightly *Swastika*, Dr Mookerjee described in graphic language the plight of the East Bengali Hindus, and the false propaganda dished out by the Pakistani government and media about them. He called it rubbing salt into the Hindu wound. About the thousands of Hindu women kidnapped or abducted, Pakistan was letting it be widely known that these women had, of their own free will, left their families and married Muslim men and embraced Islam. Dr Mookerjee remarked that such a tendency was not known at all before Partition, but after Pakistan came into being it had apparently acquired the character of an infectious disease! One newspaper of East Bengal had even printed an article on how Hindu women had lately been exhibiting such alacrity in marrying Muslim men that these men, despite the utmost reluctance, were being forced to accept them as their wives.

The communists, who had a substantial presence in West Bengal even at that time, were meanwhile trying to paint the persecution of Hindus in East Bengal as a rebellion of the have-nots (meaning the Muslims) against the haves (Hindus). This was of course in keeping with their doctrine that man is an economic animal, and all fights are truly class fights, even if they are fought ostensibly in the name of religion. Dr Mookerjee effectively rubbished this theory and described the experience of a refugee from Pirojpur in East Bengal (this was after the signing of the pact). The man told Dr Mookerjee that within the jurisdiction of just one police station there had been as many as sixty cases of dacoity within a single month, that is two dacoities per night on an average. This area is inhabited almost exclusively by members of the scheduled castes, none of whom are particularly well-to-do, and some dirt poor, mostly cultivators and fishermen. These dacoities were staged principally with a view to scare the Hindus to leave the country. The man had also told him that it was no longer possible for any Hindu to continue to live in East Bengal while preserving the honour of their women. Dr Mookerjee also described how scaring, dishonouring and brutalizing Hindu women had become the principal modus operandi for the Muslims to torment and drive away the Hindus. He also regretted the existence of apologists among Hindus in India who callously and mindlessly remarked that there must have been some provocation from the women's side too, or else such things could not happen.

Dr Mookerjee therefore felt that the foremost need of the hour was to mobilize public opinion and to ask the Government of India to impartially examine forthwith the actual effects of the Indo-Pakistan Agreement and stop the continuous one-way traffic of Hindus from East Pakistan. He emphasized that this exodus from East Pakistan would not only wreck the economy of West Bengal but also gravely imperil the stability of the Indian nation. He had already made his demand for one of the three alternatives. Now he called upon the Government of India to implement a comprehensive plan of relief and rehabilitation of refugees which must be so integrated as to be able to serve the cause of the entire population of West Bengal. It was thus that he hoped to be able to rebuild and recreate a new Bengal which would be healthy, prosperous and powerful.

But a person of Dr Mookerjee's stature and mindset could not be content with just making demands, both before the public and on the floor of the Parliament. He was burning up inside with indignation at the total disregard the then government showed for the Hindus of East Bengal despite the tall promises that Nehru had made in his 'Tryst with Destiny' speech. True, Dr Mookerjee was a constitutionalist, but he simply could not accept the use of brute majority by Nehru to play the weak-kneed, defensive politics he had adopted in respect of India's relations with Pakistan. By now another problem involving Pakistan had started taking its place in his mind like a dark cloud in one corner of the sky. That cloud was Kashmir, and Nehru's capitulation before the two-faced politics being played by Sheikh Abdullah filled him with righteous rage. But he had a problem. He had stature, he had acceptability, he had popularity, he had several burning issues. Only, he had no party.

There was no question of going back to the Hindu Mahasabha which had declined to follow his suggestions, and moreover whom he himself had advised to eschew politics. The Mahasabha had also simultaneously proved, as Lord Wavell had correctly summed up,[2] to be 'a curious body, many of whose rank and file seemed to be Congressmen, and on big political issues would follow Gandhi rather than S.P. Mookerjee or Savarkar'. The communists and the socialists were, of course, out of the question. A party called Ram Rajya Parishad had made some headway in Rajasthan and Madhya Bharat,[3] but it largely drew its sustenance from feudal elements, appealed to orthodox sentiment and was far too conservative and obscurantist for Dr Mookerjee's taste. It would have to be a different party, a brand-new party, with no baggage of the past, and one with which he could ideologically feel at ease.

So his search began in the summer of 1950. A document entitled 'Wanted—A National Front' and proposing a 'Bharat Mahasabha', dated Almora, 29 June 1950, was sent to him for his 'perusal and opinion if convenient'. This document was found among his personal papers, but no clue is available as to its authorship. According to the document, the Bharat Mahasabha warmly welcomed the different races, creeds and religions in the country of India, provided they declared their sworn loyalty to India and proclaimed their respect for the cow and the Ganges in return for the advantages derived from them. The 'Indian' included not only the offshoots of Hinduism—the Sikhs, the Buddhists, the Jains, etc.—but also those who belonged to other creeds like the Muslims, the Christians, the Parsis, etc. The Mahasabha had a particularly high place reserved for the 350-million-strong scheduled castes who, although forming an integral part of the great fraternity of Indians, had never got a fair deal. The Mahasabha was definitely opposed to the vivisection of the country and it very much desired to unsettle this settled fact, though it advocated taking a realistic view of things.

Dr Mookerjee was receiving similar proposals and exhortations from different parts of the country. Meanwhile, a certain organization, and a highly disciplined, powerful and idealistic one at that, which had so far assiduously steered clear of politics, indeed considered it to be a deterrent to their chosen objective, had begun toying with the idea of associating its members with politics while insulating the organization itself from it. This was the Rashtriya Swayamsevak Sangh (RSS), which literally means 'Nationalist Volunteers' Organization', although being a *swayamsevak* (as the members of the organization call themselves) according to the teachings of the organization meant something much more than merely a 'volunteer'.

Few organizations in India, political or social, have been through such travails as the RSS. It has been banned three times, maligned roundly, thoroughly misunderstood and drawn enormous flak from its detractors and the associated media. It has been called communalist, downright fascist, Hindu revivalist, ultra-right, ultra-nationalist, a secret society, anti-Muslim, anti-minority, a bunch of country bumpkins in khaki knickers and many other epithets, and (worst of all) has been constantly sought to be associated with the assassination of Gandhi in a Goebbelsian exercise. However, its members, the swayamsevaks, have been unwavering in their loyalty and the organization has not only resurrected itself but gained in strength following each of the three bans. Its detractors have been mostly those of the left or left-of-centre, ranging from the pale pink Nehruvians to the deep red communists. They also include leaders like Lalu Prasad of Bihar, convicted in the 'fodder scam', who is said to have taken his state back to the Stone Age.

In truth this is largely hostile propaganda, if one looks at its stated objectives as explained in the foregoing. True, it does not venerate Gandhi by raising him to the level of a demigod as the Congressites do, and does not accept him as the 'Father of the Nation'. But it does admire him as a great mass leader and one who tried to inculcate Indian values into the educated Indian psyche. It also has a particularly poor opinion of Jawaharlal Nehru (which is not at all surprising—the loathing had to be mutual) and considerable admiration for Patel.

In fact, Patel had been hugely impressed by the idealism and iron discipline of the swayamsevaks and wished to draw them into the Congress. The RSS leadership, which was so far averse to involvement in any kind of politics, had meanwhile seriously started considering a political role for itself. During the ban, Eknath Ranade, a member of the RSS Kendriya Karyakari Mandal (Central Executive) and Patel secretly parleyed with this in mind. The government had openly insisted, as a precondition for lifting the ban, on a written constitution for the RSS acceptable to the

government, and two associates of Ranade, P.B. Dani and Balasaheb
Deoras, with the approval of M.S. Golwalkar, had prepared a draft.
After some further negotiations, partly open and partly secret, the
constitution was rewritten by Mauli Chandra Sharma, Ranade and
Deen Dayal Upadhyaya, then a young *pracharak*.[4] It was accepted
by the government and the ban on the RSS was lifted.

But the talks of merging or forming an alliance with the
Congress bore no fruit. The Congress itself was deeply divided
on the issue, and initially, while Nehru was abroad, the Congress
Working Committee (CWC) had voted that swayamsevaks
could join the party as primary members while continuing to
be swayamsevaks. About a month later, on 17 November 1949,
the CWC reversed its decision and ruled that in order to become
primary members swayamsevaks would have to sever connections
with the RSS. Obviously no swayamsevak could accept such a
condition and the entire proposal fell through.

The largely traditionalist leadership of the RSS had always
held that the organization had no politics and was devoted to
purely social work. During the first round of negotiations on
lifting the ban, Golwalkar explained his personal opposition,
indeed aversion, to a political role for the RSS to the
government. Several options now faced the RSS leadership.
It could (1) transform itself into a political party, (2) form
a political affiliate, (3) make some kind of arrangement with
the Hindu Mahasabha or another compatible political group,
(4) abstain from any political involvement or (5) continue to
negotiate with the Congress. The first was rejected summarily.
The possibility of cooperation with the Hindu Mahasabha was
never seriously considered. The Mahasabha had performed
very poorly in the post-war Central Legislative Assembly elections; a cloud of suspicion hung over it because of its alleged
involvement in a conspiracy to kill Gandhi; and, outside of
Bengal and Maharashtra, it was controlled by rich landlords

and businessmen who were not anxious to see it develop into a
mass-based political party.

After excluding the Hindu Mahasabha from consideration,
some RSS activists, especially Vasantrao Krishna Oke, the Delhi
state pracharak, and Balraj Madhok, a young pracharak from
Kashmir, met Dr Mookerjee and proposed the formation of a new
nationalist party. The initial contact with him was probably not
with the clearance of the top RSS leadership, which was even then
somewhat apprehensive about its pracharaks hobnobbing with
politicians. However, the mention of the 'RSS mind' mentioned
in the interview with Balraj Madhok (unless he had the dates
totally mixed up) shows that collaborating with the organization
was never far away from Dr Mookerjee's mind even before the
informal approach by Oke was made.

It is not as if Dr Mookerjee was a total stranger to the RSS.
In April 1940, he attended an RSS *shakha* at Raja Dinendra
Street in Calcutta and was impressed by the soldierly discipline
of the swayamsevaks. Balasaheb Deoras, who later became the
third Sarsanghchalak of the RSS, was present at that meeting.
Dr Mookerjee was aware that it was the most organized, trained,
disciplined and efficient non-political national organization of
the Hindus in the country, and its approach to the problems of
culture, nationalism and partition had his fullest approval. The
very next month he was returning from a Hindu Mahasabha
meeting in Bombay en route to Calcutta when he came to know
that Dr Hedgewar, founder of the RSS, had fallen seriously ill
and was bedridden at the home of Babasaheb Ghatate at Nagpur.
Golwalkar at the time was running an Adhikari Shiksha Varg
(Officer Training Camp for RSS functionaries) at Nagpur, and
Dr Mookerjee decided to stop by at Nagpur and meet them.
But at the time Dr Hedgewar was so ill that he could not do
much more than exchange pleasantries and died soon afterwards.
Dr Mookerjee did however query whether the RSS could help the

Hindu Mahasabha in its task, and Dr Hedgewar affirmed that the RSS had to stay away from politics. There had been contacts between the two organizations before Dr Mookerjee had joined the Mahasabha, and Dr Hedgewar had maintained close ties with Vinayak Damodar Savarkar and Dr Balkrishna Shivaram Moonje of the Mahasabha. The same year Dr Mookerjee addressed a rally of swayamsevaks in Lahore in the Punjab. By then the RSS had become a powerful force in the Punjab, and he described the organization as the 'only silver lining in the cloudy sky of India'. It was, therefore, almost divinely ordained that the leader and the organization would meet, and meet they did, shortly after Dr Mookerjee's resignation.

In the summer of 1950, a meeting was arranged between Dr Mookerjee and Golwalkar at the residence of a swayamsevak in Calcutta. The late Bansi Lal Sonee, then a young pracharak, who later served in the Bharatiya Janata Party for a long time, had been present at the meeting and had recalled that Dr Mookerjee was trying to speak in halting Hindi. During the meeting, they had differences, but they tried to iron them out with a frankness rarely seen among political leaders in India. Dr Mookerjee had earlier stated at a press conference that the Hindu Mahasabha was 'communal' inasmuch as it believed in Hindu Rashtra (Hindu state). Golwalkar told him that the RSS also believed in the Bharatiya Rashtra being Hindu Rashtra, though perhaps not so strongly as the Hindu Mahasabha. As such, would he like to keep the RSS too at arm's length? If he did that he would not be able to secure the cooperation of swayamsevaks, all of whom believed in this idea. However, Dr Mookerjee acknowledged that he had made an inadvertent remark and expressed full agreement on the Hindu Rashtra ideal. Golwalkar in turn agreed to assist him and promised to lend him some of his best swayamsevaks, staunch and tried workers, for setting up his party. Also, Golwalkar had later stated in an article by him in the Hindi weekly *Panchjanya*[5] that Dr Mookerjee agreed

with him that restoration of the Hindu Rashtra was in no way
inconsistent with the establishment of a modern democracy.

Among the swayamsevaks lent by Golwalkar to Dr Mookerjee
were Atal Bihari Vajpayee, who later became the Prime Minister
of India; Pandit Deen Dayal Upadhyaya, who nursed the party
after Dr Mookerjee's untimely death and brought it to maturity;
Sundar Singh Bhandari, an organizational genius; Jagdish Prasad
Mathur, who looked after the public relations of the new party;
Bhaurao Deoras, who built the party in north India; Jagannath
Rao Joshi, and several others.

But the party was yet to be formally founded, and both the
leader and the organization were proceeding rather cautiously,
step by step as it were. Each had firm beliefs, political
compulsions and some baggage from the past, and they needed
to anticipate and smooth out the wrinkles that would inevitably
arise when they came together. The two sides had to develop
an understanding between themselves—a political party hastily
cobbled together, more often than not, does not last long—a
lesson that, much later, was learnt when the Janata Party that
Jayaprakash Narayan created in 1977 began fragmenting in less
than two years! Following this trend, after the broad agreement
between Golwalkar and Dr Mookerjee had been reached in
the Calcutta meeting, the RSS invited him to preside over its
annual function held at New Delhi on 3 December 1950. In the
function he warmly praised the recent performances of the RSS,
an organization devoted to the development of the *Bharatiya*
culture and the spirit of unity and solidarity among all classes of
Hindus throughout India. Suffering and sacrifice had only added
to its strength and vitality, he observed, and it perhaps stood more
consolidated than ever before. Dr Mookerjee, in the national
interest, called for an intensification of the spirit of unity that
existed amid diversities of states, languages, habits and customs.
Hindus had lost their political freedom because of disunity and

jealousy among themselves, he said. He further called for revival and consolidation of their past Hindu culture and civilization and rejected criticism of the same as reactionary and retrograde and born out of ignorance or an inferiority complex.

Dr Mookerjee said the universal appeal and ennobling message of the Bhagavad Gita, Ramayana and Mahabharata, based on a spirit of truth, service and sacrifice, must form the foundation of Hindu revival, which was a task of supreme importance in the development of free India. He called upon selfless swayamsevaks to campaign for creating a strong and healthy public opinion in solving the social, economic and political problems facing India, such as black marketing, profiteering, high prices of food, lack of clothing and shelter, etc. He referred to India's partition that brought misery and humiliation to millions and led to grave social, economic and political consequences. Due to historical reasons, this partition was conceded by one party which was then governing India with markedly manifest fascist tendencies, leaving no space for democracy. He called for giving full liberty to all parties, not wedded to the cult of violence, to propagate their viewpoints. He emphasized that Hindus had got the opportunity to rule their own country after nearly 1000 years and they have to prove themselves worthy of this hour in history.

Dr Mookerjee had thought up, tentatively of course, a name for his proposed party. First, he thought he would call it the 'Young India Party', then changed it to 'All-India Peoples' Party'. The RSS suggested that the name should be in Hindi and that the flag should be *keshariya* (saffron). Some had suggested the name 'Bharatiya Lok Sangh'. But Dr Mookerjee, according to Madhok, is said to have remarked, '*Lok* means *bhirh*, crowd, let the name be "Jana Sangh", the party of the people.' That is how the name Bharatiya Jana Sangh came about.

He conceived it as not only a party of swayamsevaks with he as the leader, but as a federation of all political parties and organizations which could possibly be made to unite and form an opposition to the Congress party in the interests of democratic functioning. Among the parties he had in mind were his old party, the Hindu Mahasabha; and of course the RSS; also the Socialist Party, the Ram Rajya Parishad (from Madhya Bharat and Rajasthan), the Forward Bloc, the Revolutionary Socialist Party (both from West Bengal), the Kisan Sabha, the Soshit Party (of eastern Uttar Pradesh) and the Ganatantra Parishad (from the former princely states of Orissa). Since 1947 the Congress was running the Government of India by virtue of a transitional arrangement arrived at between the past British administration in India and the Congress. Now that the Constitution had been adopted, elections had to be held. The Congress was anxious to hold them as early as possible before the other parties had time to organize and give them competition. And Dr Mookerjee was out to beat them at this game. He therefore arranged a convention in Calcutta and invited all the parties in the Opposition, barring the communists, to join the federation. Invitees to the convention included, besides the leaders of these parties and organizations, prominent personalities such as P.R. Das, K.C. Neogy, Dr John Mathai, Hanuman Prasad Poddar, Dr Choitram Gidwani, Sir C.P. Ramaswami Iyer, Dr M.R. Jayakar, a sizeable number of other politicians, editors of English and Indian-language newspapers and distinguished lawyers.

Among the people that Dr Mookerjee discussed the idea of a new party with around this time were Lala Yodh Raj, the chairman of the Punjab National Bank, Balraj Madhok and Pandit Mauli Chandra Sharma, all three of whom were influential in Delhi and Punjab politics; Lala Hansraj Gupta, the RSS chief for Delhi and managing director of Bharat Prakashan (Delhi) Limited; Mahashay Krishna, the veteran journalist and leader of the Arya Samaj; Chowdhry Siri Chand, the nephew and political heir of Chowdhry Chhotu Ram, the Jat leader of Haryana and a leader of the erstwhile Unionist Party; and Lala Balraj Bhalla, an old revolutionary and educationist. Some of them were in favour of confining the new political party to Punjab, the Patiala and East Punjab States Union (PEPSU), Himachal Pradesh and Delhi to begin with. Dr Mookerjee, on the other hand, while appreciating the special needs and problems of Punjab, PEPSU, Delhi and Jammu and Kashmir resulting from an influx of refugees and the government's weak policy towards Pakistan, was in favour of forming an all-India party at an early date. He was confident that he could form a party in his own province of West Bengal, which faced similar problems, in no time. But such regional parties would fail to make much impact on national politics and policies.

It was, therefore, decided on his suggestion that preparations for an all-India party should be begun forthwith. The basic principle, ideology and programme were discussed and a subcommittee was appointed to prepare a draft manifesto and a constitution in the light of these discussions. It was at the meeting of these men that the proposed party was provisionally christened Bharatiya Jana Sangh (Indian People's Party). Dr Mookerjee felt that the new party should stand for Hindu Rashtra, a noble concept that had no communalist undertones and stood for Indian cultural, geographical and historical unity. But he was willing to use the adjectives 'Bharatiya' and 'Indian', which were more acceptable to those under Western influence, rather than its synonym 'Hindu', until the latter description was generally accepted by people. It was also decided to form the Jana Sangh in as many states as possible so that it could take shape and start growing.

At this time tragedy struck. Sardar Vallabhbhai Patel, the Deputy Prime Minister of India, the hard-headed realist in Indian politics and the principal countercheck to Nehru's airy-fairy 'secular' idealism, breathed his last on 15 December 1950. This increased Nehru's clout within the party tremendously and disheartened all Congressmen opposed to him, who thought it now best and most politic to fall in line with him. With his death, Dr Mookerjee also lost a sincere well-wisher on whom he could count despite belonging to diametrically opposite parties. Now Dr Mookerjee could not delay the formation of the party any further and wanted to proceed with it post-haste. His initially projected line of action was to organize regionally first and then to rally all the regional organizations to a central convention. But the RSS leadership, with its greater stress on organizational working, still wanted to take its time to usher it into existence. Had the Jana Sangh been formed early, many of the parties that Dr Mookerjee had in mind could perhaps have been amalgamated. However, with all these pulls and pushes operating, things began to move at their own pace at different corners of the huge country that is India.

Meanwhile pressure was mounting on him from all sides to not delay the launch of the new party any further. The Ganatantra Parishad of Orissa was pressing him hard (though ultimately they did not join his party). So were many other elements in Madras Presidency and West Bengal. In Calcutta, several prominent political leaders held a gathering at Asutosh Memorial Hall where they formed themselves into a provisional council and authorized Dr Mookerjee to form a provisional working committee and appoint its office-bearers. He selected Makhan Lal Sen and Charu Chandra Bhattacharya as provisional secretaries.

Hanuman Prasad Poddar of Gorakhpur, UP, wrote to Dr Mookerjee that despite having independent aims and ideals, different opinions and probably some sentimental differences too, the Jana Sangh, Ram Rajya Parishad, the RSS and the Hindu Mahasabha should sink their differences for the present and offer a united front against the Congress in the coming elections so as to capture some 30 to 40 per cent of the seats. He also urged the leaders of these four Hindu parties—among them Swami

Karpatriji, M.S. Golwalkar and Dr N.B. Khare—to meet in a big city like Delhi or Calcutta and come to an agreement for fighting the elections.

The leaders of Punjab and Delhi had meanwhile decided to form the Jana Sangh in Punjab and PEPSU immediately, and establish branches in Himachal Pradesh and Delhi after forming a national Jana Sangh. Accordingly, a convention of some 300 representative citizens of Punjab, PEPSU, Himachal Pradesh and Delhi was called at Jullundur on 27 May 1951 to form the party for these four contiguous states, which in practical terms were one unit. The response was most encouraging—almost all of them responded to the invitation. The convention resolved to form itself into a single party. Political work in the region started immediately following the convention. Pandit Mauli Chandra Sharma undertook a non-stop whirlwind tour of Punjab and PEPSU, covering about thirty towns and making over fifty speeches in barely a month. People everywhere responded with zeal. The membership drive proceeded successfully and by the end of July 1951 there were already about one lakh members. Every district in the four states of Punjab, PEPSU, Himachal and Delhi had a Jana Sangh by then.

The Madhya Bharat Rashtriya Sabha also responded positively and on their behalf advocate Anand Behari Mishra, MLA and leader of the Opposition, expressed interest in Dr Mookerjee's venture and assured him that the Madhya Bharat state might prove a unique field for his programme. Kunwar Jaswant Singh of the Jaipur-based Rajasthan Kshatriya Mahasabha, who was the former Prime Minister of the princely state of Bikaner and Dr Mookerjee's colleague in Parliament and the central cabinet, also expressed happiness at the foundation of a national party by the latter in Bengal and sought details about the formation of the new party. Dr Mookerjee in reply advised Singh's organization to work vigorously in Rajasthan, inform him of their activities

from time to time and keep contact with Pandit Mauli Chandra
Sharma in Delhi.

The Democratic Swaraj Party that had been established in
Bombay in 1933, based upon the political, economic and social
philosophy, policy and programme advocated by B.G. Tilak, C.R.
Das, Vithalbhai Patel, Lajpat Rai and N.C. Kelkar, was prepared
to fight the upcoming elections in cooperation with all the non-
Congress groups which agreed with it in principle. Its leader
Jamnadas Mehta called an informal conference in Maharashtra on
23 and 24 June 1951, inviting about 150 leaders from all across
the state of Bombay, including Saurashtra, Gujarat, Bombay,
Maharashtra and Karnataka, and also the Central Provinces and
Berar. Dr Mookerjee presided over the informal conference held
in Bombay. In August, conventions were held in Lucknow and
Indore for forming the party in Uttar Pradesh and Madhya Bharat.
The Lucknow convention elected Pandit Deen Dayal Upadhyaya,
an RSS pracharak, as the first general secretary of the Uttar Pradesh
Jana Sangh, with Rao Krishna Pal Singh as president.

By this time, however, the Congress, now totally under
Nehru's thumb, began to get apprehensive about the growth of this
new party and decided to try to thwart the process. The reception
committee for the Jullundur convention of May 1951 had made
arrangements to hold it in the compound of the Anglo-Sanskrit
High School, within the municipal limits of Jullundur. But just
twenty-four hours before the convention was scheduled to meet,
the district magistrate, allegedly under instructions from some
senior Congress leaders, banned all meetings within the municipal
limits of the town. The venue, therefore, had to be shifted
overnight to the compound of a cold storage plant just outside
the municipal limits. There also appeared to have been some
concerted media campaign to create confusion in the ranks of the
new party. Some English-language newspapers printed a report of
Pandit Mauli Chandra Sharma and Balraj Madhok having made

a declaration that the Bharatiya Jana Sangh, Punjab, would work with the Congress and had nothing to do with the Bengal Jana Sangh. Dr Mookerjee was aghast at this and asked Pandit Mauli Chandra Sharma whether they had dropped the idea of an all-India organization. Replying to Dr Mookerjee on 10 July, Sharma replied that the press report was wrong and had been contradicted, but the contradiction did not receive the same publicity 'for obvious reasons'. Sharma emphasized that they must evolve into an all-India party without delay, and that was what he and Dr Mookerjee had been stressing all along.

Dr Mookerjee was still unsure as to whether he had the authority to claim that he had an all-India party. Ultimately, on Madhok's request and authorization, he wrote a letter to the election commissioner saying that they were organizing in different provinces and it was expected that they would soon merge into an all-India organization. He forwarded to Madhok a copy of the letter sent to the election commissioner. He must have breathed a sigh of relief when the Election Commission of India announced on 7 September 1951 that the All-India Bharatiya Jana Sangh as a national party had been allocated the deepak (lamp) symbol for the forthcoming general election.

Immediately following this, a meeting was held in Delhi on 9 September 1951 and was attended by Dr Mookerjee and by the presidents, secretaries and some other prominent workers of the provincial Jana Sanghs of Punjab, PEPSU, Himachal Pradesh, Delhi and the newly formed units in Uttar Pradesh and Madhya Bharat. In the meeting it was decided to give an all-India form to the party to which provincial Jana Sanghs might be affiliated. The task of organizing an all-India convention for the purpose of establishing the national party was entrusted to the Jana Sangh of Punjab, PEPSU, Himachal Pradesh and Delhi, which thereupon decided to hold a convention in New Delhi in October and appointed its general secretary, Balraj Madhok, as its convener. In the weeks which followed, provincial conventions were also held at Jaipur, Nagpur and Patna to form provincial Jana Sanghs for Rajasthan, Madhya Pradesh and Bihar in western, northern and eastern India, respectively. The Bharatiya Jana Sangh thus came into existence in all the states of north India excepting Assam and Vindhya Pradesh (another Part 'B' state), before it took an all-India shape.

Meanwhile, the front-ranking leaders of the proposed party, Lala Hansraj Gupta, Pandit Mauli Chandra Sharma and Balraj Madhok, secured the consent of Dr Mookerjee, whose stature and strength none in the country could match, to be elected as its first president at the ensuing all-India convention. From that day, he put his heart and soul into building the new organization which he visualized as the spearhead of the nationalist forces in the country. Day after day Dr Mookerjee sat for long hours with Pt Sharma and Madhok to give final touches to the draft manifesto of the Jana Sangh to be placed before the all-India convention. Eminent well-wishers of the new party from all over the country made their own contributions to the manifesto. Hemendra Prasad Ghosh, veteran journalist of Calcutta, noted his suggestions in the draft. Dr M.R. Jayakar, vice chancellor of Poona University, while describing the draft manifesto as 'excellent', advised Dr Mookerjee to tone down the resemblance of his programme to that of the Hindu Mahasabha and to state the position of minority communities in his organization more amply so that the impression was not created that his party was another form of the Mahasabha, only 'more carefully planned and disguised'.[6]

The all-India convention finally took place on 21 October 1951 in Raghomal Arya Kanya Higher Secondary School, New Delhi. About 1000 special invitees from among the citizens of Delhi and another 500 delegates from different parts of India attended the convention. The All-India Bharatiya Jana Sangh was formally launched by a unanimous vote at the convention.

Similarly, the constitution and the manifesto of the party were also adopted by a unanimous vote. And finally the name of Dr Mookerjee was proposed as president by Lala Balraj Bhalla of Punjab and seconded by a number of prominent delegates from different parts of India and similarly carried by a unanimous vote.

In his presidential address before the historic gathering Dr Mookerjee said:

> Our party must continue to function [even after the forthcoming general election] carrying a message of hope and goodwill to all classes of people and try to draw out from them their best efforts in rebuilding a happier and more prosperous free India . . . One of the chief reasons for the manifestation of dictatorship in Congress rule is the absence of well-organized opposition parties which alone can act as a healthy check on the majority party . . . Bharatiya Jana Sangh emerges today as an all-India political party which will function as the principal party in opposition . . . we have thrown our party open to all citizens of India irrespective of caste, creed or community. While we recognize that in matters of customs, habit, religion and language Bharat presents a unique diversity, the people must be united by a bond of fellowship and understanding inspired by deep devotion and loyalty to the support of a common motherland . . . While it will be dangerous to encourage growth of political minorities on the basis of caste and religion, it is obviously for the vast majority of Bharat's population to assure all classes of people who are truly loyal to their motherland that they will be entitled to full protection under the law and to build equality of treatment in all matters social, economic and political. Our party gives this assurance unreservedly . . . Our party believes that the future of Bharat lies in the proper appreciation and application of Bharatiya sanskriti and maryada.

Explaining further the composition and character of the Bharatiya Jana Sangh, he declared that he and his colleagues had thrown the party open to all citizens of India irrespective of caste, creed or community.

Regarding the most acute problem of the deteriorating economic condition of the people, he explained that his party stood for a well-planned decentralized national economic plan on the lines of the Sarvodaya scheme. The party was against concentration of economic power in the hands of small groups and cartels. It would observe sanctity of private property and give private enterprise a fair field, subject to national welfare. It would exercise state ownership and state control when found necessary in the public interest. The party would stand for progressive decontrol and checking social and economic exploitation. It would also demand fair and equitable distribution and creation of an atmosphere where all might work jointly for increased production.

In his address he expressed very definite views regarding Pakistan saying:

> We already know that the partition of Bharat was a tragic folly. It has served no purpose and has not helped to solve any problem, economic, political or communal. We believe in the goal of reunited Bharat . . . So long as Pakistan continues we will urge a policy of strict reciprocity. Our party lays great stress on the need for a satisfactory solution on post-partition problems of minorities of Pakistan and evacuee property which the Congress Government systematically tries to shirk. Our approach to these problems is not at all communal. They are mainly political and economic and have to be settled between the two States in a fair and straightforward manner.

Referring to Kashmir, which had already begun to loom large as a serious problem on the political horizon, he declared, 'Our party feels that the case should be withdrawn from the United Nations and there should be no further question of plebiscite. Kashmir is an inalienable part of India and should be treated as any other State.'

He was very critical of Nehru who had already started using the buzzword 'communal' against Dr Mookerjee and his associates.[7]

Having repeatedly sacrificed Indian nationalism at the altar of Muslim communalism and even after partition having surrendered to the whims and howls of the Pakistan Government it does not lie in the mouth of Pandit Nehru to accuse others of communalism. There is no communalism in India today, except the new policy of Muslim appeasement which had been started by Pandit Nehru and his friends for the purpose of winning their vote at the forthcoming election. We have provincialism and other types of class or caste difference in the country today. Let us jointly try to remove these evils so as to lay a foundation of a truly democratic India.

He concluded his remarkable address with these words:[8]

We enter upon our task with full faith, hope and courage. Let our workers constantly remember that only through service and sacrifice will they be able to win the confidence of mass of people. The great task of revitalizing and reconstructing Bharat awaits us. The mother calls her children irrespective of class, caste or religion to come to her and serve her. However dark the present may be, Bharat has a great destiny to fulfill in the years to come. May our party whose symbol in the forthcoming election is a humble earthen *Pradeep*[9] try to carry

this light of hope and unity, faith and courage to dispel the
darkness that surrounds the country. The journey has just
begun. May providence endow us with strength and fortitude
to remain ever on the right path, not cowed down by fears or
tempted by favours and to help make Bharat great and strong
specially so that she may become fit and noble instrument in
the preservation of wealth and prosperity.

The same day in the evening he addressed a huge outdoor meeting
at Gandhi grounds[10] in which he recalled that Subhas Chandra
Bose had launched the Indian National Army on that very day,
i.e., 21 October. He hoped that the Bharatiya Jana Sangh would
carry on the fighting tradition of the INA in the service of the
country.

He also referred to Nehru's threat, 'I shall crush your Jana
Sangh.' In reply Dr Mookerjee said, 'I say, I will crush this
crushing mentality of yours.'[11]

13

Party President and Parliamentarian, 1951–53

The first task before the president of the new party was to form his team. To this end he nominated the following members for the provisional working committee:

President: Dr Syama Prasad Mookerjee
    General secretaries: Bhai Mahavir and Mauli Chandra Sharma (both of Delhi)
    Members: Lala Balraj Bhalla (president, Punjab unit), Deen Dayal Upadhyaya (general secretary, Uttar Pradesh unit), Dada Dave (Madhya Bharat), Bapusaheb Sohni (president, Berar unit), Vimal Chandra Banerji (president, Mahakoshal unit), Ghisu Lal (Ajmer), Chiranjiva Lal Mishra (president, Rajasthan unit), Raj Kishore Shukla (Vindhya Pradesh), Shiv Kumar Dwivedi (president, Bihar unit), P.H. Krishna Rao (vice president, Mysore unit), Balraj Madhok (general secretary, East Punjab unit), Mahashay Krishna (Delhi), Rang Behari Lal (president, Delhi unit), Rao Krishna Pal Singh (president, Uttar Pradesh unit) and Manmatha Nath Das (West Bengal).

This list indicates several interesting features of the party's early leadership structure. Even at this stage, its northern bias was clear.

A majority of the members came from a solid block of territory coterminous with the Hindi-speaking belt, with an eastward extension through Bihar to West Bengal. The remainder of the country was represented by office-bearers of only two units—Berar, in the south-west of Madhya Pradesh, and Mysore. There were no members at all from the Part A states of Bombay, Madras, Assam and Orissa or from the Part B states of Hyderabad, Saurashtra and Travancore-Cochin. Further, there were several RSS recruits in this team (Mahavir, Madhok, Upadhyay and Sohni). According to Madhok, Mahavir had been nominated as one of the two general secretaries as a result of a tacit understanding between Dr Mookerjee and the leaders of the RSS.

As for the programme of the Jana Sangh, its main trends were already known due to its functioning in the provincial sphere in different parts of India for the last few months. The draft manifesto of the All-India Bharatiya Jana Sangh was settled in detail and then adopted after consultation with the representatives who assembled at the all-India convention. As far as economic and social issues were concerned, it was for adopting a liberal rather than a conservative approach, envisaging reforms which would enhance the independence and freedom of producers but assuming a restricted role for the state in the regulation of economic life. In the field of industry, the manifesto declared that those industries especially concerned with essential defence needs should be publicly owned, but for other large industries private enterprise under general state control should be encouraged in the interest of consumers and producers alike. Thus pragmatism replaced socialism as a premise.

The parts of the programme which referred to issues concerning Hindu nationalists were relatively moderate in emphasis in order to widen the acceptability of the document. When promising special aid 'to the backward sections of the people', the manifesto stated the party's belief in the equal rights of all Indian citizens 'irrespective of caste, creed or community', and also that it would not recognize minorities and majorities based on religion. It qualified its advocacy of Hindi as the national language by offering 'full encouragement' to other Indian languages so as not to antagonize Bengal and Madras. It adopted a relatively mild stand on the Hindu Code Bill (then a hotly debated subject), proposing only that the kind of far-reaching changes envisaged by the measure should not be made in the absence of popular and electoral approval.

Among the party's top priorities was the immediate building up of India's military strength through provision of military training to both young men and women, nationalization of the defence forces, creation of a large territorial army and speedy development of defence industries. The party's foreign policy would be guided primarily by enlightened national self-interest. True to the traditions of India and Hindutva, it would work for the maintenance of world peace and mutual understanding. In particular reference to Pakistan it recommended firm policies in dealing with that country (what would generally be termed today as 'hawkish'), declaring that it would work for a united India through all legitimate means, but as long as Pakistan remained a separate entity, the Jana Sangh would stand for a strict policy of reciprocity and not one of appeasement, as hitherto pursued to the detriment of the country's national interests and honour.

The draft constitution, as submitted by the drafting committee and adopted by the convention, defined the object of the Bharatiya Jana Sangh to be the rebuilding of India, on the basis of Bharatiya sanskriti and maryada, as a prosperous, powerful, united and progressive nation, able to withstand the aggressive designs of others and to pull her weight in the council of nations for the establishment of world peace. To establish itself in all the parts of India, the Sangh would work through constituent bodies like local committee, district committee, provincial committee, provincial working committee, all-India committee and all-India working committee. The term of all constituent bodies and their office-bearers would be one year. A session of the Bharatiya Jana Sangh would ordinarily be held annually at the time and place decided upon by the all-India working committee, the highest executive of the Sangh responsible to the all-India committee and carrying into effect the policy laid down by it. The Delhi convention resolved that, till the various constituent bodies provided in the constitution were duly established, the *pradhan* of the provisional all-India committee would appoint the all-India working committee. The committee, so appointed, would have the power to appoint ad hoc provincial committees to carry on the work of the Sangh in various provinces and it would be one of their primary duties to strive for the organization of local and district committees in their respective provinces.

Meanwhile, the Congress, apprehensive of the impact the Jana Sangh's campaign might have on the people, especially the refugees in Punjab and Bengal, started a counter-campaign of misrepresentation of the character, aims and objects of the new party. In this they were joined by the socialists and the communists who were ideologically opposed to the robust nationalism of the new party. All this made it imperative for Dr Mookerjee to extensively tour the country, beginning with the Punjab, to explain the programme and policies of the Jana Sangh immediately after the Delhi convention. Presiding over a mass meeting in Calcutta Maidan on 2 December 1951 under the auspices of the Bharatiya Jana Sangh, Dr Mookerjee explained in detail the pragmatic and constructive programme of the party, with special reference to the peculiar problems of Bengal. He emphatically declared that the Jana Sangh was the only political organization to have a realistic approach towards the problems of Bengal, especially in relation to post-partition matters, which the Congress regime had failed to tackle. He also stressed the imperative need for protecting the minorities who were still in Pakistan.

Nehru's charge that the Jana Sangh was a communal body was being repeated in a parrot-like manner by his partymen. Repudiating this charge Dr Mookerjee said that the history of the Congress during the last thirty-five years was nothing but an abject surrender to Muslim appeasement and communalism. The membership of the Jana Sangh was open to all communities who were prepared to accept its policy of 'one country, one nation and one culture', and they were assured the fullest protection and equality of opportunities. Dr Mookerjee called upon Muslims and other minorities in West Bengal to join the Jana Sangh in large numbers.

It was a difficult task for Dr Mookerjee to undertake an extensive tour of the country as the party neither had the resources nor the organization to ensure him comforts and fast means of transportation. The press, particularly the English press, was positively hostile, having taken the cue from the Prime Minister and being in receipt of government largesse— the term 'paid news syndrome' had not been invented then, but the disease was already very much prevalent. However, one respected newspaper, the *Statesman*, of Delhi and Calcutta, published an article by Dr Mookerjee titled 'The Bharatiya Jana Sangh' on 21 December 1951. This was a breakthrough of sorts. In this article published just before the first general elections, he summed up the party's domestic and foreign policies which gained speedy publicity. One of Dr Mookerjee's ambitions was to place the Jana Sangh at the centre of the opposition to the Congress within the framework of the Constitution. In the article, he explained why his party, which was declared an all-India political organization in Delhi in the third week of October 1951 and had started functioning in several provinces just a few months earlier, had succeeded in enlisting in its favour within that short interval a strong volume of public opinion in different parts of India. According to him it was because it had unequivocally put its finger on the weak spots of the Congress administration, and its straightforward references to certain vital matters of national policy had touched the hearts of the people, voicing their suppressed feelings and anxieties.

The Jana Sangh had been created in the nick of time to fight the general election of 1952. By then, Patel was dead, and Nehru was the unquestioned leader of Congress and the country, marginally less than a king of sorts. Because of ideological differences and a personal allergy to Dr Mookerjee he had chosen to make him and the Jana Sangh his principal enemy in the election and had directed all his energies at fighting and vilifying this nascent party. Madhok recalled that he had asked Dr Mookerjee why he was not replying to his abuses. His answer[1] was, 'Why should I reply? These are fulminations of a diseased mind. In fact, he is doing a service to us, at least he is naming us every day, and the media publishes our name. Our name is reaching people, which it otherwise could not reach.'

Of course, Dr Mookerjee was aware of the enormous difference between his party and the powerful Congress in regard to resources and also the possibility of non-Congress votes being divided among different parties to the advantage of the Congress. The latter was a fallout of the 'first-past-the-post' system that India's Constitution-makers had adopted, or rather borrowed from Britain, in preference to the proportional representation system. As is well known, this system can cause a total imbalance between the popular votes bagged by a party and the number of seats won by it. The election to the Delhi municipal committee in 1952 had fully demonstrated how this distribution of votes could work to the advantage of the ruling party. Nevertheless, Dr Mookerjee decided, manfully, to go ahead and fight the election.

Dr Mookerjee had set an extremely punishing schedule for himself for campaigning. Balraj Madhok, who accompanied him on many of these tours, states that he used to cover as much as 200–300 miles by train or car, travelling at night and addressing a dozen meetings during the day. During this period, he used to wake up at 5 a.m., be ready for work by 6.30 a.m., and work non-stop until 10 p.m. He attracted large audiences wherever he went. Nehru possibly travelled more than him but in doing so he made full use of government transport, bungalows and other appurtenances—in those days the election process had not been refined, as it has now been done, to the extent of disallowing the use of government vehicles and planes for election campaigns.

Kidar Nath Sahni, then a young *vibhag pracharak* of the RSS, who later rose to occupy several important posts in the Jana Sangh, BJP and the government had accompanied him on a number of his electoral tours. In one of them he had travelled to Rohtak and from there on to Ferozepur. It was a night train, and Dr Mookerjee expected to get some rest during the journey, but at almost every station there were people waiting to meet him, sometimes just a few, at some places hundreds. But no matter what the number was, he always spoke to them, and if the crowd was substantial, addressed them in a speech. Sahni says he was astounded at the energy and patience of the man—not once did he get irritated or complain that this was getting to be too much. At Ferozepur he stayed with Rai Sahib Kundan Lal Ahuja, a well-wisher of the party. There was a college there called Deva Samaj College whose principal was a Bengali and a former student of Sir Asutosh. He invited Dr Mookerjee to his college, and the latter obliged, in spite of a very tight schedule. In the speech that he delivered there he mentioned that he had always wanted to meet Sri Aurobindo in Pondicherry, but could never manage it. After Sri Aurobindo's death Dr Mookerjee managed to make a trip to Pondicherry (still a French possession) and was granted his wish to see the place where Sri Aurobindo used to meditate. He was amazed to see, Dr Mookerjee said, that the figure before which

Sri Aurobindo sat while in meditation was not a deity but a huge map of India. Such was the patriotism of the man.

On his way out of Ferozepur when he reached the railway station he found that his luggage had not come, but the train was about to leave. He did not show any signs of being flustered and quietly boarded the train. His partymen chased the train in a car and brought his luggage to the next stop. At Ludhiana he addressed a huge gathering where, Sahni recalls, a young man called Tilak Raj gave a beautiful rendering of a song which went, 'Yeh deepak to jwalta hi rahega (this lamp [the Jana Sangh election symbol] will burn for ever)'. Dr Mookerjee was visibly moved by the song.

Madhok has contrasted Dr Mookerjee's style of electioneering with that of Nehru's. Madhok seemed to think that Nehru was rather obsessed with power at this stage. As opposed to him, Dr Mookerjee always remained cool in spite of his physical travails. At times, when this strain became unbearable he would turn around and say, 'Balraj, you are going to kill me today', and then go on with his scheduled programme without betraying any uneasiness. He delivered his election speeches in Hindi in which he was not very adept and which he spoke with a distinct Bengali accent but he plodded on nevertheless. Once in Jullundur, recalls Sahni, he insisted on speaking in Hindi although the audience was clamouring that he speak in English.

He particularly took Nehru to task on two accounts. One was his foreign policy and the other was his countercharge against Nehru's charge of communalism. Nehru's foreign policy was based, as it seems in retrospect, on what is termed today as mere 'lofty moral posturing'. Dr Mookerjee particularly lambasted Nehru on two of his grand follies: first, welcoming the Chinese annexation of Tibet and thereby removing this very important buffer state between the two great powers; and secondly, giving a long rope to Pakistan during the Kashmir war through his declaration of the unilateral ceasefire. Posterity has amply proved his foresight in these matters, as it has in regard to several other policies of the government mentioned earlier, though pro-Congress and pro-Nehru–Gandhi family historians[2] have deftly tried to gloss over these 'Himalayan Blunders' of Nehru.

Dr Mookerjee further argued, 'If it is communalist to love one's community and *not* think ill of other communities, if we feel that an attempt should be made to unite 40 crores of Hindus living in India that have been liberated after 1000 years, if we try to recover our lost position in a manner which is one hundred per cent consistent with the dynamic principles of Hinduism which Swami Vivekananda said, I am proud to be a communalist.' About Nehru he had further said in a meeting with the elite of the Punjab in Simla, 'Pandit Nehru claims that he has discovered India but he is yet to discover his own mind that has heavy over-coating of what is un-Indian and un-Hindu.'[3] In the course of his electioneering, Dr Mookerjee also got an opportunity to watch at close quarters the men, young and old, who constituted the Jana Sangh at the town, district and provincial levels. He could see the problems between young cadres drawn mainly from the RSS and the older people with diverse social and political backgrounds drawn from elsewhere. He was quick to grasp the untiring zeal, humility and hard work of the young workers drawn from the RSS which impressed him. As an educationist he understood the working of young minds. He also realized that it was not easy for older people who had grown up in a different atmosphere to reconcile with the young swayamsevaks. He, therefore, started training the young leaders with a view to building a second line of leaders. Madhok has remarked that this act was fundamentally different from Nehru who took deliberate steps to ensure that no individual, whether young or old, however capable and deserving, came anywhere close to him so as to jeopardize his unchallenged hold over the Congress party and the government. A question often asked during the 1950s (but not after the Chinese aggression of 1962) was, 'After Nehru, who?' Nehru deliberately kept this question hanging with a sweet smile; but while on his deathbed, he is said to have remarked, 'After me, my mantle should fall on Indu [Indira Gandhi].'

Vigorous electioneering brought out certain characteristics in Dr Mookerjee which had earlier been observed only inadequately. His unflappability in the face of irritants like continuous demands for addresses, allowing him no time for rest or even sleep, as recalled by Sahni, has already been mentioned. Sahni also recalled that he had no reservations about staying with people regardless of their station in life or business, so long as they were sincere. During the phase of electioneering in Punjab (which then included Haryana and Himachal), on his way down from Simla, he halted at Solan, had tea with the vice chancellor of Punjab University, and stayed in the guest house of Mohan Meakin Breweries. He also remembered small things in the midst of all the hustle and bustle he was going through. There was one Sen, a reporter of the *Hindustan Standard*, a Calcutta daily accompanying him. Dr Mookerjee would off and on inquire whether his needs were being taken care of. At Simla, while moving around on the Mall Road, he noticed a shop selling walking sticks, and bought several for his elderly relatives and friends in Calcutta. On letting go of his hired car, without being asked he gave a certificate to his chauffeur, vouching for his driving skill.

After vigorously campaigning for days and weeks together and addressing a dozen meetings on some days without even the minimum of comforts, Dr Mookerjee could give very little of his time and attention to his own constituency of Calcutta South. On 6 December 1951, he issued an appeal regretting his inability to approach voters personally however much he wished and hoping for their support in his earnest endeavour to properly safeguard the true interests of their country along with those of various sections of the people. About 23 per cent of the voters of the constituency were Muslims who had been misguided by the Congress propaganda to look upon the Jana Sangh as their worst enemy. The Congress had fielded a millionaire and an industrialist, Mriganka Mohan Sur, as their candidate. The Sur family had wide interests in various engineering industries in West Bengal. The communists also had a strong candidate in Sadhan Gupta, a blind but brilliant barrister. However, Dr Mookerjee never had the slightest doubt about his own election and once remarked in Bengali during one of the very few election speeches he could make in his constituency, 'You will vote for me, of course; but I ask you to support my party too.'[4] As expected, the voters, conscious of his services to Bengal and India, returned him with a thumping majority.

The overall results of the party in the 1952 parliamentary election were, however, almost a sad repeat of Dr Mookerjee's fateful result in the 1945 election to the Central Assembly. The Jana Sangh, having put up candidates in ninety-four out of the 489 seats, polled 3.06 per cent of the valid votes and could manage a total of only three seats in the Lok Sabha, two from West Bengal and one from Rajasthan. Among other national non-Congress parties, the Socialist Party got 10.6 per cent, the Communist Party 3.3 per cent, and the Kisan Mazdoor Praja Party (KMPP) 5.8 per cent, compared with the Congress party's whopping 45 per cent. The Jana Sangh got a total of thirty-five out of 742 candidates put up in the assembly elections from a total of 3283 seats and secured 2.77 per cent of the valid votes. Of these, nine were from West Bengal and eight from Rajasthan. In East Punjab, where the Jana Sangh appeared to be the strongest, it could not secure a single seat. As for the reasons for this debacle, Madhok has remarked that the infancy of the organization, the lack of an organizational structure (other than that of the RSS), the inexperience of young workers and the financial stringency of it had their parts to play.

As opposed to this, the Congress and the communists had their experience and in addition the Congress had the advantage of being the party in power. In 1952, there was no restriction on the use of official resources for electioneering by the candidates of the ruling party as there is today in India. Madhok has also said that there was misuse of official machinery and reports of tampering of ballot boxes. In those days, the practice was to have separate ballot boxes for each party with the symbol of the party pasted on it. The voter was required to put his ballot into the box of the party he was voting for. This was India's very first general election, the conductors of the election were inexperienced, and the safeguards against such tampering, especially by the ruling party, were very few. The independence of the Election Commission was also not as pronounced in those days as today.

However, there was no denying the fact that the Jana Sangh had given the most determined and clean fight to the Congress wherever it had entered the election arena. One silver lining in the dismal performance of the Jana Sangh in the election was that it was recognized as one of the four national parties by the Election Commission on the basis of the number of votes polled. No mean feat for a newborn party. The election had brought the nascent party in the front rank leaving many of the older parties behind. Born optimist that he was, Dr Mookerjee argued that they had gained a lot from the election results. To him, the chief gain was that the name and ideology of the party had reached the remotest villages, especially in the areas it had contested elections, and that it had secured a foothold in the country and also in the hearts of the people.

With a view to create a combined opposition parliamentary party under the pre-eminent leadership of Dr Mookerjee, an invitation was issued to most of the non-communist members in the Opposition for an exploratory meeting in New Delhi, before the inauguration of Parliament. The invitation was issued under the joint signatures of Dr Mookerjee, N.C. Chatterjee, president of the Hindu Mahasabha (father of later Lok Sabha speaker Somnath Chatterjee), Rajendra Narayan Singh Deo of Patna, leader of the Ganatantra Parishad, Sardar Hukam Singh, leader of the Akali Dal, Jaipal Singh, leader of the Jharkhand Party and a few independents. This meeting was held on 28 March 1952 in the Constitution Club on Balraj Madhok's booking and was attended by about twenty individual members and group leaders who together represented a sizeable chunk of the non-communist Opposition in Parliament.

Dr Mookerjee was the leader of the Jana Sangh which was ideologically at the opposite pole from the communists, even further removed than the Congress. Yet, such was his personal charm that Hiren Mukherjee, a prominent parliamentarian belonging to the Communist Party of India, became friends with Dr Mookerjee. Hiren Mukherjee recalled in an article[5] written much later about Dr Mookerjee's humour that he had quipped once, 'Do you know Hiren, they have allotted accommodation to me in Tughlak Crescent—not, mind you, in Tughlak *Road*, but Tughlak *Crescent* and I do not bat an eyelid!' Hiren Mukherjee also recalls that while because of ideological as well as temperamental difference there was between him and Jawaharlal Nehru a sort of mutual allergy, there was also mutual admiration. With the communists, there was a friendly combination against the government that is known today as 'floor coordination'. On issues such as preventive detention for political reasons, the communists and Jana Sanghis joined hands. Hiren Mukherjee also recalls his gift for repartee. One example was that, pillorying the government for detention of political opponents without trial, he heard a voice from the government side, 'face the truth', and his instant reply was, 'How can I, for I face the treasury benches!'

Side by side with his working indefatigably for the formation of his new party, he continued to be the superb parliamentarian that he essentially was, and proved literally to be a thorn in the flesh of the government, especially his bête noire, Jawaharlal Nehru. On 28 March 1951, speaking in the Lok Sabha on the demands for grants of the Ministry of External Affairs, he lambasted[6] the government's soft Pakistan policy, especially its ambivalence and its trade pact with Pakistan, saying:

> I have never known this extraordinary spectacle of any self-respecting country being at war with another country and at the same time hugging that country to its bosom when the people of that country are preparing to wage war at the other . . . Three and a half years have passed since then [the beginning of the hostilities in Kashmir] . . . We should bear in mind not the money alone but the blood and toil of our people in Kashmir . . . A plebiscite was offered by Pandit Jawaharlal Nehru. But one cannot have a plebiscite and a war at one and the same time.

On the question of India–Pakistan trade, he thundered:

> If I am not mistaken, every day about 250 wagons are moving from India to West Pakistan carrying coal. What for? Not only to enable Pakistan to carry on her industries or other useful occupations but also to get ready to attack Kashmir or to carry on its policy in respect of Kashmir should such an occasion arise. Does any country follow such a suicidal policy?

One of his most memorable speeches[7] was on the matter of the Hindu Code Bill delivered on 17 September 1951. He had forcefully espoused the idea of an all-India Civil Code and observed that in refusing such a code we suffer from a new disease which may be called 'secularitis'. 'How far it is open to the parliament . . . to enact a law which will be applicable to only one section of the community?' he asked. 'I doubt very much that some of the provisions which have been suggested in this code can be proposed to be made applicable to other communities, in particular to Muslims.' He continued, 'We are passing the question of monogamy. I believe it is nobody's case that monogamy is for Hindus alone or for Buddhists alone or for Sikhs alone.' He went on to say that those who were advocating monogamy were obviously doing so on the basis that this system is civilized in principle and it should be made applicable to all—if not to all persons of the civilized world, then at least to all citizens of India who are liable to be governed under law passed by the Parliament. Therefore why should there not be a separate bill dealing only with monogamy and make it applicable to all citizens? It obviously cannot be anybody's contention that monogamy is good for Hindus only and not for others! He said:

> Stand for one social doctrine. If you believe that monogamy as a social system is the best that India should have then do not try to look at it through the Hindu door. Look at it through the human door and make it applicable to all. Behave like a secular State at least in this instance. Take courage in both hands and see that monogamy will be made applicable to all citizens of India . . . if you accept this as a principle apply it just now to the whole of India.

It is important to note here that the Hindu Code Bill which had been introduced in the Parliament in 1951 was held up and taken for consideration much later, split into four separate bills and passed as the Hindu Marriage Act, Hindu Succession Act, Hindu Minority and Guardianship Act and Hindu Adoptions and Maintenance Act between 1952 and 1956. But no government so far has been able to, or has wanted to, do anything about the practices of polygamy and *teen talaq*, the practice of instant, unilateral divorce by a Muslim husband.

No matter what the results for the party were, Dr Mookerjee's stature, expectedly, was nothing less than towering in the new Parliament. In his maiden speech on 21 May 1952, he made a sincere and passionate plea for a correct approach towards the Opposition and said:

> [As] I was looking to this house for the last two days, I feel, as must have been the feeling of many members of this house that here we witness the epitome of free India . . . it is one of the greatest experiments in history that we are making. Everyone of us, no matter to which group or party we may belong, must be able to look at the problems from the widest standpoint and while appreciating the difference among the rest, we must try to resolve these difficulties and come to the conclusions which will be to the good of the country.

He also briefly referred to the main problems and issues then besetting the country such as food scarcity in the Rayalaseema area of Madras Presidency and in parts of West Bengal. He also drew attention to the growing dangers of casteism, provincialism and communalism all of which posed a grave danger to the unity and integrity of the country. He pointed out 'that the very communalism, casteism and provincialism which have been very rightly condemned in the President's address were taken full advantage of in every suitable place by the Congress party for winning the election'.

He also referred to the problem of Jammu and Kashmir which had begun to threaten the very integrity and unity of India. He appealed to the Prime Minister to consider the forces which were then at war in Kashmir and which had been revealed for everyone to see by Sheikh Abdullah's declaration that the Indian Parliament had no jurisdiction over the state. Nehru as usual was irritated. 'I know more of Kashmir than Dr Mookerjee,' he interrupted. Dr Mookerjee's retort[8] was instant and characteristic:

The whole difficulty is that the Prime Minister knows more about anything throughout the world than anybody else and he will not accept any advice from anybody . . . If I make a suggestion, he says: 'I know more than you' . . . I would like to know, are Kashmiris Indians first and Kashmiris next or they are Kashmiris first and Indian next, or are Kashmiris first, second and third and not Indians at all? This is a very important point which we have to settle.

He also referred to the sorry state of Hindus in East Bengal which was again getting serious. He had received information that another exodus of Hindus from East Bengal had started but Nehru said that figures proved otherwise.

As for the other problem exercising Dr Mookerjee's mind, the reality was that at that stage the condition of the Hindus in East Bengal, as it appeared to him, seemed to have the least priority in Nehru's mind. He had gone and signed the Delhi Pact with Liaquat Ali, following which Dr Mookerjee and K.C. Neogy had resigned and that made the success of the pact a matter of prestige for him. He was determined to prove that following the pact all was well with the Hindus of East Bengal. And why? Because Liaquat Ali said so; and if the actual situation happened to be different, well, bad luck. In truth, admitting that the Hindus in East Pakistan were being persecuted amounted to saying that Dr Mookerjee was right, Nehru was wrong, the pact was a stupid mistake. And how could the uncrowned king of India say so?[9] Therefore, when Dr Mookerjee said that he had information that another exodus had started, and it was the duty of a responsible Prime Minister to get up and say that the Government of India will take that into consideration and see how to prevent it, an infuriated Nehru answered,[10] '[T]he honourable member is challenging my statement!' Dr Mookerjee in reply said that this challenge and counter-challenge will be carried on for the whole of the session.

Bijoygarh is a location in the Jadavpur area of what then was one of the southern suburbs of Calcutta. The place was settled by refugees from East Bengal, and held against stiff opposition from the West Bengal government and attempts to oust them— whence the name, *Bijoy* (*Vijay* in Hindi) meaning 'victory'. On 19 November 1952, Dr Mookerjee, speaking here before a crowded meeting of East Bengal refugees, said that at that time Pakistan was in the grip of a financial crisis and it was the right time for the Government of India to impose economic sanctions to make it behave itself in the matter of the treatment of its Hindu minority in its Eastern Wing.

Chanakya, the guru of statecraft in India, would have said the same thing. Nehru, of course, knew better.

Four days later, on 23 November, many thousands of men and women assembled at the Ramlila Grounds, New Delhi, in observance of East Bengal Day. Speaking here, Dr Mookerjee demanded the imposition of economic sanctions against Pakistan and suspension of trade relations with that country.

History afforded no other example of recognizing separate nationality based on the religion of a section of a country's population and sacrificing the cherished right of millions of people who passionately believed in United India . . . Subsequent events required a full and frank resurvey of the situation and not the adoption of an ostrich-like attitude. Inaction or appeasement in circumstances was neither dignified nor honourable but cowardly and hypocritical.

He also recalled the horrible migration and carnage between the two Punjabs immediately after Partition. There was a forcible exchange of population through a bloodbath and the government succumbed to it. The East Bengal Hindus, Dr Mookerjee continued, numbering about a crore and forty

lakh had never wanted Partition and had fought for the liberation of United India. They were given solemn assurances by
the Congress party and other national leaders that if Pakistan
oppressed or tortured them, the government of free India
would be there to save their lives and honour. Time had
now come to test whether this was a solemn pledge made by
honourable men or a cruel hoax made by political oppor-
tunists. During the last five years about 3 million people had
been periodically turned out of their homes and thousands
killed and dishonoured. The Government of India had entered
into pacts and agreements with Pakistan for safeguarding
minority rights on three successive occasions. Like other pacts
those were unilaterally broken by Pakistan time after time, yet
the Indian government never woke up to reality. Criticizing
the weak and vacillating policy of the Government of India,
he said that it had definitely worsened the situation and had
encouraged the Pakistan government to have its own way at
every step. Who could ever conceive that a foreign government
which has occupied by force a portion of territory of another
state, as Pakistan has done with regard to Kashmir, would still
be deemed a friendly state and no effective sanctions would
be imposed against it? 'This dual policy of war on the soil of
Kashmir and surrender and appeasement elsewhere in Pakistan
has lowered India in the estimation of her own people and
made her an object of ridicule,' he added.

We now have to look at the Parliament, specifically the Lok
Sabha or Lower House, that had come into being as a result of the
1952 elections. The Congress was the overwhelmingly powerful
government party with a whopping total of 339 members in a
house of 466, and their unquestioned leader was Nehru—no
wonder that he felt and acted like the king! The Opposition,
on the other hand, was a real motley crew. The communists,
a powerful group by contemporary standards, had eighteen

members. The socialists had twelve and the Kisan Mazdoor Praja Party (KMPP) of Acharya Kripalani, who had broken away from the Congress, had ten. Their merger to form the Praja Socialist Party (PSP) raised their combined strength to twenty-two. The communists tried to form an alliance with them and even offered the leadership of the combined group to a PSP nominee as bait. But the socialists, who had grown wiser after their experience of alliance with communists during 1935–40, spurned this offer.

The Bharatiya Jana Sangh, the only other all-India party, had only three members. The Ram Rajya Parishad, mainly based in Madhya Bharat, also had three, the Hindu Mahasabha had four and the provincial or sectional parties like the Ganatantra Parishad of Orissa, the Akali Dal representing a section of the Sikhs of Punjab, the Jharkhand Party of the tribals of Bihar and the Tamil Nadu Toilers' Party had five, four, three and four members, respectively. The independents, who numbered thirty-three, were as their very title indicated, incapable of united action. Some of them conscientiously felt that they should remain completely independent. Others wanted to use their independence to good purpose by taking sides at will or at the command of their self-interest. Another notable feature of this motley Opposition was that it lacked talent; most of the top leaders of the communists, the socialists and the KMPP had been unable to get in. The one man in the Opposition who stood pretty much above all others was Dr Mookerjee.

And by the time the first session of the Parliament ended in August 1952, there was no doubt left in anybody's mind on this score. The press, controlled by the party in power, was by no means friendly to him, admitted this fact and many of the papers editorially commented on it. The most remarkable tribute came from an English national daily which commented that the 'mantle of Sardar Patel had fallen on Dr Syama Prasad Mookerjee'. It was a most befitting tribute because Dr Mookerjee had been exercising the same sort of sobering and restraining influence on the Nehru government from the outside that Sardar Patel had been doing from within as long as he lived. The approach of Dr Mookerjee to most of the national problems was essentially the same as that of Sardar Patel to whom he paid a glowing tribute in his speech on Kashmir on 26 June. Both were practical men of affairs, deeply rooted in the soil of India, who never allowed considerations of name and international fame to get the better of their judgement regarding the real interests of the country. Madhok has also remarked that Sardar Patel continued to work with Nehru even after Dr Mookerjee's resignation from the cabinet because he was aware that his withdrawal would mean the end of the Congress. Love of the organization, in the making of which he had shed his lifeblood, kept him tied to Pandit Nehru against his better judgement.

In the first session of the first elected Lok Sabha, of the several memorable speeches that Dr Mookerjee had made, the one on redrawing the state boundaries deserves special mention. As on several other occasions, it demonstrated the political foresight and statesmanship of the man. He severely criticized the policy of 'drift' followed by the government in this regard and said:[11]

> Before things deteriorate I will beg of this House that this question should be gone into . . . It is no use adopting an ostrich-like policy and thinking that everything is going on all right. If you say: 'Let us not redistribute the boundaries of India for any consideration', if that is the policy of the Government, let them announce it and face the consequences. Then the people will know where they stand. If you say there is to be redistribution consistent with the declarations that Congress has made for the last 35 years, then do not leave the matter to be decided by the parties concerned but take the initiative in your own hands. This is my appeal to

Pandit Jawaharlal Nehru. Let him take the initiative in his own hands, appoint a commission, appoint advisers or call information conferences of the leading representatives of the areas concerned and try to adjust matters in such a way that they may come to a decision which will be mutually acceptable to all. It is not a question of making some debating point from the Congress side or the non-Congress side. It is a first-class national issue which has got to be settled on a national basis not on party basis.

It is rather clear that Nehru and his government hardly did anything substantial but evidential proof seems to suggest that they eventually allowed things to drift, just as Dr Mookerjee had apprehended, until the martyrdom of Potti Sriramulu, who fasted until death to separate the Telugu-speaking areas of Madras Presidency to form a new state. The campaign of lawlessness and destruction that followed in its wake forced the government's hands. It belatedly decided to appoint a States Reorganization Commission, which in 1957 redrew the state boundaries all over India. Even after this the clamour for further divisions did not stop. The next step was the division of bilingual Bombay state into Gujarat and Maharashtra, followed by the division of Punjab, Assam and so on. But all these took place after some agitation or other shook the government and forced its hands as it did in the case of Andhra. Dr Mookerjee's statesmanship and foresight lay in his suggestion that the government lay down a policy in this regard instead of drifting and then being swayed by this agitation or the other, thus paving the way for more agitations.

That Dr Mookerjee did not criticize for criticism's sake, and that he was more than ready to praise the government where praise was due, which is another way to say that it was constructive criticism, was amply demonstrated by his speech[12] on the First Five-Year Plan on 18 December 1952. He paid handsome tributes to the authors of the plan. At the same time, he drew attention to the uncertain and undependable premises in respect of finance on which the plan had been built and the scant attention paid to the basic questions of education, health and industrial self-sufficiency. Here again, his foresight was proved when subsequently it was observed that, as a result of rampant capital expenditure by the government without any regard to returns, the sterling balance of the country had been depleted and it had to be subjected to extremely high rates of taxation to finance developmental activities. This high taxation, in turn, paved the way for tax avoidance, evasion and corruption. His remarks on scant attention to education and health were nothing less than prophetic, as has been proved by the fact that even after seventy years of independence the country has not been able to ensure literacy and clean drinking water for all.

He drew pointed attention of the government to the question of popular enthusiasm and people's cooperation and participation in the plan without which it would not be able to achieve its objective. The public cooperation, he pointed out, would come only if the party in power would handle the plan on national and not on party lines.

> If you come forward with a sincere call that you really want to build up an economy meant not mainly for the privileged or the favoured few but for the millions of downtrodden people, not on paper but in reality; if you take such a message to them there is bound to be public cooperation . . . We want that the country should develop. We know that political freedom will be meaningless . . . if it is not followed by economic freedom and by social equality. But let us proceed not on party lines. Let there be more tolerance, let there be more appreciation of the other man's point of view.

Another one of his great speeches[13] of the session was the
one he made on the Preventive Detention Bill which was
being piloted by K.N. Katju. It not only brought the whole
Opposition, including the communists, under his wings but
completely floored Katju. Dr Mookerjee's opposition to the
principle of detention without trial sprang from his inborn
love of democracy and freedom. What amazed and annoyed
the treasury benches most was his resourcefulness in collecting
apt passages from their own speeches and writings as also
from those of their forebears like Pandit Motilal Nehru to
condemn the principles underlying the bill which, he declared,
'is repugnant to any democratic constitution in any part of the
civilized world except at a time of emergency or crisis'. Some
recall (though it is not on record) that he had his share of
impish fun when, while quoting Pandit Motilal, he deliberately
skipped his first name, causing Jawaharlal to jump up and
say, 'I never said that!' Whereupon it was Dr Mookerjee's
pleasure to point out that the 'Nehru' being spoken of was
not him but his late illustrious father. He also quoted, with
telling effect, the words, 'Detention on mere undisclosed
and often on groundless suspicion without charge or trial is
opposed to all notions of natural justice and all canons of
civilized administration' from a book without revealing its title
or author, which prompted Katju to ask about the book the
honourable member was quoting from. Whereupon it was Dr
Mookerjee's pleasure to say that he was quoting from a book
authored by none other than Kailash Nath Katju. Katju, of
course, would not listen to his own voice of reason. Secure in
the overwhelming majority of his party, he shook his head at all
his arguments and pleadings which drew from Dr Mookerjee
the famous retort:[14] 'He [Katju] will never learn anything,
forget everything and make a mess of everything.'

The story of the Hindus of East Bengal has already been related in brief but not the story of Jammu and Kashmir which will assume increasing importance in this biography. It will, therefore, now be necessary to cut to the issue to understand the situation. A short introduction to the state would also, at this stage, be in order.

Jammu and Kashmir was the largest 'native' state in British India in terms of area, covering 84,471 square miles. It had the following broad geographical divisions: Jammu, a Hindu-majority area, inhabited by Dogri-speaking people following Hindu cultural traditions and local customs, and the famous 'Vale of Kashmir', with an overwhelmingly Sunni Muslim majority (93 per cent) and a small minority (7 per cent) of Hindus known as Pandits. Both communities spoke the common language Kashmiri and wrote in Urdu. The Muzaffarabad–Mirpur region, forming the westernmost fringe of the valley, along the Jhelum River, was a Punjabi-speaking Muslim-majority area with a large Sikh-minority population. Gilgit and Baltistan, in the far north at the junction of two famous mountain ranges, the Hindu Kush and the Karakoram, bordering the Pamir plateau, were sparsely populated mountainous areas. Ladakh, forming the north-eastern corner of the state, practically isolated from the rest except by the tenuous Zoji La Pass, was partly Tibetan Mahayana Buddhist, and partly Shia Muslim, who were religion-wise and linguistically quite different from the Sunni Kashmiri Muslims. There were other very sparsely populated or almost unpopulated mountainous areas in the state, such as the Zanskar region and Aksai Chin. Apart from the principal elements of the population mentioned, there were other small tribal groups such as the Gujjars and Bakarwals, each with their customs and language.

During the last stage of British rule, the state was ruled by Dogra king Hari Singh. The accession of this state to India was mishandled by Nehru and turned into a perpetual problem for India. However, there was another aspect of the problem. During Hari Singh's reign, the Pandits of Kashmir and the Dogras of Jammu enjoyed some unwritten privileges which the Kashmiri Muslims grudged. After the government led by Sheikh Abdullah was installed at Srinagar, the balance of power shifted overwhelmingly to the Kashmiri Muslims' side and the government decided to even the score. A period of persecution and deprivation of Dogras and the people of the Jammu region ensued. The Pandits were left alone for the moment—their misfortune would hit them many years later, in the late 1980s. However, a large number of them left the valley and dispersed all over India in search of livelihood.

The issue of the Dogras and others of the Jammu area was taken up by the Jammu and Kashmir Praja Parishad, and was duly resisted by Sheikh Abdullah's government. Nehru had exhibited a faith in Sheikh Abdullah that can very well be described as nothing short of baby-like—until August 1953, when he decided to unseat and arrest him. Because the Jana Sangh supported the agitation by the Praja Parishad, Nehru was angered and immediately started clanging the 'communal' bell—naturally enough, since the agitation was by Hindus who felt deprived and persecuted by a principally Muslim government. For those afflicted by the disease Dr Mookerjee described as 'secularitis', a Muslim could do no wrong.

But of course Dr Mookerjee would not take it lying down. Referring to the charge of communalism used to malign him and his organization as also the Praja Parishad, he asked the Prime Minister to tell him exactly what was communal about him and his party and their stand instead of this incessant tom-tomming and making vague charges.

I know the Prime Minister levels the charge of communalism on all of us. Whenever he cannot meet an argument that is the answer that he has to give. I am quite prepared, I am not making a challenging suggestion, because I am getting sick of this charge which is unfounded . . . let us fix a date for a debate and let us discuss the matter. Let Government bring forward its charges. Let us have a chance of replying.[15]

Protesting against the repression and the persecution of the Dogras, he said:

You will not be able to destroy the Dogras. I have seen some of them, fine elements. It brought tears to my eyes. I saw some men and women, great people, patriotic people, fearless people . . . I have seen Pandit Premnath Dogra whom I respect with all my heart. Even now my appeal to the Prime Minister, is this: Let us forget the past. Let him take up the matter. He can rise equal to the occasion. He can deliver the goods with Shaikh Abdullah . . . and I appeal to the Prime Minister to move before it is too late.

But this chapter would not be complete without a mention of his Lok Sabha speech[16] of 7 August 1952. This was a long and comprehensive one in which he dealt with the Kashmir problem at length in all its dimensions. In the speech he pointed out the glaring inconsistencies and anomalies in the Kashmir policy of the government. But more than anything else, he pointed to the arrogance of Sheikh Abdullah, and the government's meek acquiescence to the same and the dangers inherent in such action— or inaction.

He began his speech with a frank admission that he, as a member of the Union cabinet, was a party to the reference of the Kashmir dispute to the United Nations, thereby needlessly internationalizing a bilateral dispute. But at the same time, he said

that there were circumstances surrounding this decision which he
was not at liberty to state. He said:

> It has been said that I was a party when the decision was taken to
> refer the Kashmir issue to the U.N.O. That is an obvious fact.
> I have no right and I do not wish to disclose the extraordinary
> circumstances under which that decision was taken . . . We did
> not go to the U.N.O. with regard to the question of accession,
> because accession then was an established fact . . . Somehow,
> we should withdraw ourselves, so far as consideration of the
> Kashmir case is concerned, from the U.N.O.

Thereafter he emphasized the aspect that since accession of the
state to India was final, and not included in the reference, there was
no reason for Kashmir to have any 'special status', which was at
the root of the inconsistency in the government's policy. In the
process he lambasted the two-faced policy of the government
and said:

> We say that Kashmir is a part of India. It is so. So, a part of
> India is today in the occupation of the enemy and we are helpless!
> We are peace-lovers, no doubt. But peace-lovers to what
> extent?—that we will even allow a portion of our territory
> to be occupied by the enemy? . . . Is there any possibility
> of our getting back this territory? We shall not get it through
> the efforts of the United Nations, we shall not get it through
> peaceful methods, by negotiations with Pakistan. That means we
> lose it, unless we use force and the Prime Minister is unwilling to
> do so. Let us face facts—are we prepared to lose it? It has been
> said that there is some provision in the Constitution, that
> we are bound by the pledges which have been given. Pledges?
> Undoubtedly, so many pledges we have given . . . If we talk of
> pledges, we have given pledges on many other occasions. We

gave pledges to the minorities in East Bengal. That was given after the attainment of independence. The Prime Minister said the other day that even if Kashmir had not acceded to India, when Kashmir was attacked by the raiders, on humanitarian grounds the Indian army could have marched to Kashmir and protected the distressed and oppressed. I felt proud. But if I make a similar statement, or even a similar suggestion for the purpose of saving the lives and honour of nine million of our fellow brethren and sisters—through whose sacrifices, to some extent at least, freedom has been achieved, I am a communalist, I am a reactionary, I am a warmonger!

He went on to say:

Shaikh Abdullah spoke in the Constituent Assembly of Kashmir about three or four months ago, words which have not been withdrawn, but words which created a good deal of misgivings in the minds of all Indians irrespective of party affiliations. I do not know whether the Prime Minister saw this:

We are a hundred per cent sovereign body. No country can put spokes in the wheel of our progress. Neither the Indian Parliament nor any other Parliament outside the State has any jurisdiction over our State.

. . . And then the flag. The flag has a significance. It will not do for the Prime Minister to say that it is a matter of sentiment. It was announced in the papers three days ago that the Indian flag will fly only on two ceremonial occasions and otherwise the State flag alone will fly there. It you feel that the unity and integrity of India are not affected and it will not lead to fissiparous tendencies being generated, accept it and do it for all. But why do it as a matter of surrender to Sheikh Abdullah's demand?

He wanted to call himself the Prime Minister. That is
how he first started. Some of us did not like it. We know one
Prime Minister of India including Kashmir, that is the Prime
Minister who is sitting here. How can you have two Prime
Ministers, one Prime Minister in Delhi and another Prime
Minister in Srinagar . . . As regards the emergency provision,
it is an amazing stand. If there is an emergency on account
of internal disturbance, the President of India will not have
the last say. Why this fear of the President of India? Can
you contemplate a more gratuitous insult to the President
of India? . . . I shall conclude, by making this constructive
suggestion . . . I submit that we must proceed according
to certain standards. First of all there is no question of the
President by virtue of his power to make orders altering the
provisions of the Constitution in material respects . . . You
consider all these items and make your provisions so elastic
that you can apply them either to the whole of India or you
can apply them to only such parts where the Parliament
of India will feel that such special treatment is necessary.
Proceed in accordance with a constitutional manner, not
just play with the Constitution. It is a sacred document, and
it is a document on which much labour and much thought
were bestowed. If you feel some changes are necessary in
order to take into consideration the new set-up that is slowly
developing in India, whether in Kashmir or other parts of
India, by all means let the people of the country have a chance
to express their opinion.

Lastly, mindful of the fact that the Sheikh was a Kashmiri
Muslim, and was apt to discriminate against the remainder of
the population of the state, namely the Dogras, the Ladakhis, the

Gujjars, the Bakarwals and the Shia Muslims of the Kargil area, he had the following words of warning:

> The same right which you are claiming for Kashmir may also be demanded by the people of Jammu and Ladakh. Let us proceed in a friendly spirit. Sheikh Abdullah himself said about a month ago that he will have no objection if the people of Jammu and Ladakh really felt that they would go to India . . . Let it be possible for the people residing in those areas to make up their minds which way it will be good to proceed, and it will also be consistent with the same principles of self-determination which constitute the basic claims of Sheikh Abdullah, supported by the Prime Minister.

14

Praja Parishad's Jammu
Agitation, 1952–53

The extraordinary situation in Jammu and Kashmir, created largely by Pandit Jawaharlal Nehru's unusual act of unilateral ceasefire, had been exercising Dr Mookerjee's mind even while he was totally busy with giving a shape to his newborn party and thereafter fighting the 1952 election. With these tasks now behind him, and the situation in East Bengal presenting no new crises, he perceived the imminent danger in the situation in Jammu and Kashmir and began to devote increasing attention to the state. The National Conference, led by Sheikh Abdullah, was ruling the state, and Nehru vested him with blind and unquestioning support, presumably in the hope of getting his support for the integration of the state into the Indian Union. It was the same old story, the same tradition of the Congress of appeasement and genuflection that began with Gandhi's support to the retrograde Khilafat movement and continued into the Gandhi–Jinnah talks of 1944. And it was a policy that always failed—as it failed in Kashmir too. For the moment, the Sheikh was enjoying himself tremendously and doing and saying pretty much what he pleased. Absolute power is said to corrupt absolutely, and the Kashmir government was no exception. Serious problems, as a result, began to develop in the state.

There were, as Dr Mookerjee astutely observed, two principal dimensions to the crisis in the state. One stemmed from Sheikh Abdullah's pretensions to independence of the state vis-à-vis India. The other was the preferential treatment he gave to the Vale of Kashmir and Kashmiri Sunni Muslims as compared to the other parts of the state, principally the Jammu region, whose people he considered almost pariah. The process had begun in 1948, after Nehru's unilateral ceasefire. Sheikh Abdullah had been installed as 'Head of Emergency Administration' by Maharaja Hari Singh while signing the Instrument of Accession. Immediately after assuming charge he addressed his first meeting with the government officers saying,[1] 'Pakistan is not our enemy and we have the same respect for Mr Jinnah that we had previously. We want the Kashmir issue to be settled by dialogue and if for this purpose I have to go to Karachi to meet Mr Jinnah I am willing to go there.'

He should have been deposed and arrested for this single utterance. However, this set the tune for his and his partymen's subsequent conduct, which allegedly became more and more belligerently anti-Indian. The extent to which they went can be gauged by some of their subsequent speeches. On 24 March 1952, for example, Mirza Afzal Beg, the revenue minister in Sheikh Abdullah's cabinet, declared in the state constituent assembly, 'The Jammu and Kashmir State will be a Republic within the Indian Union . . . So far as the Constitution of the State is concerned we aim at making its framework such that the State will be a Republic like other republics. According to our plans the State will have its own President, a separate National Assembly and a judicial set-up.' This was soon followed by the pompous declaration[2] on 29 March in the assembly by Sheikh Abdullah himself, who had returned a few days earlier from Paris, where he had been sent by the Government of India as its delegate to the UNO. He said, '[We] are a hundred percent sovereign body. No country can put spokes in the wheels of our progress—neither Indian Parliament nor any other Parliament outside the State has any jurisdiction over us.' He followed this up with a more damaging speech[3] at Ranbirsinghpura on 10 April in the course of which he said: 'Kashmir's accession to India will have to be of a restricted nature so long as communalism has a foot-hold on the soil of India.' He called the arguments in favour of full accession to be 'childish, unrealistic and savouring of lunacy'. And then he made a comment on India by saying, 'Many Kashmiris fear what will happen to them and their position if, for instance, something happens to Pandit Nehru. We do not know. As realists, we Kashmiris have to make provision for all eventualities.'

One of the first steps Sheikh Abdullah took to establish his hegemony and that of his party over the whole state was to send Hari Singh's last Prime Minister, Mehr Chand Mahajan,[4] packing, away from Jammu to Delhi. He assumed charge, with Nehru's support and consent, as the Prime Minister of Jammu and Kashmir on 17 March 1948—*Prime* Minister, not *Chief* Minister, like in any other state. Abdullah's party, the Jammu and Kashmir National Conference, passed a resolution on 27 October 1950 for setting up a constituent assembly for the state, to be constituted of elected representatives of the people of the state. Meanwhile Yuvraj (Prince) Karan Singh, twenty-one-year-old son of former Maharaja Hari Singh, was appointed the Sadr-i-Riyasat (Head of State) of Jammu and Kashmir. And although the Constituent Assembly of India had finished its work and given the country a constitution, the constituent assembly of Jammu and Kashmir remained busy in trying to give *that country* a constitution. Further, by the Sheikh's order, the flag of his party, the Jammu and Kashmir National Conference, not the Indian tricolour, flew atop all government buildings. So by 1952, the country, of which Jammu and Kashmir was an integral part, had two

Prime Ministers, Nehru and Abdullah; two heads of state, the President of the Republic of India and the Sadr-i-Riyasat of Jammu and Kashmir; two Constitutions, one of which was still unfinished; and two flags.

Has any nation of the world, which claims a certain part of it as an integral part of that nation, ever subjected itself to such indignity? It is against this indignity that Dr Mookerjee had thundered,[5] '*Ek desh mein do Vidhaan, do Pradhan aur do Nishaan nahin chalenge* (In one country two Constitutions, two Prime Ministers and two flags shall not be tolerated).'

One set of people over whom Sheikh Abdullah held little or no sway were the Dogras of Jammu, the second largest ethnolinguistic group of the country after the Kashmiri Sunni Muslims. The hero of their hearts was Pandit Premnath Dogra, the selfless fighter for Dogra rights. With Balraj Madhok he had founded the Jammu and Kashmir Praja Parishad party. Madhok had later moved to Delhi and became instrumental in the founding of the Jana Sangh, but Pandit Premnath Dogra remained in Jammu and led the Praja Parishad. Aside from Dogra rights, the party fought ceaselessly for full integration of the state into India.

Shortly after being anointed Prime Minister of Jammu and Kashmir, Sheikh Abdullah arrested Pandit Premnath Dogra without any charges and held him without trial.[6] The Praja Parishad launched a peaceful and non-violent satyagraha[7] in protest. Hundreds of men and women from all parts of Jammu courted arrest during this event. Finally he was released by the Kashmir government, towards the end of 1948, on the intercession of the Government of India and the party was given the assurance that no hurdles would be put in the way of its normal democratic activities. A few months later, the decision to elect a constituent assembly for the state was announced. The Praja Parishad decided to contest the elections to this assembly and began to make preparations for it in right earnest. But after the party candidates filed their nominations, forty-two out of the total of fifty-nine nomination papers were rejected by the returning officer on the most arbitrary and whimsical grounds. The Praja Parishad tried to bring the matter to the notice of the Government of India, but received no worthwhile response.

Abdullah had a genuine and unconcealed dislike, bordering on hatred, for the Dogras of Jammu. This has been commented upon not only by the director of the Intelligence Bureau B.N. Mullick who was later deputed to Jammu and Kashmir by Nehru (see later in this chapter), but also by the Sadr-i-Riyasat Dr Karan Singh. In his *Autobiography*, Dr Singh writes about the Praja Parishad agitation, 'Their slogan of the complete integration of the state with India was expressed in the rallying cry, "*Ek Vidhan, Ek Nishan, Ek Pradhan*" (One constitution, one flag and one president).' This agitation gathered momentum over the next few months as it effectively capitalized upon the sense of outrage felt by the Dogras not only at having lost their predominant position in the state but also in having at one stroke been placed at the mercy of their arch-enemy, Sheikh Abdullah. The Sheikh, for his part, not only made no efforts to mollify the feelings of the Jammu people but also continued with his hostile and aggressive attitude.

At this time Dr Mookerjee was on the point of resigning from the ministry over the issue of the Nehru–Liaquat Pact, and his mind was full of the East Bengal crisis. Meanwhile the Praja Parishad had made up its mind to boycott the elections. When a dialogue did take place between the Praja Parishad leaders and Dr Mookerjee, the latter, ever the constitutional politician, said it was a mistake that the forum of the constituent assembly of Jammu and Kashmir, illegal as it was, ought to have been taken advantage of. But by that time the nominations had been filed. Thus Sheikh Abdullah got a chance to fill up the entire constituent assembly with his henchmen.

Dr Mookerjee was deeply perturbed by these developments. Neither was he happy with the unexpected turn the discussions regarding Kashmir had taken at the United Nations. The United Nations Security Council had adopted a resolution 91 on 30 March 1951 that it would not consider elections (referring to the elections to the Jammu and Kashmir constituent assembly) held only in 'Indian administered Kashmir' to be a substitute for a free and impartial plebiscite including the people of the 'entire state Jammu and Kashmir'. He felt that the matter was being mishandled at both the domestic and the international end. Meanwhile, as a result of relentless pressure from him and others on the Jammu and Kashmir government through the Government of India, the former was forced to release Pandit Premnath Dogra from jail. Dogra then travelled to New Delhi to place his case before the leaders of public opinion in India.

He met Dr Mookerjee in his suite in the Western Court early in May 1952. Madhok describes this meeting, judged by subsequent results, as nothing less than 'momentous'. Dogra described in detail to Dr Mookerjee the events that had preceded and succeeded Sheikh Abdullah's rise to power which the latter was mostly unaware of. He described how Abdullah could not enter Jammu without getting an assurance of support from him; how Abdullah pressed him to join the National Conference as a prerequisite to his being taken into his cabinet; and how his refusal to sell his conscience for loaves and fishes of office made him his enemy. He also explained how the hand of cooperation offered by the Praja Parishad for the defence and betterment of the state and her people was spurned by Sheikh Abdullah.[8]

Madhok further states that the whole thing came as a revelation to Dr Mookerjee. He began to see for the first time in clear perspective the real purpose and motive behind Sheikh Abdullah's utterances referred to above. He saw the justice of the stand taken by the Praja Parishad and its wider implications for the unity and integrity of India as a whole. He was also highly impressed by the sincerity of the seventy-year-old Pandit Dogra and was visibly moved by his appeal for support to his party's cause. Thereafter when Pandit Dogra invited him to visit Jammu he readily agreed. The former apparently also tried to see Nehru, but Nehru, ever mindful of Sheikh Abdullah's feelings rather than anyone else's, allegedly refused to even meet a person of Pandit Dogra's stature.

Dr Mookerjee, once convinced of the Dogra cause and the Sheikh's diabolical designs, immediately got down to business. He began with getting a resolution passed by the working committee of the Bharatiya Jana Sangh on 14 June 1952, which emphasized that Jammu and Kashmir was an integral part of India and declared[9] that 'the decision of the State Constituent Assembly concerning an elected President and a separate flag . . . are in violation of India's sovereignty and the spirit of India's Constitution'.

On 26 June, that is, three days before the appointed All-India Kashmir Day, Dr Mookerjee made the first of his several speeches[10] on Kashmir in the Parliament. Earlier on the same day, the people of Delhi staged a huge demonstration before the Parliament to condemn Sheikh Abdullah's separatist policies. In the course of this speech, Dr Mookerjee dealt with, one by one, the questions of a separate flag, an elected constitutional head of the state in the place of the hereditary Maharaja and Article 370 of the Indian Constitution on the basis of which Sheikh Abdullah wanted a separate constitution for the state. He completely shattered the case of Sheikh Abdullah and his supporters in the central cabinet. Referring to the question of the flag, he pointed out: 'You cannot have divided loyalty. Sheikh Abdullah has said: "We shall treat both flags equally." You cannot do it. It is not a question of fifty-fifty, it is not a question of parity. It is a question of using one flag for the whole of India—an India that includes Kashmir. There is no question of having a separate Republic of Kashmir having a separate flag.' Referring to the move to replace the hereditary Maharaja by an elected head of the state, he declared:

> The Maharaja is gone. There is no question of the continuance of his autocratic administration . . . But if you want that no Maharaja should remain in any part of India even as a constitutional head over a particular unit let it be done soberly, properly and constitutionally. If the Parliament of India considers that the Constitution of India should be amended and there should be no Maharaja's rule, no Rajpramukh[11] in any part of India, let us discuss it.

Article 370 of the Constitution, expressly a 'Temporary and Transient' provision of the Constitution, introduced at the insistence of the Sheikh himself when he was participating in the Constituent Assembly debates, came in for trenchant criticism by Dr Mookerjee. This article has a tumultuous history relating to its passage through the Constituent Assembly and the abrogation of this article has been an issue with Dr Mookerjee's party and its successor. The article, on plain reading, detracts from the basic premise that the state of Jammu and Kashmir forms an integral part of India; in that it specifies that, except for defence, foreign affairs, finance and communications (matters specified in the Instrument of Accession) the Indian Parliament needs the state government's concurrence for applying all other laws. Thus the state's residents live under a separate set of laws, including those related to citizenship, ownership of property and fundamental rights, as compared to other Indians. Furthermore, Indian citizens from other states and women from Jammu and Kashmir who marry men from other states cannot purchase land or property in the state.

The genesis of this article lay in Sheikh Abdullah's apprehension that if Hindus and Sikhs, who migrated from Pakistan to India, were allowed to settle in the state of Jammu and Kashmir, they would transform the Muslim majority in the Valley into a minority, and his personal fiefdom would thus cease to exist. He therefore pressurized Pandit Nehru to get the article, which barred the entry of non-Kashmiris into the state of Jammu and Kashmir, incorporated in the Constitution of India. If this pernicious Article 370 had not been incorporated, Hindu and Sikh refugees from West Punjab would have settled in the Valley, and the problem of Kashmir would not have arisen at all. This is what realpolitik dictated. Pakistan has done it for Pakistan-occupied Kashmir, permitting Punjabi Muslims, including refugees from India, to settle there and in the so-called Northern Areas; and Bangladesh under General Ziaur Rahman did it for the Chittagong Hill Tracts where Bengali Muslims from the plains were encouraged to settle in the hills, thus outnumbering the indigenous Buddhist Chakma tribals. Only India, under Pandit Nehru's punditry, chose to do otherwise.

The draft article was violently opposed by many in the Constituent Assembly. However, even after this, Sheikh Abdullah had tried to stiffen the provisions further in favour of the Kashmir government (which, of course, meant himself), saying that he had to discharge his duty towards his people, and that in any case the working committee of the National Conference was not agreeable to the draft. Sardar Patel now got tough, summarily shot down the changes and stuck to the original draft. Thereafter the original draft went through without a murmur.

In his speeches Dr Mookerjee pointed out that what the Congress had said about Article 370 in the Constituent

Assembly was quite different from what they were now saying in support of Sheikh Abdullah. In respect of persecution of Dogras he drew the attention of the nation to the suppression of civil rights; elimination of Hindi, because he identified the language with the Hindus of Jammu who actually spoke the Dogri language, and gerrymandering[12] of the Jammu region on communal lines.

Kashmir Day was observed on 29 June 1952 with great enthusiasm all over the country. There was a very favourable response to it from the press as well as the public, which made Nehru sit up and take notice. Dr Mookerjee also addressed a mammoth meeting in Delhi. Disturbed by these developments, Nehru felt compelled to summon Sheikh Abdullah to Delhi to devise ways of blunting Dr Mookerjee's movement, and possibly also to ask the Sheikh to practise some moderation in speech, if not in action. The Sheikh first hedged and sent a team of his henchmen, then came down to Delhi himself on 16 July. Nehru wasn't able to drum any sense into him. Rather, he managed to twist Nehru to extract more concessions from the Government of India, which were nothing less than draconian. Nehru conceded to him the right to have separate citizenship, a separate flag, an elected head of the state in the place of the hereditary Maharaja and a separate constitution. In return he gave nothing to the Government of India except some vague promises with a lot of 'ifs and buts'. This agreement between the Jammu and Kashmir administration and the Government of India came to be known as the 'July Agreement'. It was indeed tragic to see how Nehru had allowed himself to be so malleable in the hands of Sheikh Abdullah.

Dr Mookerjee could see that the concessions granted to the Sheikh amounted to limiting the applicability even further of the Indian Constitution to the state of Jammu and Kashmir, and overriding the sovereignty of India in respect of one of its constituents. He also felt that these were the first steps towards constitutional disengagement of the state from India, which could be exploited by the disruptive forces elsewhere (as they have been—witness the terrorism in Kashmir, Mumbai, Delhi, and the Hurriyat and other aberrations). He got an opportunity to give vent to his feelings and ideas on this agreement in the Parliament on 7 August 1952. He put several questions to Nehru—the first about the areas of the state forcibly occupied by Pakistan and the second about the areas ruled by Sheikh Abdullah. Regarding the first, he asked:[13] 'Is there any possibility of our getting back this territory? We shall not get it through the efforts of U.N.O.; we shall not get it through peaceful methods, by negotiations with Pakistan. That means we lose it unless we use force and the Prime Minister is unwilling to do it. Let us face facts—are we prepared to lose it?' He further said:

> May I ask—was not Shaikh Abdullah a party to this Constitution of India? He was a member of the Constituent Assembly; but today he is asking for special treatment. Did he not agree to accept this Constitution in relation to the rest of India including 497 States. If it is good enough for all of them, why should it not be good enough for him in Kashmir?

Nehru, of course, had no answers to these questions and therefore took recourse to evasion and parroting, in his customary manner, about the 'special status' of Jammu and Kashmir. He convinced none—not even his own partymen. However, he tried a different tactic this time to hide his discomfiture on the substantive questions put to him by Dr Mookerjee. He resorted to outright condemnation of the Praja Parishad as an organization. He said that the party had no following or locus standi among the people.[14]

The Praja Parishad had by this time announced its decision to hold a convention of its workers in Jammu on 9 and 10 August 1952 and had invited a number of members of Parliament and leaders of public opinion in India to attend that convention. This would also provide an opportunity to political leaders with little exposure to the problems of Jammu and Kashmir to see for themselves the following the Praja Parishad had among the masses and the feelings of the people of Jammu in general. Dr Mookerjee was also one of the invitees and had already gladly accepted the invitation. He announced his decision to go to Jammu in the Parliament on the same day. This made some of those Congress leaders and members of Parliament who knew the real situation, nervous. They tried to persuade Dr Mookerjee to drop the idea. Some of them told him: 'Why are you lowering your position, Doctor Sahib? You will not find even five hundred people to receive you! Praja Parishad has no following at all.' But Dr Mookerjee was not swayed and left Delhi by Kashmir Mail on 8 August. U.M. Trivedi, Babu Ram Narain Singh, both members of Parliament, a good number of press representatives, and Balraj Madhok were to accompany him. He travelled third class, along with the rest of the party, remarking[15] to a surprised journalist, 'You know, ours is a poor organization, the saving made in this way helps us to meet other necessary charges.'

Dr Mookerjee had a very eventful journey all the way up to Pathankot by train and thereafter by car to Jammu. Many stations saw thousands of people waiting to greet him and they insisted upon his saying a few words to them. Dr Mookerjee did not disappoint any of them. Pandit Premnath Dogra had come all the way from Jammu to receive him at Pathankot and welcome him into the state. He crossed Madhopur bridge on the Ravi at about 3 p.m., marking his entry into Jammu and Kashmir. No sooner had he set foot in the territory of the state, the crowd burst out in resounding slogans: *Bharat Mata Ki Jai* (victory to Mother India), *Kashmir Bharat Ka Ang Hai* (Kashmir is part of India) and *Ek Desh Men Do Vidhan, Do Nishan, Do Pradhan* (Two constitutions, Two flags, Two Chiefs in one country will not be tolerated). He went on to Kathua and in a speech there, said:

> Before I left Delhi many Congress friends had told me that I should not visit Jammu because Praja Parishad has no following among the people. I would ask them to come here and see whether Praja Parishad has any following or not . . . You want Indian Constitution, you want Indian flag, you want Indian President to be your President. These are just and patriotic demands. They will have to be met. So far as I am concerned I can only assure you that I will do all I can.

And then he uttered words[16] that proved prophetic and at the same time ominous: '*Hum Vidhan Lenge Ya Balidan Denge*—I will secure for you the Constitution of India or sacrifice myself.' The seventy-mile journey from Kathua to Jammu was a continuous procession. All along the route, people from remote villages waited to greet the one Indian leader who had responded to their appeals and had come to understand their feelings and sentiments, their woes and problems. They had put up welcome arches on the roads with photos of Pandit Premnath Dogra, the name 'State Kesri' prominently displayed on them. After every mile or two, Dr Mookerjee had to stop and say a few words. At Hiranagar and Samba, two tehsil places on the wayside, he had to address mammoth meetings. He finally reached Jammu, quite late, at about 7.15 p.m. The unprecedented enthusiasm of the people who had travelled long distances to have a glimpse of him had delayed him.

An enormous ovation awaited Dr Mookerjee as he, in his flower-bedecked jeep, reached the Tawi bridge, the outpost for the city of Jammu. An ocean of humanity greeted him with loud and resounding 'Jai-s'. The two-and-a-half-mile route from the bridge to the house of Pandit Premnath Dogra, his host, was tastefully decorated and the whole city had turned out to have a glimpse of the one all-India leader who was not afraid to take up their cause. As he reached his destination at about 11 p.m., tired and exhausted after a long day's strenuous journey, in the course of which he had delivered no less than twenty speeches, he had become fully convinced of the popularity and strength of Pandit Premnath Dogra and of the organization he headed. He had also become fully aware of the people's sentiments and feelings about Sheikh Abdullah's move to have a separate flag and constitution for the state. Within a few minutes of his arrival, the deputy commissioner of Jammu came to invite him on behalf of Sheikh Abdullah to visit Srinagar the next day and have talks with him. Sheikh Abdullah, it appeared, had been informed by his officers about the charged atmosphere in Jammu and he wanted to place his point of view before Dr Mookerjee before the latter gave his advice and guidance to the Praja Parishad convention. Dr Mookerjee accepted the invitation on the condition that he would return to Jammu the same day in order to enable him to keep his other engagements there.

He left Jammu by plane for Srinagar at 11 a.m. on 10 August and reached there by noon. He was taken to Sheikh Abdullah's residence directly from the airport where he had talks lasting about six hours with him and his deputy, Bakshi Ghulam Mohammed. The plane had to return to Delhi in the evening. It waited for him for some time but as the talks continued longer than expected he let it go and decided to go back to Jammu by car at night. Before leaving Srinagar he also had a long talk with Yuvraj Karan Singh, who was then being pressed to become the Sadr-i-Riyasat—the president of the state. He was, however, just a lad of twenty and did not know what to do. Dr Mookerjee left Srinagar at about 8 p.m. by car, slept for a few hours at Batote and reached Jammu by 9 a.m. He was scheduled to leave the same afternoon.

There are no records, contemporary or otherwise, of what exactly transpired in those talks. This much, however, is known that at one point of time during the course of the talks Sheikh Abdullah began to get overbearing and was softened by Bakshi Ghulam Mohammed. Dr Mookerjee, on his part, did not appreciate the communalist position taken by Abdullah and told him to his face that his policies and utterances made him look more like Jinnah, who refused to accept a strong centre or even a weak centre on the plea that it would be controlled by the Hindus. He particularly advised him not to take any hasty steps about a separate flag for the state, a subject on which the people of Jammu had very strong feelings.

He had been travelling continuously for about thirty-six hours with very little rest and little sleep in between, but there was no time to lose. Upon his return to Jammu he met Pandit Premnath Dogra and some other top leaders of the Praja Parishad and gave them the gist of his talks with Sheikh Abdullah. He advised them not to take any precipitate action or bring matters to a head. Pandit Dogra reminded him of the temper of the people he had met and informed him how all the delegates at the convention had been demanding some sort of direct action, such as satyagraha. Dr Mookerjee's reply was characteristic of the constitutional politician that he had been all his life. Satyagraha, he said, was an extreme step and it must be resorted to only after all other means have been exhausted. He was, he added, going to meet Prime Minister Nehru, and place before him the facts and his reading of the situation. Within the state, he advised them to concentrate on organizing and educating the people. He hoped that better counsel would prevail upon Sheikh Abdullah. However, if Abdullah persisted in his separatist polices, he assured them, he would lend his support to any action they might take. He spoke in the same strain to about fifty thousand people who had assembled in the scorching heat of the grounds to listen to him. His speech evoked mixed feelings as the crowd had been ready for some direct action. The special correspondents of the *Statesman* and the *Hindustan Standard,* who had gone there with him to study the situation, writing about his visit said that he had done his best to pacify the people whose impatience had reached the highest point, and had thereby rendered a great service to the cause of mutual understanding and peaceful settlement.

The following months proved to be a frustrating period for Dr Mookerjee in regard to Kashmir. Immediately after his return to Delhi, he had a long tête-à-tête with Nehru. He told him that it was no use minimizing the gravity of the situation. The Praja Parishad, he informed him, was not the organization of a few disgruntled and expropriated landlords as he would have liked people to believe. It was a democratic political organization, with capable leadership and a mass following. It was a force to be reckoned with in Jammu, he told him, and it would be most inadvisable to go on a path of confrontation with the Parishad.

As apprehended, neither Sheikh Abdullah nor Nehru paid the slightest heed to what he said. Secure in their respective seats of power by brute majority, Abdullah persisted in implementing and Nehru in giving him silent support for the schemes he had in mind which virtually made Jammu and Kashmir an independent state with its own constitution, national assembly, Supreme Court and flag. The Praja Parishad leaders were able to secure a copy of a draft constitution that he had prepared. Pandit Dogra tried to draw the attention of the Indian authorities through a memorandum to the President of India, to no effect. Pandit Premnath Dogra met Dr Mookerjee at Jullundur on 8 November 1952, where the latter had gone in connection with the Punjab Provincial Jana Sangh conference and placed before him the facts of the deteriorating situation and the growing feeling of the people that things could not be set right without a struggle.

Later, between January and February 1953, Dr Mookerjee, Nehru and Sheikh Abdullah had a tripartite exchange of correspondence, with Dr Mookerjee trying to convince Nehru of the necessity to at least consider the demands of the Praja Parishad. Neither Nehru nor Abdullah were moved, with Nehru siding blindly with Abdullah in whatever he said, and calling the Praja Parishad and its agitation 'communal'. So great appears to be the influence of the Sheikh upon Nehru that he turned down even Vice President Radhakrishnan's advice to try to reach an amicable settlement. Dr Mookerjee, on his part, told Abdullah that he had heard about the two-nation theory from Jinnah, but now Abdullah was trying to push some three-nation theory, which he termed a 'dangerous symptom'. Nehru was nothing less than curt and threatening in his last letter. He wrote,[17] 'If indeed the agitation continues it will be for *us* [emphasis added] to consider what other and further steps Government can take in the matter', in the process clearly bracketing himself and Abdullah together. Referring to Dr Mookerjee's request for a personal meeting, he wrote, 'I regret that tomorrow and for the next day or two I am completely occupied. I confess also that, reading your letter, I find it a little difficult to discover any common ground for a talk.' It is to be noted that the use of the pronoun 'us', bracketing himself and Sheikh Abdullah together, spoke volumes about his basic attitude. To this, Dr Mookerjee replied, 'Let me assure you we are ready to face the consequences of your wrath and fury. The arrest of a number of our workers in the Punjab yesterday under the Preventive Detention Act is an indication of the things that are to come. It reflects a strange functioning of democracy in our country where the Preventive

Detention Act has to be made use of for curbing legitimate political opposition.' The situation, nevertheless, remained just the way it was, and Dr Mookerjee seemed to have given up hope of settling the matter amicably.

Intelligence Bureau chief B.N. Mullick, however, gives a strange account which seems to indicate that Nehru was perfectly aware of what Abdullah was and was not; and also what the Praja Parishad was and was not. According to his book *My Years with Nehru: Kashmir*, he was deputed by Nehru in early 1953 to soften the Sheikh and the Praja Parishad in their respective stands (probably while Nehru was making short work of Dr Mookerjee's entreaties). He was partly successful with the latter who agreed to tone down their agitation, but with the Sheikh he drew a complete blank. His words:[18]

> I was surprised to find him [Abdullah] a completely changed man from the time I first met him in September 1949. He received me coldly and then gave me a long lecture. He made violent accusations against the Dogras of Jammu in general and the ex-ruler and the Praja Parishad in particular. He spoke contemptuously of the RSS and Jana Sangh of India . . . I could not persuade him to desist from indulging from his theme of the hatred of Dogras and giving expression to his great contempt for them. He himself would have probably liked the entire Dogra community to migrate to India and make over their lands to persons of his choice . . . On my return to Delhi I reported in detail to the Prime Minister what had happened in Jammu and my failure to bring about any change in the Shaikh's attitude . . . He [Nehru] was however distressed that the Shaikh still continued his hostility to the Hindus of Jammu and gave vent to these feelings publicly. The Prime Minister commented that all this was due to the Shaikh's communal background and though politically he had

tried to turn a new leaf, his heart had never been able to get over his earlier predilections.

According to Madhok, by now a conviction seemed to have begun to grow in Dr Mookerjee that perhaps Nehru was not always susceptible to constitutional means, that arguments, logic and public opinion often appeared to have no meaning for him. Time and again he had been an agitator all his life and would rather bow before force and agitation and not necessarily before reason.[19] He, therefore, told Pandit Dogra that he had tried his best to secure justice for them but had failed and he no longer had any right to bind their hands. However, he advised circumspection and also assured him that the Jana Sangh would stand by them and do everything possible to mobilize public opinion in the country because it was convinced that the cause of the Praja Parishad was the cause of the whole of India.

Pandit Premnath Dogra bid goodbye to Dr Mookerjee at Jullundur with a heavy heart and with the knowledge that he would have to lead the people of Jammu in the struggle to a bitter end. Shortly afterwards Sheikh Abdullah's government announced its decision to ceremoniously hoist the National Conference Party flag, which had since been adopted with a minor alteration as the state flag, on the State Secretariat at Jammu on 17 November but did not follow it up. Meanwhile Pandit Dogra declared that none but the Indian National Flag shall fly over Jammu and gave a clarion call to the people to prepare and get ready to make sacrifices for the vindication of their right to be one with their country. Sheikh Abdullah's government now began its policy of repression of which the people of Jammu were to be victims. Nehru, always ready to oblige the Sheikh, lent him companies of Central Reserve and Punjab Police. Pandit Dogra and S.L. Sharma, the president and the organizing secretary of the Praja Parishad, were arrested in November 1952 when in a public meeting they hoisted the Indian tricolour in the main square of the city. This was the signal for the start of the Praja Parishad satyagraha.

In the midst of all this Dr Mookerjee took two days off from his political schedule to attend the 28th session of the *Nikhil Bharat Banga Sahitya Sammelan* (All-India Bengali Literary Conference) at Cuttack, Orissa, which he had been invited to preside over. In his presidential address at the Sammelan, he dwelt upon the role and position of regional languages vis-à-vis Hindi, the national language of the country. He stood for paying full attention to the development of all the regional languages and was opposed to any kind of imposed uniformity and considered it contrary to the Indian tradition. But he regarded Hindi as the natural lingua franca of the country and wanted it to be developed and encouraged to such an extent that it could become an effective medium of expression in all provinces of the country. He also held the view, by no means popular with Bengalis, that Devanagari, being the script of Sanskrit, should be adopted as the script for all Indian languages. He attached greater importance to a common script as a contributory factor for national unity than to the unity of language itself.

While he was busy on the Kashmir question crossing swords with Sheikh Abdullah and Nehru, it also remained a compulsion to nurse his newborn party to adulthood. The leaders of the party and the swayamsevaks of the RSS were working hard to this end. The first plenary session of the Bharatiya Jana Sangh was held at Kanpur, at a place appropriately christened 'Deep Nagar' (after the party's symbol of the lamp, 'deepak') in the last week of December 1952. Meanwhile he had been re-elected to the post of president of the party. He received a huge welcome at Kanpur when he arrived in the city. One thousand delegates had assembled at the session and they were all eager to hear him. On his part he had, on his agenda, securing their

support to extending the active support of the Jana Sangh to
the struggle being waged by the Praja Parishad for the cause of
Indian unity. It was also a challenge and an opportunity for him
to galvanize the Jana Sangh and make it an effective instrument
for the protection of the rights and liberties of the Indian
people. It also provided him the occasion to make his views on
national and international problems known to the rank and file
of his young organization and establish a close personal touch
with its workers.

He set the tone for the meeting in his presidential address,
in which he said, without mincing words, that while the doors
of membership of the party were always open for people of all
religious denominations, the party would never balk or hesitate
to take up the cause of Hindus if it felt that they were being
subjected to injustice. It is here that he openly challenged the
Nehruvian-left construction of secularism that has been sanctified
by so many parties and sections of the media in the subsequent
years, the bottom line of which is, 'A minority in India can do no
wrong.' Addressing the gathering in forceful, though *toota-phoota*
(pidgin) Hindi[20] (and with a terribly Bengali accent), he said:[21]

> It will be a fatal mistake to confine the membership of any
> political party in free India to sections of the people based on
> caste, community or religion. But while extending its hand
> of equality to all citizens, Jana Sangh does not feel ashamed
> to urge the consolidation of Hindu society nor does it suffer
> from an inferiority complex to acknowledge proudly that
> the great edifice of Indian culture and civilization which has
> stood the test of thousands of years and has been built most
> of all by the labour, wisdom and sacrifice of Hindu sages,
> savants and patriots throughout the chequered history of our
> Motherland.

He dealt with the First Five-Year Plan just launched, and said that even though the plan did not fulfil his expectations in parts, it deserved support. He spoke at length on the problems of Kashmir, East Bengal and rehabilitation of refugees. Regarding Kashmir, where the Praja Parishad satyagraha was gaining momentum, he pleaded for sympathetic understanding of the fears and doubts of the people of Jammu.

> Even at this late stage I would appeal to Mr Nehru and Shaikh Abdullah to cry a halt and not to stand on false prestige. They must open negotiations with the Parishad leaders and arrive at a settlement which will be fair and just to all. Meanwhile our active sympathy must be extended to all those in Jammu who are facing bravely the wrath of the authorities silently for a noble cause.

Referring to the plight of Hindus in East Pakistan who 'if they live there as at present will live as serfs or converts', he deplored the spirit of helplessness shown by India. 'It is tragic,' he said, 'that our stock should be so low in the eyes of Pakistan that it dares humiliate us in season and out of season and our Government should stand by as a helpless spectator incapable of taking any effective action.' He also warned that activities of fifth columnists within India were steadily on the increase.

Dr Mookerjee also deprecated the overly internationalist stance of Nehru, and said, 'Internationalism can thrive only if there is a sound base of national solidarity. We should, therefore, strive hard to keep our home front safe and sound.' Even later, in the correspondence[22] exchanged between him, Nehru and Sheikh Abdullah in January–February 1953, and referring to Nehru's fears about 'international complications', he had politely ridiculed Nehru when he said:

No one today will claim that your handling of the Kashmir problem has enhanced our international prestige or has won for us wide international support and sympathy . . . instead of being haunted by false internationalism, firmly create conditions for national solidarity based on a fair adjustment of different viewpoints and interests. If you succeed in this it will give you greater might and prestige even in international dealings.

He had no difficulty in getting the party to endorse his views on extending support to the agitation launched by the Praja Parishad. In fact, the younger delegates, in their overenthusiasm, wanted the Jana Sangh to give an ultimatum to the Government of India, either to take concrete steps to meet the patriotic demands of the Parishad within a fixed period or face the satyagraha by the Jana Sangh in its support in the rest of India as well. However, Dr Mookerjee, ever the constitutional politician, counselled patience. It was, therefore, resolved that he should write to Nehru and Sheikh Abdullah in a final bid to find a solution. It was in pursuance of this resolution of his working committee that Dr Mookerjee started his correspondence with Nehru and Sheikh Abdullah, which, as already said, proved to be fruitless.

Madhok says that even Dr Sarvepalli Radhakrishnan, an old friend and admirer of Dr Mookerjee, then the Vice President of India, tried to intercede on behalf of Dr Mookerjee—to no effect. Nehru seemed incurably prejudiced in favour of Abdullah and against Dr Mookerjee, and was moreover assured of his brute majority with no rival in sight. And quite probably he was also a victim of abject sycophancy[23]—a problem that he himself had apprehended way back in 1947 when he invited Dr Mookerjee to join independent India's first cabinet (see Chapter 10). But that was a time when Gandhi and Patel were alive to keep a check on him—and this was 1953!

A notable feature of the Kanpur session was the rise of young leaders in the party. The foremost among them was a quiet, self-effacing RSS pracharak called Deen Dayal Upadhyaya. A man of soaring idealism with a tremendous capacity for organization, he had already started three periodicals in Hindi—a monthly *Rashtra Dharma*, a weekly *Panchjanya* and a daily *Swadesh*. Also a prolific writer, he subsequently wrote a drama *Chandragupta Maurya*, a biography of Shankaracharya and translated a Marathi biography of Dr Keshav Baliram Hedgewar, the founder of the RSS, into Hindi. He became the first general secretary of the Uttar Pradesh branch of the party and was chosen as all-India general secretary at Kanpur. The qualities of the man so deeply impressed Dr Mookerjee as to apparently elicit his famous remark, 'If I had two Deen Dayals, I could transform the political face of India.'

He also recruited at Kanpur a young and very articulate swayamsevak as his private secretary. His name was Atal Bihari Vajpayee. One day that young man would become the Prime Minister of India leading a coalition led by the successor party to the Bharatiya Jana Sangh, and the first non-Congress one to last a full term.

With the plenary session over, Dr Mookerjee again applied his mind to the Jammu problem and the Praja Parishad agitation. During the months of January–February 1953 he tried his best to bring Nehru to his senses by appealing to his concern for national interests, and entered into a tripartite correspondence involving himself, Nehru and Sheikh Abdullah. The result, as already stated, was zero. Therefore, by February he had made up his mind to take the agitation to the streets and appeal directly to the people, especially in north India, and to rise against the

injustice being meted out to the Dogras of Jammu by Sheikh
Abdullah's government. Nehru was possibly apprehensive of
this and immediately took recourse to repressive measures,
under the Preventive Detention Act and otherwise. Section 144
of the Criminal Procedure Code, forbidding the assembly of five
or more persons, was promulgated in a number of major cities,
putting a stop to all political meetings or rallies, and meetings
and processions were expressly banned in Delhi. The East
Punjab government imprisoned most of the Jana Sangh leaders
under the Preventive Detention Act. Dr Mookerjee now gave
the call for observing 5 March 1953 as Kashmir Day, which
was promptly banned. Meanwhile, in four by-elections held to
state assemblies, the Jana Sangh won three and lost the fourth
by a narrow margin. The Congress government took fright
and lifted the ban on the 5 March meeting. The meeting was
held at Queens Garden and attended by some fifty thousand
people, many of whom did not know that the ban had been
lifted and had come prepared to court arrest and face repressive
measures. It was presided over by Swami Karpatriji of the Ram
Rajya Parishad and was addressed by, besides Dr Mookerjee,
Pandit Mauli Chandra Sharma and Nirmal Chandra Chatterjee.
The other speakers, referring to the immortal epic Mahabharata,
compared Dr Mookerjee to Shri Krishna who had gone to
great lengths to persuade the ruling Kurus to do justice to the
Pandavas.

Dr Mookerjee announced in the meeting, against the
sentiments of the assembly which was eager for some action, that
an urn carrying the ashes of those killed in a police firing upon
peaceful demonstrators in Jammu by Abdullah's police would
be carried the next day in procession from Delhi railway station
to Chandni Chowk. It would be led by Dr Mookerjee, Nirmal
Chandra Chatterjee and Nand Lal Shastri. The government again
took fright and reimposed the ban on meetings and processions,

and took Dr Mookerjee into custody the next day for defying the ban. Nirmal Chandra Chatterjee, one of the leading lawyers of the country, then filed a habeas corpus application before the Supreme Court of India which heard it and set him free on 11 March.

The agitation, meanwhile, continued and gathered momentum in Punjab, Delhi, UP and other parts of India. In Jammu a campaign against payment of taxes had also begun. The Dogras are a warlike people, and had been classified as a 'Martial Race' (which the Kashmiri Muslims were not) by the British, and the Indian army boasted a Dogra regiment. Many of them began to press the underground secretary of the Praja Parishad, Durga Das Verma, to allow them to meet violence with violence. 'We are soldiers,' a number of them wrote[24] to him, 'and have seen fighting in different parts of the world. We have been so far obeying your instruction to remain non-violent spectators when our women are insulted before our very eyes.' A statement issued by a number of retired civilians including an ex-inspector-general of police, who visited the scenes of such occurrences on their own, confirmed these reports. Soon after, a delegation of some retired ministers and high dignitaries of the state visited Delhi and drew the attention of the people and the Government of India to the fast deteriorating situation in Jammu.

Dr Mookerjee made a last appeal to Nehru in the course of his speech in Parliament on 26 April to take the initiative to settle the question. He told Nehru that he would be satisfied if he invited Premnath Dogra and explained to him his viewpoint and difficulties instead of talking about them. Albeit, no response was received.

The permit system of entering Jammu and Kashmir was anathema to Dr Mookerjee, not only on principle but also because it was misused to deny entry to deserving people. Only a few months back a permit to visit Jammu had been refused to U.M. Trivedi and G.V. Deshpande and prior to them to the fact-finding mission consisting of a number of legislators, including the deputy speaker of Rajasthan. He was aware of the fact that the permit system had, in reality, been introduced to prevent Pakistani agents and spies from entering Kashmir and it could not be lawfully used to deny entry to responsible men like members of Parliament into that state. He, therefore, wrote a letter to the defence minister asking him the legal position about the permit system. Again, no reply was received. He, therefore, decided to enter the state without a permit.

Before going forth he received a number of admonitions not to do so. This was not unusual, but this time they seemed to have come from knowledgeable quarters and with an extra measure of intensity. He paid a hurried visit to Calcutta to pay his respects to his aged mother before undertaking the journey. In Calcutta he paid a visit to the Bharat Sevashram Sangha, the Hindu monastic and philanthropic organization whose founder, Swami Pranavananda, had been instrumental in bringing him into politics. The head of the mission, Swami Satchidananda, repeatedly told him not to go. On his way back he stopped for a day at Patna. There he expressed his intention of going to Jammu to his host Thakur Prasad. Thakur Prasad's aged father, who had served as diwan in a number of states, tried to dissuade Dr Mookerjee from going to Jammu and finally said, 'Go, if you must. But please see that you do not take anything there unless it is first tasted by one whom you trust.' But the most telling of such admonitions is said to have come from a Congresswoman, Sucheta Kripalani, wife of Acharya J.B. Kripalani and a Bengali herself, a mention of whom was made in connection with the Noakhali atrocities of 1946. Her reaction has been described in the next chapter.

The scene is remarkably similar to the one in Shakespeare's *Julius Caesar* just before the Roman statesman's assassination. Just as he, after hearing all the fears that his Queen Calpurnia told him of, and the warnings of the soothsayer who said, 'Beware the ides of March', said,

> Yet Caesar shall go forth . . .
> Cowards die many times before their deaths;
> The valiant never taste of death but once.
> Of all the wonders that I yet have heard.
> It seems to me most strange that men should fear;
> Seeing that death, a necessary end,
> Will come when it will come.

and walked up to the Senate House in Rome to be stabbed to death by the conspirators; so did Dr Mookerjee walk up to the bridge across the Ravi at Madhopur to court arrest before an officer of Sheikh Abdullah's police; and, just like Julius Caesar, never returned alive.

15

Martyrdom and Thereafter, 1953

Dr Syama Prasad Mookerjee, unbeknown to himself, set out on his last and fateful journey from Delhi railway station at 6.30 a.m. on 8 May 1953 as the passenger train, carrying him and his entourage to Punjab on his way to Jammu, steamed out of the station. The compartment in which he sat had been bedecked with flowers and Jana Sangh flags. Guru Datt Vaid, Atal Bihari Vajpayee, Tek Chand, Balraj Madhok and a few pressmen were there with him. Shortly before his departure, he issued a statement explaining his purpose of going to Jammu, namely to find out for himself the extent and depth of the Praja Parishad agitation and the repression let loose on the citizens of Jammu by Abdullah.

Explaining why he had not applied for an entry permit, the statement[1] said:

> Mr Nehru has repeatedly declared that the accession of the State of Jammu and Kashmir to India has been hundred per cent complete. Yet it is strange to find that one cannot enter the State without a previous permit from the Government of India. This permit is granted even to Communists who are playing their usual role in Jammu and Kashmir. But entry is barred to those who think or act in terms of Indian unity and nationhood.

Regarding his aim in going to Jammu, the statement said:

> My object in going to Jammu is solely to acquaint myself with
> what exactly had happened there and the present state of affairs.
> I would also come into contact with available local leaders
> representing various interests, outside the Praja Parishad. It will
> be my endeavour to ascertain what the intention of the people
> of Jammu is, and to find out if at all there is any possibility
> of the movement being brought to a peaceful and honourable
> end, which will be fair and just not only to the people of the
> State but also to the whole of India.

He was thus, contrary to what Nehru and Abdullah had sought to project, not out to provoke the agitators and take them on the path of further confrontation with Abdullah's government. Ever the constitutional politician, he wished to bring the agitation to an end whereby both the warring parties would be able to save their faces. Only, in entering the Indian state of Jammu and Kashmir he had refused to take the permit to be issued by the Government of India.

The first stop on his itinerary was nearby Ambala, in Punjab (now Haryana). While on the train, however, Dr Mookerjee remembered that before leaving Delhi he had promised Professor Walter Johnson,[2] a visiting American dignitary, that he would send him papers on the Jana Sangh; and also more importantly, that he ought to send some official intimation to Abdullah about his entering the state. In fact, he had fixed up a meeting with Johnson on 13 May, but possibly on the apprehension that he may be arrested, also told him that he may not be able to keep the appointment. In any case, he shot off a telegram[3] to Abdullah which read, 'I am proceeding to Jammu. My object in going there is to study situation myself and to explore the possibilities of creating conditions leading to peaceful settlement. I will like to see you also if possible.' He sent a copy of the telegram to Nehru.

The train reached Ambala at about 2 p.m., and there was such a huge crowd on the platform that Dr Mookerjee had a hard time getting down. Even before he got down the president of Ambala Town Jana Sangh, advocate Raghbir Saran, showed him the latest issue of the *Illustrated Weekly of India*[4] which carried on its cover the pictures of Dr Mookerjee and Jayaprakash Narayan with the caption, 'After Nehru, Who? Mookerjee or J.P.?'

From Ambala he drove down to Karnal via Shahabad and Nilokheri where he had to make unscheduled stops and make speeches. From Karnal he sent a short letter to his sister-in-law Tara Devi, describing the reception he had had so far. He also expressed his worry about his dear Hasu, his younger daughter, whom he had left back in Delhi. He had a special soft corner for this one, the quiet, withdrawn girl who had never known a mother's love, and had moreover recently recovered from a bout of tuberculosis. He spent the night at Karnal and the next day drove to Panipat and addressed a huge meeting there; then he took a train to Phagwara, where he received a reply[5] to the telegram he had sent Abdullah. It read, 'Thanks for your telegram. I am afraid your proposed visit to the State at the present juncture is inopportune and will not serve any useful purpose.' Nehru did not bother to send a reply, or even an acknowledgement.

After Phagwara, the next stop was Jullundur where he addressed a press conference. He also sent back Madhok from Jullundur and boarded a train for Amritsar. In the train an elderly person introduced himself as deputy commissioner of Gurdaspur (the district in which Pathankot is situated) and told him that the Punjab government had decided not to allow him to reach Pathankot. Upon hearing this Dr Mookerjee proceeded to make arrangements for his arrest, and decided, after consultations, that Guru Datt Vaid, the well-known Ayurvedic physician and author who was then president of Delhi state Jana Sangh, and Tek Chand, a young energetic worker from Dehra Dun, would accompany him and court arrest with him. But strangely, he was not arrested, neither at Amritsar nor at Pathankot nor anywhere on the way. A huge crowd of over 20,000 received him at the Amritsar railway station where he halted for the night. He met the local workers and talked to them. He was emphatic that he would go to Jammu whether Abdullah liked it or not. The journey from Amritsar to Pathankot was yet another triumphant march. Thousands of people greeted him at every station. He arrived to an unbelievable reception at Pathankot. A sea of people with folded hands stood on both sides of the bazaar through which his jeep passed. Just before his departure a ninety-year-old lady blessed him in Punjabi with the following words: *'Oye Puttar! Jit ke avin, aiwan na avin* (My Son! Do not return until you are victorious).'

Soon after his arrival at Pathankot, the deputy commissioner of Gurdaspur, who seemed to have preceded him, sought an interview with him. He informed Dr Mookerjee that he had been instructed by his government to allow him and his companions to proceed and enter Jammu and Kashmir state without a permit. He himself appeared quite surprised that the orders that he was due to receive had been reversed. Little did he, or anyone else present there, know that the diabolical scheme that had been hatched had it that Dr Mookerjee would be arrested in Jammu and Kashmir state and not in Punjab, so that he would remain outside the jurisdiction of the Indian Supreme Court.

The next stop was the border check post at Madhopur on the River Ravi, one of the five great rivers of the Punjab, marking the boundary between the states of Punjab and Jammu and Kashmir. There was a bridge across the river, and the boundary lay at the midpoint of the bridge. Dr Mookerjee and his companions reached the check post at 4 p.m. The deputy commissioner of Gurdaspur and other officers present there saw them off at the bridge. But as soon as the jeep reached the centre of the bridge, they found the road blocked by a posse of the Jammu and Kashmir state police. The jeep stopped and a police officer, who said he was the superintendent of police, Kathua, handed over to him an order of the chief secretary of the state, dated 10 May 1953, banning his entry into the state.

'But I intend to go to Jammu,' Dr Mookerjee declared.

Thereupon the police officer took out an order of arrest under the Public Safety Act of the state signed by Prithvinandan Singh, inspector-general of police, dated 10 May, which stated that Dr Mookerjee 'has acted, is acting or is about to act in a manner prejudicial to public safety and peace',[6] and that 'in order to prevent him from so acting . . . Captain A. Azeez, Superintendent of Police, Kathua' was being directed to arrest Dr Mookerjee and remove him under custody to the Central Jail at Srinagar. 'All right,' said Dr Mookerjee on reading the order and got down from the jeep. Guru Datt Vaid, Tek Chand and others also got down. Atal Bihari Vajpayee, his private secretary, had been with him up to this point. In his last message as a free person Dr Mookerjee told Vajpayee and others to tell the country that he had at last entered the state of Jammu and Kashmir, though as a prisoner, and to carry on his work in his absence.

The police jeep halted for a short while at Lakhanpur. The threesome was put in another closed jeep which rushed towards Srinagar through Tawi bridge and Jammu city. The people of Jammu had assembled in thousands near Tawi bridge to receive their hero. They waited for him till night but did not notice a closed jeep passing the bridge at dusk. They reached Udhampur at about 10 p.m. and Batote at about 2 a.m., slept the night there, and reached Srinagar Central Jail at about 3 p.m.

From there he and his two companions were escorted by the superintendent of the jail, Pandit Siri Kanth Sapru, to a small cottage near the Dal Lake where he, one of the most prominent members of the Indian Parliament, the president of one of India's national parties, was to spend the last forty days of his life as a prisoner of Sheikh Abdullah, ostensibly just for having committed the offence of acting 'in a manner prejudicial to public safety and peace'.

It is important to note here that many are under the impression that Dr Mookerjee was imprisoned for entering Jammu and Kashmir state without a permit. This is a canard deliberately spread by Sheikh Abdullah himself, as he had done in a broadcast, for reasons best known to him. Dr Mookerjee mentioned this in a handwritten note to his counsel U.M. Trivedi for the drafting of his habeas corpus petition. In fact, on 11 May the state government of Jammu and Kashmir issued an ordinance through the Sadr-i-Riyasat that it is an offence to enter the state without a state permit, but as the order of Prithvinandan Singh, inspector-general of police reveals, Dr Mookerjee was not (and could not have been) arrested under that ordinance. On the day of the arrest, the only permit that could have been issued was one by the Government of India and not by the government of Jammu and Kashmir. But as we have already seen, the deputy commissioner of Gurdaspur told him that the Government of India had already decided to allow Dr Mookerjee to enter Jammu and Kashmir state without a permit. This reveals a very strange and suspicious chain of circumstances that have been discussed later in this chapter.

Meanwhile Madhok had been arrested and put in Ambala Central Jail. A habeas corpus petition was moved on his behalf and he was freed. When he came to know that Dr Mookerjee had been arrested and imprisoned in Jammu and Kashmir, he lost his nerve and ran to the one person from whom he thought he could always seek advice. That person was Justice Mehr Chand Mahajan, erstwhile Prime Minister of Jammu and Kashmir and then a judge of the Indian Supreme Court. He was from Kangra and spoke Dogri, the language of Jammu, and Madhok unthinkingly rushed to him, little realizing that as a sitting judge of the highest court of the country his powers were severely circumscribed by the canons of judicial conduct. Mahajan was, understandably, flabbergasted. He said in Dogri,[7] 'Balraj, please have some regard for my position, I am a judge of the Supreme Court! Just one week back I released you on a habeas corpus, and now here you are at my residence, asking me to do something!' Madhok said, 'Sir, what can I do, you are the only man whom I can see.' Then Mahajan told Madhok, 'Had he been arrested in Gurdaspur district, Pathankot or anywhere, the Supreme Court could have released him within a week, maybe earlier; but the Supreme Court has no jurisdiction over the Jammu and Kashmir state. What will happen, I can't say. My only advice is, send some advocate immediately and have a habeas corpus application made.'

The news of the arrest created a stir all over the country. Protests, meetings and hartals took place in Delhi and other places. This gave a new impetus and direction to the satyagraha. Satyagrahis began to proceed to Jammu without a permit and court arrest. But neither Abdullah nor Nehru was moved. Abdullah (whether with or without the consent or knowledge of Nehru, we shall never know) had a scheme up his sleeve which he was determined to follow up.

The place in which Dr Mookerjee was incarcerated was really a small cottage which was converted into a sub-jail almost in the middle of nowhere, near Nishat Bagh, far away from Srinagar city. It was situated on the slope of the mountain range flanking the Dal Lake. It could be reached only by mounting a steep flight of stairs which must have been a hard task for Dr Mookerjee with his bad leg, and proved to be much harder later. It had one main room about 10 feet by 11, in which Dr Mookerjee was lodged and two small side rooms which accommodated his co-detenues Guru Datt Vaid and Tek Chand. There was no room in this 'sub-jail' for a fourth bedstead. When Pandit Premnath Dogra was brought there on 19 June a tent had to be pitched in the compound outside to accommodate him. The whole compound was covered with fruit trees and vegetable beds leaving only a small lawn, smaller than a tennis court, for the detenues to move about. It was at a distance of about 8 miles from the city. There was also no arrangement for adequate medical aid. A doctor could come from the city only when requisitioned. About 100 yards away from the cottage was a canal and a sub-section of the waterworks department, which had a telephone. That telephone served this improvised jail in the wilderness as well, but was available for use only during office hours. Only one newspaper—*Hindustan Times*—was supplied to him though later he was permitted to receive the *Hindustan Standard* of Calcutta. They seldom reached him in time and were usually late by two or three days, as was his mail. These were brought to him by the superintendent of the jail personally. The authorities were most callous in respect of his mail. On an average it took about a week for a letter, particularly if written in Bengali, after it had reached Srinagar, to be delivered to him. Some letters that were posted from Calcutta on 10 June and which bore the Srinagar postmark of 12 and 13 June, were returned undelivered after his death. On his protest at this inordinate delay in delivering his mail to him, he was told that the person who censored his mail written in Bengali was not always available. Thereupon, he suggested that, to avoid delay, he could supply the authorities with the English rendering of the letters written in Bengali, which came only from his family members and contained no politics, for the purpose of censorship. But no heed was paid to this suggestion. So he had to take to writing even personal letters in English, for the benefit of Sheikh Abdullah's censor.

What a way to treat one of the most important, possibly the most important, member of the Opposition in the Indian Parliament!

Madhok states that many letters to and from him were completely suppressed. It was later discovered that Abdullah had ordered that Dr Mookerjee be given no additional facilities without his express orders. None of his friends or relatives was allowed to meet him while he was in jail. His eldest son, Anutosh, applied for a permit to visit Srinagar to see him. By that time there was a change in the rules of issue of the permit, and it had to be done by the government of Jammu and Kashmir. It was refused. Some of his relatives were in Srinagar at that time. They too sought an interview with him but were also refused. The only persons from outside who were taken to him for the purpose of interview were Sardar Hukam Singh, whose visit was purely political and U.M. Trivedi, barrister, who met him as his counsel. Madhok also reports that a half-mad sadhu was inflicted upon him whose nonsense he was forced to hear. It was probably done to tell the world after his death that interviews were allowed to him.

It was his long-cherished desire to write a biography of his father, and he began work on it. He also used to write his diary regularly. He took it with him to the hospital as well when he was removed there on 22 June. It would have been the most authentic source of information about his life and work, thoughts and ideals and above all his own feelings, and about the events that culminated in his tragic death. But it was kept back by the Kashmir government after his death and has still not been returned in spite of repeated requests.

On 24 May, Nehru and Dr Katju visited Srinagar for 'rest'. They never thought to visit their august prisoner and see how he was being treated there. Later, after his death, Nehru said he had inquired about him and was told that he was in great comfort, in a 'picturesque villa' on the Dal Lake. 'Being told' was enough for Nehru.

The pain in his leg, thought to be due to varicose veins, got more severe by 3 June. In a letter dated 6 June addressed to Tara Devi, he wrote:

I was on the whole keeping well, but the pain in the right leg has again worsened during the last two days. Moreover for some days I have been running [a] temperature in the evening. There is a burning sensation in the eyes and face. I am taking medicine. I get to eat only boiled vegetables. Fish [almost a staple food for Bengalis] is not available. The doctor has instructed me not to stand on my legs in order to give them some rest. As a result I get absolutely no exercise, and therefore lost all appetite. I wake up very early and around 5.30 a.m. I get up, go to the garden and recite the *Chandi stotra* . . . the whole day hangs heavy on me . . . all that I get to do is to read, recite the Bhagavad Gita, some writing.

He was feeling despondent and depressed because of the confinement and having nothing to do—it can well be imagined what a punishment it must be for such an active person to be doing nothing from morning till night.

On the receipt of this letter in Calcutta on or about 12 June, Dr Mookerjee's brother Justice Rama Prasad saw Dr B.C. Roy, apprised him of his health and requested him to contact Kashmir. Dr Mookerjee always had a problem with the pain in his leg but it had never earlier been accompanied by fever. Because of loss of appetite he was getting weaker every day. Barrister U.M. Trivedi had gone to Srinagar on 12 June to argue his habeas corpus before the Jammu and Kashmir High Court. The government insisted that he would have to take instructions from him in the presence of the district magistrate. The Indian Evidence Act lays down that communication between a client and his lawyer is totally privileged and no one can be compelled to disclose it, even in court. Trivedi refused to take instructions in the presence of the district magistrate, and had to move the high court again to permit him to take instructions in private. After the high court struck down the government's orders, Trivedi interviewed him for three hours on 18 June. He found Dr Mookerjee, who had braved so many adversities in his life, weak and cheerless.

Pandit Premnath Dogra who was taken from Jammu to Srinagar on 19 June to meet him was also struck by his poor state of health and low appetite. He asked him the reason and was informed that it might be due to lack of exercise. This was his main complaint from the very beginning, something to which Abdullah's government just turned a deaf ear. He was fond of taking walks—it was his principal form of exercise. The hut where he was incarcerated had a very small compound, most of it covered with fruit trees and vegetable beds, and two or three minutes of walking would bring him to the end of his path. As a result of lack of exercise he had lost all appetite and possibly also developed the pain in his leg. The government would have lost nothing by permitting him to walk outside the compound. They did not do so—out of cussedness, or worse?

The same night he developed a pain in his chest and back and a high temperature. On the morning of 20 June the authorities were informed about it. Thereupon, doctors Ali Mohammed and Amar Nath Raina reached the sub-jail at 11.30 a.m. The former diagnosed the trouble as dry pleurisy and prescribed streptomycin injections. Dr Mookerjee protested that his family physician had advised him not to take streptomycin as it did not suit his system. But Dr Mohammed said that that was a long time back; lately a lot of new facts had come to light regarding this drug, and he need not worry. At about 3.30 p.m. the medicine was received and the jail doctor administered one full gram of the medicine into Dr Mookerjee. In addition he was also administered some powder, possibly some painkiller (no prescription was made available to anyone), which, Dr Mohammed said, was to be taken twice a day, but could be taken up to six times if the pain persisted or became severe. According to Guru Datt Vaid, Dr Mookerjee requested the superintendent of the jail on that day to send the news of his illness to his relatives. But no such intimation was sent nor any bulletin issued by the government till after his death.

The next day, on 21 June, excepting the jail doctor who was only an assistant surgeon, no other doctor, not even Dr Mohammed, visited him. The jail doctor administered another one gram of streptomycin. His temperature rose and the pain increased during the day.

Because of this sudden relapse he could not talk much with Pandit Premnath Dogra who had been brought to Srinagar for consultations with him regarding withdrawal of the movement. There had been some internal developments in the state favourable to the movement. The state cabinet was apparently divided into two camps—Sheikh Abdullah and Mirza Afzal Beg on one side and Bakshi Ghulam Mohammed, Pandit Shyam Lal Saraf and Girdhari Lal Dogra on the other. The latter wanted an understanding with the Praja Parishad to checkmate the designs of the former. Pandit Dogra had been brought to Srinagar to meet Dr Mookerjee in spite of Abdullah's opposition. Dr Mookerjee was then thinking of drawing up proposals in consultation with Pandit Dogra for the consideration of the Jana Sangh and Praja Parishad colleagues outside who, he held, must be consulted before any decision was taken.

At about 4.45 a.m. on 22 June an attendant woke up Vaid and told him that Dr Mookerjee wanted to see him immediately. Vaid rushed to his room and found that his temperature had gone down to 97° F and he had perspired profusely. He felt his pulse and found it very feeble. He administered him some hot cardamom tea and clove water which gave him some relief. Dr Mookerjee told him that he had slept fairly well till about 4 a.m., when he woke up and felt a severe pain in his chest and had broken into a sweat. He was also feeling so giddy that he thought he would lose consciousness. He thought he should not disturb anyone at that ungodly hour, but was progressively feeling so weak that he was forced to wake up Vaid. Apparently he had had a severe heart attack, a myocardial infarction as it is medically known— possibly the second or third one after the ones he had in 1945 at Barrackpore (see Chapter 7).

At 5.15 a.m. the jail superintendent was informed about his deteriorating health and was requested to come with a doctor immediately. Dr Ali Mohammed reached there at 7.30 a.m. He suggested to the superintendent that Dr Mookerjee should be immediately removed to the nursing home. The superintendent asked him to get orders from the district magistrate. Thereupon both Guru Datt and Tek Chand requested him to get permission for them also to be moved to the hospital. But Dr Mohammed refused to do so and is said to have remarked:[8] 'I understand your anxiety, but you don't worry. He will be in better hands there.' Meanwhile Trivedi came to see him at about 10 a.m. At that time Dr Mookerjee was propped up in bed, and Trivedi found him in a good mood. They had discussions about his case for about an hour.

At about 11.30 a.m. the jail superintendent reached there with a taxi (not an ambulance), and they *walked down the steep steps* from his room to the taxi. Dr Mookerjee was removed, not to any nursing home but to the gynaecological ward in the state hospital about 10 miles away. He was kept in a room on the first floor (probably he was made to walk up the stairs). One Dr Jagannath Zutshi, a house surgeon, was detailed to look after him, though not exclusively.

What took place in the hospital is still shrouded in mystery. Barrister Trivedi came to see him at 5.30 p.m. after completing his arguments in the court. Justice Killam was hearing the matter. Trivedi was confident that Dr Mookerjee would be set at liberty the next day when the judgment was to be delivered. Trivedi said later that he did not find him the way he found him in the morning, but Dr Mookerjee said he was feeling better than in the morning. The district magistrate dropped in and gave him some letters, about fifteen in number. He read the letters, signed some papers and a couple of cheques. He was doing all these propped up in bed, and the medical superintendent, Dr Girdhari Lal, told Trivedi that he should not be sitting in that position. After signing the letters he placed his hand on his heart, and grimaced, as if in pain. Trivedi stayed with him till about 7.15 p.m. and asked the attending doctor what his true medical state was. The doctor reassured him by saying that there was no immediate cause for concern. As he was about to leave, Dr Mookerjee asked him to get him some reading material of his choice. Trivedi shook hands with him trying to feel his temperature, which he found to be normal. There was a nurse on duty in the room and some policemen on duty outside. Trivedi asked for permission to visit him at 9 a.m. on 23 June, but the doctor told him that his X-ray was scheduled at 9 a.m., so he should come and see him at 8 a.m. That was the last time Trivedi saw Dr Mookerjee alive.

When he left at about 7.30 p.m., Dr Mookerjee was weak but cheerful. Doctors in attendance told Trivedi that the worst had passed and that he would be X-rayed next morning and would be all right in two or three days.

But on 23 June at about 3.45 a.m. Trivedi was told by the police superintendent that Dr Mookerjee was in a bad state and the district magistrate had asked him to be at his bedside immediately. He was picked up from his hotel to go to the hospital. Pandit Premnath Dogra and the two co-detenues of Dr Mookerjee in the sub-jail, Guru Datt and Tek Chand, were also asked about the same time to get ready to go to the hospital. They reached there about 4 a.m. and were informed that Dr Mookerjee had breathed his last at 3.40 a.m.

This is what Madhok wrote about his last days in his life-sketch titled *The Portrait of a Martyr* and Guru Datt Vaid and barrister U.M. Trivedi said in statements made on 25 June.[9]

Apparently, when Dr Mookerjee had made known his intention to visit Jammu, Sucheta Kripalani paid him a visit. Sucheta, it would be remembered, was Bengali, and had married Acharya J.B. Kripalani, and had assisted Gandhi during his visit to pogrom-affected Noakhali in 1946 (see Chapter 8). This is what Madhok said (on tape):

> Sucheta Kripalani had told him, so many others had told him, that you won't go, Nehru will not allow you to return safe from there. Dr Mookerjee told Sucheta, 'I have no personal enmity against Nehru, I am working for a cause, why should he have any vendetta for me?' Then Sucheta told Dr Mookerjee, 'You don't know Nehru, I know Nehru, he looks upon you as his main rival and he will try to remove you from the field if he can and he is capable of anything.'[10]

Madhok was not explicit as to whether he had heard this conversation with his own ears. Quite possibly Sucheta spoke in Bengali, which Madhok does not follow.

And then again, on tape:

> So, when Trivedi was staying in Nedou's Hotel, one day a Pandit came to him. He said, 'I am a *Jyotishi* [astrologer], Dr Mookerjee is not going to return safe, please get him released as early as possible' . . . In the same evening, a police officer came, he said, 'I am so and so, but please don't disclose my identity, Sheikh Abdullah has a plan, Dr Mookerjee may not be allowed . . . [inaudible]. His habeas corpus is being discussed today. Please see that you get the judgment tonight itself.' He insisted that [the] judgment is going to be given today, and you see, that he is probably going to be released, that is, judgment is given today itself and he is released.

This biographer had also interviewed Sabita Banerjee, Dr Mookerjee's eldest daughter, at her flat in Koregaon Park, Pune, on 24 April 2010, and she had a somewhat different tale to tell. She was a widow at that time, about eighty-four, but perfectly fit, absolutely lucid and used to live all by herself with only a help. Her daughter Manju lived in another flat in the same block of buildings. Her interview was transcribed and got checked by her. She died about a year later. This is what she had to tell about the last days of her father.

After Dr Mookerjee's death his eldest son Anutosh asked for a permit to visit Kashmir. In the application one has to always mention one's father's name, and presumably for that reason his request for a permit was refused. Then Sabita and her husband, Nishith, decided to visit Kashmir in his place, but quietly, posing as tourists, with their two children. They did not apprehend any trouble [and they did not have any] because then, in married women's applications, the husband's name and not the father's name was mentioned.

They had a nerve-racking experience there. They had decided, for fear of trouble and possible arrest, that they would not reveal their identity. They took up residence in a big houseboat on the Jhelum. A friend of Dr Mookerjee from his days in London, one Jatindra Nath Majumdar, happened to be visiting Kashmir at the time, also as a tourist. He came to visit the Banerjees in their houseboat, and they were chatting in Bengali when a bearer of the houseboat came to serve tea. Majumdar mentioned Dr Mookerjee in front of the bearer and asked her if she had seen the house where he had lived. Sabita winked at him so as to suggest that he should shut up, but she was still secure in the belief that the bearer would not understand anything as he did not know Bengali. As soon as Majumdar left the bearer asked them if they knew Dr Mookerjee. She said

they didn't and that they were talking about him only because
he was Bengali. The bearer said that he could show them the
house where Dr Mookerjee spent his last days. And he did.

They took a taxi to a hillock by the side of the Dal Lake,
and climbed up the stairs to the sub-jail at the top of the
hillock, she all the while feeling how her dear Bapi [father]
must have felt with his bad leg when he was forced to climb
those steps. It was a small isolated bungalow at the top of the
hill, windswept and forlorn. In the sub-jail they found three
cots in one room, side by side. Sabita asked the bearer about the
whereabouts of the doctor who treated him in his last days. The
bearer refused to divulge anything, but said that he could take
them to a person who had been there when he died. Possibly
Miss Rajdulari Tikkoo, his regular nurse at the gynaecological
ward at the state hospital. Dr Mookerjee always insisted on a
Hindu nurse.

They went to her house in Srinagar. Two women were
living there, the nurse and her mother. As soon as Sabita
revealed her identity the nurse said she would not say anything
and asked them to leave. By now the Banerjees were extremely
emotionally charged. Sabita burst into tears, and begged the
nurse to tell her, saying that she would never reveal her name.
Then the nurse gave it all out.

Dr Mookerjee had fallen ill and was taken to the 'maternity
home' as she described it. There, on his last day, she was on
duty. He was sleeping. The doctor left, leaving instructions that
whenever he woke up he was to be administered an injection,
for which he left an ampoule with the nurse. After some time
he did wake up, and [she said to Sabita, 'I don't know why
I did it'] she pushed that injection. As soon as she did it, Dr
Mookerjee started tossing about, shouting at the top of his
voice, *Jal jata hai, humko jal raha hai* (I'm burning up, I'm
burning).' 'I rushed to the telephone to tell the doctor and ask

for instructions.' He said, '*Theek hai, sab theek ho jaiga* (It is all right, he will be all right).' Meanwhile Dr Mookerjee had fallen into a stupor. And that was the end of him.

Then she said, 'I have committed a great sin, and I had to tell it to you. But I will leave this house immediately, because you will get back to Calcutta, and talk about this, and all what I told you is bound to get out. Then I'll be murdered.' In fact that is what she did. The next day when Sabita and Nishith went to look her up both the mother and the daughter were gone. The nurse had refused to give her name.[11]

According to a report printed in the *Organiser* on 20 July 1953 and translated and reproduced in Uma Prasad's book, Rajdulari Tikkoo, the nurse, tried to get hold of a doctor when Dr Mookerjee's condition became critical but no doctor was available. Tikkoo then asked an orderly called Noor Ahmed to fetch Dr Zutshi. Dr Zutshi came immediately, and telephoned Dr Ali Mohammed for instructions. Meanwhile Dr Mookerjee's condition deteriorated further and he died at about 2.15 a.m., not 3.40 a.m. Dr Mohammed arrived about half an hour after his death. The source of this report is not mentioned.

The communiqué issued after his death by the Kashmir government on 23 June, gave the report of doctors Ali Mohammed and Ram Nath Parhar, who were said to have been attending upon him. It said that Dr Mookerjee was admitted to the hospital about midday on 22 June. Upon an examination of his blood and urine, and an electrocardiogram, the doctors came to the conclusion that he had had a coronary attack. He was administered sleeping pills, antibiotics and oxygen on demand. His general condition improved, and was fairly good at 4 p.m. Barrister Trivedi and the district magistrate visited him in the evening. Around 9 p.m. he was fairly all right but exhibited hypotension and tachycardia. Oxygen was administered to him at 11 p.m. to allay restlessness which

had started at that time, and his BP had gone down to 100/80. He
was injected with intravenous glucose and aminophylline. Around
1 a.m. he felt intense pain in the heart and became restless. His
pulse was very feeble and BP was 90/70. Oxygen was continued and
1 cc of pethidine was administered to allay his pain. By 2.30 a.m.
his respiration and pulse had become extremely feeble, and he was
administered coramine and aminophylline intravenously. The
position remained the same at 3 a.m., his pulse could barely be
felt, and intravenous coramine was again injected. By 3.20 a.m
his respiration had become very feeble and irregular. Oxygen was
continued. His pulse and respiration stopped at 3.40 a.m.

This communiqué was followed by a short and perfunctory
statement by Sheikh Abdullah on 26 June and by a detailed
statement by Pandit M.L. Saraf, the minister in charge of health
and prisons, on 1 July. In the latter the Pandit has tried to explain
that Dr Mookerjee had been given all possible facilities during his
detention and there was no bungling in his medical treatment. He
quoted selectively from Dr Mookerjee's letters trying to prove that
he was enjoying his stay at the sub-jail.

Meanwhile a heart-rending tragedy was being enacted at 77
Asutosh Mookerjee Road, the Calcutta residence of the Mookerjees,
which has been described in a book by Dr Mookerjee's younger
brother, Uma Prasad. It was around 5.45 a.m. in Calcutta when
the telephone rang at the Mookerjee household and the operator
announced a trunk call from Srinagar for Justice Mookerjee. Rama
Prasad rushed to the phone, and the rest of the household also
assembled around him. Their mother, Jogomaya, was on the ground
floor, beginning her daily puja. She was also brought near the
telephone. She was smiling wanly, very eager and hopeful of talking
to her dear son. But Rama Prasad was not smiling. Instead he was
shouting at the top of his voice, 'Yes, Justice Mookerjee speaking.
What . . . what . . . ?' Then he told his mother that her son was not
well, and she should go downstairs and get busy with her puja.

Actually the calls from Calcutta to Srinagar were routed via New Delhi. The New Delhi operator said she had received a message from Sheikh Abdullah in Srinagar that Dr Syama Prasad Mookerjee was dead, and Sheikh Abdullah wanted to know how his dead body was to be disposed of. Rama Prasad, in a state of total bewilderment, asked the operator to find out who the originator of this news was, and how Dr Mookerjee had died. The New Delhi operator contacted Srinagar and said it was one Durga Prasad Dhar, the deputy home minister of Kashmir, who was passing on the news. Three days back Dr Mookerjee had contracted pleurisy, and he was removed to a hospital a day earlier; there he had had a sudden heart attack and died at 3.40 a.m. on 23 June. Rama Prasad said that the body must be sent to Calcutta and demanded more information. The operator relayed the reply that someone in the Kashmir government would get back to him in half an hour.

According to a news item published in the *Amrita Bazar Patrika*[12] of 24 June, the Kashmir government sent a flash message to the Government of India and not to the Mookerjee household. It was A.V. Pai, the Union home secretary, who asked them to contact the family, and only after that did Rama Prasad get the call.

Barrister Trivedi said in his statement on 25 June that he arrived at the hospital at about 3.55 a.m. and found that the door to Dr Mookerjee's cabin was closed and a doctor was sitting in the visitors' room. He asked him to sit down but said nothing more. After about a minute Trivedi asked him how Dr Mookerjee was. The police superintendent was also present and said he was being administered oxygen. Trivedi said he wanted to enter the cabin. The superintendent went inside and came back with a doctor. The doctor told Trivedi that Dr Mookerjee had breathed his last about five minutes before Trivedi arrived.

Upon being told that Dr Mookerjee was no more, Trivedi entered the cabin, went near the body and lifted the shroud covering him to look at his face in its eternal sleep. Within five minutes the district magistrate arrived. Trivedi told him that the body must be taken to Calcutta immediately, and he must arrange it, failing which Trivedi would speak to the Government of India to do it. They should also inform his family immediately so that his mother got the news before it was announced over the radio. Home minister Bakshi Ghulam Mohammed also reached the hospital. Trivedi asked Bakshi to release Pandit Premnath Dogra, Guru Datt and Tek Chand immediately and to permit them to travel in the same aircraft with the body. Bakshi agreed and asked them to get back to the sub-jail and get their things ready.

Deputy Home Minister D.P. Dhar had already left to telephone Dr Mookerjee's family in Calcutta. Trivedi came back to the hotel and telephoned the representatives of All India Radio, the *Times of India* and United Press of India to come and meet him. They arrived in five minutes and were told of the tragedy. He then tried to call Mauli Chandra Sharma in New Delhi and Praja Parishad leaders in Jammu but failed to get through. He then went back to the hospital and met D.P. Dhar who said he had spoken to Dr Katju and informed him. In the meantime about five hundred people had assembled in front of the hospital. The body was taken out through a back door. Trivedi asked for the articles used by Dr Mookerjee, and got his wristwatch, pen and a suitcase. He could not locate the attaché case. The suitcase was unlocked. A pair of slippers was lying outside. His spectacles were there but not their case.

They started towards the airport by about 8.40 a.m. The Hindus among the police officers present—among them the superintendent, deputy superintendent, a sub-inspector and a head constable—asked Trivedi to make sure that no Muslim touched the body and volunteered to do it themselves. Most of the ministers of the Jammu and Kashmir government, except Sheikh Abdullah, had already assembled at the airport. Some of them were looking very upset. Abdullah arrived at about 10.15 a.m and handed over a specially embroidered, very expensive, Kashmiri shawl, which was then laid on the body. There was some difficulty in getting an Air Force Dakota to carry the body, both because of want of orders and also bad weather. Finally Bakshi Ghulam Mohammed took all responsibility on himself and ordered the wing commander in charge of the local Air Force establishment to make the aircraft available.

The aircraft, with its sad cargo, and immeasurably saddened passengers, took off from Humhama airport, Srinagar, at about 10.40 a.m., and after stops for rest and refuelling at Jullundur, Adampur and Kanpur Air Force bases, reached Dum Dum airport in Calcutta around 8.55 p.m. amid cries of his relatives, friends and admirers. The first thing his eldest son Anutosh did was to throw away the shawl that Sheikh Abdullah had brought. A sea of humanity besieged the body, and the truck carrying it could reach 77 Asutosh Mookerjee Road only as late as 4 a.m., seven hours later, a distance normally covered in less than an hour. Jogomaya broke down at the sight of the lifeless body of her illustrious son and yelled in anguish at Harendra Coomar Mookerjee, the Governor of West Bengal and earlier a professor of the Calcutta University, appointed by Dr Mookerjee himself. The fifty-second birthday of the departed leader was just two weeks away, on 6 July.

That night many people slept on the road in front of 77 Asutosh Mookerjee Road, waiting for the body to arrive. The next day saw a deluge of humanity accompanying the body from the house to the Keoratala cremation ground, near Kalighat. Bidhan Chandra Roy, the Chief Minister of West Bengal, who was very close to the family, came to accompany the body. The crowd yelled at him, holding all Congressmen responsible for his death, and he had to go to the cremation ground by a different route. Some said they had heard Roy mutter to himself at Keoratala, 'told him so many times, don't go, don't go'. As mentioned earlier, Pandit

Lakshmi Kanta Maitra, a Congress MP but an ardent admirer of Dr Mookerjee, had watched the funeral procession. He was so fond of the man that, struck by grief, he literally fell ill at the sight of the body, and died within a month.

Dr Mookerjee's eldest son, Anutosh, followed by others of the family, did the *mukhagni*, the ritual touching of the flame to his mouth. And then the pyre was lit and the body finally consigned to flames. And thus ended prematurely, even before he was fifty-two, the journey of the great man who could have saved the country from many of the ills that overtook it in the subsequent years.

* * *

Condolence messages and tributes to the departed leader poured in from all over the country. His close and dear friend of many years Dr Sarvepalli Radhakrishnan wrote one of the most poignant pieces. Radhakrishnan, then the Vice President of India, necessarily had to have his remarks circumscribed by requirements of official propriety, but he nevertheless made his feelings plain when he wrote[13] about him, 'In his public life he was never afraid of expressing his inmost convictions. In silence the cruellest lies are told. When great wrongs are committed it is criminal to be silent in the hope that truth will one day find its voice. In democratic society one should speak out, especially when we are developing an unequalled power of not seeing what we do not wish to see.'

The poet and actor Harindranath Chattopadhyay, brother of Sarojini Naidu, wrote:

> A giant has departed. Lo!
> The sun of a colossal intellect has set
> The giants are departing one by one
> To whom our mourning nation owes a debt.

Messages expressing sympathy and appreciation for his qualities and regret for his untimely death were received from several public men, some of them his sworn political adversaries, such as A.K. Gopalan, Maulana Abul Kalam Azad, Jayaprakash Narayan, Lal Bahadur Shastri, Acharya J.B. Kripalani and Frank Anthony; and of course from his colleagues and friends like V.D. Savarkar, M.S. Golwalkar, M.R. Masani, Pandit H.N. Kunzru and others. There was a full court reference at the Calcutta High Court in which Chief Justice P.B. Chakravartty paid him glowing tributes. His sometime colleague and sometime adversary Fazlul Haq sent a telegram from East Pakistan saying it was as if he had lost a brother.

A memorial meeting was arranged on 28 June at the senate house of the university by the sheriff of Calcutta. More than a lakh people assembled for the meeting. Governor Harendra Coomar Mookerjee, who had taught Dr Mookerjee at Presidency College, came to address the meeting. But his car could not reach the spot because of the crowd, and he had to walk the last bit to reach the hall. He began his prepared speech by stating that he was merely the constitutional titular head of the state government, when someone from the audience interrupted and asked him,[14] 'We demand to know from you whether your former student Dr Mookerjee was communal or narrow-minded.' Mookerjee looked at the heckler, pocketed his speech and started speaking extempore. He spoke for about thirty-five to forty minutes, frequently stopping to wipe tears. He said that however much his political adversaries tried to malign him by calling him communal or narrow-minded, he was nothing of the sort. Sukharanjan Sengupta, a veteran journalist of West Bengal, has remarked that on that day the entire audience was awash in tears. The *Statesman* of Calcutta reported a couple of days later that the central government had been discomfited by some parts of the Governor's speech, and the Union home ministry had asked for a complete transcript of his speech from the state government.

No chronicle on Dr Mookerjee's life and death would be complete without a discussion on two subjects: first, whether he died a 'natural death' or was it a case of homicide due to negligence, or worse still, a deep-seated conspiracy. This has been discussed at length by many, and part of that will be recounted. The second subject is much less known. It is called the Tram Agitation, a strategic and successful move made by the communists to shift the focus of public attention in West Bengal away from the death of Dr Mookerjee.

The untimely or violent death of any great man or prominent personality is always followed by conspiracy theories, some well founded, some pure flights of fancy. The conspiracy theories behind the assassination of US President John F. Kennedy in 1963 refuse to die down even today, more than fifty years after the act. But that does not mean that all conspiracy theories have to be rejected out of hand. It was obvious that there were suspicious circumstances surrounding Dr Mookerjee's death, loud protests from the Prime Minister of India notwithstanding. The theories, proceeding from the eminently plausible to the relatively far-fetched, would give us some insight into those circumstances.

The first question is, why was Dr Mookerjee not arrested in Gurdaspur district, but was allowed, in fact encouraged, to enter Jammu and Kashmir state? When he was arrested, the state ordinance which made it an offence for someone to enter the state without a permit had not yet been promulgated, and the only law on the books to prevent a person from entering the state without a permit was the Government of India regulation to that effect. Therefore, when he made it clear to the district officials of Gurdaspur that he was about to enter Jammu and Kashmir, they should have arrested him, as the deputy commissioner of Gurdaspur thought he would. But he did not; instead he said that the orders of the government were to let him enter the state. In fact just one month earlier, in April 1953, when Barrister U.M. Trivedi and G.V. Deshpande, both Jana Sangh MPs, tried to enter Jammu and Kashmir without permits they were arrested as early as Jullundur under the Preventive Detention Act—but not Dr Mookerjee! Why?

The second question: if, as the order of arrest signed by the IG of Jammu and Kashmir Police, Prithvinandan Singh, said, 'Dr Mookerjee has acted, is acting or is about to act in a manner prejudicial to public safety and peace', then the sensible thing to do would have been to block his entry into the state. There was no way he could have forced his way in, and he could not have acted 'in a manner prejudicial to public safety and peace' from outside the state. Instead, he was allowed to enter the state and then detained for a period of two months—by what logic?

These two clearly lead one to the conclusion that there was indeed a conspiracy to trap him in Jammu and Kashmir, outside the jurisdiction of the Supreme Court of India, as Justice Mahajan had pointed out to Madhok. And both the governments, that is of India and Jammu and Kashmir, were conspirators in this. N.C. Chatterjee said as much in so many words on the floor of the Lok Sabha, which is described later in the chapter.

Next question: Dr Mookerjee was no ordinary detenue. He was a member of the Indian Parliament and one of the most prominent members at that, and a former Union cabinet minister of India. And he had already suffered one, possibly two heart attacks. Why was he incarcerated in that decrepit bungalow, so far away from civilization, with no doctor in attendance, without even the facility of a telephone? Why was he not given permission to walk outside the compound when he repeatedly complained that he needed to walk and there was no space inside the compound? Why were his letters not delivered on time? Why were his son, colleagues and relatives not allowed to see him? Why was he—and this is extremely serious and commented upon by Dr N.B. Khare—made to *walk* from his bed in the sub-jail to the waiting taxi and possibly up the stairs to the gynaecological ward of the hospital on the first floor? Why was he removed to the state hospital in an ordinary taxi instead of an ambulance on 22 June? It is not known if any Intensive Cardiac Care Unit (ICCU) existed at that time—possibly it did not. But there certainly must have been something like a VIP ward where Dr Mookerjee could have received round-the-clock attention with a doctor in constant attendance. Surely Sheikh Abdullah, or before his time the Maharaja, would not have been put in that dingy cabin in that gynaecological ward, with fresh paint coming off the cot, if they fell ill? So why was Dr Mookerjee given such a treatment?

And why were his diary and papers not made available by Sheikh Abdullah to the family after his death?

These are incontrovertible facts. What do they say about the attitude of Abdullah who had issued orders not to give Dr Mookerjee any extra facility without his express orders? Was it just plain cussedness, unutterable callousness—or worse?

The next is not a question but an observation. Pandit Jawaharlal Nehru and Kailash Nath Katju (both of them, incidentally, Kashmiris) acted nothing less than dishonourably in not looking up Dr Mookerjee when the two visited Srinagar on 24 May, supposedly for 'rest'.

N.C. Chatterjee (father of former Lok Sabha speaker Somnath Chatterjee) made a surprising disclosure on the floor of the Parliament in the Lok Sabha on 18 September 1953. He first indicted the Jammu and Kashmir state government by saying:[15]

> I am charging that the Kashmir government had been treating Dr Syama Prasad Mookerjee as if he was a convicted felon . . . Dr Mookerjee had fundamental political differences with New Delhi and with Kashmir. But he was no criminal who deserved no consideration even in his illness. Even under the British Imperial regime a leader of his status could not have been kept behind the bars when he was ill.

Then he went on to make that disclosure about Nehru who was away at the time of Dr Mookerjee's death, attending the coronation of Queen Elizabeth II of Britain in London.

> Nehru was on the point of leaving Geneva for Cairo when the news of Dr Mookerjee's death reached him . . . when a journalist apprised Nehru of the newsflash that came from India to the effect that Dr Mookerjee passed away at Srinagar while in detention, Nehru 'whistled' and jumped up from his sitting position and walked away from the place, brandishing merrily his baton . . . When Nehru returned from his foreign tour . . . he [the journalist] observed that he had come back to the country 'happy' and did not utter a single word about the calamity that struck the country in his absence.

If we now progress from the realm of the factual and the certain to that of probabilities, possibilities, conjectures and revelations, as well as of uncorroborated statements, the picture becomes even murkier. Did Sucheta Kripalani warn Dr Mookerjee, or the unnamed police officer Trivedi, as Madhok has alleged? Did Dr B.C. Roy know something when he allegedly told Dr Mookerjee not to go to Kashmir? And did things go the way as Sabita Banerjee described, with Dr Mookerjee writhing in pain as soon as the nurse administered the last injection? Did Thakur Prasad's (Patna—see Chapter 14) father suspect something? All these people are dead now, and perhaps we shall never know, but perhaps some light could have been shed if there had been a full-fledged inquiry. That aspect is dealt with later.

There is also scope for wondering, for those who believe, about the mystical. The president of the Bharat Sevashram Sangha, Swami Satchidananda, forbade Dr Mookerjee to go. Madhok had spoken about a *jyotishi* who visited Trivedi. And The Mother of Pondicherry told[16] Manoj Das Gupta, a trustee of the ashram, '*Ils l'ont tué*', which in French means, 'They have killed him.'

Now as to the medical angle: several doctors have opined that the treatment was improper, to say the least. Dr N.B. Khare has said that the moment the doctors suspected that Dr Mookerjee had coronary trouble, they should not have moved him at all; instead he should have been treated where he was. Next, when on 22 June around noon the doctors concluded that he had had a heart attack, they should have administered aminophylline immediately; instead they did it at 11 p.m., that is eleven hours later. And finally, when following an injection of aminophylline his BP had gone down from 100/80 to 90/70, they should have started treatment for shock and administered dextran intravenously. Finally, Dr Khare opined that the demand that had been voiced throughout the country for an inquiry into his death was perfectly justified.

Dr Nalini Ranjan Sengupta, one of the most prominent doctors of Calcutta at the time, opined that after Dr Mookerjee had suffered the heart attack at 4 a.m. on 22 June, he should have been kept under continuous medical supervision. The fact that he was removed in a taxi from the sub-jail seems to indicate that the doctors did not understand at all that this was a coronary attack. He should have been administered morphine as an anticoagulant; instead he was given pethidine, which is a poor substitute, and that too at 1 a.m., eighteen hours after the attack. He also remarked that the doctors attending him were little better than quacks in regard to treatment of coronary attacks.

Dr Amal Kumar Ray Chowdhury, another prominent doctor of Calcutta, was of the opinion that there had been misdiagnosis and bungling by the doctors. What was diagnosed as dry pleurisy was a complication of a coronary problem or pneumonia that must have started quite a few days earlier. He also opined that the patient should have been administered morphine, and his prothrombin time should have been noted.

A medical board headed by Dr Ambalal Sharma of Ajmer opined that administering aminophylline when the systolic pressure was as low as 100 was a mistake. A similar board of Gwalior headed by Dr Kamal Kishore opined that morphine should have been given instead of pethidine; and Dr Mookerjee should under no circumstances have been allowed to sit up, as he had done on the evening of 22 June—in fact absolutely no movement of the body, except for urination and defecation should have been allowed. They also agreed that administering aminophylline when his blood pressure was so low was a grave mistake. Dr T.N. Banerjee, principal of Patna Medical College, also opined that there had been improper treatment.

Opinions by current-day physicians are somewhat different. It is important to remember that enormous strides in internal medicine have been made since 1953, and cardiology today is a distinct specialization. Dr R.N. Das, a leading physician in the field of internal medicine in Calcutta, has pointed to a third possibility. He opined that in view of Dr Mookerjee's obesity and severe and persistent pain in his leg the possibility of deep vein thrombosis (DVT) cannot be ruled out. Varicose veins, unless infected, should not cause so much pain or inability to walk, and there is no evidence of any such infection. DVT causes a blood clot to form in one of the deep veins (away from the surface), especially in the lower limbs. If that clot travels with the bloodstream to the lungs a severe pulmonary embolism may take place which may lead to cardiac arrest and eventually death. Dr Das also opined that administering aminophylline to a patient of myocardial infarction or unstable angina could precipitate tachycardia (rapid heart rate) and should not have been done, and that fact was known even in 1953. The drug aminophylline has now gone totally out of use for cardiac patients. As for administering pethidine as against morphine, Dr Das stated that it made little difference, so long as the dose injected was adequate. Dr Shuvo Dutta, a leading cardiologist of Calcutta, also generally agreed with Dr Das.

Both doctors are quite certain that his death ultimately took place by cardiac arrest, and not from anaphylactic shock from streptomycin, as some doctors had suspected. They are equally certain that the treatment he got was definitely at least a contributory cause to such cardiac arrest. Making a cardiac patient walk down and up the stairs on foot and letting him sit up in bed and do paperwork is unheard of, and was unheard of even in those days. Administering aminophylline and DVT (if it was present) would also have contributed to cardiac arrest.

According to Sukharanjan Sengupta, Dr B.C. Roy had telephoned Sheikh Abdullah and asked him to furnish the prescriptions and names of the doctors who had treated Dr Mookerjee. After getting the information he had remarked adversely on the treatment and the professional competence of the doctors. This remark of a prominent Chief Minister and also an outstanding physician was said to have caused Nehru quite some discomfiture.

For non-medical lay persons it may be difficult to understand who is right and who is not. But that there was a serious botch-up seems quite probable, and this would have come out had there been a proper inquiry into his death. Now thereby hangs a tale.

Whenever a leading public figure dies or disappears under suspicious circumstances there is always an inquiry, usually under the provisions of the Commissions of Inquiry Act 1952. As many as three such commissions had been constituted to conduct inquiry in relation to the disappearance of Netaji Subhas Chandra Bose—the Shah Nawaz Committee (1956), the G.D. Khosla Commission (1970) and the Manoj Mukherjee Commission (1999). Mahatma Gandhi's assassination was probed by the Kapur Commission, Indira Gandhi's by the Thakkar Commission, Rajiv Gandhi's by two commissions—J.S. Verma Commission and M.C. Jain Commission. All these assassinations (except Netaji's disappearance), it must be remembered, took place in public view, and therefore there was no doubt left in anyone's mind as to how the person died—the inquiry was needed to find out the background and the conspiracy behind it. Dr Mookerjee's untimely and suspicious death, on the other hand, took place in secret, far away from family and friends, in hostile territory, beyond even the jurisdiction of the Supreme Court of India. It is therefore natural that Dr Mookerjee's family, colleagues, admirers, partymen and unrelated men who take an interest in public affairs would demand an inquiry into it.

The initiative was taken by Dr Mookerjee's mother, Jogomaya Devi, who, in reply to Nehru's condolence message dated 30 June 1953, addressed him on 4 July. She wrote:

I am not writing to you to seek any consolation. But what I do demand of you is justice. My son died in detention—a detention without trial. In your letter you have tried to impress that Kashmir Government had done all that should have been done. You base your impression on the assurances and information you have received. What is the value, I ask, of such information when it comes from persons who themselves should stand trial? You say, you had visited Kashmir during my son's detention. You speak of the affection you had for him. But what prevented you, I wonder, from meeting him there personally and satisfying yourself about his health and arrangements?[17]

His death is shrouded in mystery. Is it not most astounding and shocking that ever since his detention there, the first information that I, his mother, received from the Government of Kashmir was that my son was no more, and that also at least two hours after the end? And in what a cruel cryptic way the message was conveyed! Even the telegram from my son that he had been removed to the hospital reached us here after the tragic news of his death. There is definite information that my son had not been keeping well practically from the beginning of his detention. He had been positively ill a number of times and for successive periods. Why did not, I ask, the Government of Kashmir or your Government send any information whatsoever to me and my family?

Even when he was removed to the Hospital they did not think it necessary to immediately intimate us or Dr Bidhan Chandra Roy. It is also evident that the Kashmir Government had never cared to acquaint itself with the previous history of Syama Prasad's health and provide for nursing arrangements and emergency medical attendance in case of need. Even his repeated attacks of illness were not taken as a warning. The result was disastrous. I have positive evidence to prove that he had, to quote his own words, a 'sinking feeling' on the morning of 22nd June. And what did the Government do? The inordinate delay in getting any medical assistance, his removal to the Hospital in a most injudicious manner, the refusal to allow even his two co-detenues to be by his side in the Hospital are some of the glaring instances of the heartless conduct of the authorities concerned.

The responsibility of the Government and their own doctors cannot be in any way evaded or lightened by some stray quotations from Dr Mookerjee's letters chosen at random [she was referring to Saraf's statement of 1 July], that he was keeping well. What is the value of such quotations? Does anybody seriously expect that he—of all persons—and that while in detention far away from his dear and near ones would ventilate his grievances through letters or diagnose his own malady? The responsibility of the Government was immense and serious.

I charge them that they had utterly neglected and failed to discharge this bounden duty. You speak of the comforts and amenities given to dear Dr Mookerjee in detention. It is a matter to be inquired into. The Kashmir Government had not even the courtesy to allow free flow of family correspondence. Letters were held up with inordinate delay and some mysteriously disappeared. His anxiety for home news, particularly of his ailing daughter and my poor self, was distressing. Will you be astonished to learn that on the 27th June last, we received here his letters dated 15th June, despatched by the Kashmir Government in a packet on the 24th June, that is, a day after sending his dead body? The packet also brought back to us the letters addressed by myself and others here to Dr Mookerjee which had reached Srinagar on the 11th and 16th June, but had never been delivered to him. It was purely a case of mental torture. He had been repeatedly asking for sufficient space for walking. He was feeling ill for want of it. But he was persistently refused it. Is not this a method of physical torture too? I am filled with surprise and shame to be told by you that 'he was being kept, not in any prison but in a private villa on the side of the famous Dal Lake in Srinagar'. Strictly confined in a small bungalow with a little compound, guarded day and night by a body of armed guards—such was the life that he was leading. Is it seriously maintained that a golden cage should make a prisoner happy? I shudder to hear such desperate propaganda. I do not know what medical treatment and assistance had been given to him. The official reports, I am told, are self-contradictory. Eminent physicians have expressed their views that it was, in the least a case of gross negligence. The matter requires a through and impartial inquiry.

I do bewail here the death of my beloved son. A fearless son of Free India has met his death while in detention without trial under most tragic and mysterious circumstances. I, the mother of the great departed, demand that an absolutely impartial and open inquiry by independent and competent persons be held without delay. I know nothing can bring back to us the life that is no more. But what I do want is that the people of India must judge for themselves the real causes of this great tragedy enacted in a free country and the part that was played by your Government.

Nehru, in answer, was all sugar and honey, filled to his gills with compassion for the bereaved mother—but refused the inquiry! The reply, dated 5 July, is, to say the least, astounding:

> I can well understand a mother's sorrow and mental anguish at the death of a beloved son. No words of mine can soften the blow that you must have felt . . . I did not venture to write to you before without going into the matter of Dr Mookerjee's detention and death fairly carefully. I have since inquired further into it from a number of persons who had occasion to know some facts. I can only say to you that I arrived at the clear and honest conclusion that there is no mystery in this and that Dr Mookerjee was given every consideration.[18]

Can one imagine a more wishy-washy, perfunctory reply to a solemn and rightful demand for an inquiry into the suspicious death of one of the foremost national leaders? 'I have since inquired further into it from a *number* of *persons* who had *occasion* to know some *facts*'—what number? Which persons? What kind of occasion and which facts? Was his personal satisfaction, upon talking to an unspecified number of unnamed persons with unknown exposure, enough? Was he talking to a child? *I* have inquired, who do you think *you* are to question me? '*I* can *only* say to you that *I* arrived at the *clear and honest* conclusion'—in other words, in my discretion *I* have decided to say no more! And after *my clear and honest conclusion* all arguments must stop. Both Gandhi and Patel were dead, and now with Dr Mookerjee's death, the last person who could question him was gone.

Veteran journalist Durga Das has written[19] that 'there were only three effective spokesmen of the Opposition during the Nehru era. They were S.P. Mookerjee, Kripalani and Lohia. The first was a real leader because he spoke for the largest group which opposed Nehru's policies. In oratory and debating skills he surpassed all others who have followed him.'

After this, Jogomaya gave up. In her last letter to Nehru dated 9 July she wrote:

Your letter . . . is a sad commentary on the whole situation. Instead of helping to clear up the mystery, your attitude deepens it. I demanded an open inquiry. I did not ask for your 'clear and honest conclusion'. Your reaction to the whole affair is now well known. The people of India and I, the mother, have got to be convinced. There is a rooted suspicion in the mind of many. What is required is an open, impartial, immediate inquiry.

The various points raised in my letter remain unanswered. I had clearly told you that I had positive evidence to prove certain very relevant and important facts. You do not care to know or look into them. You say that you had inquired 'from a number of persons who had occasion to know some facts'. It is strange that even we—the members of his family—are not regarded as persons who can throw at least some light on the matter! And yet you call your conclusion to be 'honest'! . . . It is futile to address you further. You are afraid to face facts. I hold the Kashmir Government responsible for the death of my son. I accuse your Government of complicity in the matter. You may let loose your mighty resources to carry on a desperate propaganda, but Truth is sure to find its way out and one day you will have to answer for this to the people of India and to God in Heaven.[20]

Rama Prasad telegraphed and wrote to Bakshi Ghulam Mohammed asking him to return Dr Mookerjee's personal diary and manuscript writings. Bakshi replied that all his belongings had been taken away by U.M. Trivedi and Tek Chand, and Rama Prasad should contact them. But neither Trivedi nor Tek Chand found any diary.

Dr Karan Singh, the Sadr-i-Riyasat, later wrote in his autobiography:[21]

> Soon thereafter came the shocking news of the death of Dr Syama Prasad Mookerjee in detention. I was not informed of his illness or his removal to hospital, and only learnt of his death from unofficial sources after his body had been flown out of Srinagar. The circumstances in which he died in the custody of the State Government were a cause of grave resentment and suspicion. Jammu was furious because Dr Mookerjee had been martyred while fighting for the Praja Parishad cause and there was open talk that his death had not been from natural causes.

N.C. Chatterjee's speech in the Lok Sabha on 18 September 1953 has already been mentioned. In his speech he pointed out that the extent to which the Government of India wanted Dr Mookerjee to enter Jammu and Kashmir state and get arrested there is borne out by the fact that when he was about to cross the Ravi bridge, his driver got nervous and said that he did not have a permit to enter the state. The district magistrate then said that he should proceed and the permit will follow. Chatterjee charged the Government of India with clear complicity, saying:[22]

> [The] District Magistrate of Gurdaspur actually escorted Dr Mookerjee and his party right upto the border, and it seems that he was pushed into the State of Jammu and Kashmir as a result of some understanding or some arrangement between

the Government of India and the Government of Jammu and Kashmir State . . . Sir, this clearly shows that there was some complicity, combination, co-ordination, conspiracy between the Government of India and the Government of Jammu and Kashmir . . . It may have been perfectly good strategy to push him out of the jurisdiction of the Supreme Court of India in order to avoid a repetition of another legal discomfiture as had taken place on the occasion when the Supreme Court ordered Dr Mookerjee's release and my release. But that makes this Government of India equally responsible.

Among others who demanded the inquiry were Jayaprakash Narayan, Purushottam Das Tandon, Hari Vishnu Kamath, M.R. Jayakar, Master Tara Singh, Sucheta Kripalani, Pandit Hriday Nath Kunzru, S.S. More and others. Atulya Ghosh, the Congress president of West Bengal, and Dr B.C. Roy also obliquely asked for an inquiry. All, as apprehended, to no effect whatsoever. Nehru would not budge.[23]

Was Nehru trying to shield anyone? It could be argued that he was trying to do so—but then, how does one explain the fact that just forty-seven days later, on 8 August 1953, Abdullah himself was dismissed as Prime Minister? It is impossible to accept that the decision to sack and arrest him was taken in these forty-seven days, and was not in Nehru's mind during Dr Mookerjee's captivity! It is true that Abdullah was dismissed by the Sadr-i-Riyasat, Dr Karan Singh, and not by Nehru— but it is obvious that the twenty-two-year-old figurehead could not have lifted a finger against the powerful Abdullah without Nehru's nod. Abdullah was even denied the opportunity to prove his majority on the floor of the house, and his dissident cabinet minister Bakshi Ghulam Mohammed was appointed Prime Minister. Abdullah was thereafter arrested and later shuttled from jail to jail at different places in India for eleven years, accused of conspiracy against the state in the infamous 'Kashmir Conspiracy Case'. According to him his dismissal and arrest were engineered by the central government headed by Prime Minister Nehru. He has quoted B.N. Mullick's statements in his book *My Years with Nehru* in support of his statement. It is, of course, pretty obvious otherwise.

N.C. Chatterjee said in the conclusion of his speech that when Abdullah was arrested, he told some intermediaries that he was unjustly accused of causing the death of Dr Mookerjee and he was innocent, and would give out the truth, revealing who was responsible for Dr Mookerjee's death. However, Abdullah, for reasons best known to himself, never carried out this threat.

It is submitted for general consideration that from the foregoing it would not be unreasonable to come to the conclusion that Nehru played out the following scenario very adroitly: First, on the one hand, his dispatching B.N. Mullick to Jammu and Kashmir to 'soften Abdullah and the Praja Parishad' shows that he knew that Abdullah was communal, anti-Jammu, anti-Dogra and anti-Indian and that the Praja Parishad agitation had substance. Yet at the same time he supported Abdullah to the hilt during the Dr Mookerjee–Nehru–Abdullah correspondence phase of January–February 1953 to keep Abdullah on the right side so as to have him ready to carry out his designs. He probably also shrewdly gauged that this would drive Dr Mookerjee to try to enter Jammu and Kashmir, and Dr Mookerjee took the bait. Then he refrained from arresting him in Gurdaspur, let him enter Jammu and Kashmir and used Abdullah to arrest him and put him out of the jurisdiction of Indian courts. Abdullah most definitely could not have behaved with such abominable callousness with a person of Dr Mookerjee's stature without Nehru's nod—whisking him away in a jeep and keeping him under detention under the most trying circumstances, while reciting the rot about his 'picturesque bungalow', which Nehru also repeated. And finally, Abdullah gave him unarguably very, very poor, and arguably lethal, medical treatment. Thus Nehru used Abdullah to get rid of Dr Mookerjee, refused an inquiry into his death and then got rid of the expendable Abdullah.

This sequence does not sit well with Nehru's popular image. Yet, the turn of events seems to suggest that there was indeed a deep-seated conspiracy to end the life of the man who had proved to be Nehru's worst bête noire after Patel. We shall never know.

One small fallout of the death of Dr Mookerjee was that the permit required for Indian citizens to enter Jammu and Kashmir was abolished. Abdullah did come back to power many years later, but that is another story.

That leaves only the Tram Fare Agitation to be mentioned in the aftermath of Dr Mookerjee's death. In June 1953, the Calcutta Tramways Co. Ltd, a British-owned company, raised its second-class fares by one pice (one sixty-fourth of a rupee). The Communist Party of India opposed it and called a strike on 13 July. In its wake they took out a number of processions, burnt some thirteen tramcars and threw acid bulbs at tram passengers. Dr B.C. Roy, the Chief Minister of West Bengal, at this time was away in Vienna to get his eyes operated on. The agitation was handled very ineptly by the state government in his absence.

Till this agitation the death of Dr Mookerjee was *the* most burning issue in West Bengal. Posters criticizing Nehru and his cabinet minister Rafi Ahmed Kidwai had appeared all over the state. The population was seething with anger. Taking advantage of the proverbially short public memory, the Tram Fare Agitation started, gradually pushing the Dr Mookerjee issue to the background. The communists got enormous political mileage and leapt into centre stage in West Bengal, effectively upstaging the memory of Dr Mookerjee. The refugees from Islamic persecution in East Bengal, for whom Dr Mookerjee had thrown away his cabinet berth, were won over and gradually became the mainstay of the Communist Party. It was remarked in jest by a historian that the communists managed to run over Dr Mookerjee with a tramcar. Doubtless this brought enormous relief to Nehru. Sukharanjan Sengupta, the veteran journalist, has wondered in his book if the Intelligence Bureau of the central government (presumably under Nehru's orders, maybe Mullick's pilotage) played any role in strengthening the hand of the communists in this manner.

The communists eventually installed themselves firmly in power in 1977 (before that they had two short spells of power in 1967–70) in the state to rule it continuously for thirty-four years. The total political orientation, the ethos, of the state became leftist, and the memory of Dr Mookerjee and his sacrifices was effectively all but erased among his very own people, the Bengali Hindus. Among the few who knew of him, many regarded him as a 'communal' politician who did 'divisive' and not 'inclusive' politics. In fact, it had become fashionable to call oneself 'secular' and not 'Hindu'. How could such a thing happen to a people who had suffered the worst kind of Islamic persecution, much worse than the Punjabi refugees?

To find an answer to this paradox, at a quiet, private breakfast meeting, this author had put this question to an eminent left-oriented historian of international repute, now dead. The historian is a very perceptive person, himself an upper-caste Bengali Hindu of East Bengali origin, totally opposed to the RSS and the politics of the BJP, but he has some grudging admiration for Dr Mookerjee. The reply he gave was as strange as it was eye-opening. 'Who wants to remember,' he asked in a rhetorical question, 'that his mother and sister were raped in front of his eyes and he could do nothing about it?' What emerged by way of his analysis of the paradox during the conversation that followed, is that the East Bengal refugees, in order to cleanse themselves of their angst, had rationalized their persecution and their own inaction by absolving the perpetrators of all guilt, transferring it to their ancestors (they treated the Muslims so badly) and sought refuge in being 'aggressively secular'. A kind of modified Stockholm syndrome, perhaps!

However, Syama Prasad's memory survives in his party and among some of the people.

His ideals and legacy, however, survived glowingly elsewhere in India; with the result that the BJP, successor to the Bharatiya Jana Sangh that he had founded, came to power in the central government under the stewardship of his one-time private secretary Atal Bihari Vajpayee, and became the first non-Congress government in India to last a full term between 1999 and 2004. Then in 2014 the party shot to power with a decisive majority under the leadership of Narendra Damodardas Modi, decimating Nehru's Congress to a miserable forty-four seats.

His party has kept up, subject to compulsions of coalition politics, its struggle for abrogation of Article 370 of the Constitution. It has also actively kept alive the memory of his struggle for the integration of Jammu and Kashmir. His *balidaan*, sacrifice, has not gone in vain. True sacrifices never do.

Epilogue

As said earlier, none of Syama Prasad's children or further descendants have showed the slightest predilection for either politics or education, or even law, all of which were Syama Prasad's forte; or for that matter, for public life in any form. Still, after reading a biography, some curiosity always lingers in the reader's mind as to what happened to the succeeding generations (see Genealogical Table).

Syama Prasad and his wife, Sudha Devi, had five children, of whom the youngest, a boy, died in his infancy from diphtheria. Sudha Devi died soon thereafter, leaving the children to an infernally busy father who chose not to remarry for their sakes. Tara Devi, wife of his elder brother Rama Prasad, brought them up with all the care of a mother. The eldest among them, Anutosh (Santu), married the daughter of the construction magnate Shib Banerjee, and with his help set up his own business. His wife also died at a young age while undergoing an operation. He had two sons, Subha Prasad and Soura Prasad, and two daughters, Supriya and Sharmila. Subha Prasad is an industrialist and lives in New Alipore, Kolkata. His son, Agrotosh, the latest in the direct male line, lives in London and works as an actuary. Soura Prasad also moved to the United Kingdom, but his whereabouts are not known at present.

The younger son, Debtosh (Ontu), had moved to Germany and married and divorced there. His daughter, Mita, still lives somewhere in Germany. Both Anutosh and Debtosh are now dead.

Of the daughters, the elder Sabita (Bua) had been married to Nishith Banerjee, an engineering executive who worked with Tata Engineering and Locomotive Co. Ltd (now known as Tata Motors Ltd) in Jamshedpur and Guest Keen Williams Ltd, Kolkata. They had built a house in Parnasree, Behala, Kolkata, but later moved to Pune, Maharashtra, next to her daughter, Manju, and her husband, Biman Mookerji. Sabita died during the writing of this book, but this author had an opportunity to interview her about a year before that. Sabita's son, Anup, lives in Chicago, USA. The younger daughter Arati (Hasi) married Paresh Bhattacharji, a civil engineer, who moved to the USA. He worked in Puerto Rico for some time, and then for the New York City Planning Commission. Arati died in 2013 in New York. Her only son, Sandip, is a lawyer with a New York firm.

The Mookerjee house that Sir Asutosh built at 77 Asutosh Mookerjee Road stands to this day, and houses a number of public institutions associated with Sir Asutosh and his progeny. The Ganga Prasad House at Madhupur, of which Syama Prasad was so fond, had fallen into disuse and was getting encroached upon. It was eventually sold off and dismantled by its new owners. Only a plaque stands at the site to commemorate its days of glory. The Puri house was passed on to one of his successors who dismantled it and built a hotel there.

Notes

Introduction

1. The details of these books, and more, are in the Bibliography appended to this book.

Chapter 1: Ancestry and Early Life

1. The ceremonial wearing of this thread marks the second birth of a Brahmin boy. It is for this reason that Brahmins are known as *dwija*, which means twice-born.
2. Nikhilesh, Guha, *Dr Syama Prasad Mookerjee in the Eyes of His Contemporaries* (Kolkata: Asutosh Mookerjee Memorial Institute), p. 149.
3. A Bengali Muslim of humble origin, often a convert from a lower-caste Hindu or Buddhist, as distinguished from Ashraf, a high-born one, the ones who claim Turkish, Afghan, Persian or Arab ancestry.
4. Uma Prasad Mookerjee, ed., *Syamaprasader Diary o Mrityu Prosongo* (Kolkata: Mitra & Ghosh, 1988), pp. 51.
5. Syama Prasad Mookerjee, *Leaves from a Diary* (New Delhi: Oxford University Press, 2000), p. xviii.
6. Ibid., pp. 165–66.

7. *Sakta* is derived from Shakti, another name of Goddess Kali, the Hindu deity most commonly worshipped in Bengal. *Padavali* means a set of verses.

8. Ram Prasad Sen was a poet and composer of *Shyama Sangeet*, a variety of Bengali lyric worshipping the Goddess Kali.

9. Guha, *Dr Syama Prasad Mookerjee*, p. 150.

Chapter 2: Student Days and a Short Married Life, 1906–33

1. *Kishore Maitri* (Kolkata: Mitra Institution Bhawanipur Branch and Asutosh Mookerjee Memorial Institute, 2001), p. 81.

2. Uma Prasad Mookerjee, ed., *Syamaprasader Diary o Mrityu Prosongo* (Kolkata: Mitra & Ghosh, 1988), p. 5.

3. Sen (1890–1959) initially taught at the University of Calcutta. In 1939, he was appointed the keeper of Imperial Records (which later became the National Archives). In 1949, he resigned from that post and became a professor at the University of Delhi. He is the author of several major works, mostly on the history of the Marathas. In 1956, the Indian government commissioned him to write a history of the First War of Independence of 1857–59. The work, titled *Eighteen Fifty-Seven*, was published in 1957.

4. Purnendu Banerjee (1917–2000) was the eldest son of Syama Prasad's second sister, Amala and her husband Pramatha Nath Banerjee, an educationist and minister (for some time) in Fazlul Haq's cabinet. Purnendu later joined the Indian Foreign Service and served, among other positions, as the permanent representative of India at the United Nations.

5. Anil Chandra Banerjee, *A Phase in the Life of Dr Syama Prasad Mookerjee, 1937–46* (Kolkata: Asutosh Mookerjee Memorial Institute, 2000), p. 121.

6. Syama Prasad Mookerjee, *Leaves from a Diary* (New Delhi: Oxford University Press, 2000), p. 213.

7. Tara Devi was the daughter of Lalit Mohan Chatterjee and a descendant of the great Sanskrit scholars Madan Mohan Tarkalankar and Jogendra Nath Vidyabhushan. She was also the first cousin of Jatindra Nath Mukherjee (Bagha Jatin), mentioned earlier in this chapter, and an aunt of Soumitra Chatterjee, the Bengali film star.

8. Mookerjee, ed., *Syamaprasader Diary o Mrityu Prosongo*, pp. 14–15.

9. Sarvepalli Gopal, *Radhakrishnan, A Biography* (New Delhi: Oxford University Press, 1989), p. 183.

Chapter 3: University Years, 1924–38

1. Uma Prasad Mookerjee, ed., *Syamaprasader Diary o Mrityu Prosongo* (Kolkata: Mitra & Ghosh, 1988), p. 15.

2. Acharya Prafulla Chandra Ray (1861–1944) was a famous academician and chemist and the Palit professor of chemistry in the university. He was also a great enthusiast with regard to nurturing entrepreneurship among Bengalis, founded Bengal Chemical and Pharmaceutical Works, probably the very first pharma company of India, and was a pioneer in many fields of applied chemistry. He was totally dedicated to academics and his students, and died a bachelor. He donated all his life's earnings to charity. *Bap ka beta*, an expression in Hindi, means 'worthy son of a worthy father'. The title 'Acharya' (meaning 'a very learned man') is an unofficial and informal one conferred upon him.

3. Dinesh Chandra Sinha, Letter dated 6 February 1925, in *Shotoborsher Aloy Syamaprasad* (Kolkata: Srishti Prakashan, 2002), p. 38.

4. Mookerjee, ed., *Syamaprasader Diary o Mrityu Prosongo*, p. 17.

5. *Kishore Maitri* (Kolkata: Mitra Institution Bhawanipur Branch and Asutosh Mookerjee Memorial Institute, 2001), p. 219.

6. Reena Bhaduri, ed., *Syama Prasad Mookerjee, Educational Speeches*, 2nd ed. (Kolkata: A. Mukherjee & Co., 2016), p. 110.
7. Dinesh Chandra Sinha, 'Shikshachintar Onyotom Ogropothik Syamaprasad', *Desh*, 4 July 2001, p. 25.
8. Bhaduri, ed., *Syama Prasad Mookerjee, Educational Speeches*, p. 44.
9. *Kishore Maitri*, p. 223.
10. In fact, the national anthem of Sri Lanka, 'Namo Sri Lanka Matha', written by Ananda Samarakoon, a disciple of Tagore at Visva-Bharati, was also inspired and influenced by Tagore.
11. Helen M. Nugent, 'The Communal Award: The Process of Decision-Making', *South Asia: Journal of South Asian Studies* 2 (1979): pp. 112–29.

Chapter 4: Entry into Politics, 1939–41

1. Syama Prasad Mookerjee, *Leaves from a Diary* (New Delhi: Oxford University Press, 2000), Entries dated 21 October 1944; 6 December 1945, pp. 38, 45–46.
2. 'How can an organization [the Congress] which subsists on Hindu support but considers it a sin to think or speak on behalf of Hindus contend with another [Muslim League] whose sole purpose is to establish Muslim domination, carry forward the Islamic flag?' Freely translated from Umaprasad Mookerjee, ed., *Syamaprasader Diary o Mrityu Prosongo* (Kolkata: Mitra & Ghosh, 2001), p. 58.
3. Amales Tripathi, *Swadhinatar Mukh* (Kolkata: Ananda Publishers, 1998), pp. 64, 112; V.P. Menon, *The Transfer of Power in India* (Chennai: Orient Longman, 1957), p. 49.
4. Prominent Indo-Anglian author of the celebrated books *Autobiography of an Unknown Indian, The Continent of Circe and Thy Hand, Great Anarch*, Nirad C. Chaudhuri at the

time was the secretary to Sarat Chandra Bose, the provincial Congress president and Netaji Subhas Chandra Bose's elder brother, and had the opportunity to observe the political goings-on in the province at close range.

5. Anil Chandra Banerjee, *A Phase in the Life of Dr Syama Prasad Mookerjee, 1937–46*, pp. 29–33.

6. Ibid. Also Nirad C. Chaudhuri, *Thy Hand, Great Anarch* (London: Chatto & Windus, 1987).

7. Ibid. pp. 29–30.

8. Leonard A. Gordon, *Brothers against the Raj: A Biography of Indian Nationalists Sarat and Subhas Chandra Bose* (New Delhi: Rupa, 1997), p. 394.

9. The letters stood for Indian Civil Service which, together with the IP (Imperial Police), constituted the 'steel frame' of British administration in India. It was a cadre of very highly paid and highly trusted bureaucrats, about half of whom were British and the other half Indian.

10. Proceedings of the Bengal Legislative Assembly, LIII, No. 2, 10 August 1938, p. 99, quoted by Gordon, *Brothers against the Raj*, p. 365.

11. Balraj Madhok, *Portrait of a Martyr: A Biography of Dr. Shyama Prasad Mookerji* (New Delhi: Rupa, 2001), p. 26.

12. This thesis postulated that India is not one nationality but a conglomeration of some eighteen nationalities, and each one of them had the inherent right to secede. Based on this thesis, the communists extended their full-throated support to the Pakistan demand of the Muslim League, presumably in the hope that they would blossom in Muslim Pakistan, a chance that Hindu India had denied them. Their hope was belied and practically all of them had to leave East and West Pakistan.

13. The Poona Pact (1932) was an agreement signed at the Yeravada Jail, Poona (now Pune), between Gandhi and Ambedkar,

whereby the scheduled castes (then called depressed classes) were given reservation with regard to seats in the legislature.

14. The leader of this group, Jogendra Nath Mandal, joined the Muslim League and became the central minister for law and labour in Pakistan after Independence. However, after the government-engineered anti-Hindu pogrom of 1950 in East Pakistan, he protested and was threatened with imprisonment by Liaquat Ali Khan, the Prime Minister. He managed to escape to India with Dr Mookerjee's assistance and sent his resignation from India.

15. Balraj Madhok (1920–2016) was born in Skardu, Baltistan, Pakistan-Occupied Kashmir. He joined the Rashtriya Swayamsevak Sangh in 1938, and became a pracharak (full-time worker) in 1942. In 1951, he joined Dr Syama Prasad Mookerjee in the formation of the Bharatiya Jana Sangh, and remained a trusted lieutenant of him. In 1966–67, he rose to become the president of the Jana Sangh. When the Jana Sangh merged with the Janata Party he left it for ideological reasons and unsuccessfully tried to revive the Jana Sangh.

16. The Congress and the Muslim League (presided over by Jinnah) fought the 1937 elections to the United Provinces assembly on the basis of 'independent cooperation'. However, the Congress, after winning an absolute majority, refused to form a coalition with the League. It has been commented that this one action 'revived simmering Muslim suspicions of Hindu absorptive tendencies', and paved the way for Pakistan. See Mookerjee, *Leaves from a Diary*, p. 38.

17. Mookerjee, *Leaves from a Diary*, p. 45.

18. Ibid., p. 100.

19. Dr Mookerjee's statement in Parliament following his resignation from the Union Cabinet, 19 April 1950.

20. Mookerjee, *Leaves from a Diary*, p. 43.

Chapter 5: Finance Minister of Bengal, 1941–42

1. Syama Prasad Mookerjee, *Leaves from a Diary* (New Delhi: Oxford University Press, 2000), p. 45.
2. The principal scheduled castes in undivided Bengal were the Rajbangshis in north Bengal and Namasudras in south and east Bengal.
3. Mookerjee, *Leaves from a Diary*, p. 55.
4. Abul Mansur Ahmad, from Mymensingh, was a prominent anti-League Muslim leader of Bengal during the fateful days of undivided Bengal and post-partition East Pakistan. He was also a close associate of Fazlul Haq. He rose to become a cabinet minister in Pakistan's central cabinet under Suhrawardy. His autobiography, *Amar Dekha Rajneetir Ponchas Bochhor* (in Bengali, meaning Fifty Years of Politics as I Have Seen It) is a storehouse of information on the times, of course from his point of view.
5. Mookerjee, *Leaves from a Diary*, p. 58.
6. Ibid., p. 57.
7. Anil Chandra Banerjee, *A Phase in the Life of Dr Syama Prasad Mookerjee, 1937–46* (Kolkata: Asutosh Mookerjee Memorial Institute, 2000), pp. 102–20.
8. Banerjee, *A Phase in the Life of Dr Syama Prasad Mookerjee,* p. 110.
9. Banerjee, *A Phase in the Life of Dr Syama Prasad Mookerjee,* p. 122.

Chapter 6: The Great Bengal Famine, 1942–43

1. Calcutta's main business district, now called Netaji Subhas Road.
2. Anil Chandra Banerjee, *A Phase in the Life of Dr Syama Prasad Mookerjee, 1937–46* (Kolkata: Asutosh Mookerjee Memorial Institute, 2000), p. 137.

3. Ibid., p. 106.

4. Ashok Mitra, *Tin Kuri Dosh* (Kolkata: Dey's Publishing, 1988), the autobiography of Ashok Mitra of the ICS, later census commissioner of India.

5. Not to be confused with the economist Ashok Mitra, sometime finance minister of West Bengal in the Left Front government, rendered famous by his statement, 'I am not a gentleman. I am a communist.'

6. A *taktaposh* is a Spartan bedstead, consisting of a few cheap hardwood planks nailed together to form a horizontal surface, supported on four wooden posts nailed to them. It was the custom in Bengal to store luggage, non-perishable foodstuff and the like below such taktaposhes.

7. Syama Prasad Mookerjee, *Rashtrasangram o Ponchasher Manwantar* (Kolkata: Mitra & Ghosh, 1998), p. 14.

8. Ibid., p. 16.

9. Ibid., p. 91.

10. *Phan* is the supernatant starchy liquid left after rice has been boiled in an open container. It is usually thrown away. Nowadays rice is often boiled in pressure cookers which does not produce phan.

Chapter 7: Difficult Years, 1944–46

1. Syama Prasad Mookerjee, *Awake Hindusthan* (New Delhi: Dr Syama Prasad Mookerjee Research Foundation, 2009), pp. 153–55.

2. Prashanto Kumar Chatterji, *Dr Syama Prasad Mookerjee and Indian Politics* (New Delhi: Cambridge University Press, 2010), p. 137.

3. Vasant Moon, *Dr Babasaheb Ambedkar*, trans. Asha Damle (New Delhi: National Book Trust, 2009), p. 153.

4. Chatterji, *Dr Syama Prasad Mookerjee and Indian Politics*, p. 139.

5. Syama Prasad Mookerjee, *Leaves from a Diary* (New Delhi: Oxford University Press, 2000), p. 77. This, in fact, proved prophetic because Gandhi's ill-advised (by Rajagopalachari) overture to Jinnah later in September 1944 resulted in exactly this, when the staunch anti-League Muslim leaders were forced to join the League, and the Muslims of India, almost to a man, became supporters of the League. Also see Mushirul Hasan, *India's Partition: Process, Strategy, Mobilization* (New Delhi: Oxford University Press, 1994), p. 15: 'The person who consistently opposed the mixing of religion with politics . . . remained on the fringes of Indian politics during the massive pan-Islamic upsurge of the early 1920s, was now prepared to press the *ulama* into service.'

6. Anil Chandra Banerjee, *A Phase in the Life of Dr Syama Prasad Mookerjee, 1937–46* (Kolkata: Asutosh Mookerjee Memorial Institute, 2000), pp. 64–65.

7. Nikhil Chakravartti later chose journalism over politics, and edited a leftist journal called *Mainstream*. His wife, Renu, incidentally a niece of Dr Bidhan Chandra Roy, was, however, a Member of Parliament from the undivided Communist Party of India. This association reveals the extent to which the communists were in collusion with the Muslim League. See Sunanda Sanyal et al., *The Sickle and the Crescent*, mentioned in the Bibliography. Abul Hashim later became famous for his co-authorship, with Sarat Bose, of the (thankfully) abortive scheme for united independent sovereign Bengal, which is discussed in depth in Chapter 8.

8. Uma Prasad Mookerjee, ed., *Syamaprasader Diary o Mrityu Prosongo* (Kolkata: Mitra & Ghosh, 1988), p. 46.

9. Ibid.

10. Dr Radha Binod Pal was a jurist of international repute and a member of the Tokyo Tribunal for the trial of Japanese war criminals in World War II. He took a dissenting view, holding

that it is the victors who decide what is right and what is not. He is highly regarded in Japan for this view.

11. Dr Bidhan Chandra (B.C.) Roy became the Chief Minister of West Bengal shortly after Independence (1948) and continued till his death in 1962. He was also a legendary physician and was said to possess extra-sensory powers of diagnosis. He was active in Congress politics before Independence. He is highly respected for his efforts to rebuild West Bengal after a traumatic partition, and particularly for his efforts in rehabilitating Hindu refugees from Islamic persecution in East Pakistan.

Chapter 8: The Great Calcutta Killings and the Noakhali Carnage, 1946

1. Bidyut Chakrabarty, *The Partition of Bengal and Assam, 1932–47* (London: RoutledgeCurzon, 2004), p. 99; Bhabani Prasad Chatterjee, *Deshbibhag: Poshchat o Nepothyo Kahini* (Kolkata: Ananda Publishers, 1993), p. 86.

2. Leonard A. Gordon, *Brothers against the Raj: A Biography of Indian Nationalists Sarat and Subhas Chandra Bose* (New Delhi: Rupa, 1997), p. 566, quoting a sociology PhD dissertation by Richard D. Lambert, University of Pennsylvania, 1951.

3. Mizanur Rahman, *Krishna Sholoi* (Dhaka: Sahana, 2000).

4. Amales Tripathi, *Swadhinatar Mukh* (Kolkata: Ananda Publishers, 1998), pp. 86, 185.

5. Chakrabarty, *The Partition of Bengal and Assam*, p. 259, n. 29.

6. Partha Chatterjee, *The Present History of West Bengal, Essays in Political Criticism* (New Delhi: Oxford University Press, 1998), p. 35. For a different view on this, see Joya Chatterji, *Bengal Divided: Hindu Communalism and Partition, 1932–47* (New Delhi: Cambridge University Press, 1995).

7. Abul Mansur Ahmad, *Amar Dekha Rajneetir Ponchas Bochhor* (Dhaka: Khosroz Kitab Mahal, 1999), p. 196.

8. Maulana Abul Kalam Azad, *India Wins Freedom (Complete Version)* (Hyderabad: Orient Longman, 1988), p. 170.

9. Spoken to J.B. Kripalani, Congress president and husband of Sucheta, who played an outstanding role in arranging relief to the victims of the pogrom. Kripalani says he felt like hitting Burrows, but restrained himself. See D.P. Mishra, *India's March to Freedom* (New Delhi: Har-Anand Publications, 2001), p. 566.

10. Dinesh Chandra Sinha, *Noakhalir Mati o Manush* (Kolkata: Gyan Prakashan, 1992), pp. 95–96.

11. Louis Fischer, *The Life of Mahatma Gandhi* (New York: Harper and Row, 1983), p. 450.

12. Syama Prasad Mookerjee, *Leaves from a Diary* (New Delhi: Oxford University Press, 2000), p. 226.

13. The St Bartholomew's Day massacre was a targeted set of assassinations in France in 1572 of Protestant Huguenots by Catholics. Estimates of deaths in the massacre vary from 10,000 to 70,000.

14. Sinha, *Noakhalir Mati o Manush*, p. 122.

15. A custom prevailing in Hindu society at the time was that anyone who converted out of Hinduism, even if he was forced to do so, could come back to the fold by doing prayashchitta. This involved observing certain expensive rituals, such as yajna and the like. Return to Hinduism is today actively administered by several organizations, among them the Arya Samaj and the Vishva Hindu Parishad.

16. Ashok Dasgupta and Dinesh Chandra Sinha, *The Great Calcutta Killings and the Noakhali Genocide* (Kolkata: Tuhina Prakashani, 2013), pp. 247–49.

17. Fischer, *The Life of Mahatma Gandhi*, pp. 451, 454.

18. Ram Manohar Lohia, *Guilty Men of India's Partition* (New Delhi: Rupa, 2009), p. 22.

19. Ibid., p. 23.

20. Larry Collins and Dominique Lapierre, *Freedom at Midnight* (New Delhi: Vikas Publishing House, 1976), p. 120.

Chapter 9: The Architect of West Bengal, 1947

1. R.C. Majumdar, *The History and Culture of the Indian People, Vol. XI, Struggle for Freedom*, general ed., (Mumbai: Bharatiya Vidya Bhavan, 1988), p. 606.

2. Benami means a system of ownership of property in India whereby the real owner is different from the ostensible owner (*benamdar*). The system was lawful in India at that time, but has now been abolished.

3. The only Indian member of the House of Lords then.

4. An outstanding historian.

5. Eminent philologist, later a national professor of humanities.

6. A prominent member of the Bengal Congress from the Marwari community.

7. A father figure among journalists in Bengal.

8. Prashanto Kumar Chatterji, *Dr Syama Prasad Mookerjee and Indian Politics* (New Delhi: Cambridge University Press, 2010), p. 196.

9. *Amrita Bazar Patrika*, 23 April 1947.

10. Amales Tripathi, *Swadhinatar Mukh* (Kolkata: Ananda Publishers), pp. 86, 185; Bidyut Chakrabarty, *The Partition of Bengal and Assam 1932–47* (London: RoutledgeCurzon, 2004), p. 259, n. 29; Partha Chatterjee, *The Present History of West Bengal, Essays in Political Criticism* (New Delhi, Oxford University Press, 1998), p. 35.

11. The acronym EBDO stood for Elected Bodies Disqualification Order, a promulgation by Field Marshal Ayub Khan in 1958 after he usurped power over Pakistan in a coup in 1958, clamped martial law on the country, and abolished all elected bodies and replaced them with military administrators.

Chapter 10: Central Minister of Industry and Supply, 1947–50

1. Earl Attlee, Prime Minister of Britain when India got her freedom, had occasion to visit Calcutta in 1953, and stayed at the Raj Bhavan (Governor's residence). P.B. Chakravartty, chief justice of the Calcutta High Court, was then the acting Governor. He asked Attlee, among other things, about the extent to which Gandhi's Non-cooperation movement and Quit India movement had been instrumental in ending British rule. Attlee is said to have replied, with his pipe clenched between his teeth, 'm-i-n-i-m-a-l'. It is widely held that the formation of the INA and the Naval Mutiny of 1946, which destroyed British confidence in the loyalty of their Indian troops, were what finally caused them to pack their bags and go. Gandhi's movement was certainly one of the factors, however 'minimal'.

2. Balraj Madhok, *Portrait of a Martyr: A Biography of Dr. Shyama Prasad Mookerji* (Mumbai: Jaico Publishing House, 1969), p. 70.

3. The RSS, founded in 1925 by Dr K.B. Hedgewar and nurtured to its great strength by his successor M.S. Golwalkar, is a regimented organization admired and maligned with equal intensity, depending on which side of the 'secular' divide one is on. Its declared objective is to unify and organize Hindus irrespective of their caste or language, and build men of character (*manushya-nirman*, as they themselves describe it). The central government had banned it three times—in 1948, following Gandhi's assassination, in 1975 during Indira Gandhi's infamous Emergency and in 1992, following the demolition of the disputed shrine at Ayodhya. Each time the government has found the ban unjustified and has been forced to withdraw the same. A common mistake is to confuse it with the Hindu Mahasabha; the two are organizationally unconnected.

4. Of course the ordnance factories were there, but they were
   defence-oriented and purely government-run, and Sindri
   Fertilizer and subsequent industries were envisaged to be
   differently constituted in order to free them of bureaucratic
   red tape. It is here that Dr Mookerjee showed considerable
   innovation. However, subsequent experience showed that red
   tape had returned by the back door to haunt these industries.
5. *Constituent Assembly Debates, Book No. 4* (New Delhi: Lok
   Sabha Secretariat, Reprinted 2014), p. 1391.

Chapter 11: The Pogrom in East Bengal and Resignation from Cabinet, 1950

1. It is important to understand that this was not a riot, but
   a pogrom, a one-sided looting, raping and killing spree.
   The word 'pogrom', assimilated from Russian into English,
   originally meant the organized massacre of Jews, as was
   practised in Russia and parts of Eastern Europe, and is now
   applied to any such massacre.
2. Michael Brecher in *Nehru: A Political Biography* (New Delhi:
   Oxford University Press, 2011), pp. 427–29, 429n, writes:
   'Statistics on the Bengal migration of 1950 must be viewed with
   caution, for both parties were anxious to place the responsibility
   on their neighbour . . . Here seemed to be an ideal opportunity
   to "avenge the wrong" of 1947. Within the central cabinet
   this extremist view had powerful support, not only from self-
   proclaimed communalists like Dr S.P. Mookerjee, but also from
   the Sardar . . . Within a few months [of the Pact] the flood of
   refugees subsided and many returned to their homes.' Later in a
   note: 'Dr Mookerjee was the most forceful spokesman for Hindu
   communalism in recent Indian politics . . . While on one of his
   visits to Kashmir in *1954* he was taken seriously ill and died *before
   he could be brought to Delhi* [emphasis added in both].' The gross

factual inaccuracy, not to speak of bias, is palpable and is further brought home by incidents like the Santahar massacre and similar incidents. For a detailed treatment of the situation in East Bengal post Delhi Pact, the reader is referred to the author's *My People, Uprooted: The Exodus of Hindus from East Pakistan and Bangladesh* (New Delhi: Synergy Books India, 2016), pp. 255–67.

3. Prabhas Chandra Lahiri, *Pak-Bharater Ruprekha* (Chakdaha [Distt Nadia, West Bengal]: Shyama Prakashani), p. 202; Sukharanjan Sengupta, *Bongosonghar Ebong* (Kolkata: Naya Udyog, 2002), p. 149; Sandip Banerjee, *Deshbhag, Deshtyag* (Kolkata: Anushtup, 1994), p. 66; Roy, *My People, Uprooted,* p. 222.

4. Eyewitness interviews, Ranjit Kar, 1999; Shyamalesh Das, 1999; Ramendra Lal Basu, 1998; Dinesh Chandra Sinha, *Roktoronjito Dhaka-Barisal Ebong* (Kolkata: Codex, 2012); Roy, *My People, Uprooted,* p. 222; Sukharanjan Sengupta, *Bongosonghar Ebong* (Kolkata: Naya Udyog, 2002), p. 153.

5. A.J. Kamra, *The Prolonged Partition and Its Pogroms* (New Delhi: Voice of India, 2000), p. 63; Roy, *My People, Uprooted,* p. 218.

6. This is adequately explained in the seminal work by Jayanta Kumar Ray, *Democracy and Nationalism on Trial: A Study of East Pakistan* (Simla: Institute of Advanced Studies, 1968), pp. 25–28, 32, 151. Also see Prashanto Kumar Chatterji, *Dr Syama Prasad Mookerjee and Indian Politics* (New Delhi: Foundation Books/Cambridge University Press, 2010), p. 252; Lahiri, *Pak-Bharater Ruprekha,* p. 148.

7. Jawaharlal Nehru, *Jawaharlal Nehru's Speeches Volume 2* (New Delhi: Publications Division, 1963), p. 135.

8. Ibid.

9. The year of publication of his seminal work *Democracy and Nationalism on Trial: A Study of East Pakistan.*

10. See note 6 above.

11. A scheduled caste leader from Barisal in East Bengal, Jogendra
    Nath Mandal (1906–56) had joined the Muslim League, and
    had been used by the party to whitewash their misdeeds as
    to the persecution of Hindus. However, the 1950 pogrom,
    when no less than 10,000 Hindus had been killed in his own
    district of Barisal, proved to be too much even for him. He
    had drawn Liaquat Ali's attention to it, whereupon Liaquat
    first said he was exaggerating and then threatened to throw
    him in jail. Mandal subsequently escaped to West Bengal and
    sent his resignation from there.

12. Nehru, *Jawaharlal Nehru's Speeches Volume 2*, pp. 137, 142.

13. Ibid., p. 144.

14. Sukharanjan Sengupta, 'Ponchasher Danga: Shyamaprasad
    Keno Podotyag Korechhilen', in *Shotoborsher Aloy Syama
    Prasad* (Kolkata: Srishti Prakashan, 2002), p. 119; Sengupta,
    Bongosonghar Ebong, p. 162.

15. Louis Fischer, *The Life of Mahatma Gandhi* (New York:
    Harper and Row, 1983), p. 401.

16. Binoy Mukhopadhyay (1909–2003) is in fact quite well known
    in contemporary Bengali literature by his pseudonym Jajabor
    (meaning 'nomad' in Bengali). As press adviser he had access to
    information relating to all the goings-on in official circles during
    the tumultuous years immediately preceding and following
    the independence of the country. As such all his observations
    are authentic and very valuable. His interview appeared in the
    24 April 1993 issue of *Desh,* an ABP publication.

17. Binoy Mukhopadhyay (Jajabor), Interview in Bengali
    fortnightly *Desh* to Niladri Chaki, 24 April 1993, pp. 51–66.

18. Durga Das, *India from Curzon to Nehru and After* (New
    Delhi: Rupa, 2009), p. 384.

19. Pandit Lakshmi Kanta Maitra (1895–1953) was a Congress
    member of the Central Legislative Assembly from 1934
    onwards, a member of the Constituent Assembly and a

follower of Patel, but had enormous admiration for Syama Prasad Mookerjee. His relation with Nehru, though, was always lukewarm. He used to say that Syama Prasad was a man with a heart like an ocean. He was so fond of the man that struck by grief he literally fell ill at the sight of Syama Prasad's dead body in Calcutta, and died within a month. However, his son Kashi Kanta Maitra, a minister (1972–77) in the West Bengal government and an advocate, was unable to confirm if he had a discussion with Syama Prasad before his speech, though he said that it was fairly probable.

20. *Parliamentary Debates, Part II, Volume I to IV, 1950, 17 March*, p. 1704.
21. Ibid., p. 1726.
22. Ibid., p. 1727.
23. Ibid., p. 1741.
24. This daily, of the Anandabazar Patrika group of Calcutta, has since ceased publication.
25. Chatterji, *Dr Syama Prasad Mookerjee and Indian Politics*, p. 204.
26. *Parliamentary Debates, Part II, Volume I to IV, 1950, 19 April*, pp. 3017–22; *Syama Prasad Mookerjee Papers* (New Delhi: Nehru Memorial Museum and Library), Instalment 1(c), Sl. No. 3, pp. 1–13; Balraj Madhok, *Portrait of a Martyr: A Biography of Dr. Shyama Prasad Mookerji* (Mumbai: Jaico Publishing House, 1969), pp. 103, 107–13; Roy, *My People, Uprooted*, pp. 493–503.
27. Binoy Mukhopadhyay (Jajabor), Interview in Bengali fortnightly *Desh* to Niladri Chaki, 24 April 1993, pp. 51–66.
28. There has been such a concerted effort to obfuscate the exodus of Hindus from East Bengal that no official statistics are available on this movement in which people in excess of one crore (10 million) were displaced, some 50,000 murdered, countless women brutalized or kidnapped and thousands forcibly converted. However, this author has tried to collate statistics available from

census and other data in order to extract approximate figures. See Roy, *My People, Uprooted*, pp. 240–43, 465–69.

Chapter 12: The Bharatiya Jana Sangh Is Born, 1951

1. *Syama Prasad Mookerjee Papers* (New Delhi: Nehru Memorial Museum and Library), Instalment 1(c), Sl. No. 4, pp. 1–13; Prashanto Kumar Chatterji, *Dr Syama Prasad Mookerjee and Indian Politics* (New Delhi: Cambridge University Press, 2010), p. 270.
2. Anil Chandra Banerjee, *A Phase in the Life of Dr Syama Prasad Mookerjee, 1937–46* (Kolkata: Asutosh Mookerjee Memorial Institute, 2000), pp. 64–65.
3. Madhya Bharat (different from present-day Madhya Pradesh) was an erstwhile Part 'B' state consisting of several former princely states such as Bhopal, Indore and Gwalior. The Constitution in 1950 created four kinds of states—Part 'A' states consisting of former provinces of British India, such as West Bengal, Bombay, or UP; Part 'B' states which were either single former princely states, such as Hyderabad or Mysore, or were a combination of such states, such as Rajasthan or Madhya Bharat; Part 'C' states which were small princely states such as Ajmer or Coorg; and Part 'D' states, small centrally administered units such as Andaman and Nicobar Islands. All these distinctions were abolished by the States Reorganization of 1957.
4. Pracharaks in the RSS are full-timers (all male) who devote themselves to RSS work, do not marry and are taken care of by the organization. However, some of them do go back home after a few years and marry. The topmost posts in the organization are manned by people from among those who stay on for their lives.

5. The Hindi weekly *Panchjanya* was launched in Lucknow under the auspices of the Rashtra Dharma Prakashan on Makara Sankranti day, 14 January 1948, and is, to use the popular line, still going strong. The first editor was Atal Bihari Vajpayee, but it was Pandit Deen Dayal Upadhyaya who took upon himself the role of an editor, proofreader, compositor, binder and printer. The article in question appeared in the 26 June 1956 issue of the weekly.

6. Chatterji, *Dr Syama Prasad Mookerjee and Indian Politics,* p. 301.

7. Balraj Madhok, *Portrait of a Martyr: A Biography of Dr. Shyama Prasad Mookerji* (Mumbai: Jaico Publishing House, 1969), p. 109.

8. Ibid., p. 110.

9. The Bengali word for 'lamp', the symbol of the new party. Dr Mookerjee, in spite of his advocacy of Hindi, was weak in the language which is why he did not use its Hindi word 'deepak'.

10. In front of Gurdwara Sis Ganj, in Old Delhi. The grounds have shrunk considerably now in making way for parking lots and other facilities.

11. Madhok, *Portrait of a Martyr,* p. 110.

Chapter 13: Party President and Parliamentarian, 1951–53

1. Interview of Balraj Madhok, New Delhi, 2009. Also see Balraj Madhok, *Portrait of a Martyr: A Biography of Dr. Shyama Prasad Mookerji* (Mumbai: Jaico Publishing House, 1969), p. 112.

2. For an exposé of the depths to which some of these so-called 'historians' had descended to curry favour with the ruling elite of India, read Arun Shourie's *Eminent Historians: Their Technology, Their Line, Their Fraud* mentioned in the Bibliography.

3. Madhok, *Portrait of a Martyr,* p. 118.

4. The author has heard this from his father who was a voter in south Kolkata in 1952. The author, incidentally, has lived almost all his life in south Kolkata.

5. *Dr Syama Prasad Mookerjee*, Eminent Parliamentarians Monograph Series (New Delhi: Lok Sabha Secretariat, 1990), p. 24.

6. *Parliamentary Debates, Part II, 28 March 1951*, pp. 5273–80.

7. *Parliamentary Debates, Part II, 17 September 1951*, pp. 2705–24; *Dr Syama Prasad Mookerjee*, Eminent Parliamentarians Monograph Series, pp. 82–98.

8. Madhok, *Portrait of a Martyr*, p. 132.

9. Madhok has also remarked, 'Nehru had developed a Fascist tendency to intolerance and also an exaggerated sense of self-righteousness. This tendency in him had become very marked since the death of Sardar Patel.' See ibid., p. 129.

10. Madhok, *Portrait of a Martyr*, p. 133.

11. Ibid., p. 135.

12. *Parliamentary Debates, Part II, Vol. 6, 18 December 1952*, pp. 2657–73.

13. *Parliamentary Debates, Part II, 9–22 July and 30 July–2 August 1952*, pp. 3445–4422, 5200–5764.

14. *Parliamentary Debates, Part II, 2 August 1952*, p. 5210; Madhok, *Portrait of a Martyr*, p. 136.

15. Madhok, *Portrait of a Martyr*, p. 139.

16. *Parliamentary Debates, Part II, 7 August 1952*, pp. 5885–99; *Dr Syama Prasad Mookerjee*, Eminent Parliamentarians Monograph Series, pp. 109–23.

Chapter 14: Praja Parishad's Jammu Agitation, 1952–53

1. Interview with Madhok, New Delhi, 28 August 2008.

2. *Parliamentary Debates, Part II, 7 August 1952*, pp. 5885–99; *Dr Syama Prasad Mookerjee*, Eminent Parliamentarians

Monograph Series (New Delhi: Lok Sabha Secretariat, 1990), pp. 109–23 at p. 114; Balraj Madhok, *Portrait of a Martyr: A Biography of Dr. Shyama Prasad Mookerji* (Mumbai: Jaico Publishing House, 1969), p. 150.

3. Madhok, *Portrait of a Martyr*, p. 150.
4. Mehr Chand Mahajan was subsequently appointed as a judge of the newly formed Supreme Court and rose to become the third Chief Justice of India.
5. Madhok, *Portrait of a Martyr*, p. 159.
6. Ibid., p. 146.
7. Satyagraha literally means 'quest for truth', and had been popularized by Gandhi as a non-violent means of agitation. It encompasses non-violent dharna (sit-in), processions, courting arrest, demonstrations, etc. Dr Mookerjee, as a constitutional politician, was generally opposed to these means, except as a last resort.
8. Madhok, *Portrait of a Martyr*, pp. 151–52.
9. Ibid., p. 154.
10. Ibid., p. 154; Prashanto Kumar Chatterji, *Dr Syama Prasad Mookerjee and Indian Politics* (New Delhi: Cambridge University Press, 2010), p. 325.
11. The Constitution provided for Part B states which were singly Indian states before (e.g. Hyderabad, Mysore) or were a collection of substantial Indian states (e.g. Rajasthan, Saurashtra). The nominal head of the governments of these states were designated as Rajpramukh, and this post was occupied by the former ruler of the state (e.g. The Nizam, in the case of Hyderabad) in the first category of Part B states and the former ruler of one of the important states in the second category (e.g. The Maharaja of Jaipur, in the case of Rajasthan). In contrast, the head of a Part A state (a state of erstwhile British India) was designated as Rajyapal or Governor. All these distinctions were abolished after the States Reorganization of 1957. Jammu and Kashmir,

however, although earlier an Indian state, had no Rajpramukh, but the son of the former ruler was made Sadr-i-Riyasat.

12. Gerrymandering is a political term of American origin, and means cutting up electoral districts or constituencies in an odd manner to give unfair advantage to a particular political party.

13. *Parliamentary Debates, Part II, 7 August 1952*, pp. 5885–99; *Mookerjee*, Eminent Parliamentarians Monograph Series, pp. 109–23 at p. 110.

14. Madhok, *Portrait of a Martyr*, p. 160.

15. Ibid., p. 158.

16. Ibid., p. 160.

17. Reena Bhaduri, ed., *Kashmir Issue: Correspondence, Speeches and Reports, 1947–53* (Kolkata: Asutosh Mookerjee Memorial Institute, 2003), p. 90; ibid., p. 205.

18. B.N. Mullick, *My Years with Nehru: Kashmir* (New York: Allied Publishers, 1971), p. 110.

19. This had also proved contemporaneously true in respect of Potti Sreeramulu's agitation for a separate Telugu-speaking state where he had capitulated only after Sreeramulu died following his fast, and widespread violence broke out.

20. Dr Mookerjee, a staunch supporter of Hindi as he was, had problems with the language as many Bengalis do, and could never get the accent and particularly the gender right. However, he got around the problem of vocabulary by following Pandit Mauli Chandra Sharma's advice who told him to use chaste (*tatsama, or same as Sanskrit*) Bengali words and expressions whenever he could not remember an appropriate Hindi word or expression. He did it, and was perfectly understood by Hindi-speaking audiences.

21. Reena Bhaduri, ed., *Kashmir Issue*, pp. 200–01; Madhok, *Portrait of a Martyr*, p. 195.

22. Bhaduri, ed., *Kashmir Issue*, pp. 94–95.

23. After the death of Gandhi, Sardar Patel and finally Dr Mookerjee there was no one left in or out of the Parliament to speak up to Nehru. Some of his cabinet colleagues must have foreseen that his Industrial Policy Resolution of 1956 would usher in the notorious Licence-Permit Raj in India; they also must have had reservations about his neglect of agriculture and the removal of illiteracy and his emphasis on heavy industries, blindly copying the Soviet model; and also his *Hindi-Chini bhai bhai* in spite of China's cartographical aggression on India. There is, however, no such reservation on record. Even Maulana Azad, pretty much his equal, willed that the parts of his autobiography, *India Wins Freedom,* critical of Nehru should be published only thirty years after Azad's death.

24. Madhok, *Portrait of a Martyr,* p. 222.

Chapter 15: Martyrdom and Thereafter, 1953

1. Balraj Madhok, *Portrait of a Martyr: A Biography of r. Shyama Prasad Mookerji* (Mumbai: Jaico Publishing House, 1969), p. 226.
2. Walter Johnson at the time was on the faculty of Chicago University and was the co-chairman of the national committee for (Adlai) Stevenson for President. After Stevenson's defeat to Dwight D. Eisenhower, Johnson accompanied Stevenson on his world tour in 1953.
3. Madhok, *Portrait of a Martyr,* p. 228.
4. A popular newsmagazine of India belonging to the Times of India group. It ceased publication in 1993.
5. Madhok, *Portrait of a Martyr,* pp. 229–30.
6. Order dated 11 May 1953 by Prithvinandan Singh, inspector-general of police, Jammu and Kashmir, reproduced in Uma Prasad Mookerjee, ed., *Syamaprasader Diary o Mrityu Prosongo* (Kolkata: Mitra & Ghosh), p. 230.

7. Interview with Madhok, New Delhi, 28 August 2008.

8. Madhok, *Portrait of a Martyr*, p. 241; Interview with Madhok, New Delhi, 28 August 2008.

9. Balraj Madhok's account in his *Portrait of a Martyr* is supplemented by my interview of him on 28 August 2008 in New Delhi. Madhok got it from Guru Datt Vaid, Tek Chand and U.M. Trivedi. This is technically hearsay, but has to be given due importance as none of the eyewitnesses were available for interview.

10. Interview of Madhok, ibid.

11. Interview of the late Sabita Banerjee, Syama Prasad's elder daughter, 24 April 2010, at her residence at Koregaon Park, Pune.

12. *Amrita Bazar Patrika* (English) and *Jugantor* (Bengali) were nationalist daily newspapers of Kolkata owned by the Ghosh family of Bagbazar, Calcutta. The former was published simultaneously from Calcutta and Allahabad and played a significant role in assisting Dr Mookerjee in his struggle for West Bengal (see Chapter 9). The house itself has ceased to exist and the dailies have discontinued publication.

13. Sarvepalli Radhakrishnan, 'Syama Prasad—A Man of Unshakeable Purpose', in *Dr Syama Prasad Mookerjee in the Eyes of his Contemporaries*, ed. Nikhilesh Guha (Kolkata: Asutosh Mookerjee Memorial Institute, 2016), pp. 89–90.

14. Sukharanjan Sengupta, *Bhanga Pather Ranga Dhulay* (Kolkata: Punashcha, 2010), p. 88.

15. Reena Bhaduri, ed., *Kashmir Issue: Correspondence, Speeches and Reports, 1947–53* (Kolkata: Asutosh Mookerjee Memorial Institute, 2003), pp. 293–311 at p. 303.

16. Manoj Das Gupta, *Dr Syama Prasad Mookerjee: A Pure and Manly Life* (Pondicherry/Kolkata: Sri Aurobindo Ashram Trust/New House), p. 53.

17. Mookerjee, ed., *Syamaprasader Diary o Mrityu Prosongo*, pp. 214–19.
18. Ibid.
19. Durga Das, *India from Curzon to Nehru and After* (New Delhi: Rupa, 2009), p. 373.
20. Mookerjee, ed., *Syamaprasader Diary o Mrityu Prosongo*, pp. 214–19.
21. Karan Singh, *Autobiography* (New Delhi: Oxford University Press, 2003).
22. Bhaduri, ed., *Kashmir Issue*, pp. 293–311 at pp. 298–99.
23. Mookerjee, ed., *Syamaprasader Diary o Mrityu Prosongo*, pp. 198–222.

Bibliography

Books and Periodicals in English

Advani, L.K. *My Country, My Life.* 1st ed. Delhi: Rupa, 2008.

Ambedkar, B.R. *Dr. Babasaheb Ambedkar's Writings and Speeches.* Vol. 8. 1st ed. Edited by Vasant Moon. Mumbai: Education Department, Government of Maharashtra, 1990.

Andersen, Walter K., and Shridhar D. Damle. *The Brotherhood in Saffron: The Rashtriya Swayamsevak Sangh and Hindu Revivalism.* New Delhi: Vistaar Publications, 1987.

Autumn Annual (Bilingual, in English and Bengali). Presidency College Alumni Association. Vol. XXIX (2000–01). Kolkata: Presidency College Alumni Association.

Banerjee, Anil Chandra. *A Phase in the Life of Dr Syama Prasad Mookerjee, 1937–46.* 1st ed. Kolkata: Asutosh Mookerjee Memorial Institute, 2000.

Banerjee, Purnendu Kumar. *Sir Asutosh, Our Grandfather.* 1st ed. Mumbai: Bharatiya Vidya Bhavan, 1992.

Baxter, Craig. *The Jana Sangh: A Biography of an Indian Political Party.* Philadelphia: University of Pennsylvania Press, 1969.

Bharat Keshari Dr. Syama Prasad Mookerjee. A Souvenir. Kolkata: Syama Prasad Smarak Samiti, 1999.

Bose, Nirmal Kumar. *My Days With Gandhi.* 1st ed. Hyderabad: Orient Longman, 1974.

Brass, Paul R. *The New Cambridge History of India: The Politics of India since Independence*. 2nd Indian ed. New Delhi: Foundation Books/ Cambridge University Press, 1994.

Butler, David, Ashok Lahiri and Prannoy Roy. *India Decides*. 1st ed. New Delhi: Living Media India Ltd, 1989.

Centenary Souvenir of Syama Prasad Mookerjee. Kolkata: Syama Prasad Smarak Samiti, 2001.

Chagla, M.C. *Roses in December, an Autobiography, with Epilogue*. 10th ed. Mumbai: Bharatiya Vidya Bhavan, 1994.

Chakrabarti, Prafulla Kumar. *The Marginal Men: The Refugees and the Left Political Syndrome in West Bengal*. 2nd ed. Kolkata: Naya Udyog, 1999.

Chandra, Bipan, Mridula Mukherjee, Aditya Mukherjee, Sucheta Mahajan and K.N. Panikkar. *India's Struggle for Independence*. 1st ed. New Delhi: Penguin Books, 1989.

Chatterjee, Santimoy and Jyotirmay Gupta. *Meghnad Saha in Parliament*. 1st ed. Kolkata: The Asiatic Society, 1993.

Chatterji, Prashanto Kumar. *Dr Syama Prasad Mookerjee and Indian Politics: An Account of an Outstanding Political Leader*. 1st ed. New Delhi: Foundations Books/Cambridge University Press, 2010.

Chaudhuri, Nirad C. *Thy Hand, Great Anarch*. 1st ed. London: Chatto & Windus, 1987.

Cohen, Stephen P. *The Idea of Pakistan*. 1st ed. New Delhi: Oxford University Press, 2004.

Collins, Larry and Dominique Lapierre. *Freedom at Midnight*. 1st ed. New York: Simon and Schuster, 1975.

Das, Durga. *India From Curzon to Nehru and After*. 1st ed. New Delhi: Rupa, 1981.

Das, Durga, ed. *Sardar Patel's Correspondence, 1945–50*. Vol. 6. 1st ed. Ahmedabad: Navjivan Publishing House, 1973.

Das Gupta, Manoj. *Dr Syama Prasad Mookerjee, A Pure and Manly Life*. 1st ed. Kolkata: New House, 2001.

Elst, Koenraad. *Negationism in India: Concealing the Record of Islam*. 2nd ed. New Delhi: Voice of India, 1993.

Fischer, Louis. *The Life of Mahatma Gandhi*. 1st paperback ed. New York: Harper and Row, 1983.

Ghosh, Acharya Devaprasad. *Shifting Scenes.* 1st ed. Kolkata: Acharya Devaprasad Smaran Samity, 1958.

Ghosh, Sarup Prasad. *Swami Vivekananda's View on the Role of Religion and Caste in India's Socio-Political Life: A Contemporary Perspective.* 1st ed. Kolkata: Ramkrishna Pustakalaya, 2006.

Gordon, Leonard A. *Brothers against the Raj: A Biography of Indian Nationalists Sarat and Subhas Chandra Bose.* 1st ed. New Delhi: Rupa, 1997.

Graham, Bruce. 'Syama Prasad Mookerjee and the Communalist Alternative'. In *Soundings in Modern South Asian History,* edited by D.A. Low. Berkeley: University of California Press, 1968.

Harish Chander, Padmini. *Dr. Syama Prasad Mookerjee: A Contemporary Study.* 2nd ed. New Delhi: Noida News, 2001.

Hughes, Thomas Patrick. *A Dictionary of Islam.* New Delhi: Munshiram Manoharlal, 1999.

Madhok, Balraj. *Portrait of a Martyr: A Biography of Dr. Shyama Prasad Mookerji.* Centenary ed. New Delhi: Rupa, 2001.

Malkani, K.R. *Dr. Syama Prasad Mookerjee: A Great Life Greatly Lived.* Eminent Parliamentarians Monograph Series. New Delhi: Lok Sabha Secretariat, 1990.

Maulana Abul Kalam Azad. *India Wins Freedom.* 1st ed. Hyderabad: Orient Longman, 1988.

Menon, V.P. *The Transfer of Power in India.* 1st ed. Chennai: Orient Longman, 1957.

Mishra, D.P. *India's March to Freedom.* 1st ed. New Delhi: Har-Anand Publications, 2001.

Mookerjee, Syama Prasad. *Awake Hindusthan.* 1st ed. New Delhi: Dr Syama Prasad Mookerjee Research Foundation, 1945.

Mookerjee, Syama Prasad. *Leaves from a Diary.* 1st ed. New Delhi: Oxford University Press, 1993.

Mookerjee, Syama Prasad. *Kashmir Issue: Correspondence, Speeches and Reports (1947–53),* edited by Reena Bhaduri. 1st ed. Kolkata: Dr Syama Prasad Mookerjee Research Foundation and Asutosh Mookerjee Memorial Institute, 2003.

Mookerjee, Syama Prasad. *Selected Speeches in Bengal Legislative Assembly 1937–47.* 1st ed. Kolkata: Asutosh Mookerjee Memorial Institute, 2002.

Mountbatten, Pamela. *India Remembered.* 1st ed. New Delhi: Roli, 2009.

Mukerjee, Hiren. *Was India's Partition Unavoidable.* 1st ed. Kolkata: Manisha, 1987.

Mukherjee, Madhusree. *Churchill's Secret War.* 1st ed. Chennai: Tranquebar Press, 2010.

Mukhopadhyay, Kali Prasad. *Partition, Bengal and After, The Great Tragedy of India.* 1st ed. New Delhi: Reference Press, 2007.

Mullick, B.N. *My Years with Nehru: Kashmir.* 1st ed. New York: Allied Publishers, 1971.

Nath, Purnendu Nath and Chaudhury Shibnath, ed. *Portrait of a Patriot: Selected Speeches of Page, D., Singh, A.I., Moon, P. and Khosla, G.D.* 1st ed. The Partition Omnibus. New Delhi: Oxford University Press, 2002.

Pandit Lakshmi Kanta Maitra. 1st ed. Kolkata: Pandit Lakshmi Kanta Maitra Birth Centenary Celebration Committee, 2002.

Ray, Jayanta Kumar. *Democracy and Nationalism on Trial: A Study of East Pakistan.* 1st ed. Simla: Institute of Advanced Studies, 1968.

Relief Coordination Committee, Relief Organizations Fight Bengal Famine, Kolkata, 1943.

Roy, Tathagata. *My People, Uprooted: The Exodus of Hindus from East Pakistan and Bangladesh.* New Delhi: Synergy Books India, 2016.

Sanyal, Sunanda and Soumya Basu. *The Sickle and the Crescent: Communists, Muslim League and India's Partition.* 1st ed. London: Frontpage, 2011.

Sen, Amartya. *Poverty and Famines.* 1st ed. 3rd impression paperback. Oxford University Press, 1999.

Sen, L.P., Lt Gen. *Slender Was the Thread: Kashmir Confrontation 1947–48.* 1st ed. Hyderabad: Orient Blackswan, 1994.

Shourie, Arun. *Eminent Historians, Their Technology, Their Line, Their Fraud.* 1st ed. New Delhi: ASA, 1998.

Singh, Jaswant. *Jinnah: India, Partition, Independence.* 1st ed. New Delhi: Rupa, 2009.

Singh, Karan, Dr. *Autobiography.* 1st ed. New Delhi: Oxford University Press, 2003.

Sinha, Dinesh Chandra and Ashok Dasgupta. *1946: The Great Calcutta Killings and Noakhali Genocide, A Historical Study.* 1st ed. Kolkata: Himansu Maity, pub., 2011.

Sinha, Narendra Krishna. *Asutosh Mookerjee, A Biographical Study.* 1st ed. Kolkata: Asutosh Mookerjee Centenary Committee, 1966.

Smith, Vincent A. *The Oxford History of India.* 4th ed. 10th impression. Edited by Percival Spear. New Delhi: Oxford University Press, 1992.

Sundaram, Captain V. *An Airman's Saga.* 1st ed. Mumbai: Bharatiya Vidya Bhavan, 1998.

Swami Vivekananda. *The Complete Works of Swami Vivekananda.* Vol. I. Mayavati Memorial ed. Kolkata: Advaita Ashrama, 1989.

Tunzelmann, Alex von. *Indian Summer: The Secret History of the End of an Empire.* 1st ed. London: Pocket Books, 2007.

Vijay, Tarun, ed. *Thus Spoke Syama Prasad.* 1st ed. New Delhi: Dr Syama Prasad Mookerjee Research Foundation, 2009.

Weiner, Myron. *Party Politics in India.* Princeton: Princeton University Press, 1956.

Wolpert, Stanley. *Jinnah of Pakistan.* 1st ed. New Delhi: Oxford University Press, 1988.

Zavos, John, Thomas Blom Hansen and Christophe Jaffrelot. *Hindu Nationalism and Indian Politics.* 1st ed. New Delhi: Oxford University Press, 2004.

Books and Periodicals in Bengali

Ahmad, Abul Mansur. *Amar Dekha Rajnitir Panchash Bachar.* 8th ed. Dhaka: Khoshroz Kitab Mahal, 1999.

Ali, Syed Mostafa. *Atmakatha.* 1st ed. Dhaka: Utso Prakashan, 2012.

Ali, Syed Murtaza. *Amader Kaler Katha.* 1st ed. Dhaka: Sahitya Prakash, 2005

Bagal, Jogesh Chandra. *Muktir Shondhane bharat, ba Bharater Nobojagoroner Itibritto*. 1st ed. Kolkata: S.K. Mitra & Bros, 1940.

Banerjee, Chandan, ed. *Syama Prasad Ke Na Jana Aparadh*. 1st ed. Sebika Prakashan, 2000.

Banerjee, Hiranmay. *Udbastu*. 1st ed. Kolkata: Sahitya Samsad, 1970.

Chatterjee, Bhabani Prosaad. *Deshbibhag: Poschat O Nepottho Kahini*. 1st ed. Kolkata: Ananda Publishers, 1993.

Chatterjee, Rudra Pratap. *Kashmir Manche Syama Prasad*. 1st ed. Barasat: Aditya Ranjan Ghatak, pub., 2000.

Dalit Neta Jogendra Nath Mondal Padatyag Korechhilen Keno? 1st ed. Kolkata: Vivekananda Sahitya Kendra, 1999.

Das, Ramen. *Syamaprasad Ki Sampradayika?* 1st ed. Kolkata: Nath Brothers, 2000.

Das, Sandip. Article. *Desh*. 4 July 2001.

Das, Shyamalesh. *Bharat Keno Bhag Holo*. 1st ed. Kolkata: Medha Prakashan, 2005.

Das, Shyamalesh. *Doordarshi Rajneetik Dr. Syama Prasad*. 1st ed. Kolkata: Sribhumi Publishing Co., 1997.

Dr. Syama Prasad Mookerjee Smarak Samity ed. and pub. *Bharat Keshari Dr. Syama Prasad*, 1991.

Dr. Syama Prasad Mookerjee Smarak Samity ed. and pub. *Shotoborsher Aloy Syama Prasad*. 1st ed. Kolkata: Shrishti Prakashan, 2001.

Dutt, Bhabatosh. *Aat Doshok* (Eight Decades) (Bangla). 1st ed. Kolkata: Pratikshan Publications, 1993.

Golwalkar, Madhav Sadashivrao. *Shri Guruji Samagra* (Translation). Vol. 12. 1st ed. Kolkata: Bharatiya Samskriti Trust, 2007.

Guha, Nikhilesh, ed. *Syama Prasad, Jonmo Shotoborshe*. 1st ed. Kolkata: Pandulipi, 2000.

Gupta, Ashoka. *Noakhalir Durjoger Diney*. 1st ed. Kolkata: Naya Udyog, 1999.

Islam, Nazrul, *Banglay Hindu-Musalman Samparka*. 1st ed. Kolkata: Mitra & Ghosh, 1994.

Lahiri, Prabhas Chandra. *Pak-Bharater Ruprekha*. 1st ed. Chakdaha, Nadia: Shyama Prakashani, 1968.

Mitra, Ashok. *Tin Kuri Dash*. 1st ed. Kolkata: Dey's Publishing, 1988.

Mookerjee, Syama Prasad. 'Jyotirmay Bharater Dibya Shrashta Acharya Swami Pranavanandaji Maharaj'. *Monishider Drishtite Acharya Swami Pranavananda*. 1st ed. Edited by Swami Atmananda. Kolkata: Bharat Sevasharam Sangha, 1996.

Mookerjee, Syama Prasad. *Rashtrasangram O Ponchaser Monnontor*. 1st ed. Kolkata: Mitra & Ghosh, 1998.

Mookerjee, Uma Prasad, ed. *Syama Prasader Diary o Mrityu Prosongo*. 1st ed. Kolkata: Mitra & Ghosh, 1988.

Mukhopadhyay, Binoy (Jajabor). Article. *Desh*, 24 April 1993. Interview by Niladri Chaki.

Purba Banga o Hindu Samaj. Belur: Ramakrishna Mission, 1946.

Rahaman, Mizanur. *Krishna Sholoi* (Black Sixteenth) (Bangla). 1st ed. Dhaka: Sahana, 2000.

Rahman, Hossainur. *Adhunikata o Dharmanirapekkhota*. 1st ed. Kolkata: Mitra & Ghosh, 2001.

Rahman, Sheikh Mujibur. *Ausamapta Atmajiboni*. 1st ed. Dhaka: University Press, 2014.

Ray, Annada Sankar. *Jukto Bonger Sriti* (Memories of United Bengal) (Bangla). 2nd ed. Kolkata: Mitra & Ghosh, 1990.

Ray, Kabishekhar Kalidas, Reena Bhaduri and Amitabha Chatterjee, ed. *Syama Prasad*. 2nd ed. Kolkata: Dr Syama Prasad Mookerjee Research Foundation, 2008.

Roy, Debojyoti. *Keno Udbastu Hote Holo*. 1st ed. Kolkata: Vivekananda Sahitya Kendra, 2001.

Roy, Tathagata. Article, *Desh*, 4 July 2001.

Sahityaratna, Sushanta Kumar. *Bharat Keshari Syama Prasad*. 1st ed. Kolkata: Sahityam, 2001.

Salaam, Azad. *Hindu Sampraday Keno Deshtyag Korchhe*. 1st ed. Kolkata: Swatantra Prakashani, 1999.

Sanyal, Arun. *Sikshabrati Syamaprasad*. 1st ed. Kolkata: Modern Column, 1999.

Sengupta, Mihir. *Bishadbrikkho*. 2nd ed. Kolkata: Subarnarekha, 2005.

Sengupta, Sukharanjan. *Bangla: Fazlul Haq thekey Jyoti Basu*. 1st ed. Kolkata: Sujan Publications, 1995.

Sengupta, Sukharanjan. *Bhanga Pather Ranga Dhulay.* 1st ed. Kolkata: Punashcha, 2010.

Sengupta, Sukharanjan. *Bongosonghar Ebong (1946–50).* 1st ed. Kolkata: Naya Udyog, 2002.

Sinha, Dinesh Chandra. Article. *Desh*, 4 July 2001.

Sinha, Dinesh Chandra. *Asutosh Mukhopadhyayer Siksha Chinta.* 1st ed. Kolkata: Kolkata University, 1992.

Sinha, Dinesh Chandra. *Noakhalir Mati o Manush.* 2nd ed. Kolkata: Noakhali Sammilani, 2010.

Sinha, Dinesh Chandra. *Proshongo Kolkata Bishwabidyalay (1857–2007).* 1st ed. Kolkata: Kolkata University, 2007.

Sinha, Dinesh Chandra. *Syamaprasad, Bangabibhag O Pashchimbanga.* 1st ed. Kolkata: Grantharashmi, 2001.

Sinha, Santanu. *Syama Prasad: Byartha Balidan?* 1st ed. Kolkata: ABVP, 1994.

Tripathi, Amales. *Swadhinatar Mukh.* 1st ed. Ananda, 1998.